487679

302·2301 JOH
1 WL

ONE WEEK LOAN

NEWS NARRATIVES AND
NEWS FRAMING

WITHDRAWN

D1439928

CK
CK

6457479

Communication, Media, and Politics

Series Editor
Robert E. Denton, Jr., Virginia Tech

This series features a broad range of work dealing with the role and function of communication in the realm of politics, broadly defined. Including general academic books, monographs, and texts for use in graduate and advanced undergraduate courses, the series will encompass humanistic, critical, historical, and empirical studies in political communication in the United States.

Recent Titles in the Series

Strategic Political Communication: Rethinking Social Influence, Persuasion, and Propaganda
Karen S. Johnson-Cartee and Gary Copeland
Inventing a Voice: The Rhetoric of American First Ladies of the Twentieth Century
Edited by Molly Meijer Wertheimer
Communicating for Change: Strategies of Social and Political Advocates
John P. McHale
Political Campaign Communication: Principles and Practices, Fifth Edition
Judith S. Trent and Robert V. Friedenberg
The Rhetoric of Redemption: Kenneth Burke's Redemption Drama and Martin Luther King, Jr.'s "I Have a Dream" Speech
David A. Bobbitt
Reelpolitik II: Political Ideologies in '50s and '60s Films
Beverly Merrill Kelley
New Frontiers in International Communication Theory
Edited by Mehdi Semati
Entertaining Politics: New Political Television and Civic Culture
Jeffrey P. Jones
News Narratives and News Framing: Constructing Political Reality
Karen S. Johnson-Cartee

Forthcoming

Presidential Candidate Images
Edited by Kenneth L. Hacker
Leading Ladies of the White House
Edited by Molly Meijer Wertheimer
Bring 'Em On: Media and Politics in the U.S. War on Iraq
Edited by Lee Artz and Yahya R. Kamalipour
Women's Political Discourse
Molly A. Mayhead and Brenda DeVore Marshall
The 2004 Presidential Campaign
Edited by Robert E. Denton, Jr.
Making Sense of Political Ideology
Bernard L. Brock, Mark E. Huglen, James F. Klumpp, and Sharon Howell
Politeness and Political Debate
Edward A. Hinck, Shelly S. Hinck, and William O. Dailey
Bush at War
Jim A. Kuypers
Media and the Staging of American Politics
Gary C. Woodward

NEWS NARRATIVES AND NEWS FRAMING
Constructing Political Reality

Karen S. Johnson-Cartee

ROWMAN & LITTLEFIELD PUBLISHERS, INC.
Lanham • *Boulder* • *New York* • *Toronto* • *Oxford*

MOUNTBATTEN LIBRARY
SOUTHAMPTON INSTITUTE

SUPPLIER COUTTS

ORDER No

DATE 1 4 DEC 2004

ROWMAN & LITTLEFIELD PUBLISHERS, INC.

Published in the United States of America
by Rowman & Littlefield Publishers, Inc.
A wholly owned subsidary of The Rowman & Littlefield Publishing Group, Inc.
4501 Forbes Boulevard, Suite 200, Lanham, MD 20706
www.rowmanlittlefield.com

PO Box 317, Oxford OX2 9RU, UK

Copyright © 2005 by Rowman & Littlefield Publishers, Inc.

All rights reserved. No part of this publication may be reproduced, stored in a
retrieval system, or transmitted in any form or by any means, electronic, mechanical,
photocopying, recording, or otherwise, without the prior permission of the publisher.

British Library Cataloguing in Publication Information Available

Library of Congress Cataloging-in-Publication Data

Johnson-Cartee, Karen S.
  News narratives and news framing : constructing political reality / Karen S. Johnson-Cartee.
      p. cm. — (Communication, media, and politics)
  Includes bibliographical references and index.
  ISBN 0-7425-3662-9 (cloth : alk. paper) — ISBN 0-7425-3663-7 (pbk. : alk. paper)
  1. Journalism—Social aspects. 2. Journalism—Objectivity. I. Title. II. Series.
  PN4749 .J64 2005

                                                         302.23—dc22
                                                         2004007175

Printed in the United States of America

⊗™ The paper used in this publication meets the minimum requirements of American
National Standard for Information Sciences—Permanence of Paper for Printed Library
Materials, ANSI/NISO Z39.48-1992.

Contents

Acknowledgments

T O THE MANY STUDENTS WHO HAVE SERVED as the guinea pigs for most of my ruminations, I hope I have brought as much light into your lives as you have into mine. May you all continue to be liberated political communicators.

And to Charmie Johnson, my dear aunt, who spent summers making sure a little girl from Bramwell, West Virginia, had the necessary academic skills to succeed in the world outside the mountains.

And to my beloved parents, Edsel and Betty Johnson, and my dear husband, Michael, who graciously put up with my absentmindedness, reams of paper on the floor, and frequent disappearances into my office.

My thanks to Gary A. Copeland for his careful reading of this manuscript. His editorial assistance as always proved invaluable. And my thanks to Mike Little, a talented graphic artist and valued colleague, for his help in designing the artwork.

Introduction

I N HIS REVIEW OF THE POLITICAL NEWS RESEARCH LITERATURE in the 1990 *Handbook of Political Communication*, Dennis lamented that "social construction of reality theory is concerned with the way news influences consumer perceptions of the social world but it has generally failed to give serious attention to content structure" (166). Dennis (1990) also acknowledged, however, a growing area of research, which he associated with the developing body of work associated with Nimmo and Combs (Nimmo 1974; Combs 1980; Nimmo and Combs 1980, 1983; Combs and Nimmo 1993), that is interested in the content and structure of news narratives and that analyzes them as a cultural phenomenon. This approach (with the emphasis on social or public knowledge) necessitated an emphasis on news content and its subsequent use or misuse by the attendant public. Such scholars had focused on the mythology, ritual, symbolism, and rhetoric found in news content and had considered the potential implications such devices have on news consumers' images of the political world.

Dennis viewed such work as distinct from the research produced by the Chicago School, because social construction of reality theory has its historical roots in the writings of Kenneth Burke (1945, 1950). However, it should be noted that the *Handbook of Social Psychology* (Lindzey and Aronson 1985) as well as most other significant compilations of symbolic interactionism and its many offshoots (from narrative theory to ethnomethodology to frame analysis) place Burke's work and the growing body of dramatism under the umbrella of symbolic interactionism (Combs 1973; Lindzey and Aronson 1985; Littlejohn 1992). Burke was a contemporary of George Herbert Mead; although they did not teach, research, or publish together and although they came from vastly different academic disciplines (Burke from theater and speech, and Mead from social psychology), they had arrived at remarkably similar conclusions about language, meaning, culture, and society. Indeed, a host of doctoral thesis literature reviews linking symbolic interactionism and dramatism exists (e.g., Combs 1973; Johnson [a.k.a. Johnson-Cartee] 1984). This work is, in part, the process of crafting and explicating the theoretical linkages between symbolic interactionism, dramatism, and narrative theory.

This task is an important one in light of the many advances made by sociologists in the area of news analysis and framing theory, in particular during the past twenty years. Although ignored by Dennis (1990) in his news analysis review, their work constitutes a significant body of knowledge. Gamson and Lasch (1983), Gamson and Modigliani (1989), and a host of other noted scholars find the theoretical and philosophical grounding for framing theory in both the narrative paradigm (within the umbrella of symbolic interactionism; see Blumer 1969; Duncan 1962, 1968; Hall 1972; Mead 1934; Meltzer 1972) and what has come to be called the social construction of reality theory (Berger and Luckmann 1966; Gergen 1982, 1985a, 1985b, 1999, 2001; Schudson 1991). However, in much of their work, this connection or shared philosophical grounding is made implicitly rather than explicitly, and this work is an attempt to remedy that.

Because we view the news product as the outcome of a social construction process, the book is beneficial not only for those engaged in news criticism and news reporting, but also for those seeking to influence the news product such as political activists, elected officials, or public relations practitioners. I will also consider the ramifications of the news construction process on our political, economic, and social realities.

1

The Social Construction of Reality

THE AUSTRIAN-BORN PHENOMENOLOGIST Alfred Schutz (1970) writes:

> The world of my daily life is by no means my private world but is from the out-set an intersubjective one, shared with my fellow men, experienced and inter-preted by others: in brief, it is a world common to all of us. The unique biogra-phical situation in which I find myself within the world at any moment of my existence is only to a very small extent of my own making. (163)

For Schutz (1962), people operating in the world engage in situations that call for a "reciprocity of perspectives" (315–316). In other words, people explore "we-relationships" in which they construct "ideal-types" of behavior patterns, ascertaining appropriate social behaviors. People then imagine social actions and the consequences of those actions. When considering action, a person as-sesses his or her own past, present, and future expectations for one's own per-sonal conduct as well as that for others, and it is through this assessment that one constructs his or her own social reality.

Social Interactions

Reality, then, is created through the social process of communication (cf. Berger and Luckmann 1966; Schutz 1970; Watzlawick, Beavin, and Jackson 1967). What one knows and what one thinks one knows are both shaped by the communication process. Thus, what one responds to is a subjective reality created through the process of social interaction (see Gergen 1985a, 1985b).

Scholars interested in this area of social inquiry are said to be social constructivists. "Social constructionism is principally concerned with elucidating the processes by which people come to describe, explain, or otherwise account for the world in which they live" (Gergen 1985b, 3–4). In short, social constructionism is an exploration into the nature of human knowledge, social knowledge, or both (Gergen 1985b).

First, social constuctionists question or attack the taken-for-granted world of everyday life. This is because what we know about the world is colored by our social interactions with others, the naming, defining, and altering of our own personal realities during our lifetimes. Such an approach analyzes the nonverbal and verbal languages we use to constitute our realities.

Second, social constructionists maintain that "*the terms in which the world is understood are social artifacts, products of historically situated interchanges among people*" (Gergen 1985b, 5; emphasis in original). And third, social constructionists maintain that "*the degree to which a given form of understanding prevails or is sustained across time is not directly dependent on the empirical validity of the perspective in question, but on the vicissitudes of social processes* (e.g., communication, negotiation, conflict, rhetoric, etc.)" (Gergen 1985b, 6; emphasis in original).

In academic inquiry, social constructionists reject the naïve realists of the positivist-empiricist movement in social science, arguing that by naming, labeling, and categorizing observable behavioral phenomena such realists have in fact forced upon the world their own previously determined order (Burr 1998; Gergen 1985b). In short, the empiricist assumption that "'facts' can be gathered by disinterested and neutral observation" (Cromby and Nightingale 1999, 6) is now regarded by many as being hopelessly naïve. In both sociology and psychology, the social constructionist movement has grown substantially during the past twenty years (Burr 1998; D. Edwards, Ashmore, and Potter 1992).

Although empirical research is still very much alive, those who do conduct such research should now recognize the inherent limitations of such analysis (Burr 1998; Gergen 1998, 2001). Frequently, those who pursue empirical research do so out of the fear of social constructionism legitimating or reinforcing the status quo (Burr 1998). Because social constructionism analyzes how social knowledge is historically and culturally constituted, many researchers find it inherently conservative. However, social constructionists often differ as to the proper endgame of their analysis. One camp is content to describe and explain, yielding no recommendations as to future social and political activity (e.g., Gill 1995). Another camp chooses to analyze "social processes that are already shaped by influences such as power relationships and material resources" (Cromby and Nightingale 1999, 6; Harré 1999) to ultimately provide not only a political critique but also a political proscription for social change (see Cromby and Nightingale 1999). For those desiring a more activist social scientific community, such proscriptions are alternative constructions to contemporary social reality (Burr 1998; Gergen 1999, 2001; Nightingale and Cromby 1999).

Often social constructionism focuses on the language used in a given culture, for the culture's language determines to a large extent what can be known and what can be achieved by a society (Whorf 1956). This **linguistic relativity** is known as the **Sapir-Whorf hypothesis.** As Whorf notes:

> It is quite an illusion to imagine that one adjusts to reality essentially without the use of language and that language is merely an incidental means of solving specific problems of communication or reflection. The fact of the matter is that the "real world" is to a large extent unconsciously built upon the language habits of the group. (1956, 134)

Nimmo and Combs (1983) have interpreted the work of Watzlawick, Sapir, Whorf, and others who view reality as being created through communication to mean:

> (1) our everyday, taken-for-granted reality is a delusion; (2) reality is created, constructed, through communication not expressed by it; (3) for any situation there is no single reality, no one objective truth, but multiple subjectively derived realities. (3)

While theoretical differences exist among social constructionist researchers, Cromby and Nightingale (1999) have argued that they do agree on the primacy of the social processes, including language, in constructing reality. They write:

> Social constructionists argue that the world we experience and the people we find ourselves to be are first and foremost the product of social processes. Neither God nor individual consciousness but society itself is the prime mover, the root of experience. It is the social reproduction and transformation of structures of meaning, conventions, morals, and discursive formation of structures of meaning, conventions, morals and discursive practices that principally constitutes both our relationships and ourselves. This implies that language, both as the dominant carrier of categories and meanings and as the medium which provides much of the raw material for our activity, is central. (Cromby and Nightingale 1999, 4)

Mediated Interactions

While the works of Schutz (1967) and Berger and Luckmann (1967) have many theoretical commonalities, their works represent two academic traditions, the European and American approaches to the study of language, knowledge, culture, and society (see Adoni and Mane 1984; J. Turner 1974). However, in recent years, the emphasis has been placed not on social interactions but on mediated interactions in an individual's construction of his or her social reality. Lippmann ([1922] 1965) and Kessel (1965) have argued that the "pictures in our heads" or the images that we hold in modern society are primarily created through an individual's contact with the media rather than direct experience. For most people, political knowledge is constructed through the mass media. Many people have never met their city council member or mayor in person but don't doubt they exist, because the media have told them they do. Even lands far away and cultures outside of our own personal experience suddenly become real as we attend to the mass media. And we behave toward what we have learned as if it were real (real in the sense of personal validation of existence). Most Americans have never set foot on the continent of Africa; yet, when famines occur on that continent, thousands upon thousands of Americans will send money, medical supplies, and food to help those in need. Clearly, then, the mass media provide us with the mosaics from which we build our own personal reality (Brody and Page 1975; Kraus and Davis 1976; M. E. McCombs 1979). Individuals attend to the mediated mosaics, filter them through their own perceptual screens, and discuss them with others. The end result of this process is what Nimmo and Combs (1983) have called a **mass-mediated reality**. Thus, meaning has been socially constructed through a process often dominated by the mass media. Because of this, research analyzing the images found in mass-mediated messages reveal important social indicators.

Dependency Theory of Mass Media Effects

As early as 1935, Lasswell observed that the complexities of modern life had led even the most sagacious among us to turn to the mass media for guidance; he wrote: "Everywhere the labyrinth of modern living ensnares specialist and layman in the common necessity of acting without knowledge" (187). Clearly, one may not know everything about everything, because the flood of information available in contemporary society is overwhelming. Consequently, we try to attend to and store pieces of information likely to prove useful to us in our everyday lives, whether pertaining to family life, purchasing decisions, career advancements, or social situations.

Eighty percent of Americans report that their primary source of information is the news media (Dautrich and Hartley 1999, 22). "A January, 1997 survey found that 50 percent of the public relied on television news as their primary source of information, and 24 percent relied mostly on newspapers" (Dautrich and Hartley 1999, 24). Sixty percent of voters say they read a newspaper daily, and 22 percent report they read a weekly news magazine such as *Newsweek* or *Time* once a week (Dautrich and Hartley 1999, 27). Dautrich and Hartley (1999) found that 29 percent of respondents frequently use a variety of "elite news" sources such as ABC's *Nightline*, PBS's *NewsHour*, *Inside Politics* on CNN, C-Span, and National Public Radio's *Inside Edition*.

In a survey of voters in February 1996, the researchers found that 5 percent of respondents said they visited a "politically oriented home page," and 12 percent had visited news organizations' websites (Dautrich and Hartley, 1999). In the presidential campaign of 2000, 104 million Americans utilized the Internet for election information (Whillock and Whillock 2002), a sharp increase from that seen during the 1996 campaign. Yet D. Weaver and Drew (2001) found that in the presidential campaign of 2000, Internet usage had little impact on "issue knowledge, campaign interest, or intention to vote" (796). Such findings may be indicative of how Internet news sites are constructed. "Relative to traditional newspapers, Internet-based papers provide fewer cues about news story importance and give readers more control over story selection" (Tewksbury and Althaus 2000, 457). Wu and Bechtel (2002) found that news consumers are more likely to utilize Internet news sites when they are seeking information about "ongoing, breaking news—stories that command people's attention" (73). For instance, when John F. Kennedy Jr.'s plane went down in 1999, the *New York Times on the Web* reported record-high site visits (Wu and Bechtel 2002). "For now, the Internet is a source of information for only a small proportion of the electorate" (Dautrich and Hartley 1999, 34). Yet some scholars remain very optimistic about the Internet's future in contributing to public knowledge about politics. For instance, Whillock and Whillock (2002) confidently predict that "the Internet will discover its unique capabilities and in doing so will find itself important in the company of traditional forms of information dissemination" (167).

Sociodemographic factors affect how much political news is consumed. Typically, those with higher degrees of education, occupational stature, and economic means consume more political news than, say, blue-collar workers. Thus, it is likely (as Gamson 1996 notes) that the higher-educated individual with greater economic means would have the greatest exposure to news narratives. While political news may not always be the primary source of political knowledge about a public issue, "it is very rare for people to ignore media discourse in framing it" (131).

Dautrich and Hartley (1999) in their review of empirical studies examining news consumption found that the majority of research findings suggest that most people turn to the news for entertainment rather than serious attempts to educate themselves about the events of the day. Consequently, the majority of Americans turn to television news for their public affairs information; researchers have long recognized that television viewing is communication-play rather than the communication-work associated with newspaper reading (Stephenson 1967).

In the political realm, as the American political process has grown increasingly complex and conflictual, political leaders frequently call upon voters to act on issues or areas of knowledge with which they are unfamiliar. Such occurrences cause voters to experience anxiety because people feel uncomfortable when dealing with ambiguity, and thus most people, if the requests for action(s) are deemed important, are compelled to gain familiarity or some degree of understanding about the uncertainties confronting them. And this often means turning to the mass media for information and guidance. People want to be seen by others as being able to function effectively in their world. Whether it is being able to recall last year's World Series events or being able to discuss the latest steps in the "War on Terror," most people want to appear informed.

Since Lasswell's observations in 1935, our society has grown increasingly more specialized, technological, globalized, and conflictual; as a result, time has become even more precious. For this reason, people rely increasingly on the mass media to provide them with essential information that is deemed necessary to conduct their daily lives (see Ball-Rokeach and DeFleur 1976, 6–7). The character or nature of this reliance on the mass media is determined by the individual's perceived interests and needs; thus, for a person interested in politics, political news becomes essential or more centralized in the individual's information-seeking behaviors than for someone who is primarily interested in gardening. Media dependency occurs because societal members need to efficiently utilize time to maximize their effectiveness in goal attainment. Such observations about contemporary life led Ball-Rokeach and DeFleur (1976) to propose the dependency model of mass media effects. According to Ball-Rokeach and DeFleur (1976), the audience is "dependent" on the mass media to satisfy a variety of important needs in contemporary society: (1) to understand the world in which they live; (2) to function meaningfully and effectively in that social, political, and economic arena; and (3) to escape the cares and travails of contemporary life through a presentation of fantasy and escape. Thus, not only do the mass media provide information, but they also provide readily available avenues for entertainment such as game shows, soap operas, or reality television shows. Such programming does not necessitate participation in group structures such as team sports like basketball.

However, while the media dependency model does emphasize the influence of the mass media in contemporary life, it in no way eliminates the significance of social group influence. Unlike the hypodermic needle model or magic bullet model of media effects, which are two names for the same theoretical perspective arguing for immediate and direct effects of mass-communication influence (see Johnson-Cartee and Copeland 2004), the dependency model recognizes the public's reliance on media-supplied information as well as the process by which that information is then talked about and altered by individuals who function within societal groups. Ball-Rokeach and DeFleur (1976) explain:

> As the social structure becomes more complex, people have less and less contact with the social system as a whole. In other words, they begin to be less aware of what is going on in their society beyond their own position in the structure. The mass media enter as not only economic systems engaged in deliberate attempts to persuade and entertain, but also as information systems vitally involved in maintenance, change, and conflict processes at the societal as well as the group and individual levels of social action. (4–5)

However, it should be recognized that the mass media have come to increasingly fulfill what were once considered to be the requisite societal functions of traditional communities. Denis McQuail (1994) has outlined the major social functions of the mass media within contemporary society:

Information

- providing information about events and conditions in society and the world;
- indicating relations of power;
- facilitating innovation, adaptation and progress.

Correlation

- explaining, interpreting and commenting on the meaning of events and information;
- providing support for established authority and norms;
- socializing;
- co-coordinating separate activities;
- consensus building;
- setting orders of priority and signalling relative status.

Continuity

- expressing the dominant culture and recognizing subcultures and new cultural developments;
- forging and maintaining commonality of values.

Entertainment

- providing amusement, diversion and the means of relaxation;
- reducing social tension.

Mobilization

- campaigning for societal objectives in the sphere of politics, war, economic development, work and sometimes religion. (79)

Obviously, as the media fulfill more and more societal functions, we will observe a corresponding increase in influence of the mass media on both individuals and society. And as information sources become more highly specialized, providing very specific information to highly select audiences, the centrality of that experience for those select audiences becomes ever more important. And, with that, the potential power of the mass media for influencing people's lives increases dramatically.

Levels of Media Effects

Traditionally, it may be viewed that the mass media potentially have two potential levels of effects: (1) microeffects, or those effects related to an individual; or (2) macroeffects, or those effects related to society at large. These effects are summarized as follows:

Microeffects: Effects on the Individual

Cognitive effects—Influences on what an individual knows or is aware of
Affective effects—Influences on how an individual emotionally responds to what is known
Behavioral effects—Influences on how an individual acts on what is known and felt

Macroeffects: Effects on Society

Status quo—Influences that maintain existing structures and behaviors
Catalyst—Influences that allow society to change or evolve

In the microeffects realm, for instance, the medical profession as well as the news media have increasingly focused on the amount of fat in the typical American's diet. Indeed, we have been inundated with information about fat grams, dietary restrictions, low-fat or no-fat products, and nutrition fact panels. As a result, most Americans recognize that it is important to limit the amount of fat in their diets. This may be viewed as a cognitive effect in that they have learned or become aware of this information. As a result, many of us feel guilty (an affective effect) when we eat that juicy cheeseburger or that deep-dish pizza with extra pepperoni and cheese. Or we may feel virtuous as we nibble on rice cakes and alfalfa sprouts, even though we don't necessarily enjoy it (both an affective effect—feeling virtuous—and a behavioral effect—eating hamster food). News reports, then, may change what we know, what we feel about what we know, and how we act on both what we know and what we feel.

In the macroeffects realm, DeFleur and Ball-Rokeach (1982) have argued that to understand potential societal effects, we must recognize the transactional relationships existing among audiences, media, and societal structures from a systems perspective. Such a **systems perspective** is meant to indicate an approach that views a whole as an interrelated group of objects (see Monge 1977). Dependency theory posits that for any one of the three elements (audiences, the media, or society) to attain its goals, it must depend upon the other two. As a result, contemporary researchers seek to examine how all three parties—audiences, media, and society—influence each other. Rather than looking at potential influences as one-to-one or as each with equal influence, it must be understood that the influences that each party (audiences, the media, or society) yields should be described as ratios of power that change given the culture and other environmental influences through time. Such an approach is particularly useful in highly complex societal situations where interactions and the flow of influence are not necessarily easily ascertained. For example, many Americans are surprised when visiting European nations that explicit sex shows are broadcast on television in countries with strongly Catholic populations such as Spain or Italy. The Catholic Church's stand on sex for procreation, not recreation, is widely known. And, as the Catholic Church in both countries exerts a great deal of influence on the governmental process, it seems on first analysis rather unusual that broadcast stations enjoy such latitude in their programming. But, clearly, other influences operate within the culture to change the configuration of power between the church as a societal structure, the audience's desires, and the media system's policy. It has been suggested that the history of machismo—or an emphasis on the male sexual impulse—in both Spain and Italy accounts for the very open broadcasting policy.

Uses and Gratifications Theory

Other communication researchers have concentrated on uses and gratifications theory (see A. M. Rubin and Windahl 1986). Uses and gratifications research has long investigated why an individual seeks out particular types of media programming and what gratifications are received from the attendance to or use of that programming. From watching soap operas for sexual excitement to watching the *Late Show with David Letterman* for a natural, nonaddictive sleeping pill, Americans seek out various types of mass media to satisfy perceived needs. In other words, researchers investigate the functions the mass media serve by gratifying the perceived needs in an individual's life; thus, uses and gratifications theory is often characterized as functionalist (e.g., E. Katz, Blumer, and Gurevitch 1974). However, after more than forty years of uses and gratifications research, the theory is now presented as a much less mechanistic, functional approach. McQuail (1994) has summarized contemporary uses and gratifications research in the following manner:

> (1) Personal social circumstances and psychological dispositions together influence both (2) general habits of media use and also (3) beliefs and expectations about the benefits offered by media, which shape (4) specific acts of media choice and consumption, followed by (5) assessments of the value of the experience (with consequences for further media use) and, possibly (6) applications of benefits acquired in other areas of experience and social activity. (319)

Of particular importance in the transformation of uses and gratifications theory is the refinement of the concept of **expectation**, now clarified as an "expectancy-value approach" (Palmgreen and Rayburn 1985, 303–305). Individuals attend to the mass media based on their beliefs that certain types of media and media content have attributes that are judged to be either positive or negative. Thus, we can observe a three-stage linked process of attending to the media: audience expectations of attributes (gratifications sought), media consumption, and gratifications obtained (Rayburn and Palmgreen 1984). McQuail (1994) has identified a number of motives for attending to the mass media (gratifications sought) and a number of satisfactions received from media use (gratifications obtained):

- Getting information and advice
- Reducing personal insecurity
- Learning about society and the world
- Finding support for one's own values
- Gaining insight into one's own life
- Experiencing empathy with [the] problems of others

- Having a basis for social contact
- Feeling connected with others
- Escaping from problems and worries
- Gaining entry into an imaginary world
- Filling time
- Experiencing emotional release
- Acquiring a structure for daily routine (320)

Despite such emphasis on gratifications sought and obtained, Palmgreen, Wenner, and Rosengren (1985) have argued that uses and gratifications theory is far more complicated. They write:

> While taking into account the feedback from gratifications obtained to those sought, [uses and gratifications theory] also considers (among other things) the social psychological origins of needs, values, and beliefs, which give rise to motives for behavior, which may in turn be guided by beliefs, values, and social circumstances into seeking various gratifications through media consumption and other nonmedia behaviors. The gratification processes are seen as taking place within a field of interaction between societal structures and individual characteristics, an interaction calling forward specific realization of the potentials and restrictions inherent in those structures and characteristics. (Palmgreen, Wenner, and Rosengren 1985, 16)

While most research in this area has investigated general media programming, Wenner (1985) has specifically investigated news programming. Wenner (1985) argues that individuals who attend to the news media also receive para-social and para-orientational gratifications. **Para-social gratifications** are the result of the "para-social interaction" (see Horton and Wohl 1956; R. B. Rubin and McHugh 1987) of experiencing news content as if you are a fellow news reporter, a participant in the news or a physical observer of the news event. Such gratifications "provide for personal identity and reference through ritualized social relationships with media 'actors' who coexist with news content" (Wenner 1985, 175). As news viewers, we are "beside" Wolf Blitzer or Dan Rather as he asks tough questions and demands straight answers from our nation's leaders. We often mistake such vicarious experiences as being true acts of political participation; we feel both involved and knowledgeable. And, depending upon the news outcomes, we may emerge feeling either empowered or politically inefficacious.

During and immediately after the news coverage surrounding the terrorist attacks on September 11, 2001, Americans shifted their personal feelings in relation to these horrific acts from ones of bewilderment, hopelessness, and inefficaciousness to ones of resilience, pride, and, ultimately, empowerment. As the smoke cleared and as the news media reported the many acts of heroism and self-sacrifice on the part of ordinary Americans, our nation's flag appeared on mailboxes, home and office doors, automobiles and tractor trailers, and the lapels of men and women across America. And we took strength in our solidarity. As President George W. Bush called to the 9/11 rescue teams on his bullhorn and as he assured them that he would not rest, that all Americans would not rest, until the "evildoers" were brought to justice, Americans gained renewed strength and courage to persevere.

Such **para-orientational gratifications** occur through playacting or role-playing during the course of the news attendance. Such expressive activities allow for tension reduction or ego defense. At other times, such activities may turn us away from information gain to information avoidance or simply reinforcement or the reaffirmation of our own beliefs. Such expressive activities allow us to **counterargue** or play at arguing back against the source of the message. We hold conversations in our heads in which we argue with either the news expert's assessments or the news reporter's commentary. We bring to this "conversation" our past knowledge and experiences and our corresponding stereotypes and world views. Such counterarguing often causes reinforcement of existing beliefs and attitudes. For example, news ad-watches presenting negative political television advertising attacking an individual's chosen candidate may allow the viewer to counterargue each attack point with prior knowledge, and the experience of that counterarguing reinforces the individual's choice for office.

Wenner (1985) pays far more attention to the content of the news programming than do other uses and gratification researchers. Taking a transactional view, Wenner writes that "*content* gratifications must be *processed*, and it is not possible for process gratifications to be formed without some reference to the *content* characteristics that provided information for orientation" (100; emphases in original). In other words, the viewer's use of the news and the gratifications received cannot be understood separate from the news content that evoked the viewer's interest. To illustrate his perspective, Wenner crafts a map, indicating the transactional nature of the relationships: "Content and process gratifications form the principal axes of the map" and "each axis is anchored by orientational (or self-referent) and social (or other-referent) poles" (1985, 175). Watching *Crossfire* on CNN provides the viewer with an opportunity to hear often diametrically opposite perspectives from both news sources and news commentators. Conversations on the popular talk news show are often shrill and pejorative. The boxing gloves are off, and the program presents a hard-knuckled approach to political debate. In one recent show, the audience was presented with Paul Begala, a white, liberal, left-wing commentator, taking on the Reverend Al Sharpton, a controversial Democratic presidential candidate. Begala intensively and extensively questioned Sharpton on what many people would categorize as Sharpton's inflammatory racist rhetoric and political malfeasance. This encounter provided the news audience with an important opportunity. Many white as well as black Americans have been frustrated with the news media's relative lack of critical review of the actions of the Reverend Sharpton for fear of being labeled racist in our race-polarized society. Begala's harsh critique of Sharpton came from the left, a far more "politically friendly" source in this regard. The interview provided a catharsis of sort in that, finally, Sharpton had been called on the carpet by a fellow liberal, and the American notion of equal justice was served.

Uses and Dependency Theory

Building upon such research advances in understanding multilevel media effects, A. M. Rubin and Windahl (1986) proposed a merger of uses and gratifications theory and the dependency model of mass media effects: a uses and dependency theory. As with any hybrid, they view their new theory as having strengths not found in the theories from which it was spawned and as having fewer weaknesses. They assert, "Uses and gratifications, then, adds a voluntaristic element to dependency, just as dependency adds a more deterministic flavor to uses and gratifications" (1986, 279). Although uses and dependency theory is more complex, it broadens our understanding of human behavior in a contemporary media society by providing insights into the motivations of attendant individuals.

Other Conditions That Make the Mass Media Powerful

From her research in Germany, Noelle-Neumann (1973, 1981) also envisions the power of the media to be a product of people's need to know. As the world becomes more complex, people's need for news, information, and entertainment finds succor in the media. Though Noelle-Neumann never says so explicitly, her reasoning over the renewed power of the media comes from the media's ability to provide the information that people want. The increase in television penetration into homes that were then in West Germany has been accompanied by an increased interest by the population in politics (1981). Noelle-Neumann views this increased interest as a result of television's focus on political issues.

In addition, Noelle-Neumann (1973) provides us with clues as to how to make mass-communicated messages more powerful. She says that, under certain conditions, the mass media have real and powerful effects. These conditions—ubiquity, consonance, and cumulation of mass-communicated messages—are met in a modern industrialized society. **Ubiquity** means that the mass-mediated messages give the appearance of being pervasive throughout mass media channels (Noelle-Neumann 1973). **Consonance**, as Noelle-Neumann uses the term, means that the messages from mass media news sources provide a similar picture of the world. And **cumulation** speaks to the repetition of similar messages over an extended period of time. She views the conditions of ubiquity, cumulation, and consonance as "unanimous illumination, unanimous argumentation with regard to events, people, and problems" (Noelle-Neumann 1981, 138). Such uniformity overshadows if not overwhelms potentially competing messages, and the result is media influence. Noelle-Neumann (1977, 1984) believes that an individual's perception of the majority opinion directly relates to how willing one is to publicly state one's own opinion. If an individual perceives that his opinion is shared by a majority of the population, then he will be more willing to express his opinion. Conversely, if an individual perceives her opinion to be in the minority or to be not widely shared in society, then she will be less willing to state her opinion publicly. Indeed, some research indicates that when people perceive their opinion as being in the minority, they feel pressure to conceal or hide their true opinions (Lasorsa 1991). In 2003, many Americans who opposed the intervention in Iraq found it difficult to voice their views in the early days of the war. And those who did often suffered the criticism and popularity fallout for their public pronouncements. Hollywood actor Martin Sheen faced heavy criticism when he spoke out against the war, and his popular television series *West Wing* saw a sharp drop in the ratings.

Researchers now commonly identify certain areas where the mass media have the greatest potential for powerful societal effects:

- Attracting and directing public attention
- Persuasion in matters of opinion and belief
- Influencing behavior
- Structuring definitions of reality
- Conferring status and legitimacy
- Informing quickly and extensively (McQuail 1994, 69)

In the words of two groundbreaking political communicologists, Kraus and Davis:

> The mass media create common reality by shaping the conceptual environment in which humans communicate. . . . Political reality is formed by mass communication reports which are talked about, altered, and interpreted by citizens in a society. The totality of this process constitutes reality. (1976, 211)

The Social Construction of News

This viewpoint reflects what has been called the **constructionist paradigm**, which posits that for public opinion to be understood, we must examine the artifacts of political culture—the language, symbols, and myths of public discourse. After all, words are creators. "They create situations which are no longer there, or which have never existed, and people behave as if they were real" (Berelson and Steiner 1964, 664–665). Consequently, researchers examine the "role of mass media frames in shaping political discourse and in reproducing the dominant political culture" (W. A. Gamson 1988b, 165; see also Edelman 1964, 1971, 1977; Gitlin 1978, 1980; Tuchman 1978a). This significant role is rarely recognized by the viewing public, for, as W. A. Gamson, Croteau, Hoynes, and Sasson (1992) explain:

> We walk around with media-generated images of the world, using them to construct meaning about political and social issues. The lens through which we received these images is not neutral but evinces the power and point of view of the political and economic elites who operate and focus it. And the special genius of this system is to make the whole process seem so normal and natural that the very art of social construction is invisible. (373)

Yet, ordinary people are not at the mercy of the political and economic elites, for they are active, reasoning beings capable of independent analysis. W. A. Gamson explains:

> The constructionist model reframes the relationship between media and public opinion as the interplay of two interacting systems. On the one hand, we have a system of media discourse that frames events and presents information always in some context of meaning. On the other hand, we have a public of interacting individuals who approach media discourse in an active way, using it to construct their own personal meanings about public events and issues. (1988b, 165)

In this way, such public deliberations serve to preserve both our democratic values and our democratic society.

Johnson-Cartee and Copeland (1997b), in analyzing the constructionist paradigm and its significance for students of public opinion, have explained:

> Today, voters no longer experience politics firsthand but rather through the eyes and ears of the mass media system. From the mass media we obtain, symbols, which we then interpret, redefine, and alter through our communication with

other people. What we know as our political world is not a photocopy of the objective world but rather a created world of symbols, often mass-mediated symbols. People use symbols without questioning or thinking about their origin. We use symbols nonchalantly without realizing the social, political, or personal ramifications for having used them. We often accept for ourselves the symbols created by others without analyzing the merits or appropriateness of their symbolic logic. Politics is a symbolic world. Men and women divide the goods of society among groups of people. The goods are mostly symbolic in nature but considered precious nevertheless. We construct our rules and regulations based on our symbolic knowledge of the world. Our acceptance of and promotion of various symbolic constructions have real consequences. For, we act on what we think we know and feel. (63)

As society becomes more complex, audience members are frequently confronted by news dealing with topics about which they know very little or nothing. Under such circumstances, the role of the news media in informing them is critical. And, as Bensman and Lilienfeld (1973) have warned:

This situation . . . is precisely that situation which makes possible large-scale fraud, charlatanry, and deceit by misdirection. For the conscious manipulation of information becomes possible only when access to genuine information or direct sources of experience is obscured by the complexity of events, issues, technology, size or differentiation in society. (211)

For instance, President George W. Bush's pronouncements concerning "weapons of mass destruction" (WMD) in Iraq served as the chief means by which the American public was persuaded that an invasion of that country was necessary. Yet, months after "hostilities had ended," no evidence of WMD was discovered.

In addition, Entman (1989a, 1989b) found that the public's evaluation of news is also related to how they feel about interest groups, public policies, and political leaders. And it is not just the people that mediated reports influence. Graber (1982) notes:

The perspective newspeople use in selecting and presenting their stories shape[s] politics to a significant degree. For many people in and out of government, media images become the reality on which their judgments are based. They also become the menu from which politicians select the political fare to be served to legislative bodies and publics. (11)

Consequently, reporting practices will be given greater consideration in chapters 3, 4, 5, and 6.

Redefining the Influence of Mass-Communicated News Reports: Agenda Setting, Priming, and Framing

Agenda Setting

Early theorists such as Wallas (1914), Lippmann ([1922] 1965) and Park (1940) emphasized the growing dependency of the public on the news media to orient themselves in their everyday world. Such emphasis led Bernard Cohen (1963) to suggest that the mass media performed an **agenda-setting function** for the public. Cohen wrote that the news media

> may not be successful much of the time in telling people what to think, but it is stunningly successful in telling its readers what to think about. . . . The world will look different to different people, depending . . . on the map that is drawn for them by writers, editors, and publishers of the papers they read. (1963, 13)

The first quantitative study of agenda setting is credited to M. E. McCombs and Shaw (1972), who found that those issues given prominent attention by the media were the same ones that people said were important to them during a presidential election campaign (cf. J. McLeod, Becker, and Byrnes 1974). Many researchers (e.g., Atkin 1980; Baus and Ross 1968; Iyengar and Kinder 1987; Rudd 1986) have commented on political candidates' attempts to determine the agenda for the media and ultimately the electorate.

Because agenda-setting research has been dealt with exhaustively by others, we will limit our discussion to Rogers and Dearing's (1988) synthesis of research findings. They report that agenda-setting research has revealed:

(1) The mass media influence the public agenda. This proposition, implied by the Cohen (1963) metaphor, has been generally supported by evidence from most public agenda-setting investigations, which cover a very wide range of agenda items, types of publics, and points in time.

(2) An understanding of media agenda-setting is a necessary requisite to comprehending how the mass media agenda influences the public agenda.

(3) The public agenda, once set by, or reflected by, the media agenda influences the policy agenda of elite decision makers, and, in some cases, policy implementation.

(4) The media agenda seems to have direct, sometimes strong, influence upon the policy agenda of elite decision makers, and, in some cases, policy implementation.

(5) For some issues the policy agenda seems to have a direct, sometimes strong, influence upon the media agenda. (579–580)

By naming or labeling particular "issues" during the campaign season, news consumers assign greater importance to and are more likely to access such issue-framed information when considering political options (Oskamp 1991, 294). Indeed, it has been found that simply labeling a story as campaign news will increase the news account's impact on consumers' agendas (W. Williams, Shapiro, and Cutbirth 1991). Research has found that newspaper coverage is particularly influential in the early stages of a campaign in determining the audience's agenda, and that television becomes increasingly important as the election day draws near (D. L. Shaw and McCombs 1977; W. Williams, Shapiro, and Cutbirth 1991). However, in the later stages of a presidential campaign, a single news commentary on national network television may create as much as four percentage points of opinion change (B. Page, Shapiro, and Dempsey 1987).

In the arena of politics, the news media are more influential in constructing consumers' political images within issue domains where consumers have little personal experience, such as in the area of foreign relations (Zucker 1978). Palmgreen and Clarke (1991) found that the "agenda-setting impact of the media . . . is generally weaker at the local level" (116), because voters have an opportunity to have firsthand knowledge of the issues.

Priming and Its Theoretical Antecedent Cultivation Theory

In particular, a group of researchers have focused on the role of television in influencing the "pictures in our heads" (Lippmann [1922] 1965). Gerbner and his colleagues (Gerbner and Gross 1976; Gerbner, Gross, Morgan, and Signorielli 1980a, 1980b, 1982, 1986, 1994) view television as uniquely influencing our perceptions of the world in which we live, in effect producing a homogenization of popular culture. Gerbner, Gross, Morgan, and Signorielli (1986) write:

> Television is a centralized system of storytelling. It is part and parcel of our daily lives. Its drama, commercials, news, and other programs bring a relatively coherent world of common images and messages into every home. Television cultivates from infancy the very predispositions and preferences that used to be acquired from other primary sources. Transcending historic barriers of literacy and mobility, television has become the primary common source of socialization and everyday information (mostly in the form of entertainment) of an otherwise heterogeneous population. The repetitive pattern of television's mass-produced messages and images forms the mainstream of common symbolic environment. (18)

And, despite new types of delivery systems such as cable, satellite, and VCRs, such advances only "signal even deeper penetration and integration of the dominant patterns of images and messages into everyday life" (Gerbner, Gross, Morgan, and Signorielli 1994, 17).

Gerbner and his colleagues use the term **cultivation** to "describe the independent contributions television viewing makes to viewer conceptions of social reality" (Gerbner, Gross, Morgan, and Signorielli 1994, 23). For many Americans who do not enjoy a variety of life experiences because of limited means and abilities, the use of television is "their major vehicle of cultural participation. To the extent that television dominates their sources of entertainment and information, continued exposure to its messages is likely to reiterate, confirm, and nourish—that is, cultivate—its own values and perspectives" (Gerbner, Gross, Morgan, and Signorielli 1994, 24; Morgan and Signorielli 1990). As television programming is designed for the largest possible audience, researchers have observed what they call **mainstreaming** or the convergence and entrenchment of mainstream orientations or world views among the attending public (Gerbner, Gross, Morgan, and Signorielli 1994, 25). Such mainstreaming involves the shared meanings and assumptions that people use to make sense out of their everyday lives and on which they base their actions.

Gerbner and his associates have observed a significant difference in how heavy viewers and light viewers of television conceive of social reality; they term this difference a **cultivation differential** (Gerbner, Gross, Morgan, and Signorielli 1994, 23). When heavy television viewers' beliefs about the world are compared with objective reality, sharp divergences emerge. One particular area, the perception of violence and the perceived likelihood of being victimized, provides ready evidence. Gerbner, Gross, Morgan, and Signorielli observed:

> FBI statistics . . . indicate that in any 1 year less than 1% of people in the United States are victims of criminal violence. We have found considerable support for the proposition that heavy exposure to the world of television cultivates exaggerated perceptions of the number of people involved in violence in any given week, as well as numerous other inaccurate beliefs about crime and law enforcement. (1994, 29; see also Gerbner, Gross, Morgan, and Signorielli 1980a)

However, it is important to note that the results that Gerbner and his associates have reported have not been replicated by other researchers. And the cultivation effect that Gerbner reports is eliminated when environment, race, and gender are controlled (A. N. Doob and Macdonald 1979; Skogan and Maxfield 1980; Slater and Elliott 1982; Wober 1978). In addition, when people are confronted with objective reality, the cultivation effect disappears (Slater and Elliott 1982).

While Gerbner's cultivation effect remains controversial, it is still important to recognize that there is the world of facts and figures, and there is another world made up of the residual impressions of audience members who have been exposed to mass media reports about crime. This is particularly true in understanding the role of public perception of public opinion climates, which are important to political communicators, whether public officials, political candidates, lobbyists, or social movement activists. In many situations, what the public believes to be true may be, in the sense of an objective reality, not true. Such errors in the public's judgment are thought to be the result of poor or misleading information environments, and in an industrialized society, this typically means the mass media and in particular television (see Shamir and Shamir 1997; O'Gorman 1986). For this reason, a strategic political communicator often adopts an approach to the study of public opinion that incorporates a perceptual component that takes into account "an individual's awareness, assessment or sense of relevant others' opinions" (C. J. Glenn, Ostman, and McDonald 1995, 253). We will consider such public perceptions of public sentiment later in this chapter.

Brody and Page (1975) have observed that "in a large and complex world people do not observe most major events directly. . . . But most people, most of the time, receive information about events indirectly, through mass media—particularly television" (40). Neuman (1982) reports that, clearly,

> television has emerged as the truly dominant mass medium in American society. The numbers are staggering. Ninety-eight percent of American homes have sets and those sets are turned on for an average of about seven hours a day. The average adult takes in an incredible four hours of television a day, which over the average lifetime adds up to the equivalent of eight straight years (at 24 hours a day) of television viewing. (471)

Indeed, by the late 1960s, television news emerged as the dominant source of information for the majority of Americans (J. P. Robinson and Levy 1986b). "The most striking aspect of the television phenomenon from a sociological point of view is its universality. Television is socially defined as the culture of the masses" (Neuman 1982, 472).

Most importantly, it has been observed that "the emergence of television as a prominent provider of information has fundamentally altered the organization and flow of public information in modern society" (J. P. Robinson and Levy 1986a, 13), for TV news by virtue of its format is significantly constrained. Batscha (1975) has addressed the constraints of the television news format, writing:

> Because the broadcast format promotes simplicity, capsulation, and stereotyping, the [attending] individual's map lacks certain facets of the overall picture.

Stories on complex ideas, long-term trends, and economics do not often receive air time. . . . The demand for simplicity and conciseness and the need for the visually interesting story results not only in the potential danger of presentational bias and stereotyping, but in the words of a news magazine's advertisement, in creating a public that is "overnewsed and underinformed." (223–225)

As early as 1965, CBS *Evening News* anchor Walter Cronkite warned that the constrained nature of broadcast journalism ill served the country, for people began to rely on television as their sole means of public information (J. P. Robinson and Levy 1986b). This problem is even more acute now than almost forty years ago because of the emergence of all-news channels such as CNN and MSNBC. Local television news has grown to three hours or more per day in many markets. News magazine programming has become a popular prime-time offering. And networks interrupt regularly scheduled entertainment programming to bring viewers "special reports," "breaking news," and "news updates." Sometimes, even our news gets interrupted by "breaking news." A shooting spree at an industrial facility in Meridian, Mississippi, or a major airline disaster will interrupt normal news programming. And, often, lead anchors are called back to the newsroom to handle the perceived crisis.

Yet, with all this access to television news, Americans remain woefully uninformed about the day's events (Delli Carpini and Keeter 1996). Television news provides the illusion of being informed. J. P. Robinson and Levy (1986b) write: "But it is a false sense of knowledge, for it is based only on a vaguely understood jumble of visual and auditory stimuli that leave few traces in long term memory" (17–18). Such emphasis on fast-paced commentary, stereotypical news themes, action news clips, and short sound bites may "divert the public from more useful and worthwhile forms of mental work—from knowledge, from insight, from contemplation, or from dialectic" (J. P. Robinson and Levy 1986b, 16).

Despite such widespread cynicism concerning the informational benefits of television news, for the most part broadcast journalism remains, in the words of J. P. Robinson and Levy (1986b), "the main source" or, in the worst-case scenarios, "the only source" of public information for vast numbers of our people. Therefore, the newsgathering processes involved in the "construction of news" are considered very important in that they ultimately affect how public issues are named and defined by reporters. Television's role in shaping public perceptions of not only political actors, political issues, and social forces but also public opinion makes TV news a prime social indicator (see Adoni and Cohen 1978; Adoni, Cohen, and Mane 1984; Hawkins and Pingree 1981).

Indeed, "*By calling attention to some matters while ignoring others, television news influences the standards by which governments, presidents, policies, and candidates for office are judged*" (Iyengar and Kinder 1987, 63; emphasis in original). Such influence Iyengar and Kinder (1987, 63–72; 1986) call "the priming effect." While providing no succinct definition of "the priming effect," Iyengar and Kinder (1987) provide clues as to what they mean by priming. In the complex and rapidly changing modern world, individuals cannot hope to know and to understand everything in the public arena. People are literally bombarded by televised public information, from which they select information to attend to and to evaluate. Clearly, much is winnowed out by selectively attending to what is offered by the media. Stories about weather patterns in southern Florida are routinely ignored by people living in Maine, unless they also own a condominium in the Sunshine State. In addition, news selection and attention involve a personal judgment of saliency: Is this important to me, personally? Does it concern a medication I'm currently taking? Does this event, piece of information, news story, and so on affect my life or the life of my loved ones in any way? Will the war with Iraq involve a reinstitution of the military draft, and will my son be eligible for such a draft? Or does this information appear to be historically significant; will it have lasting impact in society? Will the acts of September 11, 2001, have lasting impact on the way Americans conduct their travel plans both at home and abroad? Such judgments of saliency are just one evaluative mechanism by which individuals make sense out of the world. Because their lives are so very busy and complex, individuals also turn to heuristics, memory shortcuts, or past memory cueing to make sense of the world. In other words, they utilize accessible information that they have already stored in evaluating new information and making social judgments. Thus, most social judgments are made upon that which readily comes to mind and is easily accessible and retrievable. Thus, priming, if you will, is television news's ability to equip or to provide information in a simple and readily digestible manner. Such televised information is already placed within a familiar thematic context, an identifiable social judgment that provides individuals with memory shortcuts or heuristics from which to reach their own evaluations. During the summer of 2002, as more top executives from leading American corporations were exposed for stock manipulation, insider trading, false earnings projections, and gross personal greed, the thematic context provided by television news was a corporate world run by economic criminals. According to Shrum and O'Guinn, heavy television viewers find information learned from television highly accessible, leading them to "not only overestimate frequency or probability but also give faster responses" to various questions about "social reality" (1993, 436). We might expect that heavy television viewers during the summer of 2002 would overestimate the frequency of corporate executives' misdeeds and would be able to provide faster responses as to the nature of such misdeeds.

It must be noted that individuals turn to broadcast news not only for factual information but also for some evaluative guidelines. Television news does more than assist in establishing personal and public policy agendas in that it fosters the creation of evaluative dimensions to public discourse as well. In the words of Iyengar and Kinder (1987):

> Priming presumes that when evaluating complex political phenomena, people do not take into account all that they know—they cannot, even if they are motivated to do so. Instead, they consider what comes to mind, those bits and pieces of political memory that are accessible. Television news, we supposed, might be a powerful determinant of what springs to mind and what is forgotten or ignored. Through priming (drawing attention to some aspects of political life at the expense of others) television news might help to set the terms by which political judgments are reached and political choices made. (114)

Because people tend to turn to information sources that are convenient and accessible, they place great reliance on television news. For this reason, Iyengar and Kinder (1987) suggest that the more a problem area is primed on television news, the more likely voters will take this problem area into account in judging public officials. And, in experimental conditions, the researchers found that indeed priming was "both powerful and pervasive" (1987, 72). In their study examining social judgments made about presidents, Iyengar and Kinder (1987) conclude:

> Television news does indeed shape the standards by which presidential performance is measured. . . . The power of television news to shape the standards by which presidents are judged is greater when stories focus on the president, and less when stories focus attention elsewhere. When coverage implied that the president was responsible for causing a problem or for solving it, the priming effect increased. When coverage implied that forces and agents other than the president were responsible for the problem, the priming effect diminished. These effects were particularly apparent for problems relatively new to the American political agenda, for which public understanding is perhaps less solidly formed and therefore more susceptible to the way that television news frames the matter of responsibility. (115–116)

The researchers also examined the networks' national agendas as compared to the local news agendas. Iyengar and Kinder (1987) report that network news programs focus on the state of the economy, the president's economic policies, and the resulting implications for congressional elections. Yet, if exposed to local television news, people tend to make congressional voting decisions based upon the "story frame" of their favorite local television news. And "depending on the interests and resources of local television news, congressional elections can either

be a referendum on the president's economic performance, or purely a local contest between two distinct candidates" (Iyengar and Kinder 1987, 116). Therefore,
according to Iyengar and Kinder, television news—whether national or local—
"can alter the grounds on which elections are contested" (1987, 116).

Framing

In the communication literature, there are many uses of the terms "frame"
and "framing." These terms are not necessarily synonymous. For our purposes, "Framing is the process by which a communication source, such as a
news organization [or a political leader, public relations officer, political advertising consultant, or news consumer], defines and constructs a political
issue or public controversy" (T. E. Nelson, Clawson, and Oxley 1997, 567).
And, in the words of Tankard, Hendrickson, Silberman, Bliss, and Ghanem
(1991), "A frame is a central organizing idea for news content that supplies a
context and suggests what the issue is through the use of selection, emphasis,
exclusion, and elaboration" (11). For the purposes of analysis, framing research may be characterized as investigating either media frames or individual frames. Media frames may be viewed as rhetorical "devices embedded in
political discourse" (Kinder and Sanders 1990, 74), which are presented
through communication channels. Individual frames may be viewed as the
"internal structures of the mind" utilized to categorize and organize beliefs
and values (Kinder and Sanders 1990, 74). Often scholars look at the relationships existing between media frames and individual frames, for, in Friedland
and Zhong's (1996) words, frames operate as "the bridge between . . . larger
social and cultural realms and everyday understandings of social interaction"
(13; see also Reese 2001).

Individual Frames and Public Deliberation

Researchers had long puzzled over how ordinary citizens make choices between alternative policy positions; in many cases, their decisions didn't appear to
fit any rational model of decision making. For this reason, researchers began to
examine a variety of situational factors involved in decision making. Such situational factors are the frames or what Kahneman and Tversky (1984) have called
the "reference states" that people draw from to make decisions. Indeed, much of
the work examining media/individual issue framing draws upon this earlier
work of Kahneman and Tversky (1984) on the psychology of decision making.
In short, "The way in which choices are presented to people [by the news media
and other social actors]—the way the choices are framed—will affect the likelihood that particular options will be selected" (Price and Tewksbury 1997, 182).

Or, to put it another way, when people engage in public discourse about political, economic, or social issues, they are engaging in public deliberation or the very essence of democracy. And when people engage in deliberation or the "process of collective and open reasoning, and discussion about the merits of public policy" (Pan and Kosicki 2001, 36), they are of necessity engaged in issue framing. Individual issue frames are influenced by media presentations, popular wisdom, and past experiences of the participants involved (W. A. Gamson 1992). "Framing an issue is to participate in public deliberation strategically, both for one's own sense making and for contesting the frames of others" (Pan and Kosicki 2001, 38). Pan and Kosicki (2001) have observed:

> In public deliberations, the rise and fall in the prevalence of a frame, and consequently a particular policy option, clearly involve debates among people who sponsor or align with different frames. . . . Which frame to sponsor, how to sponsor it, and how to expand its appeal are strategic issues to participants. (39)

Different political actors vary in their framing power. The head of a teachers' union with 75,000 public school employees supporting her will have a larger voice in framing educational issues for the news media and for the state legislature than a lone teacher. A lobbyist with almost unlimited financial resources committed to reelecting favored political incumbents is more likely to be successful in influencing state legislators than an individual writing his state representative to complain about a particular policy initiative. Lobbyists who can craft strategic alliances among a variety of other associations, lobbying operatives, and legislative committee chairpersons will have an effective voice in public policy debates. And experienced "frame-makers," or those with skills in crafting and sponsoring policy frames, are more likely to have their frames accepted than those who are novices in such public deliberations. In short, "Framing potency comes from three sources: access to and control of material resources, strategic alliances, and stock of knowledge of and skills in frame sponsorship" (Pan and Kosicki 2001, 44). Different political actors bring different political "resources" to the table when engaging in public debate. According to Pan and Kosicki (2001), resources "refer to the material, social structural, institutional, and cultural means that are available to an actor to promote his or her frame and to influence the language, context, and atmosphere of public deliberation concerning an issue" (44; see chapters 5, 6, and 7).

Media Framing

While agenda setting and priming deal with how news may promote issue prioritization or increase issue accessibility, media framing research examines how news content influences and affects news consumers. "By framing social and political issues in specific ways, news organizations declare the underlying causes and likely consequences of a problem and establish criteria for evaluating potential remedies of the problem" (T. E. Nelson, Clawson, and Oxley 1997, 567–568). Some researchers study psychological responses to issue framing (Kahneman 1982; Kahneman and Tversky 1984). Others are more interested in the sociological aspects of issue framing, examining the cultural narratives, mythologies, and rituals utilized in constructing the frame (Bennett 1996; Bennett and Lawrence 1995). Others examine how ideologies and cultural values permeate the news frames (W. A. Gamson 1989; Gitlin 1980; see chapter 5).

M. R. Just, Crigler, and Neuman (1996) investigated how people went about constructing their political meanings about public issues. They found that political meanings or political conceptualizations are constructed by utilizing two highly integrated cognitive and evaluative dimensions:

> The first dimension, the frame, is primarily cognitive in nature and contains information about the structure and general parameters of the object under consideration. The second dimension, the tone, is primarily affective and represents the emotions associated with the object. (1996, 133)

While the political conceptualizations may well have been limited to short, limited cognitive elements, those that the individuals in their study possessed were intertwined with evaluative or affective meanings.

All of these research avenues are particularly significant to the political communication research arena in understanding how news frames affect an individual's personal concerns, issue preferences, or even voting decisions. Particularly when news consumers hold no prior strong beliefs or attitudes toward an issue, news framing is likely to have more influence on individual decision making. And, when news consumers face cross-pressures, leaving themselves confused and/or ambivalent about competing issue solutions, news frames may have a strong influence on individual decision making. According to Price, Tewksbury, and Powers (1997), because journalists construct news frames that reflect the cultural themes and narratives within a society, journalists fundamentally affect how news viewers or readers understand the day's events. In short, news story frames produce an observable **framing effect** upon viewers and readers who attended to the news. Such influence occurs because news reports

> stress specific values, facts, or other considerations, endowing them with greater relevance to the issue than they might appear to have under an alternative frame. In other words, frames affect opinions simply by making certain considerations seem more important than others, these considerations, in turn, carry greater weight for the final attitude. (T. E. Nelson, Clawson, and Oxley 1997, 569)

Indeed, those involved in social influence study how to best frame mass-communicated messages from both a creative and a scientific standpoint. T. E. Nelson, Clawson, and Oxley (1997) report:

> The evidence is steadily accumulating that framing is a powerful concept for explicating the activities of journalists and news organizations. It also provides leverage for understanding the behaviors of public relations specialists, "spin doctors," and other elites and professionals whose job it is to produce congenial concepts, beliefs, and opinions among the broader public. (577; see chapter 6)

Framing provides the evidence that mass media accounts do more than just prime certain issues or values' accessibility; news frames provide "psychological weight" or belief importance to specific arguments (T. E. Nelson, Clawson, and Oxley 1997; T. E. Nelson and Oxley 1999; T. E. Nelson, Oxley, and Clawson 1997). "Some kinds of information are more important than others for a particular judgment, regardless of their value" (T. E. Nelson, Clawson, and Oxley 1997, 578).

T. E. Nelson, Oxley, and Clawson (1997) argue that there are "three main cognitive routes to political communication effects" (236), writing: "Messages may change attitudes by *adding information* to an individual's stockpile of considerations about the issue (belief change), by making particular considerations temporarily more *accessible* (priming), or by altering the *weight* of particular considerations (framing)" (T. E. Nelson, Oxley, and Clawson 1997, 236). For T. E. Nelson, Oxley, and Clawson (1997), frames are not just important for any news information they may provide; rather, they are important because they tap information already stored in the long-term memory that individuals have already judged as significant. Because frames are the structuring devices of cultural narratives, they evoke what is already within an individual (see chapter 5).

> Frames tell people how to weight the often conflicting considerations that enter into everyday political deliberations. Frames may supply no new information about an issue, yet their influence on our opinions may be decisive through their effect on the perceived relevance of alternative considerations. (T. E. Nelson, Oxley, and Clawson 1997, 226)

The body of work produced by the authors Nelson, Oxley, and Clawson in various combinations have produced greater understanding about framing effects and helped clarify a theoretical area often confused with agenda setting and priming (e.g., M. E. McCombs, Einsiedel, and Weaver 1991; M. E. McCombs, Llamas, Lopez-Escobar, and Rey 1997; M. E. McCombs and Shaw 1993; McCombs, Shaw, and Weaver 1997). McCombs and associates believe that framing or what they term "frame setting" is merely "second level agenda setting" (M. McCombs and Ghanem 2001; M. E. McCombs, Llamas, Lopez-Escobar and Rey 1997), arguing that agenda setting focuses on the salience of various issues, and frame setting focuses on the salience of individual issue attributes. However, I view agenda setting as an atheoretical orientation, recognizing the correlation of issues within news reports or political advertising with those expressed by voters as being important. Framing theory is grounded within the narrative paradigm as well as the construction of social reality theory, and it accounts for the way in which political communicators utilize and construct political meanings within our society (see Maher 2001 for a similar perspective).

Similarly, Price and Tewksbury's (1997) model of framing effects distinguishes between applicability affects and accessibility effects. When news consumers attend to the news, "salient attributes of a message activate certain ideas, which are thus more likely to be used in evaluations made in response to the message" (Price, Tewksbury, and Powers 1997, 486), what Price and Tewksbury (1997) called an **applicability affect**. Once activated, a memory residue remains, making it more likely that when news consumers attend to a given issue frame, past salient attributes and their evaluations will be reactivated for the news consumers' present use, a demonstrated **accessibility effect**. "Applicability effects are conceptualized as first-order effects of stimuli (in this case, media messages), whereas accessibility effects are secondary or second-order effects of messages" (Price, Tewksbury, and Powers 1997, 486). News story framing, then, is

> an applicability effect that occurs during message processing. A framing effect is one in which salient attributes of a message (its organization, selection of content, or thematic structure) render particular thoughts applicable, resulting in their activation and use in evaluations. (Price, Tewksbury, and Powers 1997, 486)

At any one time, multiple applicable ideas compete for activation. Price, Tewksbury, and Powers (1997) explain:

> Although an author tries, in creating a message, to evoke particular thoughts and feelings, those will inevitably compete for attention with whatever is already on the minds of readers or viewers (including but not limited to those already in general circulation in the media). Audiences may thus summon to mind other ideas, previous evaluations, and the like, well beyond those stimulated by a particular frame. So a message can serve to direct in various ways, but not completely control, a message recipient's train of thought. (486–487)

Researchers have also been interested in how the public utilizes media discourse to construct their political knowledge of the world. For W. A. Gamson

(1988b, 1996), individuals actively construct their own political reality, ultimately crafting their own narrative frames as to what they believe about a given issue. In a 1996 research study involving peer group discussions of public issues (a variant of a focus group, utilizing sociodemographic peers, primarily the working class in this instance, as participants), Gamson wanted "to observe the process of people constructing and negotiating shared meaning, using their natural vocabulary" (114). Interestingly, not only news reports but also advertising slogans and movie plots proved to be information resources for the participants. When discussing nuclear power, the participants mentioned the movies *Silkwood* and *The China Syndrome*. And, when discussing affirmative action, an advertising slogan from the United Negro College Fund's campaign, "A mind is a terrible thing to waste," was frequently mentioned within group discussions (Gamson 1996). People utilize what is at hand to construct their realities, holding on to that which rings true and discarding that which is discordant.

Gamson found that participants utilized three resources in carrying on their conversations about public issues: media discourse or news reports, experiential knowledge or personal experience, and popular wisdom or perceptions of what others believed (1996, 114). Media influence varied from issue to issue. For instance, if participants were discussing an international crisis, it was far more likely that they would rely on media frames and popular wisdom than on their experiential knowledge, for they had no personal experience with the issues at hand. Similarly, Lang and Lang (1981) distinguished between low-threshold issues and high-threshold issues. **Low-threshold issues** are those that individuals have personal experience with in their everyday lives; people observe higher grocery prices, gasoline prices, and heating and cooling expenses. They understand that inflation means that their dollars don't go as far, and the cost of everything they need will likely go up as a result. **High-threshold issues** are those with which they have no firsthand experience in their lives; what they know comes to them indirectly through the mass media. For instance, Muslim extremists and terrorist training camps aren't likely to be part of the average American's daily life. Lang and Lang (1981) have argued that the news media have the greatest influence on such high-threshold issues, because people have no independent means to verify news accounts.

Personal Concerns and Framing

Iorio and Huxman (1996) analyzed how voters perceived media framing of matters they perceived as being of personal concern. They observed three conceptual processes that voters used in discussing their personal concerns: linking, collapsing, and colorizing. Voters frequently **linked** one issue with another; for instance, while discussing crime, they would point out that the nation needs more jobs so that people will not need to resort to criminal behaviors to support themselves. Or, they may have argued that providing better educational opportunities to citizens will allow people to get better jobs, again reducing the need for crime. Crime, then, is linked with poor educational opportunities and unemployment. Voters also didn't bother to remember or to discuss details; rather, they simply *collapsed* beliefs into kernels of understanding, and "differences were glossed over, distinctions blurred, and details dissolved, as concerns and issues melded into a central, elemental essence" (Iorio and Huxman 1996, 106). Voters had a hard time distinguishing between various levels of government. They were just as likely to attribute responsibility for paving potholes to the federal government as to the city government. Voters also **colorized** their accounts of personal concerns by introducing "like life" judgments by "associating concerns with both assumptions regarding how people act and with personal assessments about how life circumstances unfold" (Iorio and Huxman 1996, 107). "Respondents extrapolated from news reports and interpersonal sources and held up a mirror to judge performances, events, and news makers on the basis of their own knowledge of human behavior" (Iorio and Huxman 1996, 107). For instance, in a recent school board dispute, the school board fired the superintendent of schools, granting her a one-year, paid sabbatical before retiring. Citizens wrote outraged letters to the newspaper editor, arguing that in the real world that they know, people who get fired don't get paid not to work. In short, Iorio and Huxman conclude that voters didn't attend to news frames and utilize them in rational debate over public policy alternatives; rather, they experienced these news frames and the inevitable discussions of those frames as "overarching, politically charged, social and personal *problems* in need of resolution" (1996, 110; emphasis in original). Public issues, then, are viewed in terms of personal problems; such a finding might indicate how political news could be constructed to create greater interest among news audiences.

Indeed, Scheufele (1999) reminds us in summary of what we do know from the framing literature: (1) the similarity of media frames to individual frames is largely contingent on the issue under investigation (Iyengar 1991); (2) different priorities are frequently expressed when comparing media frames and issue frames (Neuman, Just, and Crigler 1992); and (3) multiple competing frames are also operational, being presented by influentials, groups, organizations, or interests within society but not necessarily through mass media channels (Neuman, Just, and Crigler 1992). In addition, individuals frequently introduce their own thoughts, their own analysis, when constructing their individual frames of social issues; Price, Tewksbury, and Powers (1997) found that individuals "demonstrated a capacity to introduce their own thoughts, going beyond the information provided and drawing out some basic implications on their own" (496), reinforcing my belief in a minded, active, and creative humankind.

Gamson (1992b) has suggested that groups may utilize three different framing resource pathways to construct their individual or group frames of public issues:

> *Cultural.* These discussions rely on media discourse and popular wisdom in framing the issue but do not integrate experiential knowledge in support of it.
>
> *Personal.* These discussions rely on experiential knowledge and popular wisdom in framing the issue but do not integrate media discourse in support of it.
>
> *Integrated.* These discussions rely on a full combination of resources, bringing together media discourse and experiential knowledge. (129; emphasis added)

The resource pathway or strategy chosen is largely issue dependent (Gamson 1992b), for reasons presented earlier.

In Summary

The power of the mass media to influence the way in which people view the world, particularly television, makes the newsgathering processes involved in the "construction of news" an important knowledge area for anyone desiring to understand the public opinion/news media/public policy process. These newsgathering processes affect how issues are named and defined by reporters, thus shaping the raw materials from which people inevitably draw to form their own versions of reality.

However, an analysis of the construction of news is no easy process. Bennett (1996) has observed that "the construction of news like the social construction of other human realities, is a creative and largely intuitive process involving information processing, judgment, and the timing and management of events themselves" (381). It is, therefore, essential for political observers to understand the creative, sometimes routine, often haphazard aspects of the social construction of news (see chapters 5, 6, and 7).

The Knowledge Gap Hypothesis

In 1970, Tichenor, Donohue, and Olien introduced a highly controversial but equally intriguing hypothesis that had significant implications for those studying how to better utilize mass communication for constructive social change. Originally their knowledge gap hypothesis predicted:

> As the infusion of mass media information into a social system increases, segments of the population with higher socioeconomic status (SES) tend to acquire

this information at a faster rate than the lower status segments, so that the gap in knowledge between these segments tends to increase. (1970, 159)

Clearly the hypothesis suggests, for instance, that when a public information campaign attempts to equalize information throughout a society, the disparity between those who have information about a given topic and those who do not will grow. Such an argument has grave implications, whether for those constructing a campaign to improve water purity standards in a developing nation or for those working to increase HIV awareness and prevention methods in the United States.

According to Gaziano (1983), the knowledge gap hypothesis has three explicit variables and one implicit one to consider: "the level of mass media publicity in a particular social setting, level of individuals' education, and level of individuals' knowledge. Time can be considered a fourth variable" (449). A wide range of news diffusion, agenda-setting, and public opinion studies as well as those specifically dedicated to knowledge gap analysis have produced a large legacy of knowledge gap research (for reviews, see Gaziano 1983; Viswanath and Finnegan 1996). However, given the wide variety of research circumstances and treatments used, the research remains, for the most part, inconclusive. I will focus on findings where there is at least some agreement regarding the factors researchers are grappling with in their ongoing agenda to understand the elusive phenomena known as knowledge gaps.

Early studies focused on education levels as an explanatory variable producing the observable knowledge gap (see, for instance, Deutschmann and Danielson 1960; Hyman and Sheatsley 1947). One school of thought argued that the poor and others also diagnosed as being "culturally deprived" were deficient in language and lived in societies that could only be described as dysfunctional, two conditions that researchers perceived as producing a deficiency in intellectual competence.

However, other researchers oppositely interpreted "perceived differences," arguing "that those groups ordinarily diagnosed as culturally deprived have the same underlying competence as those in the mainstream dominant culture, the difference in performance being accounted for by the situations and contexts in which the competence is expressed" (Cole and Bruner 1971, 870). If, for example, public affairs information is not perceived by "culturally deprived" individuals as being essential to their functioning in everyday life, then they will be unlikely to attend to it. An individual who is worried about putting food on the table will probably not spend the time or money to attend to the mass media. Consequently, Genova and Greenberg (1979) found that composite interest in an issue was a better predictor of knowledge than of education. In a similar perspective, Ettema and Kline (1977) incorporate motivation and functional utility of the information as explanative variables and reformulate the knowledge gap hypothesis, writing:

> As the infusion of mass media information into a social system increases, segments of the population motivated to acquire that information and/or for which that information is functional tend to acquire the information at a faster rate than those not motivated or for which it is not functional, so that the gap in knowledge between these segments tends to increase rather than decrease. (188)

This emphasis on situation-specific circumstances has been labeled "policy-relevant personal motivations" or "transsituational factors" (Lovrich and Pierce 1984, 415). In one particularly innovative study, researchers compared the effects of a campaign directed at a high-risk-for-cancer membership group with the knowledge levels of the general population. Interestingly, the study "suggested that group membership, information functionality, motivation, and education combined to affect knowledge, rather than motivation alone overcoming the effect of education" (Viswanath, Kahn, Finnegan, Hertog, and Potter 1993, 546).

In a variety of other studies, social conflict reduced substantially the size of knowledge gaps (Donohue, Tichenor, and Olien 1975; Gaziano 1988). Negativity and conflict have long been associated with higher attention and retention levels (Johnson-Cartee and Copeland 1991; Lau 1982, 1985; Lau and Pomper 2001a, 2001b, 2002; Lau, Sigelman, Heldman, and Babbitt 1999). Gaziano wrote that in circumstances of social conflict

> Knowledge gaps were narrower when the issue was: (1) specific and important to the community in which respondents lived, (2) less abstract, (3) directly affecting the lives of community residents, and (4) discussed frequently. These factors increased conflict intensity. (1988, 352)

Knowledge gaps frequently develop when either international or national topics are studied. Gaps are smaller for local issues, and they aren't necessarily related to education level (Becker and Whitney 1980). It has also been recognized that the idea of **community boundedness** or the personal identification with an issue and others affected by that issue may occur because of ethnicity or other associational properties (Viswanath and Finnegan 1996).

In addition, variations in SES levels and levels of interest may play a key role in explaining the presence of knowledge gaps. Research has indicated that when there is a high level of interest, particularly among elites, specialized occupational groups (as the communication relates to the occupation), or both, the disparity between elites and non-elites is likely to increase (Gaziano 1983, 1988, 1997). However, research has also found that low-SES individuals are just as likely to know information that is important to them personally as high-SES individuals (Genova and Greenberg 1979).

The preferred channel of communication also seems to play a role in observed knowledge gaps. Even within education groups, those individuals who routinely read the newspaper as opposed to those seeking news from other available media outlets will consistently demonstrate heightened levels of public affairs knowledge (Bogart 1980; Gaziano 1988). However, recent studies have found that "television use could decrease existing gaps in knowledge between those with more and less education" (Eveland and Scheufele 2000, 228; see also Kwak 1999; Miyo 1983, Neuman, Just, and Crigler 1992). And "television news' meager content inhibits learning by higher education groups" (Eveland and Scheufele 2000, 229). While the debate concerning the knowledge gap hypothesis continues and the majority of research findings are far from conclusive, this intriguing concept does offer insights into the political process.

Social Perceptions

The news places people in touch with a distant other, and this connection allows them to consider their own behavior in comparison to that of the other. A woman in Trenton, New Jersey, listens to an account of public child abuse in Houston, Texas. News commentators, social workers, children's rights activists, legal experts, and religious activists debate the significance of the televised child abuse reaching millions of Americans. E-mails to network anchors are read on the air, and her favorite news organization produces a prime-time special program to highlight child abuse in America and the legal system's response to it. The woman in Trenton listens to news accounts concerning people far away from her own personal reality, yet she is able because of this exposure to review and evaluate her own behavior toward her children, her parents' behavior toward her, and her personal experiences with other parents and children. She is able to compare her own experiences with those depicted on the television news programming. This process allows the woman to make social judgments or perceptions about others. We now turn to a discussion of social perceptions and ultimately their significance for the democratic process.

Since the turn of this century, researchers recognized that humans create "mental communities" (Wundt 1907, 296–298) or **generalized others** (Mead 1934) that help guide their beliefs, attitudes, and behaviors. For Mead, the generalized other would be the image of recognized symbol systems of a broader cultural system (the perceived shared norms, values, and beliefs) that serve to regulate human conduct (see J. H. Turner and Beeghley 1981). The generalized other should be viewed on a continuum in that "the other" might be as small as an occupational group or as large as the human race. For example, a person might take into account as his or her generalized other people sharing a common occupation, religion, class, region of the country, gender, age group, political affiliation, institutional affiliation, racial or ethnic identity, personality type, national identity, and so on.

For Mead, the ability of humans to assess or evaluate the beliefs and attitudes of others was key to making society possible. People will engage in role taking or the assumption of attitudes or beliefs belonging to others in regulating their own conduct. And this fact has significant implications for the health and well-being of society. J. H. Turner and Beeghley (1981) write that

> Mead argued that to the degree individuals can accurately take the role of the other and assume the perspective of common generalized other(s), patterns of interaction will be stable and cooperative. Conversely, to the degree that role-taking is inaccurate and occurs with respect to divergent generalized other(s), interaction will be disrupted, and perhaps conflictual. (482; see also Mead 1934, 321–322)

If people have unwittingly created "false" images about the attitudes, beliefs, and behaviors of others, they will act upon those images as if they were real, and as a result, these images will ultimately have real consequences. People, while capable of imagining a generalized other, are also capable of imagining public opinion shared by a group, an institution, or even a nation. We turn now to an analysis of social perception and public opinion.

Public Opinion Perceptions

C. J. Glenn, Ostman, and McDonald (1995) have identified six perspectives on perception and public opinion: (1) the pluralistic ignorance hypothesis, (2) the false consensus, (3) the looking-glass perception, (4) the spiral of silence theory, (5) the unrealistic optimism hypothesis, and (6) the third-person effect hypothesis (261–268). We will briefly consider these perspectives below.

Pluralistic Ignorance

People live in a state of what Allport (1924) called pluralistic ignorance— "a situation in which individuals hold unwarranted assumptions about the thoughts, feelings, and behavior of other people" (O'Gorman 1975, 314; see also Katz and Allport 1931; Latané and Darley 1970; D. T. Miller and McFarland 1987; Nimmo and Combs 1983; O'Gorman and Garry 1976). O'Gorman (1986) explains that

> pluralistic ignorance is not ignorance in the ordinary sense of not knowing. On the contrary, it is knowledge of others that is mistakenly considered to be correct. . . . Pluralistic ignorance refers to *shared* cognitive patterns, that is, socially accepted but false propositions about the social world. (333; see also O'Gorman 1988)

Korte (1972) has distinguished between two types of pluralistic ignorance: absolute and relative pluralistic ignorance. **Absolute pluralistic ignorance** is when two or more people misconstrue or mislabel majority and minority positions on an issue. When people label the majority of Americans as being against abortion rights for women, this is an example of absolute pluralistic ignorance. **Relative pluralistic ignorance** (while not as severe an error as absolute pluralistic ignorance) is when two or more people significantly underestimate or overestimate the size of the majority and minority positions (see also Fields and Schuman 1976–1977; Merton [1957] 1968).

Shamir and Shamir (1997) have argued that pluralistic ignorance occurs because of erroneous environmental messages: "Inadequate, misleading, or false information cues serve as invalid indicators for public opinion and produce pluralistic ignorance" (229). Particularly important, then, to an understanding of pluralistic ignorance is the analysis of the information environment to which people attend, that is, the mass media. As the dependency model of mass communication effects indicated, the mass media both maintain the status quo and provide catalysts for change. These "catalysts" are usually created by the reporting of things that are "unexpected" or "negative," because such things fit with the American news media's definition of news. Often, the media overreport "events, groups, and views that are unusual or unexpected, extreme, loud, or provocative" (Shamir and Shamir 1997, 231). When this occurs, people often develop invalid shared perceptions about public opinion. For example, the news media's coverage of the anti-abortion or right-to-life movement has led many people to believe the following erroneous statements:

1. The majority of Americans oppose abortion.
2. The majority of Americans support the Right to Life Amendment.
3. Republicans are anti-abortion.
4. Democrats are pro-choice.
5. Most abortions are third-trimester abortions.
6. Most women who receive abortions are irresponsible single women.

7. Abortion as practiced in the United States is just another form of birth control like the pill or condoms.
8. If you are Christian, you oppose abortion; or you must oppose abortion to be Christian.

Yet research reveals a much different picture. Indeed, the following may conclusively be reported:

1. The majority of Americans support some form of abortion rights for women.
2. The majority of Americans do not support the Right to Life Amendment.
3. Roughly the same percentage of voters in each party oppose abortion rights—about 28–30 percent.
4. Third-trimester abortions are relatively rare.
5. Most women who receive abortions are married women with children. These women habitually practice birth control, but for whatever reason, the birth control method failed on this occasion, resulting in an unwanted pregnancy. The majority of these women give financial concerns as the major factor in seeking an abortion.
6. Abortion as practiced in the United States is a surgical remedy when birth control mechanisms fail.
7. The majority of people self-identifying themselves as Christian are pro-choice.

Perhaps such shared erroneous assumptions or pluralistic ignorance explains why the abortion issue has not been resolved in American politics in that many voters may be fearful of speaking out for fear of ostracism or embarrassment, for they fear being labeled "anti-Christ" or "anti-Christian" (D. T. Miller and McFarland 1987; Noelle-Neumann 1991, 1993). Clearly, then, a pro-choice campaign designed to resolve the "abortion issue" should educate the American public about the "true" majority of opinion on abortion. In addition, the campaign should provide voters with the necessary psychological and coping skills to overcome their social fears of expressing their true beliefs.

False Consensus Effect

Individuals have the tendency to view their own beliefs and behaviors as being widely shared and appropriate in a given circumstance, and they judge those beliefs and actions of others that are different from their own (but under similar circumstances) as uncommon, inappropriate, and even deviant

(Ross, Greene, and House 1977). This is called the false consensus effect. Sherman, Presson, and Chassin (1984) suggest three reasons why false consensus might occur: (1) self-enhancement, or the need to perceive yourself as being like everyone else; (2) the need for social support, or the perception that other people agree with your beliefs; and (3) the need to reaffirm or validate your own opinions by widely attributing those beliefs to others. For example, the Republican presidential convention of 1992 (for George H. W. Bush and Dan Quayle) revealed a number of false consensus effects among convention speakers. Pat Buchanan told the convention audience and, through the technology of television, the world at large: "Our culture is superior. . . . Our culture is superior because our religion is Christianity and that is the truth that makes men free" (1992). In other words, Buchanan was saying that the people in the world who aren't Christian are inferior. It is no wonder that President Bush's support from Jewish voters fell from 35 percent in 1988 to 12 percent in 1992 (Clymer 1992, 28). And who is to say how such comments affected Muslims, Buddhists, Hindus, atheists, or those simply viewing themselves as religiously tolerant? But one thing was clear: traditionally presidential candidates experience the benefits of a "post-convention bump" in that their popularity dramatically improves after the convention, but this was not true in 1992 (see Holbrook 1996).

False consensus effects can have highly negative consequences for a political leader who believes that there is unanimity among his or her constituents on a particular issue, when in fact the issue is highly divisive. If the issue becomes very important to either a minority or majority of voters, the position the leader takes might well cost him or her the next election.

Looking-Glass Perception

People often erroneously assume that those they identify as being **significant others** (someone important in your own self-identification) in their life share the same opinions on issues as they themselves do. This is called the **looking-glass perception.** If we choose to belong to groups, it is usually because we view them as being important to us, as fulfilling some need we may have. And because we come to identify with those groups we belong to, we begin to identify with members of the group or to view the other members as significant others. In a recent social occasion involving a historical society's cocktail hour, I was amazed at how openly some members expressed obnoxiously bigoted comments about a wide variety of ethnic, racial, religious, and political groups. And it was clear that the individuals expressing such views feared no negative reactions from those within earshot; in short, they expected their listeners to hold the same opinions as they themselves.

Such assumptions about the thoughts and opinions of others by news reporters, political leaders, or other professional communicators such as press secretaries or public relation executives are a dangerous enterprise. Rarely does anyone have a "true fix" or a "true read" of public opinion, even those opinions shared among a public to which one belongs. Overestimation or underestimation of sentiment could lead to critical errors in decision making. For those even remotely involved in public policy making, whether as a journalist, media consultant, lobbyist, or elected official, it is best not to assume anything, for as the old adage goes, when something is assumed, it makes an "ass out of you and me" (ass-u-me).

Momentum Effect

Interestingly, evidence indicates that when people perceive others within a group as moving in a particular direction in terms of opinion on an issue, a **momentum** or **bandwagon effect** occurs in that they may then follow those who have already altered their opinion (Aronson and Linder 1965; N. L. Kerr, MacCoun, Hansen, and Hymes 1987; Price 1989). Awareness of such a mechanism is apparent in much of contemporary advertising in that frequently advertisers assure us "that everyone is doing it, eating it, buying it, or wearing it" within a certain target group. Today's Gap and Old Navy commercials illustrate the use of this technique to influence teenagers and young adults. However, there is some indication that such a bandwagon phenomenon occurs only when individuals have a heightened sensitivity to currents of opinion among a key group. For example, teenagers and young adults are operating within a highly sensitized mating environment, and therefore advertising using sex appeal and social status cues is highly persuasive for those seeking mates. The message is simple: buy Old Navy vests and get a high-status mate. Buy khakis from the Gap and get a high-status, "cool" mate. If, however, an individual is participating in a group or climate with weak identification ties, then the individual will not as conscientiously attend to opinion shifts. This creates an **antimomentum** effect in that the individual is not aware of opinion shifts and therefore will not review his or her own opinions in relation to others (Kerr, MacCoun, Hansen, and Hymes 1987), and this will not likely bring the individual into line with others.

Unrealistic Optimism

Individuals often assess themselves differently from others in terms of the probability of whether good or bad things will happen to them (Culbertson and Stempel 1985; C. J. Glenn, Ostman, and McDonald 1995; Tyler and Cook 1984).

Specifically, people tend to think that good things will happen to them, and bad things won't. In assessing risk for bad things to happen, people perceive far greater risk for others in society and little if any risk for themselves on a personal level. Tyler and Cook (1984) suggest that the media are good at making people aware of societal problems or risks, but individuals do not necessarily translate that risk into their everyday life. Taylor and Brown (1988) call this a **self-positivity bias**, because people do not believe that bad things will happen to them.

Such unrealistic optimism must be taken into account when developing persuasive risk-communication campaigns. Raghubir and Menon (1998) succinctly described this problem in an article dealing with AIDS (acquired immunodeficiency syndrome), titled "AIDS and Me, Never the Twain Shall Meet" (52). In other words, while past AIDS campaigns have been effective in making people aware of the AIDS epidemic, HIV risk–associated behaviors, and HIV risk–avoidance behaviors, these campaigns have been remarkably ineffective in changing individual sexual behaviors. People simply believe that "people like me don't get it" or "I won't get it, because I don't even know the kinds of people who get it." The incidence of HIV among American college students and nursing home residents who have engaged in unprotected sex gives testimony to the life-or-death significance of such unwarranted optimism. To be successful in altering sexual behavior patterns, public information campaign experts must create risk messages that are able to break through such perceptual screens.

In November 2001, the U.S. Postal Service felt sufficiently concerned to send out millions of notices warning mail recipients of suspicious letters or packages that might be contaminated with anthrax. As ordinary people began to die from anthrax—those having no connection with any of the targeted media organizations and federal office buildings—the unrealistic optimism turned into real fear. The dire warnings left many Americans worried about going to their mailbox.

Third-Person Effect

People often view themselves as being staunchly independent in their views. They do not perceive themselves as being susceptible to media influences; however, these same individuals will often characterize the mass media as being powerfully persuasive on the beliefs, attitudes, behaviors of others. Tyler and Cook (1984) have called this the **third-person effect** (see also Culbertson and Stempel 1985; Davison 1983; R. M. Perloff 1989, 1996). Glenn, Ostman, and McDonald (1995) explain the phenomenon:

> The "third person" may be seen as either the "other" person, who is affected by mass mediated messages, or the original person, who, not affected by the pri-

mary media message, but perceiving the probability of the media's effect on others, reacts to the impact that he or she thinks the message will have on others. (267–268)

For example, transplanted northerners who live in the Deep South often laugh at southerners rushing to the grocery store to stock up on staples such as bread, milk, and luncheon meat after weather reports of possible snow. Yet those same northerners who find southerners who fear driving in snow so humorous will also rush to the grocery store to buy bread, milk, and luncheon meat, because they believe from previous news reports that if they don't, those silly southerners will buy it all, leaving them without necessary staples.

Research indicates that individuals overestimate the effects of mass-mediated messages on others (J. Cohen, Mutz, Price, and Gunther 1988; Gunther 1991; Lasorsa 1989, 1992; R. M. Perloff, Neuendorf, Giles, Chang, and Jeffres 1992). And, ironically, research has found that at the same time, individuals underestimate the effects of mass-mediated messages on themselves (J. Cohen, Mutz, Price, and Gunther 1988; Gunther and Thorson 1992). For instance, when asked if political advertising influences their voting decisions, respondents will overwhelmingly answer negatively. Yet, when asked if political advertising influences the votes of others, the same individuals will overwhelmingly answer in the affirmative.

In Conclusion

As individuals, we are dependent on the news media to bring us the political happenings of our day. This dependency affects not only how we view politics but also the way we go about our daily lives, influencing not only our social perceptions but also our social judgments. We treat news-mediated messages as if they were real, and we act upon them without considering how or in what manner these messages were produced (see chapters 4, 5, and 6). And we often develop, through a steady diet of news messages, pictures of reality that have little to do with an objective reality (see chapters 4, 5, and 6).

Our social perceptions, particularly with regard to the social judgments of others and the public opinion process, are critical in understanding the American democratic processes. In chapter 2, we will review the significance of public opinion within the American body politic.

2

Public Opinion and Public Policy

He who loses the support of the people is a king no longer.

—Aristotle 1932, 1313a

Public opinion is often opposed to, and successfully sways politicians against, the quite sensible ideas of the qualified.

—T. Qualter 1985, 35

Historical Overview

UNLIKE ITS DEMOCRATIC COUNTERPARTS IN EUROPE, the United States does not have a tradition of fearing its people. Bloody rebellions that eventually annihilated the then current ruling elite (commercial or economic and political) in Europe were not part of U.S. history. Except for the Whisky Rebellion and John Brown's Rebellion, neither of which was a mass movement but isolated pockets of dissension, the United States has had very little spontaneous political turbulence. The Civil War, like most wars, was orchestrated by and for American ruling elites, and therefore, even though the War between the States was often characterized as a rebellion, it was more in keeping with two organized political factions settling their differences through armed combat. Without spontaneous explosions in mass opinion creating havoc in the social system as they did in Europe, the United States has continued its positive assessment of (if not captivation with) public opinion. Indeed, American political dialog, in keeping with traditional liberal democratic theory, has embraced public opinion as the cornerstone of its democracy.

Traditional liberal democratic theory has its roots in the Enlightenment; John Locke's *Second Treatise of Civil Government* and Jean-Jacques Rousseau's *Social Contract* provided what came to be the classical tenets of democratic theory. These works served as the theoretical and ideological basis for the U.S. Constitution (Bailyn 1967; Christenson, Engel, Jacobs, Rejai, and Herbert 1981; Groth 1971; Hartz 1955). The core belief of liberal democratic theory, or liberalism, is the "assumption that the individual is more important than the government and that government exists for the purpose of permitting . . . [the] individual to serve best his or her own needs and attain personal fulfillment" (Dolbeare 1981, 9). Consequently, popular sovereignty and the emphasis on public information, public debate, and public negotiation and compromise have played a central role in the development of American political thought. Liberal democratic theory (see Johnson-Cartee, Copeland, Marquez, Buford, and Stephens 1998) has exalted the average citizen's participation and the character of that participation in the public opinion process and the resulting political system. Indeed, public opinion is presented and thought of by most Americans as being an enlightened discussion characterized by the natural nobility of humans and their innate ability for reason (see Sproule 1989b, 227). And if there were problems, well, they could easily be fixed. American pragmatism and the progressive movement presented the argument that any deficiencies in individual participation in the political process would be remedied by the educational system in the United States, which socialized each individual into democratic life, providing the tools necessary for effective participation by every person, no matter his or her station in life. Such political behavior was deemed paramount by liberal political theorists, who pointed to "the free exchange, or *marketplace*, of ideas as a defining condition of liberal democracy" (Åsard and Bennett 1997, 28; emphasis in original). Consequently, rather than fearing public opinion as "something dangerous to rational national welfare," as do many Europeans who fear volatility and instability (Sproule 1989b, 228), Americans express optimism for both democracy and their lot in life. And, for the most part, lower- and middle-class Americans have not shared with their European counterparts the same degree of alienation from the commercial and political elites. During the Vietnam conflict, the traditional working classes were the last to turn against the war effort, despite paying a far greater price in terms of casualties among their young men than did members of the upper middle class, upper class, and intelligentsia who had either the resources or knowledge to avoid the draft. However, it should be noted that African Americans did experience this alienation, but by being systematically prevented from exercising their voting rights, they were prevented from effectively voicing this alienation within the system. And while the civil rights movement was a social force that the American political system had to reckon with and eventually accommodate, the movement did not reach the level of a political rebellion. The civil rights movement did not seek to overthrow the government; rather, its political activists wanted their rightful stake within the government.

To summarize, I turn to the writing of Noelle-Neumann (1979), who suggests that a belief in the significance of public opinion within liberal democratic theory fulfills four requisite functions in contemporary democratic society: (1) social integration, (2) societal stabilization, (3) societal prioritization, and (4) governmental legitimacy. A belief in public opinion provides:

1. **Social integration**—in that individuals desire to belong to identifiable groups or entities, and this desire then motivates them to engage in negotiation or compromise behaviors; therefore, these actions help establish "commonness" among others within society.
2. **Societal stabilization**—in that an interest in the beliefs, values, and attitudes of others helps establish (along with social integration) an infrastructure of consensus or an infrastructure of the status quo that allows for continuity and discourages change or instability.
3. **Societal prioritization**—in that the process of defining and structuring the public opinion process within society allows for societal members to prioritize or rank order those items deemed important for the society to consider or to act upon. Again, this practice helps maintain order and gives the illusion that the society, government, or both are responding to the public's wishes.
4. **Governmental legitimization**—in that by striving for commonness, by establishing structures to maintain stability, by upholding established norms and practices, and by reacting or adapting to demands within society, the government appears to be responding to what the people want and thus establishing or reinforcing its own legitimacy.

An Overview of American Conceptualizations of Public Opinion

Although public opinion is uniformly recognized as a powerful force in democratic politics, little consensus exists among scholars as to the exact nature of the beast. Public opinion—in both definition and specification—is probably one of the most misunderstood concepts in public life today. From social scientists to politicians, press secretaries, journalists, and finally laypersons, the term is widely used and misused in contemporary public debate (see Allport 1937; E. Katz 1983).

Perhaps German historian Hermann Oncken best characterized the ephemeral, definition-defying nature of public opinion when he wrote:

> Anyone who tries to grasp it [the concept of public opinion] and pin it down recognizes immediately that he is dealing with a Proteus, a creature that is both visible in a thousand ways and yet shadowy, that is powerless and at the same time surprisingly effective, that manifests itself in countless different ways, that always manages to escape our grasp just when we think we have a hold on it. . . . It is not possible to comprehend something that is in a state of fluctuation and flow by forcing it to fit into a set formula. . . . After all, anyone who is asked knows exactly what public opinion means. (1914, 224ff, 236; translated by Noelle-Neumann 1995)

Perhaps the protean nature of public opinion has led scholars to define it in a wide variety of ways (see P. E. Converse 1987; L. W. Doob 1966; Zaller 1994). In 1965, Harwood Childs cataloged fifty definitions of the term. Summarizing countless articles, books, and treatises concerning the nature of public opinion, Noelle-Neumann (1995, 34) suggested that public opinion conceptualizations may be categorized as public opinion characterized by discussion of its (1) rationality, (2) social comparison and social control, (3) elite pluralism and low-information rationality, or (4) participatory pluralism (see also Herbst 1993 and Noelle-Neumann 1995 for other breakdowns of public opinion conceptualizations).

Rationality

The founding fathers posited man as a rational being, an active information seeker, engaging in principled and responsible political behaviors. For the founding fathers, the individual's worth and the individual's needs were paramount. Through self-interest, the rational man would make good decisions. Consequently, they believed that it was the individual's choice to join with others to form a limited government based on a voluntary social contract that only served to provide the fulfillment of needs that an individual could not ensure himself—for instance, a national road system, a common currency, and so on (Johnson-Cartee, Copeland, Marquez, Buford, and Stephens 1998). Ultimately, all those under the social contract would benefit and prosper, because men were capable of ruling themselves wisely. Man was viewed as capable of listening, reasoning, deliberating, and reaching an informed compromise. Thus, collectively people would engage in the public opinion process to ultimately resolve conflict, ensuring the continuation of the polity.

"The concept of public opinion shaped by rationality is based on the notion of the rational, well-informed citizen capable of advancing sensible arguments and making sound judgments; it focuses on *political* life and *political* controversies" (Noelle-Neumann 1995, 43; emphasis added). Such notions ascribe to the Jeffersonian ideal that individuals through self-interest attend to the arena of political actors and the issues and values they espouse to evaluate and ultimately make their own decision as to what matters one chooses to endorse or to oppose. Consequently, conceptualizations of public opinion influenced by the rational actor premise tend to employ the flavor of that provided by Speier (1950), who defined public opinion as "opinions on matters of concern to the nation freely and publicly expressed by men outside the government who claim a right that their opinions should influence or determine the actions, personnel, or structure of their government" (376).

The belief in a rational actor premise has provided us with a view of the public opinion process as a well-oiled, readily functioning machine going about the daily affairs of the body politic, following the guiding forces of a reasoned design. Indeed, public opinion is viewed as a means of social organization. The **public** is "a group of people (a) who are confronted by an issue, (b) who are divided in their ideas as to how to meet the issue, and (c) who engage in discussion over the issue" (Blumer 1946, 188). It is helpful, therefore, to think of **opinion**, as depicted by traditional liberal democratic theory, as "a thought-out, reasoned choice between alternatives for action in a social matrix" (Price and Roberts 1987, 787). Consequently, for liberal democratic theorists, public opinion has been regarded as the "product of interactive influences, formed within 'the larger mind,' shaped by—but by no means reducible to—the many individual expressions that enter public opinion" (Price and Roberts 1987, 782; see also Cooley 1909).

The conceptualization of public opinion based on rationality fulfills a **manifest function** in American society in that it recognizes the need for citizen participation in the adjustment and adaptation of government processes and policies for the regime to remain legitimate. Liberal democratic theory posits that there should be a relationship between what people believe or want and what a representative government enacts in terms of policies. For this reason, scholars, political leaders, and social influence professionals are the natural students of public opinion (see Johnson-Cartee and Copeland 2004), gauging the trends and currents within a sea of competing interests and ideals. Such judgments influence not only what is talked about within the halls of power but also ultimately what is actually produced in terms of policy.

While definitions of public opinion emphasizing rationality posit an activist society, the reality is that only a very few people choose to participate in the public opinion process. And, furthermore, the relationship between public opinion on the one hand and governmental action or inaction on the other is a complex one, involving a multitude of forces—some direct and immediate, others less direct and collaborative, and still others broken or contradictory (see Nimmo 1978, 394–419). To understand this relationship, we must first understand politics. For Nimmo (1978):

> Politics . . . is the regulation of social conduct under conditions of conflict. The character of that regulation is continuing negotiation—negotiations of the meanings of the roles of leaders, followers, and nonfollowers: of political talk, symbols, and languages; of propaganda, advertising, and rhetoric; of channels, media, and techniques of political communication; of mass, group, and popular opinion; of the political self; of ways of taking part in politics, including voting and elections; and of the choices policy officials face and make. (419; see also Mancini and Swanson 1996)

Thus, the nature of public opinion—informed or uninformed, interested or disinterested—is critical to an evaluation of our democratic ideals as reflected by our public policies and as expressed through our body politic.

Reconsidering the Rational Voter and the Public Opinion Process

During the 1940s and 1950s, empirical researchers from Columbia University and the University of Michigan became dismayed by their research findings, which depicted widespread political ignorance and political disinterest among the general population (see Popkin [1991] 1994). In 1948, Lazarsfeld, Berelson, and Gaudet published *The People's Choice*, sending a dagger into traditional democratic theory's mythology of the rational political actor. They concluded:

> The open-minded voters who make a sincere attempt to weigh the issues and the candidates dispassionately for the good of the country as a whole—exist mainly in deferential campaign propaganda, in textbooks on civics, in the movies and in the minds of political idealists. In real life, they are few indeed. (100)

Indeed, the noted political scientist Paul Converse concluded in 1964 that "large portions of an electorate simply do not have meaningful beliefs, even on issues that have formed the basis for intense political controversy among elites for a substantial period of time" (245). Such findings led Bartels to conclude in 1996 that "the political ignorance of the American voter is one of the best documented data of modern political science" (194). Ferejohn (1990) has argued that the average American citizen knows "virtually nothing about the public issues that occupy officials from Washington to city hall" (3). Such observations rest on nearly seven decades of scholarly research, documenting the woeful ignorance of the American public concerning public affairs (Delli Carpini and Keeter 1996, 62; e.g., Bishop, Oldendick, Tuchfarber, and Bennett 1980; P. E. Converse 1970; Johnson-Cartee and Copeland 1997a; Key 1961; B. I. Page and Shapiro 1992; Patterson, 1980). Such research findings have led to sweeping generalizations of the sort provided by N. D. Glenn in 1972, who concluded that "a large proportion of the American public can not . . . intelligently vote or participate in the democratic process" (273), and of the sort provided by Whitney and Wartella, who in 1988 characterized American voters as political dummies (see also Delli Carpini and Keeter 1996; Erikson and Tedin 1995).

M. Schlesinger and Lau (2000) have argued that Americans don't use ideological or party identifications when making policy decisions. And, for the most part, they do not know details about the structures and functions of their government. However, they do think about politics; they think about politics metaphorically. In other words, they reason about policy decisions by evoking learned metaphors—metaphors provided them by political activists, policy-makers, and the news media. Schlesinger and Lau argue:

> We hypothesize that every society has a set of commonly understood ways of arranging social institutions and judging the effectiveness of their performance. Citizens . . . whether members of the general public or political elite—share a broad understanding of the nature of these "templates" for collective activity. Each of these arrangements constitutes a sort of archetype, an ideal against which people compare the consequences of actual policies or project the expected outcomes of proposed policy reforms. It is this process of comparison that makes the reasoning metaphorical. (2000, 611)

M. Schlesinger and Lau (2000) argue that five cognitive processes underlie the reasoning about policy metaphorically: "identifying causal responsibility, assigning treatment responsibility, applying norms of fairness, evoking effective responses, and establishing concrete comparisons" (622). In their analysis of the use of policy metaphors among the general public and the policy elite concerned with public health issues, they determined that

> (1) policy metaphors are coherent to both policy elites and members of the general public; (2) understanding particular metaphors appears to be distinct from favoring that metaphor as a guide for policymaking; and (3) there are shared patterns in metaphorical thinking between elites and the general public, as reflected in the relative coherence of different metaphors, the cognitive processes that are most salient for metaphorical reasoning, and the extent to which pairs of metaphors are seen as compatible with one another. (M. Schlesinger and Lau 2000, 622)

In short, while the American public remains woefully ignorant about political structures and functions, political actors, political ideologies, and political parties, they do make policy choices and state policy preferences through a process of metaphorical reasoning. Whether they can determine which candidate best represents their policy choices is another matter altogether. Lau and Redlawsk (1997) provide us with some optimism at this point. They find that roughly 75 percent of Americans do vote "correctly," if correctness is "*based on the values and beliefs of the individual voter*" and is the same as a vote choice made "under conditions of full information" (586; emphasis in original). In other words, most of the time, most Americans get it right.

Other researchers documenting the paucity of political interest, political knowledge, and political participation among American voters found other factors to be operating in favor of social control or social stability. Leon Festinger (1950) argued that despite the fact that few people choose to participate actively in the public opinion process, people do evaluate their own beliefs and opinions by comparing them to the beliefs and opinions of others, an argument that came to be known as **social comparison theory** (Festinger 1950, 1954). For Hardin and Higgins (1996),

> Social comparison theory rests on the assumptions that (1) social comparison processes are initiated when external reality is ambiguous and difficult to grasp; (2) a dualism between physical and social realities exists; and (3) physical reality takes precedence over social reality. (29)

Generally, people choose "others" similar to themselves when making such comparisons. Often people turn to **reference groups** or those groups to which an individual belongs or aspires (Riley and Riley 1959). Such reference groups exert influence on an individual's self-evaluation by providing a point of comparison and exerting influence on an individual's adoption of values, beliefs, and attitudes (Kelley 1952; Merton [1957] 1968). Reference groups are particularly important to people when they hold beliefs that are not supported by a physical reality, for they will then turn to their own reference groups to validate their own beliefs and attitudes (Festinger 1950, 1954; see also Johnson-Cartee and Copeland 2004). For example, some African Americans believe that AIDS and the HIV virus that produces this condition are the results of a conspiracy perpetrated by the U.S. Central Intelligence Agency (CIA) to rid the world of individuals of African descent regardless of where they live. Such a belief in CIA-crafted genocide is not reflected in physical reality; thus, believers in such a conspiracy must turn to others like themselves for validation. In this validation, they find solidarity with others like themselves.

In 1960, Campbell, Converse, Miller, and Stokes, in their seminal work *The American Voter*, depicted a citizenry disinterested in politics, largely passive, with little or no political knowledge, guided only by party labels and party identification when voting. But the researchers were not overly concerned about the future stability of the democratic process in the United States, for at this time party labels and party identifications were viewed as stable and long lasting, and as working to exercise a mechanism of social control. Similarly, Noelle-Neumann (1995) has argued that such social comparisons or political evaluations do exert influence on the behavior of man in society, for man is a social animal, fearing isolation or the ostracism that often comes when one is perceived as being different. And in this capacity public opinion acts as a powerful **social control** in that "it exerts pressure on the individual, who fears isolation, and on the government as well, which will also be isolated and eventually toppled without the support of public opinion" (Noelle-Neumann 1995, 43). This function of public opinion is **latent** in that it is not widely recognized as a consequence of holding opinions in society (Noelle-Neumann 1995), for most people do not recognize that they are influenced by what others think or believe.

However, such optimism concerning the durability and longevity of political labels and identifications quickly changed in 1976, with the publication of Nie, Verba, and Petrocik's alarming account of American political behavior. Instead of a passive, stable population, they portrayed a voting population coming unmoored from traditional party labels, becoming increasingly unstable, voting personal issue preferences, and increasingly expressing dissatisfaction and disillusionment with American politics. "Superficiality in issue constructs, inattentiveness to current events, and wildly fluctuating viewpoints gave scholars reason to distrust the rationality of the average American voter" (Johnson-Cartee and Copeland 1997a, 54; see B. I. Page and Shapiro 1992; Popkin [1991] 1994).

Elite Pluralism

Following the publication and replication of such voting behavior studies, many political scientists around the country began to rethink the social, political, and cultural requirements for the maintenance of a democratic nation; in effect, these political philosophers were rethinking traditional liberal democratic theory and its many assumptions. The resulting reconceptualization—**elite pluralism**—"argues that apathy and ignorance are tolerable if the society is structured to encourage and permit leaders to be drawn from all levels and all important social groups in society" (D. K. Davis and Robinson 1986, 52).

Researchers abandoned the concept of a voter being a rational actor, seeking out information, considering alternatives, and arriving at a desirable compromise. In short, they abandoned the ideal of a competent, deliberative democracy. In its place is Popkin's ([1991] 1994) view of a voter with **low-information rationality**:

Popularly known as "gut" reasoning—best describes the kind of practical think-ing about government and politics in which people actually engage. It is a method of combining, in an economical way, learning and information from past experiences, daily life, the media, and political campaigns. (7)

Popkin's ([1991] 1994) research was based in no small way on the work of famed political economic theorist Anthony Downs (1957), who in his seminal work *An Economic Theory of Democracy* argued that voters do not have the economic incentives to gather political information, conduct analysis, and make evaluations to improve or maximize their voting decisions. A vote for or against a political party or a political candidate does not translate into eco-nomic gains or benefits. Consequently, "the rational" voter will conduct his or her voting decision-making process with the least amount of effort, conserv-ing energy for more rewarding pursuits. Thus, according to Downs's argu-ment, the uninformed and relatively disinterested voter will be the norm rather than the exception. Research emphasizing the importance of party identification for some voters makes sense in economic terms. Popkin ([1991] 1994) writes: "Party identification, viewed from the perspective of low-information rationality, is an informational shortcut or default value, a sub-stitute for more complete information about parties and candidates" (14). In addition to party identification, voters also use other relatively free informa-tion, painlessly acquired in their everyday lives, when considering voting de-cisions. "They triangulate and validate their opinions in conversations with people they trust and according to the opinions of national figures whose judgments and positions they have come to know" (Popkin [1991] 1994, 7). Consequently, what they do know about politics is simply a "by-product" of living (see Popkin [1991] 1994). Popkin writes:

> The information that people acquire to negotiate their daily lives is later applied to their political judgments and choices. The specific connections that voters make between personal information, personal problems, and personal experi-ences with government, on one hand, and their political evaluations and choices, on the other, will depend upon several variables: what they believe government can do; what they know about what government is doing; what they know about what other people want from government; and what they are told by the media and political campaigns. ([1991] 1994, 22)

As a result, according to Popkin ([1991] 1994, 12), highly successful political campaigns transform the voting adage "What have you done for me lately?" into "What have you done for *us* lately?" In this transformation, Popkin sees the very "essence of campaigning" ([1991] 1994, 12), for transforming the "me" into an "us" provides a powerful political shortcut. Popkin writes:

Transforming unstructured and diverse interests into a single coalition, making a single cleavage dominant, requires the creation of new constituencies and political identities. It requires the aggregation of countless *I's* into a few *we's*. Behind the *we's*, however, are people who are still reasoning about the ways in which their lives and government policies are related. ([1991] 1994, 12; emphasis in original)

And, for some researchers, a cynical view has emerged. Murray Edelman has argued that ignorance—not knowledge of public affairs (as constructed by elites in the political construction stage of the opinion process)—is the mark of a healthy, stable society. Edelman wrote:

Public indifference is deplored by politicians and by right-thinking citizens. It is the target of civics courses, oratory, and television news shows and the reiterated theme of polls that discover how little political information the public has and how low politics rates among public concerns. . . . That indifference, which academic political science notices but treats as an obstacle to enlightenment or democracy, is, from another perspective, a refuge against the kind of engagement that would, if it could, keep everyone's energies taken up with activism: election campaigns, lobbying, repressing some and liberating others, wars, and all other political activities that displace living, loving, and creative work. Regimes and proponents of political causes know that it takes much coercion, propaganda, and the portrayal of issues in terms that entertain, distort, and shock to extract a public response of any kind. . . . . Indifference to the enthusiasms and alarms of political activists has very likely always been a paramount political force. . . . Without it, slaughter and repression of diverse groups in the name of nationalism, morality, or rationality would certainly be even more widespread than it has been. (1988, 7–8)

Participatory Pluralism

Others researchers such as Pateman (1980) and Davis and Robinson (1986) have fought the growing support for elite pluralism, arguing that in reality, today's political leaders are not drawn from all walks of life. Consequently, the unrepresented or the underrepresented such as minorities, the poor, and women are likely to feel increasingly alienated, dissatisfied, and disillusioned by the body politic. We have seen the social turmoil brought about by exclusionary politics. The Vietnam War protest movement, the civil rights movement, and to some extent the women's movement eventually brought about limited social change, but at what cost to the participants and to the system? Davis and Robinson (1986) have argued that despite these small social gains by politically disenfranchised groups, for the most part our political system has remained relatively stagnant for fifty or more years. Similarly, S. Coleman (2000), Dahl (1989), and Sartori (1987) have all argued that an informed citizenry engaged in public debate and exercising their voting rights is the very essence of popular sovereignty. Consequently, Davis and Robinson believe that the United States must return to liberal democratic theory for inspiration, future progress, and self-preservation; the nation must pursue democratic ideals, particularly those emphasizing **participatory pluralism**. They write:

> We have chosen the term "participatory pluralism" to emphasize two essential features of such theory. Citizens representing all groups of a complex social order can and should be expected to participate in the political decision-making that affects their lives and shapes their social worlds. (Davis and Robinson 1986, 53)

However, such a society—based on participatory pluralism—is only possible if the American educational system, the news media, the political campaign process, the American civic culture, and American citizens reconsider the meaning and value of living in a democracy as fully participating individuals (B. Barber 1984; Etzioni 1993; Fishkin 1995). In short, an appreciation of individual worth, self-determination, and self-responsibility must emerge from the ashes of American democracy.

Despite such widespread and conflicting conceptualizations of public opinion among political behaviorists, political knowledge, political reasoning, and political participation remain cornerstones of the American system of government (J. D. Barber 1974). And, as such, political communications, whether in the form of high school and college government classes, political biographies and documentaries, or mass-mediated news reports or other popular culture artifacts (such as Hollywood movies or television dramas), remain an essential ingredient in democratic government. For, as noted presidential scholar James David Barber has suggested, as effective citizens, we must not only have a thorough grounding in the structures and functions of government and the formal and informal means by which it works, but we must also have a knowledge of how the government is currently operating (1974). Consequently, mass-mediated political communications and the effects of those communications on public life are of critical importance to those studying the health and welfare of our democracy.

The Political Process

Politics may be viewed as the process by which human conduct is regulated, where decisions are made determining who gets what and who pays for what—all under conditions of social conflict. Ultimately, the American political process is a mechanism of social control, characterized by compromise and negotiation to maintain some semblance of public support and public order. And the American news media are key players in that process.

The significance of the news media in social change was very evident to renowned sociologist Robert Ezra Park. Park never formally presented his theory of news, public opinion, and social control to the academic community, but it is implicit in his scholarly writings (Frazier and Gaziano 1979). Park was interested in explaining the "development of public opinion and its relationships to social action or inaction" (Frazier and Gaziano 1979, 3–4). Park used an ecological, evolutionary approach when he suggested that issues had "'natural histories' or sequences of stages through which they developed, leading to both institutionalization and to social change, each being different stages or dimensions in social control" (Frazier and Gaziano 1979, 12). For Park, social unrest often occurs in the form of mass movements occurring outside the structures of government; and, at other times, it is expressed through the routinized but highly complex stages of the public opinion, mass media, and attendant public policy process (see figure 2.1, an adaptation of Frazier and Gaziano's depiction of Park's view of the public opinion process).

According to Frazier and Gaziano (1979), Park's theory explains "how social change takes place through successive stages involving the reporting of news and the initiation of public opinion" (37). Park wrote: "The ordinary function of news is to keep individuals and societies oriented and in touch with their world and with reality by minor adjustments" (1940, 141). "News functions in society both to preserve stability and to generate social change through initiation of the public opinion process by presentation of different points of view" (Frazier and Gaziano 1979, 20). Through communication and over time, different points of view are accommodated within the social tradition. Thus, according to Frazier and Gaziano, "The power of the press derives from its ability to initiate the forces of public opinion and subsequent political action" (1979, 32).

Public and Policy Agendas

The public policy process in the United States may be thought of as "agenda-building, a collective process in which media, government, and the public reciprocally influence each other" (M. McCombs and Gilbert 1986, 13). Political scientists examine power and the processes of influence in modern democracies. For this reason, not only the mass media but also political elites, the public opinion process, and the policy decision-making process are the foci of attention (R. M. Perloff 1998). According to Rogers and Dearing (1988):

> One method for understanding modern democracy is to concentrate upon mass media, public and policy *agendas*, defined as issues or events that are viewed at a point in time as ranked in a hierarchy of importance. Agenda research, concerned with investigating and explaining societal influence, has two

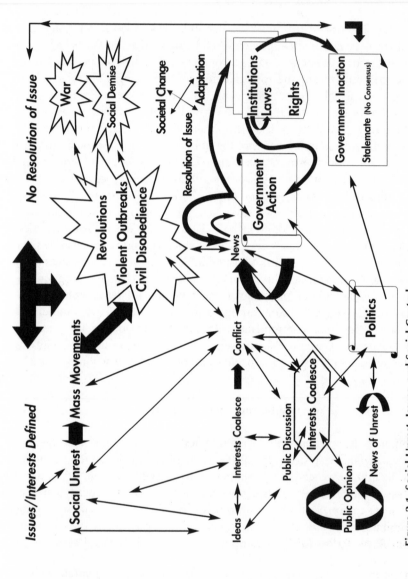

Figure 2.1 Social Unrest, Issues, and Social Control

Source: Frazier and Gaziano 1979, 35. Graphic art courtesy of Mike Little, instructor in advertising and public relations, University of Alabama.

main research traditions. . . : (1) *agenda-setting*, a process through which the mass media communicate the relative importance of various issues and events to the public (an approach mainly pursued by mass communication researchers), and (2) *agenda-building*, a process through which the policy agendas of political elites are influenced by a variety of factors, including media agendas and public agendas. (556; emphasis in original)

In their model of the agenda-setting process, Rogers and Dearing (1988) show the transactional interrelationships among the media agenda, the public agenda, and the policy agenda.

Issues and Events

E. F. Shaw (1977a) distinguished between (1) **issues,** defined as matters of concern involving repetitive news coverage of related happenings that fit together under one umbrella term, and (2) **events,** defined as discrete, finite happenings that are limited geographically and temporally. A tornado destroying a small Alabama town is an event. But if a series of tornadoes occur, accompanied by a corresponding failure of the National Weather Service to adequately notify state and local government disaster warning systems, then it becomes a public safety issue. Issues, then, are those events linked in a media context that provides a thematic structure, assigns significance and prioritization, and often contains a desired attitude toward the event network. Or, to put it more simply, the news media give events their public character—their assigned role in the media-agenda-policy process.

Some researchers emphasize the controversial nature of public issues. For example, Cobb and Elder (1971) maintain that while events may cause concern, issues tend to be controversial. They write, "An issue is a conflict between two or more identifiable groups over procedural or substantive matters relating to the distribution of positions or resources" (Cobb and Elder 1971, 82). Similarly, Eyestone (1974) writes: "An issue arises when a public with a problem seeks or demands governmental action, and there is public disagreement over the best solution to the problem" (3). Cobb and Elder (1983) report three dimensions of a conflict situation involved in an agenda-building situation:

Scope refers to the extensity of a conflict—the number of persons and groups who have actually aligned themselves in a conflict. . . . Clearly, the scope of a conflict will depend on the number of persons who value the scarce things at issue. . . . The *intensity* of a conflict relates to the degree of commitment of the contending parties to mutually incompatible positions. . . . Operationally, intensity will roughly correspond to the resources the contending parties are willing to commit to the conflict relative to their total capability. . . . *Visibility* is the variable linking a conflict with its publics. It indicates the number of persons or groups that will be aware of a conflict and its possible consequences. The visibility of a conflict will be a function of both its scope and intensity, as well as its definition. Visibility is a critical variable in that it is necessary for the expansion of a conflict, which in turn will bear on the probable access of an issue to a governmental agenda. (43–44; emphasis in original)

Yet other scholars (Kotz 1969; B. J. Nelson 1978) maintain that issues are operationalized as adversarial only because most research on issues and issue cycles has been done in cases where the opposition is particularly well organized (e.g., Cobb and Elder 1971; Groennings 1970). In some situations, an issue generates great interest and discussion, but no organized opposition emerges. For instance, Kotz (1969) found that the federal food stamp program created a great deal of public discussion; however, organized opposition was lacking. B. J. Nelson (1978) concludes that some domestic social issues may stir public debate about the merits of various programs, but there is no true adversarial component to the life cycle.

As previously mentioned, Cobb and Elder (1983) also view agenda building as stages in conflict. They identify three types of **initiators** who bring issues to our attention:

- **The exploiter**—those who create or manufacture issues for their own personal gain (e.g., a challenger running for public office wishing to be seen as a crusader on heretofore unstaked territory). For example, in January 2004, Democratic presidential candidate John Kerry urged the creation of an economic czar, a cabinet-level position designed to oversee the activities of the stock market, the SEC, mutual funds, and pension funds. Recent scandals involving American businesses and investments have left the "little guy" reeling from serious financial misdeeds involving those at the very top of the pyramid. With this announcement, Kerry positioned himself as both a take-charge activist and as someone committed to protecting the average worker.
- **Circumstantial reactors**—through unanticipated events, it becomes clear to the attentive public "that something must be done." The massacre in Columbine High School in the suburbs of Denver, Colorado, sparked another national debate about gun control.
- **Do-gooders**—these initiators have no vested interest in seeking resolution on an issue. They do not directly materially benefit from their issue activity. When tax revenues failed to provide enough money to fund the local public library and school system, a group of concerned citizens in Tuscaloosa, Alabama, formed their own fundraising organization. The

group raised enough money to renovate the public library, and a successful building contractor gave money to build a new high school. In this instance, citizens went outside the traditional governmental process to bring about change.

Recently, some researchers have taken a less cynical view of political actors seeking political and social change. Rather than viewing them as "exploiters" or "do-gooders," they see them as **policy entrepreneurs** who are working to shape public debate by framing public issues to garner support from the public, the news media, and other political actors (Kelman 1987; Mintrom 1997). According to Mintrom, "Policy entrepreneurs are able to spot problems, they are prepared to take risks to promote innovative approaches to problem solving, and they have the ability to organize others to help turn policy ideas into government policies" (1997, 740). Mintrom does not limit potential policy entrepreneurs to only elected officials; rather, he recognizes that influential members of think tanks, grassroots groups, interest groups, prominent businesses and industries, as well as elected officials may all play a role in public policy debate and resolution. Schoenfeld, Meier, and Griffin (1979) call such policy entrepreneurs "claims-makers" in that they work to stake their claim on the decision-makers' time and resources.

> If claims-makers are able to persuade others of the legitimacy of their concerns and are able to recruit early converts, a collective definition of a problem forms; and to the extent that collective definitions of problems come to supplant individualistic definitions, a social problem can be said to exist. (Schoenfeld, Meier, and Griffin 1979, 38)

At the earliest stages, these claims-makers are working to "construct a social problem" for public consumption of a social problem. It could be said that they are working at both the "conception and gestation" of a future public issue (Schoenfeld, Meier, and Griffin, 1979, 38). Typically, the claims-makers must identify a potentially advantageous triggering device to assist them in their cause.

Cobb and Elder (1983) describe **triggering devices** as the unforeseen events that often bring issues to the forefront. For Cobb and Elder (1983), it is both the watchful eye of the initiator (or claims-maker) and the triggering device that transform social problems into issues. In the domestic policy arena, triggering devices are likely to be categorized as natural catastrophes (wildfires, tornadoes), unanticipated human tragedies (the Los Angeles riots, John F. Kennedy Jr.'s airplane accident), technological repercussions (water pollution, ozone depletion), societal imbalance (hate crimes directed at gays, African American church burnings), and ecological change (the population explosion in India and China, the decimation of the African population by AIDS). In the foreign policy arena, triggering devices might be an act of war against the United States (airplanes bringing down the Twin Towers in New York, the seizing of the American embassy in Tehran, Iran), weapons technology innovations (the Star Wars missile defense system, stealth technology, and air space treaty negotiations), other international conflicts not involving the United States (civil war in Nigeria, Protestants versus Catholics in Northern Ireland), and changes in world political and military alignment patterns (fall of the USSR, reunification of Germany) (Cobb and Elder 1983).

The Systemic and Formal Agendas

Cobb and Elder (1983) maintain that there are two basic types of political agendas: (1) the systemic agenda for political controversy, and (2) the formal agenda. *"The systemic agenda consists of all issues that are commonly perceived by members of the political community as meriting public attention and as involving matters within the legitimate jurisdiction of existing governmental authority"* (Cobb and Elder 1983, 85; emphasis in original). For a matter to be on the systemic agenda, policymakers must first perceive that a large number of people are aware of and are attentive to the problem; second, must perceive that there is a widespread perception that something must be done and that such action is feasible economically, physically, and politically (e.g., must foresee that there is little or no conflict in seeking a solution to a societal ill or that the cost of the solution is not prohibitive); and, third, perceive that the problem falls within their authority as a political entity (e.g., federal legislators would not consider local property taxes in their home state to be an issue for their concern) (see Cobb and Elder 1983, 86). All three of these conditions must be met before a matter arrives on the systemic agenda.

The choice of which issues to formally consider before decision-making bodies is the crux of power within a democracy. Schattschneider writes:

> Political conflict is not like an intercollegiate debate in which the opponents agree in advance on a definition of the issues. As a matter of fact, *the definition of the alternatives is the supreme instrument of power*, the antagonists can rarely agree on what the issues are because power is involved in the definition. He who determines what politics is about runs the country, because the definition of alternatives is the choice of conflicts, and the choice of conflicts allocates power. (1960, 68; emphasis in original)

And, from the perspective of a social constructionist, the dominant framing of the public issue ultimately determines policy outcomes (see chapters 5, 6, and 7).

According to Cobb and Elder (1983), the formal agenda is composed of *"that set of items explicitly up for the active and serious consideration of authoritative decision-makers"* (Cobb and Elder 1983, 86; emphasis in original). In other words, matters that are currently being debated within legislative bodies are considered to be on the formal agenda. However, a distinction must be made between those matters under "active and serious" consideration and those "pseudo-agenda items" (Cobb and Elder 1983, 87). Lawmakers assessing an issue as meritorious with little political fallout will actively work to seek resolution on an issue. However, often pressure groups force lawmakers to put an issue on the table, but because the lawmakers themselves do not see the item as being meritorious, there is no real consideration. During the 1980s and 1990s, many conservative issues ranging from the elimination of birth control to prayer in schools to American flag observance have been placed before the U.S. Congress, yet little or no action has been taken.

Walker (1977) places an interesting spin on the evaluations that U.S. senators make in determining whether social problems are placed on the formal "active and serious" agenda. He writes:

> First, an item's attractiveness increases if it has an impact on large numbers of people. Senators must believe that the proposed legislation will have broad political appeal. Second, convincing evidence must exist that the proposed legislation is addressed to a serious problem. The more graphic and easily understood the evidence of trouble, the more creditable the sources of information from which the case is based the more appealing the aspiring item becomes. Third, the case for inclusion on the agenda will be greatly strengthened if an easily understood solution exists for the problem being addressed. Again, the more comprehensible the solution and the more honorable and prestigious its origins, the more likely it is that an item will claim a place on the discretionary agenda. If proposed legislation has all three of these desirable characteristics, its chances of appearing on the Senate's agenda are greatly increased. (430–431)

Issue Analysis

Successful political leaders, political activists, corporate executives, and political candidates all engage in issue analysis and issue management. And political journalists seeking to survey the issue environment go through a similar issue mapping; they determine the frames utilized to argue public issues and the key players involved. Such professional communicators monitor the political arena to detect key issue developments and to understand the intriguing dynamics of the public opinion/public policy process. Mack (1997) has produced an outline of a model issue options paper that I believe highlights the research, the evaluation stages, and the strategic considerations used in determining one's position on an issue (see figure 2.2). Only through conscientiously completing these steps may one hope to have a handle on the issue with all of its ramifications.

Issue Competition

Issue competition leads to what some researchers have observed as issue attention cycles. One month the topic being discussed in the news is the revitalization of our inner cities, but a dramatic event such as the massacre at Columbine will thrust gun control and gun-control legislation to the forefront

Figure 2.2 C. S. Mack's Model Issue Options Paper

- Date:
- Issue name:
    - ♣ Senate Bill No.:   House Bill No.:
    - ♣ Main sponsor(s):   Main sponsor(s):
    - ♣ Date introd.   Date introd.
- Key provisions:
    - ♣ Probable impact on our organization:
    - ♣ Is impact unique to us or shared with others? Who?
    - ♣ Other factors bearing on our decision:
- Likely proponents (legislators & interest groups)
- Rationale and arguments pro:
- Likely opponents (legislators & interest groups)
- Arguments against:
- Alternatives (legislative or other):
- Our position options:
    - ♣ Support
    - ♣ Support if following changes made (or not made):
    - ♣ Oppose
    - ♣ Oppose if following changes are made (or not made):
- Other considerations:
- Decision: Priority:

    - ♣ Fallback positions (if needed):

- Implementation by:

- Comments:

-

Source: Reprinted with permission from C. S. Mack, *Business, Politics, and the Practice of Government Relations* (Westport, CT: Quorum Books, 1997), 51.

of both news coverage and public discussion. Thus, issues compete with other potential issues for the attention of the news media, politicians, and the public. Besides Park, other researchers have also used a natural history or ecological approach to the study of issue attention cycles. In 1972, Anthony Downs published an article exploring the dynamics of the issue attention cycle. In this article, Downs maintains: "Public perception of most 'crises' in American domestic life does not reflect changes in real conditions as much as it reflects the operation of a systematic cycle of heightening public interest and then increasing boredom with major issues" (39). Central to the cycle of interest/boredom is the behavior of the U.S. news media. The media's increased attention to a particular public interest yields a similar blip on the public's awareness screen. And as the media become saturated with news stories covering the topic, the public and the media become bored, turning to other breaking news events for interest. According to Downs (1972), the issue attention cycle is characterized by five stages that usually occur in the same sequence:

> **The preproblem stage.** This prevails when some highly undesirable social condition exists but has not yet captured much media attention, even though some experts or interest groups may already be alarmed by it. . . .
>
> **Alarmed discovery and euphoric enthusiasm.** As a result of some dramatic series of events . . . or other reasons, the public suddenly becomes both aware of and alarmed about the evils of a particular problem. This alarmed discovery is invariably accompanied by euphoric enthusiasm about society's ability to "solve this problem" or "do something effective" within a relatively short time. The combination of alarm and confidence results in part from the strong pressure in America for political leaders to claim that every problem can be "solved". . . .
>
> **Realizing the cost of significant progress.** The third stage consists of a gradually spreading realization that the cost of "solving" the problem is very high indeed. Really doing so would not only take a great deal of money but would also require major sacrifices by large groups in the population. . . .
>
> **Gradual decline of intense public interest.** The previous stage becomes almost imperceptibly transformed into the fourth stage: a gradual decline in the intensity of public interest in the problem. As more and more people realize how difficult, and how costly to themselves, a solution to the problem would be, three reactions occur. Some people just get discouraged. Others feel positively threatened by thinking about the problem; so they suppress such thoughts. Still others become bored by the issue. Most people experience some combination of these feelings. Consequently, public desire to keep attention focused on the issue wanes. . . .
>
> **The postproblem stage.** In the final stage, an issue that has been replaced at the center of public concern moves into a prolonged limbo—a twilight realm of lesser attention or spasmodic reoccurrence of interest. (Downs 1972, 39–40)

Thus, according to Downs (1972), periods of intense activity are followed by dramatic drops of activity levels. However, Hogwood and Peters (1985) found that while issues usually had one "peak decade" of activity in which both government and public attention were strongly focused, in subsequent decades the interest and activity did not drop off to levels consistent with that found prior to the peak period. Rather, issues that achieve a "peak decade" are often institutionalized in terms of bureaucratic apparatus. Bureaucratic organizations devoted to the finding or implementation of "solutions" to the identified social issue conduct their daily business. The bureaucracy's budget, personnel, organizational structures, and regulatory policy are all in place; congressional oversight committees make sure the bureaucracy is fulfilling its congressional mandate. Such bureaucracies have a life of their own.

Limited Pluralism

Schattschneider (1960) lamented that for the most part, interest group or pressure group activity is limited to the very few. For Schattschneider, even though numerous pressure groups compete within the marketplace of ideas, "the flaw in the pluralist heaven is that the heavenly chorus sings with a strong upper class accent. Probably 90 percent of the population cannot get into the pressure system" (1960, 35). This suggests that those pressure groups active in the system are far more likely to support the status quo; however, such activity may in the long run undermine the stability of society. Gamson (1988b) has called this phenomenon **stable unrepresentation**. However, both Schattschneider (1960) and Gamson (1988b) warn that if 90 percent of the citizenry are outside the policy loop for most of the time, then this inefficacious political group might eventually revolt, bringing its cause before the public outside of the normal, legitimate channels of government. Under these circumstances, we could expect to see civil protest and even violence.

Schattschneider (1960) also argued that the losers in a public policy issue debate must attempt to expand the arena of the debate to include those not previously involved. For example, opponents of the government's tobacco policy supporting subsidization of the tobacco farmers began to broaden the arena of contention to include concerns about public health. In this way, people concerned with tax dollars supporting a nonessential, nonfood commodity were linked with those concerned with the government propping up a business that promotes ill health and disease. Similarly Cobb and Elder (1983) suggest that the "greater the size of the audience to which an issue can be enlarged, the greater the likelihood that it will attain systemic agenda standing and thus access to the formal agenda" (7). Cobb and Elder (1983) have identified a number of issue characteristics that increase the probability of issue expansion:

> *The more ambiguously an issue is defined, the greater the likelihood that it will reach an expanded public.* (Cobb and Elder 1983, 112; emphasis in original)
> *The more socially significant an issue is defined to be, the greater the likelihood that it will be expanded to a larger public.* (Cobb and Elder 1983, 116; emphasis in original)
> *The more an issue is defined as having extended temporal relevance, the greater the chance that it will be exposed to a larger audience.* (Cobb and Elder 1983, 117; emphasis in original)
> *The more non-technical an issue is defined to be, the greater the likelihood that it will be expanded to a larger public.* (Cobb and Elder 1983, 120; emphasis in original)
> *The more an issue is defined as lacking a clear precedent, the greater the chance that it will be expanded to a larger population.* (Cobb and Elder 1983, 122; emphasis in original; see chapter 7)

In other words, if the issue is defined in rather broad, general terms with supporting evidence to indicate the long-term, social significance of the problem, and if the issue has a nontechnical solution that has no legal or regulatory precedents, then it is far more likely that the issue will be expanded in the public's eye. In addition, Cobb and Elder (1983) suggest that for an issue to capture the imagination of the mass public, it must reach prominence quickly and should quickly be portrayed as an emotional one.

Other Competitive Voice Models

Implied within the Schattschneider (1960) and Cobb and Elder (1983) discussion is the concept of issue competition for scarce resources such as the public's and lawmakers' attention. F. L. Cook (1981) and F. L. Cook and Skogan (1991) were also interested in the competition of various issues for public attention. F. L. Cook (1981) produced a model explaining how policy issues arise: the convergent voice model. In 1991, F. L. Cook and Skogan produced a model explaining why policy issues move off the policy agenda: the divergent voice model.

The **convergent voice model** suggests that a number of matters must come to fruition before an issue successfully arrives as an item on the public policy agenda. First, groups both inside and outside the government must become aware of and display concern about a particular issue. Voters talking about the issue, creating organizations devoted to finding a solution to an issue, or notifying their political officials about their concern allow the issue to be articulated among the people. About the same time, political leaders may hold hearings, investigate the issue's merits, or issue public statements of concern. Thus the issue climate becomes "ripe . . . for the issue to gain salience" (F. L. Cook and Skogan 1991, 193). Typically such issues are what may be called "valence" issues in that people from all walks of life uniformly tend to emotionally react in a consistent manner; and because of this, the issue is really a one-sided matter in that only one position may said to be legitimately taken (B. J. Nelson 1984).

Second, the issue must be important to a number of groups, and they must be willing to voice their concerns. This demonstrates **issue momentum**—the building of issue salience across the public, which then encourages news media interest in the issue. The mass media highlight the significance of the issue to other media outlets, the general public, and the political arena. The media do this by providing base rate information as well as emotional exemplars illustrating the importance of the issue to their audiences (Gibson and Zillmann 1994a; Zillmann, Gibson, Sundar, and Perkins 1996). **Base rate information** is the quantification of the number of people or the percentage of people affected by a social phenomenon; such information may be presented with great precision involving specific numbers or ratios, or base rate information may presented in more subjective terms (for example, a majority). Exemplars are examples or stories of people affected by the phenomenon under study. Stories that combine base rate information with exemplars serve to concretize the issue for the attentive public, and in this way more and more people come to recognize a social phenomenon as a problem (see chapter 8).

Through the enlargement of the **awareness issue sphere** (those people actually aware of and potentially sympathetic to a satisfactory resolution of an issue, i.e., policy change), the third stage of the convergent voice model occurs where the issue becomes **legitimized** or worthy of both the public's and political leaders' attention. From there, the politicians go into high gear, developing both policy proposals and ultimately policy programs. At this point, the issue has reached the formal policy/political agenda status, ultimately becoming a matter of governmental law or regulation.

F. L. Cook and Skogan (1991) also posit a **divergent voice model**, highlighting why issues sometimes disappear from the policy/political agenda before becoming a matter of governmental law or regulation. Although an issue may initially have widespread support, investigative news media reports, conflicting governmental committee reports, or active antagonistic interest groups may ultimately create a climate of divergence. Thus, multiple credible voices may be arguing about the **basic issue formulation**—the definition, pervasiveness, significance, or cause of a given problem. When this happens, the once seemingly cohesive policy community begins to disintegrate, because political leaders will lose interest once it is apparent that the originally perceived political advantages of an issue are rapidly becoming disadvantages in that potential governmental actions will alienate or anger various voter groups. Once political leaders lose interest, the bureaucratic policy communities take their cue from the politicians, and the issue dies a quiet death. When political leaders and bureaucratic news sources begin to exhibit "mixed signals" about the basic issue formulation (see F. L. Cook and Skogan 1991, 201), the news media get wary about the continued news story potential of the issue in that while the news media like conflict, they like simple, easy-to-understand, easy-to-resolve conflict, not highly complex, convoluted conflict that makes reporting intelligible stories to the general public next to impossible. Without news media and political interest, the issue is doomed.

Similarly, Hilgartner and Bosk (1988) have proposed a **public arenas model** that explores how "social problems compete for societal attention" (55). Hilgartner and Bosk (1988) define a social problem "as a putative condition or situation that is labeled a problem in the arenas of public discourse and action" (55). Rather than focusing on issue stages, issue cycles, or problem histories, Hilgartner and Bosk instead focus on the competition that takes place among issues for the scarce resource of public and governmental attention. This model is of particular interest to lobbyists and governmental affairs officers, for it emphasizes the dynamism involved in the process of competition among a variety of social problem claims. They give considerable attention to the institutional arenas where such social problems are examined and analyzed: congressional committees, subcommittees, bureaucracies, and so on. Often multiple groups are involved simultaneously in the consideration of a social problem, which necessitates interdependent responsibility and negotiation. And they suggest that legislative leaders who have adopted the social problem are critical to the understanding of the evolution of an issue. These leaders—their rank and prestige within their own organization, as well as their network of contacts in the opposite chamber and within the federal bureaucracy—are an essential ingredient in issue resolution.

Hilgartner and Bosk (1988) suggest that such issue arenas have a natural "carrying capacity" that limits the number and variety of issues under active consideration; the institutional arena and individual lawmakers have carrying capacities (59). Indeed, they say that a variety of institutional, political, and cultural factors serve as guides to lawmakers and bureaucrats in deciding what to actively and seriously consider. Hilgartner and Bosk (1988) call these factors "principles of selection" (56). They provide five general principles of selection: dramatization, cultural resonance, political biases, carrying capacity, and institutional rhythms. According to Hilgartner and Bosk (1988), interest groups, political activists, and public officials must **dramatize** public issues for the news media, other political officials, other interest groups, and the public; they write:

> Public arenas place a premium on drama. Social problems presented in a dramatic way have a higher probability of successfully competing in the arenas: (a) saturation of the arenas with redundant claims and symbols can dedramatize a problem; (b) repeated bombardment of the public with messages about similar problems can dedramatize problems of that class; and (c) to remain high on the public agenda, a problem must remain dramatic; thus, new symbols or events must continually renew the drama or the problem will decline. (71; see chapter 7)

Often such issue dramatizations are steeped in **cultural resonance**, or the evoking of relevant cultural themes or mythologies. Hilgartner and Bosk (1988) observe, "In all public arenas, social problems that can be related to deep mythic themes or broad cultural preoccupations have a higher probability of competing successfully" (71; see chapters 5, 6, and 7). For example, research funding requests that are packaged to present American scientists as exploring the new frontiers of space or medicine are more likely to gain a hearing.

In addition, it should be recognized that

> all public arenas have political biases that set the acceptable range of discourse in that arena. Social problems that fall outside of or at the margins of this range are less likely to compete successfully than are mainstream ideas: (a) most of the public arenas (especially powerful ones) are heavily influenced by dominant political and economic groups. Thus, social problem definitions that reflect these biases have a higher probability of success; and (b) changes in political culture affect selection by altering the acceptable range of public discourse. (Hilgartner and Bosk 1988, 71)

For example, not too long ago, the concept of "workfare" was only discussed favorably by Republicans; but, in 1992, a presidential candidate, Democrat Bill Clinton, made it acceptable and indeed advantageous for Democratic candidates to also endorse workfare. Clinton wanted to shift the public's perceived label of the Democratic Party from the party on the left to the party in the center, and he did this by incorporating traditional rightist proposals in his agenda. Thus, he brought about a change in the acceptable range of political discourse on the part of Democratic leaders. Today, as a society, we still have not come to grips with teenage pregnancy and sexually transmitted diseases.

Unlike most of Western Europe, which long ago wholeheartedly endorsed birth control education and sexual disease protection education as means of curing these social ills, it is still not politically correct in the United States to advocate such educational programs. Instead, abstinence programs continue to be the favored answer despite increasing evidence that they do not work. Thus, funding for abstinence programs is likely to receive more widespread support on Capitol Hill than those that also call for sex education.

It should also be noted that the smaller the **carrying capacity** of an arena, the more intense the competition (Hilgartner and Bosk 1988). It stands to reason that in an arena where there is only a very limited amount of time or resources that may be devoted to active consideration, competition will be at its fiercest. We are reminded about the old adage of the fierceness of political infighting in academia; because resources are inherently limited or constrained, political infighting among academicians is said to be some of the most ferocious.

In addition to their own carrying capacities, public arenas also have their own **institutional rhythms** in that they have their own patterns of organizational life that influence the arena's receptiveness to issues (Hilgartner and Bosk 1988, 72). For example, the U.S. Congress has its own session calendar. What problems are presented, actively studied, and actively resolved is in no small way determined by the calendar's schedule.

In addition to these general principles of selection that are widely shared by public arenas, an individual arena has its own **local or unique selection principles** that "depend on its institutional characteristics, political allegiances, and occupational culture," which influence what is considered (Hilgartner and Bosk 1988, 72). For example, the U.S. Senate with its long-held tradition of individualism has its unique list of rules and procedures, which help dictate what is actively considered. The filibuster is just one of many of these procedures.

In Summary

Strategic policy players will carefully target social issues to specific arenas "by packaging their claims in a form that is dramatic, succinct, and employs novel symbols or classic theatrical tropes or by framing their claims in politically acceptable rhetoric" (Hilgartner and Bosk 1988, 72). Strategic policy players do their homework, analyze the relevant audiences, and design appropriate persuasive strategies for each audience.

The public opinion process is an ephemeral one, a quicksilver phenomenon that is largely unknowable. However, as students of the political system, we must conduct ourselves much like Sisyphus, who was condemned by the gods to eternally push, albeit unsuccessfully, a massive boulder up the mountain, for we continue to seek political understanding, to forecast trends, and to measure the public opinion process. We do this in hopes of bringing about important social change for the benefit of our people and for the maintenance of our democracy.

3

Journalism at a Crossroads

Professional Status

JOURNALISM'S PROFESSIONAL STATUS OR LACK THEREOF has been long debated among academicians, social critics, and journalists themselves (Singletary 1982). B. Barber (1963), Boyd-Barrett (1970), Greenwood (1957), Hughes (1963), and Wilensky (1964) have all provided interesting commentary on the attributes of professions operating within society. Summarizing their discussions, professions appear to:

1. have a body of knowledge, a theoretical base called their own;
2. have authority over who enters the profession through such means as educational degrees, examinations, licensing, and continuing education requirements;
3. exercise binding community sanctions on errant or incompetent members of the professional community by censure, fines, or expulsion;
4. have well-established ethical codes that serve to constrain professional behaviors by establishing legitimate professional practices;
5. have a well-defined occupational culture, with established norms, folkways, and mores; and
6. have a responsibility to advise and to act in the client's behalf rather than in personal self-interest.

Singletary's (1982) review of professional attributes and the journalism "profession" asserted that newspeople are not professionals in the strictest sense, for they are sorely lacking in a number of these professional dimensions. However, Singletary also notes that journalism, despite its shortcomings, might be viewed as an emerging profession, one struggling to come to grips with professional expectations. In addition, he argues that examining the individual performances of newspeople might be more indicative of the progress toward professional status for the field than examining the occupation itself. He (1982) concludes his investigation by arguing that many journalists see themselves as professional, operate as such, and seek the betterment of the profession. In short, while failing to meet many traditional requirements for professional status, most journalists think of themselves, their organizations, and their practices as being professionally oriented. For this reason, this text will treat journalism as a profession.

The Profession's Profile

According to a recent study by Wilhoit and Weaver (1996), journalists closely resemble, in terms of social profile, other professionals in American society. Journalists are predominately white males who are college graduates (see also Johnstone, Slawski, and Bowman 1976; Lichter, Rothman, and Lichter 1986). Yet journalists are different in terms of their high interest in politics. Ito (1996) observed that despite widespread education in the United States, the average level of participation in politics in recent years has declined in terms of political knowledge and concern. Thus, journalists are very different, for the most part, from the audiences they desire to reach, and Ito (1996) warns that the gap between journalists and their audiences is continuing to broaden.

The U.S. pool of practicing journalists, for instance, is not as racially diverse as the U.S. population. Minority journalists make up only 8 percent of practicing journalists (Wilhoit and Weaver 1996); this is true despite the fact that minority peoples in the United States in 1992 accounted for 25 percent of the population (Graber 1997, 95). And minority journalists are more likely to be women than men (Graber 1997). Wilhoit and Weaver (1996) report that women constituted "52.5% of Asian Americans, 53.2% of African Americans, 48.1% of Hispanics, and 42.9% of Native Americans" (179) practicing journalism in the United States. Women make up 34 percent of working journalists as a whole in the United States (Wilhoit and Weaver 1996).

In terms of party identification, journalists in 1992 were more than twice as likely to identify themselves as being Democrats or Independents as they were to identify themselves as being Republicans (Wilhoit and Weaver 1996). Consequently,

> economic and social liberalism prevails, especially in the most prominent media
> organizations, as does a preference for an internationalist foreign policy, caution

about military intervention, and some suspicion about ethics of established large institutions, particularly big business and big government. (Graber 1997, 95)

However, it is not party preference but educational attainment that is, according to Graber, "the single most important background characteristic that shapes newspeople's general philosophy of reporting" (1997, 95). The more education that journalists have finished, the more likely they will be liberal, appreciating the news media's role in producing an informed citizenry and accepting this social responsibility as one of their professional commitments.

Media Ownership

Since the 1930s, media ownership has proven to be a subject of great debate in the United States. As dictatorships flourished in Europe, partly as the result of governments' monopolizing news organizations, American political leaders looked to the regulatory power of the Federal Communications Commission (FCC) to protect the public from concentrated ownerships (Hickey 2003). Just as they feared the rise of dictators, they also feared big corporations controlling news and information flows to the American voters; consequently, the FCC limited media ownership in geographical localities and across the media spectrum. Recently, that debate has intensified as a result of FCC chairman Michael Powell's attempts at changing FCC rules on media ownership. A proponent of deregulation, Powell pushed through sweeping changes in June 2003 that would have resulted in even greater media consolidation with fewer owners. The U.S. Senate and the House of Representatives acted swiftly to stop the deregulation, fearing the power of unchecked media monopolies. In addition, legal challenges were introduced into the Washington, D.C., Circuit Court of Appeals (Hickey 2003). Democratic presidential hopeful Howard Dean has been at the forefront in criticizing FCC chairman Michael Powell and his deregulation campaign, and if Dean had won the nomination, concentration of media ownership would have likely been a campaign issue. Dean has argued that media conglomerates mean that "Americans get less independent and frequently less dependable news, views and information" ("Howard Dean" 2003). And Dean reminded Americans that "James Madison and Thomas Jefferson spoke of the fear that economic power would one day try to seize political power. No consolidated economic power has more opportunity to do this than the consolidated power of media" ("Howard Dean" 2003).

Media ownership and the possible consequences for the health of our democracy have long interested media scholars in the United States. Compaigne and Gomery (1982, 1995, 2000) have been in the forefront of tracking media ownership in the United States. During the past decade, media mergers and acquisitions have made major headlines in the United States, yet from Compaigne's (2000, 486) perspective, these highly profiled business deals have made only "modest shifts in the role of major players in the media industry." Some media companies such as Viacom got larger in the past decade, acquiring Paramount, Prentice Hall, and Simon and Schuster (Compaigne 2000). Others such as Knight-Ridder got smaller, divesting "itself of specialized information services as well as minor broadcasting, cable and book publishing operations" (Compaigne 2000, 487). In addition, new companies emerge on the scene: MediaNews Group, a small news organization first incorporated in 1983, became a major player when it bought newspapers sold off by Knight-Ridder and Gannett (Compaigne 2000). International media organizations are buying interests in media organizations in the United States; Australia's NewsCorp, Britain's Pearson PLC and EMI Group, and Japan's Softbank are now all players in the United States (Compaigne 2000).

While who owns what in terms of media organizations is not the focus of this work, it is important to note the major strains of media ownership criticism in the United States. For instance, Parenti (1996) has argued "there is no free and independent press in the United States" (99). Instead, Parenti sees the American news media as part of an interlocking, right-wing, corporate directorate, producing right-wing commentaries on American political life. He writes:

> Who owns the big media? The press lords who come to mind are Hearst, Luce, Murdoch, Sulzberger, Annenberg, and the like, personages of markedly conservative hue who regularly leave their ideological imprint on both news and editorial content. The boards of directors of print and broadcast news organizations are populated by representatives from Ford, General Motors, General Electric, Alcoa, Coca-Cola, Philip Morris, ITT, IBM, and other corporations in a system of interlocking directorates that resembles the boards of any other corporation. Among the major stockholders of the three largest networks are Chase Manhattan, J. P. Morgan, and Citibank. The prime stockholder of this country's most far reaching wire service, Associated Press, is the Wall Street brokerage firm, Merrill Lynch. NBC is owned outright by General Electric, a corporation that frequently backs conservative causes and candidates. In 1995, CBS was bought up by Westinghouse for $5 billion and Time Warner prepared to take over Ted Turner's CNN [since completed]. (Parenti 1996, 99)

Parenti even includes the Public Broadcasting System (PBS) in his network of right-wing conspirators, calling the organization the "Petroleum Broadcasting System" (1996, 101). Parenti argues that 70 percent of PBS's prime-time shows are funded by four giant multinational oil companies, and this underwriting necessitates a probusiness perspective. While PBS is routinely cited as one of the more left-leaning broadcasting systems, Parenti argues that this is just another "conservative hallucination" used to create a perceived liberal threat that ultimately rallies and unites conservatives (1996, 101). And he goes on to write:

> If news and commentary are so preponderantly conservative, why do rightists blast the press for its supposedly left bias? For one thing, such attacks help create a climate of opinion favorable to the Right. Railing against the press's "liberalism" is a way of putting the press on the defensive, keeping it leaning rightward for its respectability, so that liberal opinion in this country is forever striving for credibility within a conservatively defined framework. (Parenti 1996, 102)

And Parenti (1996) isn't the only political observer to see conspiracies at work in the ownership and management of the American news media. On December 2, 2003, democratic presidential hopeful Howard Dean gave a major address, arguing that eleven conglomerates owned and controlled every potential news source, from book publishers and newsmagazines and newspapers to television networks, radio chains, and cable companies to film and recording producers—the conservative big guns were in charge. Dean promised to immediately act, if elected president, to reverse the trend in an increasingly monopolistic communication marketplace by breaking up existing media conglomerates. Later that same day, Dean went on MSNBC's *Hardball with Chris Matthews* to discuss his views, attracting the interest of Matt Drudge (*Drudge Report* 2003). Both MSNBC's Matthews and rival CNN news commentators during the Lou Dobb's show seemed less than impressed with Dean's promises. And they argued that Dean's campaign promise to reform media ownership regulations wasn't likely to secure many votes for his candidacy, because the American people simply didn't care about the issue. One *Time* magazine economic writer quipped that she wished Dean had been around when the AOL–Time-Warner–CNN debacle had first been contemplated.

Functional Goals of the Profession

Journalists share a number of professional goals as they go about their daily work. These professional goals are often described by researchers as the "news functions" that journalists see themselves performing for society. For instance, Cunningham and Henry (1989), writing for the American Society of Newspaper Editors, have provided a prioritized list of news functions:

1. Provide analysis and interpretation of complex events.
2. Investigate claims and statements made by the government.
3. Get information to the public quickly.

4. Discuss national policy while it is still being developed.
5. Stay away from stories where factual content cannot be verified.
6. Provide entertainment and relaxation.
7. Concentrate on news that is of interest to the widest possible public.
8. Be an adversary of public officials by being constantly skeptical of their actions.
9. Be an adversary of businesses by being constantly skeptical of their actions.
10. Cover "chicken dinner" news. (As quoted in Tipton 1992, 135–136)

Reporters' Views of Their Work: Journalistic Roles

Dunn (1969) wrote that journalists see themselves as serving several "overarching purposes" as they go about their daily work, operating as a "(1) neutral information transmitter, (2) translator and interpreter of government to the people, (3) representative of the public, and (4) participant in policy making" (7). We will consider each of these in turn.

Journalists believe they are to serve "as an impartial, objective transmission device, dispensing information about political activities" (Dunn 1969, 8–9). Journalists believe they are objective either by their education or by their training. In other words, their own subjectivity has been weaned out of them by more experienced journalistic hands, making them suitable for objective work. Consequently, journalists view what they do as seeking the facts of a given situation and reporting them to their readers or audience. The journalistic reporting formula of "who, what, when, where, why, and how" provides further evidence of their emphasis on facts. Journalists view themselves as neither part of the story nor as creators of the story. They believe they simply report the facts as they see them (see chapter 4). Such views are classic examples of consummate self-deception, yet they remain widespread throughout the profession (see Ettema and Glasser 1998).

Journalistic objectivity and truth-seeking behaviors are often dramatized in popular fiction or movies. The reporter is portrayed "as a loner, a man free— or abandoned—to see and say the truth. Those who pay him haven't bought him. He flits or slogs his way, loyal to *his* muse, not his masters" (J. D. Barber 1978, 125; emphasis in original). Russell Baker's image of a reporter illustrates this same phenomenon:

On the road, laden down with a typewriter in one hand and a suitcase in the other and a trench coat, trudging his way through the mob, living a rather dreary life with the reality of it romanticized with good booze, sitting up nights and telling old tales. Basically, he's a guy who is riding out there with a shoeshine and a smile, and he's easily shot down. (As quoted by Lou Cannon in *Reporting: An Inside View*, as reported in Barber 1978, 125)

L. W. Doob (1948) provides us with a humorous (but some would say very accurate) description of the working journalist; he writes:

> He usually believes in himself and considers that he is making an important contribution to mankind, as indeed he sometimes is. And he tends to be a snob. He tends to be a snob because he is absolutely convinced that only the methods of American journalism represent a sure-fire path to absolute, ultimate truth. The facts, he says, speak for themselves, provided they are reported accurately and in the best traditions of his craft; his job is to get those facts and to get them quickly. (271)

Journalists see themselves as taking a web of complex and often convoluted workings of government and governmental decision making, and simplifying these processes and actions into an understandable form suitable for the average man or woman to comprehend. Journalism students are taught to write on the eighth-grade level, reaching all people by appealing to and writing for the lowest common denominator within society. In effect, journalists see themselves as translators of the highly complex and difficult to the simple and easy. They interpret what high-level government actions mean in the everyday lives of average Americans. If journalists seem paternalistic, they are.

If the people can't be present in the halls of government to watch out for their own interests, then it is the journalist's job to represent them. This public representation has taken on heroic dimensions. Conventionally, journalism skills courses teach aspiring journalists that it is their future profession's responsibility to make sure that the government remains honest and working in the public interest; this notion is popularly known as **the watchdog theory** of the press (see B. C. Cohen 1963; Dunn 1969; McCamy 1939). Journalists often depict themselves as being the public's "guardian against special interests" (Dunn 1969, 9). Special interests are viewed as more powerful than the general public, because they are organized, have formal structures, and have money to contribute to election coffers. For this reason, journalists see themselves as countering special interests' power by exposing their intentions and their political maneuverings to the public. And they play competing interest groups off each other in their reports, highlighting conflicting agendas and multiple policy positions. In addition, journalists view secrecy or behind-the-scenes deal making as working against the public interest; consequently, they seek to expose those who engage in secrecy, opening up their practices and their motives to public scrutiny (Dunn 1969).

Journalism students are taught that the news media serve as the **fourth branch of government**, assisting in the exercise of checks and balances found in our Constitution. It is, in the minds of journalism educators, the news media's job to step in and keep the executive, the legislative, and the judicial branches running smoothly, efficiently, and in the public's interest. This depiction of the news media is known as **the fourth estate** premise of the American news media (see Johnson a.k.a. Johnson-Cartee 1984).

In the past thirty years, journalists have taken the watchdog theory and the fourth estate depiction one step further in their evolving societal role; we will now consider this new role of journalists as **political arbiters**. Researchers have noted that journalists are involved in "surrogate representation" or, according to Entman, "the enforcement of government responsiveness to the public by pressing politicians to explain candidly their actions, motivations, and plans" (1981, 81–82). And they have become, as one group of researchers has described them, "the arbiters of the political system" (Grossman and Kumar 1981, 302). Journalists are no longer just concerned with collecting facts, for they are now discerning truth for the American public (P. Weaver 1974). According to Seib (1994), journalists' "ethical responsibility is to provide information—as thoroughly verified as is possible—that will illuminate political debate and give news consumers additional tools they may use in building their voting decisions" (6). For any issue debated during a political campaign, it is the news media's job to explain "what the candidate wants to do; whether it is doable; and, if done, what its impact will be" (Seib 1994, 5). This means that policy-makers routinely question and consider how the media will react to potential policy decisions before committing to one policy or another. For this reason, it may be said that not only the public but also the media work to constrain the policy-makers by shrinking the universe of potential policy solutions (Y. Cohen 1986).

Consequently, journalists have become a new type of political actor (T. E. Cook 1998). Grossman and Kumar write:

The central impact of permanent underlying forces on the media is that news organizations have become actors of considerable significance in the American political system. They plan a number of important roles including influencing the selection and removal of those who hold office, determining the public perception of the importance of many issues, and interpreting the significance of a leader's activities. Nonetheless, news organizations are neither traditional political actors nor are they a fourth branch of government. They do not have clearly defined objectives, as do interest groups, and they do not seek power in the sense of winning and holding office, as do most of the politicians. With the exception of a relatively few matters about which their owners and managers care a lot, or about which a few columnists, editors, and elite reporters do have opinions, most media organizations do not seek to determine electoral or policy outcomes. What might be said of them is that they strive to become the arbiters of the political system. They legitimize and delegitimize individuals, points of view on issues, and even institutions such as the Presidency itself. Collectively and individually, news enterprises act as if they set the ethical norms for candidates and the criteria by which policies shall be evaluated. In sum, these organizations attempt to establish the criteria of rectitude for political operations in the United States. It is no wonder that the other actors, including the President, resent them. (1981, 106–107)

This journalistic attitude is unfortunate, for it not only masks the symbiotic nature of the mass media–governmental relationship in this country but also ignores the very real and very powerful role the news media play in American politics.

Thus, for the most part, our political knowledge comes to us not through participation and personal experience but from a conceptual environment created by the mass media. This has led Ceasar, Thurow, Tulis, and Bassette to suggest that the news media actively create "the" political reality for most Americans; they conclude:

"Real" expressions of mass opinion, which in the past were sporadic, are replaced by the news media's continuous "sophisticated" analyses that served as a surrogate audience speaking to the government and supposedly representing to it what the people are saying and thinking. Driven by its own inner dynamic to find and sustain exciting issues and to present them in dramatic terms, the news media create—or give the impression of creating—national moods and currents of opinion which appear to call for some form of action by the government and especially by the president. (1982, 242)

Under certain circumstances, the news media do more than act as a political arbiter; in effect, news reporters and the organizations they represent become active participants or collaborators in the policy-making process (Molotch, Protess, and Gordon 1996). Depending on the problem or issue presented, investigative reports often influence policy-makers after publication or broadcast (F. L. Cook, Tyler, Goetz, Gordon, Leff, and Molotch 1983). And researchers have also observed that investigative reports often spawn additional news stories in the same news outlet, in effect triggering a conscious attention to related news opportunities (Protess, Leff, Brooks, and Gordon 1985). In their investigation of toxic waste investigative reporting, Protess, Cook, Curtin, Gordon, Leff, McCombs, and Miller (1987) found that journalists were personally active in the policy-making process; they wrote:

It was not the members of the public who were so aroused by the report that they pressured their representatives to act. Rather it was the active collaboration between journalists and policymakers during the prepublication phase of investigation that generated the policy outcomes. (180; see Protess, Cook, Doppelt, Ettema, Gordon, Leff, and Miller 1991; D. Weaver 1996)

Molotch, Protess, and Gordon (1996) call such policy-makers in these collaborative instances "policy partners." They write:

> A "policy partner" is usually an administrator or politician who (a) can be appraised of the nature of the developing investigation, (b) can be used as a consultant for informing the investigatory work, and (c) can be relied on to provide headline-worthy policy initiatives as "response" to the resulting exposés. (Molotch, Protess, and Gordon 1996, 54)

Both the policy partner and the working journalist benefit from the relationship. "Policy partners gain 'insider' access to media coverage in a very advantageous way; they can be 'in front' of a breaking story and establish high visibility in a favorable media context" (Molotch, Protess, and Gordon 1996, 54). According to Protess et al. (1987), the exact nature of the policy-maker–journalist relationship and the subsequent policy-maker's action(s) is influenced by "the timing of the publication in relation to political exigencies, the extent of journalistic collaboration with policymakers, the level of general public and interest group pressures, and the availability of cost-effective solutions to the problems discussed" (182).

Other direct effects on policy have also been noted. Linsky (1986) has reported that negative media coverage often accelerates the policy-making process in that political leaders suddenly find themselves with a hot issue and one on which they want to appear as being actively involved in its resolution. In some situations, he (1986) suggests that this is not always desirable; policy-makers often rush to make a decision without a thorough investigation and analysis of the problem. But there is yet another way in which the news media serve as the surrogate for the people; policy-makers often take news reports as indicative of public opinion, that is, "the views expressed in the media are equated with public opinion" (Y. Cohen 1986, 59; see also Kennamer 1992). Thus, views expressed in news reports become **public opinion indicators**. Interestingly, Kennamer (1992) has also suggested that given that policy-makers often "use press reactions to their own public relations efforts as evidence of public opinion, some of the voices of 'public opinion' they hear are simply their own voices" (11). For this reason, researchers have found that policy-makers' perceptions of public sentiment on an issue are often well off the mark (Benson 1967–1968; Erikson, Luttbeg, and Tedin 1988; Kennamer 1992; W. E. Miller and Stokes 1963). Kennamer (1992) concludes: "The upshot is that public officials may entertain perceptions that may have been derived by unsystematic means, that may not be independent of themselves, of a public opinion that may not really exist" (11). In other words, policy-makers are often guilty of pluralistic ignorance (see chapter 1). B. C. Cohen observed in 1973:

When a policy maker is attributing a decision to the dictates of public opinion, he may be explaining away a variety of complicated, delicate political constraints on his or his colleagues' behavior by passing them off onto the one "legitimate" political actor that cannot answer back, defend itself, or take offense at the charge. (12–13)

And for this reason, as Kennamer (1992) so aptly observed, policy-makers have a vested interest in manipulating the media to report public opinion as being aligned with their own policy objectives. In this manner, in effect, policy-makers seek to craft the agenda of public opinion for not only the media but also news consumers.

The journalistic assumption of surrogate representation "is unfortunate, for it masks the symbiotic nature of the mass media-governmental relationship in this country as well as ignoring the very real and very powerful role the mass media play in American politics" (Johnson a.k.a. Johnson-Cartee 1984, 43). Similarly, Negrine (1996) observed:

The private media are, in the final instance, only accountable to their proprietors for their actions, so that their increased (self) importance and enhanced role within the political process may be taking the place of, or become a replacement for, public participation in political debate and for the processes by which governments are called to account by their wider citizenry. Rather than see the media and their insertion in the "public sphere" as a solution to contemporary ills, they may in fact be part of the problem. (22)

Professional Philosophies

As a profession, journalism purports to serve the public's interest. Serving the public's interest has been operationalized as providing meaningful public information to news consumers in order that they more meaningfully participate in public dialogue about controversial public issues. As early as the eighteenth century, our founding fathers recognized the importance of a free press in the preservation of individual freedoms in a democratic society (Tuchman 1978a). The First Amendment of the Bill of Rights asserts:

Congress shall make no law respecting an establishment of religion, or prohibiting the free exercise thereof; or abridging the freedom of speech, or of the press; or the right of the people peaceably to assemble, and to petition the Government for a redress of grievances. (Constitution of the United States, Amendment 1)

The American court system has found that "there is a national commitment to principle that debate on public issues should be uninhibited, robust, and wide-open, and that it may well include vehement, caustic and sometimes unpleasantly sharp attacks on government and public officials" (U.S.C.A., Const. Amend. 1). Moreover, "The constitutional protections for speech and press do not turn upon the truth, popularity, or social utility of the ideas and beliefs which are offered" (U.S.C.A., Const. Amend. 1).

The Libertarian Tradition

The significance of the First Amendment heavily influenced early mass communication scholars seeking to classify mass media systems and their attending sociopolitical systems. Siebert, Peterson, and Schramm's *Four Theories of the Press* (1956) proved to be highly influential in structuring not only academic debate but also journalistic thought for more than forty years. The oft-quoted work portrayed the U.S. print news system as functioning within a **libertarian tradition**. It emphasized print news's freedom from governmental control and regulation. Through the "free marketplace of ideas," the nation's citizens would participate and actively determine their own political futures. This **free marketplace of ideas** was self-righting in that despite competing currents within public opinion, reason would prevail, and a rational compromise would ensure the continuation of the body politic (see McQuail 2000; Siebert, Peterson, and Schramm 1956). The free press would commit itself to operating in a **socially responsible manner**, providing news and public information geared to serving and promoting democratic ideals.

In recent years, *Four Theories* has fallen out of favor with an increasingly sophisticated academy (Blanchard 1977, 1986; Nerone 1995; Nordenstreng 1997). However, it should be noted that the work remains significant for two reasons. First is its groundbreaking argument that the "press always takes on the form and coloration of the social and political structures within which it operates. Especially it reflects the system of social control" (Siebert, Peterson, and Schramm 1956, 1). And, secondly, it should be remembered that this work structured debate on press and social systems for more than forty years, generating more sophisticated scholarship and educating countless college graduates about the linkages between societal structures and the press.

Today, Siebert, Peterson, and Schramm's social responsibility of 1956 has been operationalized in the academic literature as **advocacy journalism** (Janowitz 1975). In advocacy journalism:

> The role of the journalist is to insure that all perspectives are adequately represented in the media, for the resolution of social conflict depends on effective representation of alternative definitions of reality. The journalist must "participate"

in the advocacy process. He must be an advocate for those who are denied powerful spokesmen, and he must point out the consequences of the contemporary power imbalance. The search for objective reality yields to a struggle to participate in the sociopolitical process by supplying knowledge and information. (Janowitz 1975, 619)

Johnstone, Slawski, and Bowman, in surveying a national sample (1,125) of working journalists in 1971, estimated that between 11 and 34.9 percent of working journalists consider themselves to be advocates or news participants (1976). Advocates are more likely to be younger, urban, and liberal arts educated (Janowitz 1975). Advocacy journalism is an outgrowth of a commonly shared desire among those entering the journalism field for political, economic, and social reform. According to Janowitz, this **reformist impulse** is "accompanied not by an urge to exercise power but by a desire to bring about change through moral criticism" (1975, 622). Today, the reformist impulse has been institutionalized by professional practice and by news portrayals featured in popular books and movies (Protess et al. 1991). This quest for reform is viewed as a normal extension of our American ideal of popular democracy. "Vigilant journalists bring wrongdoing to public attention. An informed citizenry responds by demanding reforms from their elected representatives. Policy makers respond in turn by taking corrective action" (Protess et al. 1991, 3). Such notions accept the professional mythology of the news media serving as the **public watchdog**, bringing to light illegal, unethical, and unsavory matters.

In some quarters, this watchdog function is placed under the umbrella of investigative journalism. "Investigative reporting is an intellectual process. It is a business of gathering and sorting ideas and facts, building patterns, analyzing options and making decisions based on logic rather than emotion—including the decision to say no at any of the several stages" (P. N. Williams 1978, 12). A simple definition, but in practice, investigative journalism is intended to provoke outrage, to bring about social protest and social change. For Ettema (1988), Ettema and Glasser (1988), and Glasser and Ettema (1989), investigative journalism is the **journalism of outrage**. According to Protess et al. (1991):

The journalism of outrage is a form of storytelling that probes the boundaries of America's civic conscience. Published allegations of wrongdoing—political corruption, government inefficiency, corporate abuses—help define public morality in the United States. Journalistic exposés that trigger outrage from the public or policy makers affirm society's standards of misconduct. Societal indifference to investigative disclosures constitutes evidence of morally tolerable, if not ethically acceptable behavior. (5)

For instance, the national news media were surprised and ultimately angered by the public's indifference to the many scandals associated with Bill Clinton's presidency. Kurtz (1998) wrote: "In the harsh light cast by the media, Clinton was a slippery, dishonest, cash-obsessed, sex-crazed opportunist who, by sheer dint of his political skills, had managed to fool the voters, co-opt the Republicans, and outrun the prosecutors" (287). Yet, the American people failed to take their cues from the national news media, failing to condemn Clinton for his many misdeeds. Kurtz (1998) explained: "The most investigated president in recent history had somehow become one of the most popular. Clinton was riding high, despite the barrage of negative headlines, precisely because the voters' expectations had sunk so low" (289).

However, in other circumstances, investigative journalism may have significant consequences, for such investigative reports may well work to alter societal agendas. Such news reports "trigger" societal agenda-building processes (see chapter 2), where news reports, public outcry, and government actions and reactions ultimately bring about policy changes (Lang and Lang 1983). Such investigative reports are political narratives that establish the forces of evil and the forces of good. Reoccurring characters within these political narratives include:

1. Elected officials who may be held accountable to the legal requisites of their office and the moral principles of public service
2. Political office seekers whose public and private integrity may be challenged
3. Government bureaucrats expected to administer programs properly and enforce regulations in their domains
4. Business executives whose commitment to corporate responsibility may be tested
5. An array of victims, including taxpayers and consumers, who expect their public and private services to be delivered with honesty, efficiency, and fairness (Protess et al. 1991, 10)

A reading of *Time* or *Newsweek* during any given week will yield ample examples of these political characters; they are the stuff of contemporary journalism.

Such political narratives represent the **mobilization model of responsible civic journalism**. In other words, "The process is that the press tells the public what they need to know, the people then decide what they want, and the press helps communicate these decisions back to policy makers" (Linsky 1986, 8). For many, journalism is a cornerstone in the protection of American democracy (Mollenhoff 1968).

Civic, Public, or Community Journalism

In recent years, some journalists have moved from simply investigating public malfeasance and reporting it to advocating particular social, economic, or political policies. Journalists considering themselves to be advocates (Janowitz 1975) are said to be practicing what is now called **civic, public, or community journalism** (Black 1997; Graber 1997; Patterson 1995; Rosen 1996; Semetko 1995). "The advocates of civic journalism believe that reporters must tailor the news so that it informs citizens about important happenings known to be of concern to them and helps them to take collective action to resolve problems" (Graber 1997, 98; see also Patterson 1995; Semetko 1995). It is founded on the belief that "the press can do more—much more than it has been doing—to engage people as citizens, to improve public discussion, to help communities solve problems, and to aid in the country's search for a workable public life" (Rosen 1996, 2). Davis Merritt, then editor of the *Wichita Eagle*, is credited as being one of the founding proponents of public journalism; he wrote his own newspaper's staff that journalism should be about "empower[ing] people to take back control of their lives" (Rosen 1996, 39). In other words, public journalists believe that journalists should function as "civic capitalists," improving the "productivity of a community" (Charity 1995, 11). Graber observes, "Beyond turning reporters into interpreters of what the news means or should mean, it [civic journalism] also turns them consciously into participants in the political process" (1997, 98).

The push toward community journalism came as a result of an internal self-assessment by news organizations during the late 1980s and early 1990s. Traditional news such as the major dailies, national newsmagazines, and television networks began to experience downturns in readership and viewing.

> News executives, prompted by years of flat-line circulation, slipping ratings, and flagging public confidence, devised strategies to entice a fast-track, consumer-oriented generation that appeared, at least, to have little time to dawdle over the news and scant interest in public life. (Anderson, Dardenne, and Killenberg 1994, 1)

Instead of supporting traditional news forms, the public increasingly turned to entertainment news and to other "fringe" offerings to satisfy their information needs (Shaw 1993). It seems that most Americans were looking for more than the simple recitation of the day's events; they wanted context, history, interpretation, and analysis presented in an interesting and enjoyable manner (Anderson, Dardenne, and Killenberg 1994). And, just as importantly, researchers found that news consumers wanted to know (1) how these news stories fit into the greater scheme of things (what was their lasting significance) and (2) how these news stories might specifically affect them personally. In addition, news consumers wanted more information and more discussion about how to improve their daily lives. In short, according to community journalism advocates, news consumers craved true communication, a "journalism of conversation" (Carey 1987, 14) about matters that concerned them. And, most importantly, a journalism of conversation would treat people with dignity as citizens analyzing and discussing the middle ground of public issues—a far cry from the traditional journalism's freak shows, featuring the "tails of the normal distribution" (Meyer 1995, 3; see also Glasser and Craft 1996). Glasser and Craft (1996) suggest that public journalism embraces a new "news attitude"; they write:

> Public journalism strikes a hopeful tone. It stands as a corrective to a language of despair and discontent. It resists, specifically, the unmistakably ironic tone that enables journalists to report the news while conveying, quietly and discreetly, their disgust for it. (155)

Thus, public journalism proponents argue that news organizations should reinvent themselves, reconsidering and reformulating the very nature of news as a process. Anderson, Dardenne, and Killenberg (1994) explain:

> News is one of the activities through which people strive to make sense out of their lives and the world around them. All people are part of the news because they are part of their culture and because news is a participative narrative that defines the culture in all its diversity. News is not what we receive; it is the culture's story, which develops as it is told. (5–6)

This orientation toward news has been called a **radical democratic journalistic perspective**. Curran (1991) writes:

> The starting-point of the radical democratic approach is that the role of the media goes beyond that defined by classic liberalism. The media are a battleground between contending forces. How they respond to and mediate this conflict affects the balance of social forces and, ultimately, the distribution of rewards in society.
>
> A basic requirement of a democratic media system should be, therefore, that it represents all significant interests in society. It should facilitate their participation in the public domain, enable them to contribute to public debate and have an input in the framing of public policy. The media should also facilitate the functioning of representative organizations, and expose their internal processes to public scrutiny and the play of public opinion. In short, a central role of the media should be defined as *assisting the equitable negotiation or arbitration of competing interests through democratic processes.* (29–30, emphasis in original; see also Dahlgren and Sparks 1991)

Consequently, those who support radical democratic journalism have argued that the way journalists go about their craft must be fundamentally altered:

Journalists can no longer afford to act as if they are conduits of information to an uninformed, and perhaps even unformed, public. They must develop new ways to listen as well as speak, to empathize, identify, and cooperate with citizens who, once included, will become more likely to say something of substance. (Anderson, Dardenne, and Killenberg 1994, 7).

By emphasizing public conversations, community journalism advocates necessitate that news reporters and editors become community activists, organizing cooperative citizens into groups and programs that build harmonious and progressive partnerships dedicated to improving community life. In short, news organizations become community facilitators. Rosen (1996) writes: "Properly approached, public journalism is about challenging people to interact with journalists and with each other as concerned citizens rather than as victims, consumers, or bystanders" (16).

While few public journalists draw road maps on how to go about making these changes, Charity (1995) provides some interesting suggestions:

- *Reducing issues to choices*: Journalists should identify, define, and provide possible policy solutions to public problems.
- *Plumbing to core values*: Journalists should identify core values expressed through the selection of each policy solution.
- *Spelling out the costs and consequences of each choice*: Journalists should provide a thorough cost-benefit analysis for each policy solution presented.
- *Bridging the expert-public gap*: Journalists should make expert opinion intelligible to the average citizen; in short, they should translate expert opinion into everyday language.
- *Facilitating deliberation*: Journalists should provide opportunities for ordinary citizens' voices to be heard, through either the pages of newspaper or staged events such as town-hall meetings.
- *Promoting civility*: Journalists should encourage citizens to engage in respectful dialogs with others, recognizing and valuing a free marketplace of ideas. They should encourage tolerance and mutual respect. (6–7; quoted material in italics)
- *Prodding action on the public's choice*: Once the community has reached a consensus, the newspaper should champion their decision, spearheading the effort for their voices to be heard in the halls of government. (8; quoted material in italics)

However, it should be noted that this shift in orientation is not all altruistic; it does establish a road map for news organizational relevance and survival in the twenty-first century. As a result of this reorientation, journalists are experimenting with not only new community activities but also new communication styles, altering traditional means of delivering the news. Community journalism advocates see these changes as having major consequences:

> The range of invitation of a redefined, conversational journalism will produce deeper and more comprehensive accounts of social issues, not just accounts of the events that are symptomatic of them.
> The inclusion and empathy characterizing a conversational journalism will be more suited to the needs and tensions of an era of multicultural diversity. (Anderson, Dardenne, and Killenberg 1994, 15–16)

In addition, conversational journalism will be better able to participate fully within the ongoing dialogue among social scientists and humanists on how to improve the health, economic, social, cultural, and political state of humankind, enriching the democratic sphere within which Americans operate.

Community journalism advocates, those who subscribe to radical democratic journalism, criticize "old news" or traditional journalism for being linear, one-directional, or engaged, in effect, in a monologue (see Anderson, Dardenne, and Killenberg 1994; Curran 1991; Dahlgren and Sparks 1991). Such criticism implies that traditional journalism is elitist in that journalists view their jobs as crafting news stories to inform ordinary citizens about the world and their daily lives. In short, journalists were viewed as being in a better position to observe, seek out additional information, and provide an appropriate context for that information for others to later consume. And while certainly no one would argue that journalists and other news personnel are superbly educated, the fact that they are better educated than the general population also contributed to the elite criticism.

But, as a student of not only news, politics, and political rhetoric, I observe that community journalism's (and its attendant political philosophy of radical democratic journalism's) depiction of "new journalism for the 21st century" is far different than the one earlier proposed by Pateman (1980) and D. K. Davis and Robinson (1986), the participatory pluralistic press theory (see the discussion of the theoretical underpinnings of participatory pluralism in chapter 1). "A participatory pluralistic press theory would seek to identify the way in which news assists or retards intergroup politics" (D. K. Davis and Robinson 1986, 54), for pluralist scholars have long argued that a democratic society is only possible if individuals and individual interests are actively involved in the negotiation of complex and competing political issues (Bailyn 1967; Christenson, Engel, Jacobs, Rejai, and Herbert 1981; Dolbeare 1981; Groth 1971; Hartz 1955). Consequently, journalists and news organizations should be committed to broadening social understandings by providing messages in which groups "are interested and possess the background to interpret" (D. K. Davis and Robinson 1986, 54). Rather than simply writing about crime stories, journalists should provide provocative accounts of poverty, unemployment, cultural deprivation, educational system shortfalls, drug addiction, and public and mental health system failures. Such insightful accounts into the environment in which crime germinates and takes root would provide necessary information and understanding to those outside of the social environment where crime festers. Personal accounts of those living, enduring, surviving, and dying in such crime-riddled areas, as well as accounts and evaluations of other governmental programs intended to alleviate social ills, would also provide perspective. Medical doctors, public defenders, and court-appointed attorneys, as well as social workers, government program providers, and criminal justice experts, should be presented and their actions presented within this complex criminal policy arena.

A participatory pluralistic press theory argues for what Gans termed "multiperspectival" news (1979). For Gans, multiperspectival news would differ from traditional news in five ways. First, according to Gans (1979), multiperspectival news would truly be *more national*, ceasing to equate the federal government, Wall Street, and Hollywood with the nation. Instead, the nation would be represented by a vast array of national institutions, corporations, unions, voluntary associations, and organized/unorganized interests wherever they were found. Second, multiperspectival news would incorporate *bottom-up views* with the more traditional top-down views. In other words, those affected by new governmental policies or regulations—people, interest groups, institutions—would present their reactions to changes in public policy. Third, multiperspectival news would include more *output news* associated with governmental policies, plans, and the programs' practical applications, and results would also be reviewed and critiqued. Fourth, multiperspectival news would be *more representative* in that ordinary people from all walks of life would be free to express what was happening and what was important in their own lives. And fifth, multiperspectival news would provide more *service news*, news designed to fulfill certain informational news needs of various segments in society. In short, multiperspectival news would better meet the information needs of a modern democratic society.

The participatory pluralist would argue that genuine social progress will only be made when all the voices have access, when the multiplicity of realities and perspectives is provided for news consumption. Classic liberalism argues that through information and education, negotiation, and compromise, reasonable human beings can make decisions, decisions that are for the betterment of all human beings.

Participatory pluralistic journalism argues for a more informed reporter and better-educated reporter who fully accesses and utilizes the many academic and expert sources available for the production of a superior news product. Such an orientation has its roots in the writing of Walter Lippmann (1920), who more than eighty years ago envisioned an empowered news profession better suited for fostering democratic ideals within society. Similarly, Jack Fuller (1996) has argued that journalism programs should produce good writers, not simply stylistic writers. With rapidly changing communication technologies and the accompanying stylistic changes that inevitably occur, Fuller suggests that journalism programs should not concentrate so much on the styles associated with a particular medium in which they plan to work, but only on telling a good story better. "We need journalists who will be able to tell a story like the tale of the discovery of AIDS in a way that will reach and persuade both the scientists and the general audience," Fuller (1996, 181) writes. In addition, Fuller suggests that journalists should be trained in the new technologies, particularly related to the area of information sciences and retrieval. And, as did Lippmann, Fuller (1996) argues that journalists should pursue specialized training in academic disciplines that would provide a contextual framework from which to build more lucid and informative news copy. He argues for pursuing graduate degrees, whether in the arts, science, politics, public administration, or any other rigorous academic discipline. Such training provides for understanding far beyond a single discipline and provides the necessary tools for lifelong learning. Fuller (1996) explains:

> Intensive, graduate level work gives an individual the vocabulary, the analytic skills, and the confidence to deal with complex issues. It should prepare him to deal with complex issues outside the specific field in which he trains. The reporter with a strong economics background should find that, having immersed himself in this difficult discipline, he can move more quickly to understand an area of the physical sciences than if he had never before had to work with complicated masses of data and high-level mathematics. (182–183)

Such training is designed, according to Fuller, to do more than just produce good copy or more-informed reporting; it should produce men and women socialized in intellectual honesty. Fuller writes:

> No matter how vigorous newspapers become in reporting on the complexities of science, medicine, and technology, they will be no substitute for a reexamination by those institutions of their own commitment to the discipline of truth. The cause of intellectual honesty, lately a losing battle, needs to be revived in all areas of society. The confusion between what the law requires and what decency and self-respect demand must be cleared up. Legal analysis is vital, but it must be

kept in its proper place. Learned societies should become more active in these matters. (1996, 184)

Alabama politics provides a test case in point. For more than a century, Alabama politicians have chosen to maintain power or to acquire greater power by resorting to demagoguery. Alabama is a poor, backward state that has never shown any significant inclination to enter into the New South. Rather, Alabamians are content to live in the past, rejecting any social, political, or economic changes. Alabamians are highly religious, perhaps being the state most typifying what scholars have long termed "the Bible Belt." Most importantly, Alabamians, in general, have little regard for education, whether K–12 or college level. Consequently, most Alabamians who live outside of the few well-funded, nationally recognized school districts attend some of the worst schools in the nation and as a consequence are limited in their understanding of the everyday world. Nowhere is this more acute than in the areas of American history and government.

Demagogues have long maintained control in Alabama politics by playing on the basic ignorance of its people and their uncritical biblical faith. During the past twenty years, governors, lieutenant governors, and judges have engaged in lawsuits against the federal government, attempting to impose Christianity on all the people of the state. Whether school prayer or Bible study in the classrooms of state schools, or whether it is the Ten Commandments displayed in state courtrooms and the Lord's Prayer required in judicial proceedings, state leaders have used such "coded" states' rights issues to build and maintain political careers.

Millions of state tax dollars have gone to appointed nongovernmental lawyers to pursue these cases, rewarding hundreds of attorneys who have given money to campaign treasure chests. These are tax dollars that the state treasury can ill afford to lose. Facing a $700 million shortfall in 2003, the state may well be forced to close schools, college programs, state-supported nursing homes, mental health facilities, and a prison early-release program. Yet, the state's chief justice, Roy Moore, pursued a case before the U.S. Supreme Court during 2003, attempting to gain the right to keep a two-ton statue of the Ten Commandments in the state supreme court building, a statue financed by a religious organization and placed within the judicial corridors in the dead of night. The case has already cost the state $1 million in legal fees; however, the state has successfully negotiated a reduction in the attorney fees to $580,000. Yes, the state's chief justice does have the right to file in the federal court system; everyone should have access to the courts. But the greater question should be "But at what cost to the state and its people?" Constitutional law is required of all law students; did the state supreme court justice simply miss that day in class, when the professor talked about the separation of church and state? Did the learned writings of thousands of legal scholars escape his attention? Did the bar exam simply not cover the Bill of Rights the year that he stood for the bar? Or is the state supreme court justice simply an unethical politician willing to use any and all means to stir the emotions of people submerged in ignorance and religious intolerance? When the U.S. Supreme Court ruled against him and he defied the Court by refusing to remove the statue, he was eventually removed from office by a vote of the collected Alabama Supreme Court for defying the federal court ruling. He is now appealing the Alabama decision; however, a specially constituted Alabama Supreme Court denied his appeal and refused to allow Moore to resume his duties as the chief justice. And pollsters predict another successful run for public office, based on approval ratings that hover around 87 percent. Our point cannot be overemphasized: When learned men are willing to play on ignorance, ensuring its continuation in perpetuity, then all men are lessened. While Alabama newspapers are quick to cite legal precedents and lament past religious grandstanding on the part of Alabama leaders, they are slow to question the morality of what such unscrupulous, deceptive, and incompetent leadership has done to the state's welfare. If they fear retribution, they should go to the experts, and if the experts are frightened of commenting, they should go to legal experts outside the state. Participatory pluralistic journalism encourages such intellectual honesty on the part of its practitioners. On the other hand, community journalists, by simply reporting the people's overwhelming wishes, would further excite the demagogues, and as a result, the state would likely see two-ton Ten Commandments statues in every schoolroom and public building, which would only lead to more lawsuits.

Clearly, then, participatory pluralistic journalism encourages the highest professional standards without succumbing to the rather naïve logic of the community journalists that utilizes a propagandistic device that argues that the common folk or the plain folk are naturally far more sagacious than the learned (Johnson-Cartee and Copeland 2004; Jowett and O'Donnell 1992; Qualter 1985). The common-folk appeal is the argument that if ordinary, common people or plain folk believe something, support something, or act on something, then the idea, attitude, or action is somehow superior to competing ideas, attitudes, or actions. Such arguments imply that nobility exists within the simple, uneducated person and that within this nobility, wisdom and an appreciation for truth are born. Thus, an uneducated, simple person is far more knowledgeable, with opinions more valuable than those of an educated, more sophisticated individual. While not negating the value of human life or the practicality of conventional wisdom, I, if confronting a serious malady such as appendicitis or bronchial pneumonia, would not choose to drink manure tea brewed by a Green County, Alabama, woman instead of seeking professional medical help from either a board-certified surgeon or a pulmonary specialist. Having said that, however, it should be noted that insights may be gained by listening to others dissimilar from ourselves, for the discovery of communication patterns, community power structures, and community values and norms is a valuable endeavor, in that such variables are important social indicators in ethnographic studies and provide assistance in constructing informative and persuasive messages for public information campaigns targeting such communities. More importantly, disenfranchised individuals need a voice in public affairs. A multiplicity of voices should be heard in mass-communicated news reports, continuing and promoting pluralist debate. But to suggest that journalists serve as communication facilitators, engaging in conversations with a multitude of others, shepherding their individual interests into community-based programs, is an ill-founded new breed of political paternalism. Ultimately, such a misguided notion limits not only the responsibilities of others but their freedoms as well.

Furthermore, I agree with John Merrill (1997), who disagrees vehemently with community journalism proponents who argue that

> the rational liberal theory of the Enlightenment has failed and must be trashed; that individualism is a flawed foundation for journalism and must be supplanted by a more collectivized, group-oriented and cooperationist theory, which will eliminate social friction and establish a kind of communitarian heaven on earth. (56)

Liberal democratic theory hasn't failed us; we have failed to live up to the ideals it expresses (see Merrill, Gade, and Blevens 2001).

Despite the growth of community journalism academic programs and courses at universities throughout the country, community journalism proponents are still in the minority among practicing journalists today. In the majority are older journalists known as **gatekeepers**, who have been educated in professional journalism programs and who are actively involved in professional associations (Janowitz 1975). While these gatekeepers are still overwhelmingly liberal, these older journalists are not as liberal as the advocates. Janowitz writes:

> Since World War I, journalists have come more and more to consider themselves as professionals and to search for an appropriate professional model. The initial efforts were to fashion journalism into a field, similar to medicine, where the journalist would develop his technical expertise and also a sense of professional responsibility. This model and its aspirations can best be called the "gatekeeper" model. In particular, this image of the journalist sought to apply the canons of the scientific method to increase his objectivity and enhance his effective performance. (1975, 618)

Professional Organizational Culture

Journalists are influenced not only by their own educational background, political party and ideological predispositions, personality traits, and professional operating philosophies but also by their reporting environment. The reporting environment in which a journalist works serves to constrain his or her behavior. The organization's medium, whether broadcast, Internet, or print, has its own routines and constraints, which have been constructed over time by other individuals actively shaping their organizational culture. News production routines serve as guideposts for new reporters and continue to play an important role in shaping their work behaviors for the remainder of their careers.

Research indicates that a tension exists between a reporter's professional considerations and the employing news organization's operating culture. "Organizations stress routinized activities that contribute to profitability. Professionalism stresses ethical performance that contributes to social responsibility" (Pollard 1995, 682). Thus, journalists contend daily with dual control centers. This tension between organizational expectations and individual professional expectations must be seen as affecting not only the working reporter and the news product but also the news organization (Shoemaker and Reese 1991). Each reporter and each news organization operates in a state of perpetual balance and imbalance fluctuations, adjusting and adapting to each other as both internal and external pressures affect the relationship. While no one definitive conclusion may be drawn about the nature of this mutual adjustment process, it may be said that, for the most part, journalists experience more job satisfaction when they are allowed more independence and authority in the production of their news products. On the other hand, when organizational routines hold the upper hand, professionalism weakens, and when this occurs, according to Pollard (1995), the pleasure and personal meaning that journalists receive from their work suffer as well. Thus, journalists and their employers must negotiate the ravine between organizational needs and professional values.

Each news organization has its own operating culture, and for this reason, the working journalist's observance of the news organization's routines and norms becomes essential for the successful navigation of his or her own career path. When preparing for a news assignment, the journalist must take into account both organizational and professional considerations. Johnson (a.k.a. Johnson-Cartee 1984) writes:

The media organization—the newspaper, the magazine, the network—has a code of conduct or expectations of journalistic performance that individual journalists must follow. In a sense, a reporter writes for his immediate executive as well as for the public. The copy must meet the expectations of the "group" to which the journalist either belongs or aspires to belong. In addition to the norms and values of the group that influence the journalist when he or she writes the story, there are also group influences after the reporter turns in the story. For "the group" or "the news organization" then molds the story to fit the group's demands (structure, style, etc.). (40)

Thus media outlets, in effect, constrain reporters by their established expectations and routines, for each media organization has its own manner of conducting business, its own interests, and its own reporting or news agenda (Rock 1981). Obviously a reporter from the *National Review* with its staunch conservative, procapitalist perspective would observe occurrences, take them into account, and fashion them into "events" as determined by the magazine's news values far differently than, say, a reporter from the Sierra Club's *Sierra* magazine, a liberal, environmentally oriented publication. Events are merely journalistic accounts of "newsworthy happenings" (as judged by reportorial and organizational values) that provide news consumers with the public face of such happenings. If a logger chops down a redwood tree in a protected national forest in California and a reporter from the *National Review* observes the procedure, he will probably not choose to report the occurrence for, in his eyes and in the eyes of his magazine, this is not an environmental disaster but an individual entrepreneur working the resources of the land for personal gain. In other words, the occurrence would not be judged as negative and therefore would not meet the reporter's definition of news, and therefore it would not be considered an "event" or an occurrence with significance or importance far greater than that of the single act. But if a reporter from *Sierra* magazine witnessed the logger cutting down a protected redwood, the occurrence would be evaluated as an event: further evidence of the raping of our natural resources by the timber industry (see Molotch and Lester 1974). Clearly, then, "Any occurrence is a potential resource for constructing an event, and the event so constructed is continuously dependent on purposes-at-hand [objectives and worldview of the reporter and the employing media organization] for its durability [usefulness]" (Molotch and Lester 1974, 102).

For instance, Clarke and Evans (1980) found that a journalist's aggressive reporting style in covering congressional campaigns is often directly related to his or her perception of their publisher as being politically active. "The politically inclined publisher appears to be a catalytic agent. . . . We can assume that a politically charged newspaper management issues cues about how it would like to see congressional politics covered—presumably with some intensity of effort" (Clarke and Evans 1980, 118). In addition, they found that when organizational norms place a premium on reporters' aggressiveness, then collegial esteem is an inducement to adopt an aggressive reporting style.

Ultimately, the successful newsperson develops what Schudson (1995) has called "news conventions" or what Altheide and Johnson (1980) have called "a news perspective," in that they learn how to craft their stories, utilizing professional and organizationally determined desirable components. Altheide and Johnson (1980) write:

> A *news perspective: the view that any event can be summarily presented in an interesting and visually exciting way with a beginning, middle, and end, and that this can be accomplished within a few hours.* This perspective fundamentally distorts events by *decontextualizing* them from the complex situations and meanings that surround them and then *recontextualizing* them within the practical context of the newscast. Thus, the content of the original message is important, but so is the context and work involved in shaping the message to meet practical demands. (46; emphases in original)

Such news conventions are not timeless; much of what we consider today to be the absolute professional requirements such as the inverted pyramid are only recent innovations in the history of journalism (Schudson 1995). Schudson (1995) argues that such news conventions "function . . . less to increase or decrease the truth value of the messages they convey than to shape and narrow the range of what kinds of truth can be told. They reinforce certain assumptions about the political world" (55). For instance, journalists believe that they should always focus on the most powerful actor in a potential news story; consequently, the president of the United States will be the focus of any news story that in any way involves the president or his staff (Schudson 1995). Another news convention is journalistic emphasis on motives. Journalists believe that their role is to translate or interpret public events, providing meaning to news consumers who would otherwise be clueless as to the significance of public acts. The meaning of public acts is not in the passage of particular bills, the signing of bills into law, but in the deeper political motivations behind each actor's maneuvers. "The journalists' responsibility, as they see it, is to discover in the conscious plans of political actors the intentions that create political meaning" (Schudson 1995, 56).

Such news conventions also include the reporter's beliefs of what others in his or her news organization or in the news community expect in terms of news content and style. As Molotch and Lester (1974) observed:

> An occurrence passes through a set of agencies (individuals or groups), each of which helps construct, through a distinctive set of organizational routines, what the event will have turned out to be using as resources the work of agencies who came before and anticipating what successive agencies "might make out of it." (103)

For example, a copy editor knows that his immediate superior, the city editor, prefers all social problems to be expressed in baseball analogies. He then describes the occurrence in terms of a baseball event in order to please the city editor. Or the editor in chief, thinking of the bottom line and newsstand sales, insists on photographs illustrating the news story that contain attractive women or cute babies, even if these presentations fail to add meaning to the story as much as the photographs the reporter had intended to use, for beautiful women and adorable babies sell papers.

The result is that most news reporters have adopted news conventions that fundamentally distort the news story and ultimately the raw materials from which audience members create their own realities. Such news conventions worth special emphasis include market-driven journalism, talk shows, and literary journalism.

A free press, Siebert, Peterson, and Schramm (1956) once argued, is a product of a free society; a free press is also a product of a free economy, capitalism, or laissez-faire. Clearly, news organizations are profit-seeking, profit-requiring businesses; the organizational routines they construct are intended to secure profitability (Shoemaker and Reese 1991). For some, sound journalistic practices are sound business practices (Stepp 1991; Underwood 1988). For others, the commercial production of news sounds alarms, for such observers fear the compromising of journalistic principles for monetary gains or profits (Fuller 1996). We will first address the views of those who caution against the commercialization of news, and then we will return to the more profit-seeking, marketing-guided news perspectives.

Fuller (1996), in an intriguing exploration of the tension between journalists and marketing specialists (the strategists behind planned profits), suggests that the two groups are often operating at cross-purposes, philosophically. Journalists, by trade, are engaged in the creation of effective communication, if not for persuasion then at least for enlightenment. Fuller writes: "He is in the business of changing minds, if only from a state of ignorance to a state of knowledge. And that means he must master the art of getting messages through to people, which is rhetoric" (1996, 101). Historically, the founding fathers recognized the importance of a free press, and consequently, the journalists' "privileged position in law arises from its utility to the system of self-governance" (Fuller 1996, 101). On the other hand, the marketer is interested in what sells, what makes money. In short, the marketer wants to understand what the news organization's audiences want, to package the news to meet those demands, and to fulfill its customers' expectations and desires, resulting in increased profits for the news organization. For Fuller, journalists and marketers represent the "duality" of modern news organizations (1996). Both sides agree that to be effective, journalists must understand their audiences; journalists recognize that effective communication is based on understanding targeted audiences; however, for the marketer, this understanding produces

copy that is desired by the news audience, producing greater sales and profitability. This is a practice that most practicing journalists would view as
"pandering" (Fuller 1996, 117).

Fuller (1996) argues that news marketers have trivialized audience analysis
by only superficially investigating what the audience wants and neglecting, for
the most part, what the audience needs. While journalists may complain that
news marketers want to turn news copy into a commodity such as soap or
cornflakes, what they fail to recognize is that product advertisers and marketers know far more about their target audiences in terms of either wants or
needs than do news marketers about their audiences. Successful products are
marketed by aggressively taking into account both the wants and needs of potential customers. And audiences do need certain things from their news delivery systems. For instance, Fuller writes:

> There is, for example, every reason to believe that readers expect newspapers to
> be courageous and bold, to challenge conventional wisdom and question au-
> thority. There is every reason to believe that readers want their newspapers to
> know the difference between the significant and the trivial. (1996, 118)

Fuller argues that just as in the selection of an automobile, an individual
chooses a newspaper for more than the simple data that it provides; the selection is influenced by how an individual views him- or herself, how an individual expresses him- or herself, and how an individual wishes to be perceived
by others. In short, the selection of a news product is based on an individual's
perceived relationship with that news organization—just as a serious high-
performance automobile devotee wouldn't choose a Ford Escort rather than a
BMW Z4 if prices and opportunity were equalized. A political influential
wouldn't select the *MTV News* show rather than PBS's *NewsHour with Jim
Lehrer*, unless he or she had a particular reason to tune into the MTV show.
Perhaps such examples do trivialize the needs of various audiences. However,
journalists do recognize that as American citizens and potential voters, audiences have significant social, economic, and political needs fulfilled by the nation's news organizations. Fuller (1996) writes: "The journalist sees his role as
informing people of what they need to know in order to be functioning citizens, whether they want to know it or not. He takes it as his primary duty to
tell the truth about important things" (121). Such beliefs are at odds with the
news marketer, who believes that the audience should dictate news selection
and copy. But journalists do in fact benefit from news marketers, if their audience analysis is done expertly, for marketing information helps journalists
understand "*how* to say something, not *what* to say about something. Marketing helps journalists get the message across successfully; it does not determine
what message to give" (Fuller 1996, 121; emphasis in original).

While Fuller (1996) addressed marketing and business forces in relationship to newspaper readership or television viewing audiences—the earning, the maintaining, and the increasing of market share, McManus (1992, 1994) suggests that market forces within the news business are far more complicated than the picture that Fuller has presented for us. McManus argues that news must first be understood as a **commodity**, something that is bought, sold, or traded (1992, 1994). McManus suggests that news is a "double commodity" in that (1) news consumers either purchase the news by per copy fee or trade their attention to news providers for desired information, and (2) news providers sell news consumers' attention to advertisers for "rates based on the size and commercial value (income, stage of life, etc.) of the audience whose attention is delivered" (1992, 788). For newspapers and magazines, advertising revenues account for between 70 and 90 percent of their gross income; and, for television networks and their affiliated stations, advertising revenues account for nearly all of news programming income (see McManus 1992). Consequently, McManus (1992) has concluded that:

> For both newspapers and television, having advertising rather than consumers as the primary source of income means that the way to increase profit is to produce a product that has a minimal threshold appeal to the maximum number of demographically desirable consumers in the signal or circulation area. (789)

And, because advertisers are also profit oriented, they "can be expected to support the program generating the largest audience likely to purchase the products offered, at the lowest cost per thousand viewers" (McManus 1992, 79). Consequently, a premium news show that cost a premium price to produce but delivered the same quality and size of a desirable audience as a run-of-the-mill news show would not be desirable for advertisers in that the cost of the premium production would be passed on to advertisers. The advertisers have no concern with the meaning or merits of programming; rather, they are only concerned with acquiring advertising space for the lowest cost per desired thousand (see Bogart 1991; McManus 1992, 1994).

One consequence of advertising providing the revenues for news programming is that news organizations are not compelled to attract the poor and the elderly by their programming. Advertisers traditionally have little interest in such groups, because such groups are stereotyped as having either little disposable income or little inclination to acquire commercial goods (Bogart 1991; Kerner 1968). Therefore, little news programming is targeted toward the elderly and poor (Bogart 1991; Hilt 1997). However, Thorson (1995) has argued that the volume of news targeted to the elderly may well change in the near future. As the desired prime-time audience of eighteen- to thirty-four-year-olds shrinks, advertisers may well reevaluate their targeted populations.

Specifically, they may revisit the significance of the older population—fifty-five years old and above—"the fastest growing segment of American society, well-educated, and increasingly prosperous, with the lowest poverty rate of any age group in the population" (Hilt 1997, 84; see also Thorson 1995).

Another consequence of advertisers, providing the revenues for news programming is the likely pressure on news programmers to create news programs attracting the largest possible desirable audience. News, then, is likely to be popularized by emphasizing entertainment attributes such as dramatization or sensationalism (McManus 1992, 1994). Indeed, for a number of years, researchers have found news programming to be more entertainment than information or education (Bennett and Entman 2001; Combs and Nimmo 1993; Delli Carpini and Williams 2001; Henry 1981; Weimann 2000; Woodward 1997). Bennett (1996) reports that news executives often refer to their programming as **infotainment**, the merger of news with entertainment. Indeed, recent market pressures seem to dictate an infotainment approach; Manning (2001) has observed:

> Some correspondents complain that there is pressure to emphasise the sensational more in order to sell the news, even in mainstream reporting—hence the succession of scandal, corruption, and sleaze stories that have characterized political reporting in some European countries and the USA. (65; see also N. Jones 1995)

Nowhere is this more apparent than in talk radio or talk TV. With the repeal of the Fairness Doctrine by the FCC, talk shows virtually exploded into the marketplace. Kurtz (1996) writes:

> The richest and most prominent talkers include a wide assortment of pundits, commentators, experts, hacks, and hucksters, some of them cloaked in the thinnest journalistic garb. They analyze, interpret, elucidate, expound, pontificate, and predict, an unprecedented barrage of blather and bluster that has dramatically ratcheted up the noise level of political debate. (3)

The result has been that, in Kurtz's words, the United States has become a "talk show nation" (1996, 3). From the early days of Phil Donahue and Oprah Winfrey to the talk shows of such infamous talkers as Geraldo Rivera, Howard Stern, Don Imus, and Rush Limbaugh, Americans rushed to be titillated, seduced, and energized by the barrage of raw, hot verbiage such shows produced. Such shows "revel[ed] in their one-sided pugnacity, spreading wild theories, delicious gossip, and angry denunciations with gleeful abandon" (Kurtz 1996, 3). The talk show version of journalism gave up any pretense of objectivity or balanced presentations (Kurtz 1996). As a result, "The national conversation has been coarsened, cheapened, reduced to name-calling and finger-pointing and bumper-sticker sloganeering" (Kurtz 1996, 4). As the years have passed, more sophisticated talk shows have cultivated the aura of authenticity, while remaining relatively the same. Larry King, John McLaughlin, Ted Koppel, and the ever changing hosts of *Crossfire* lead the pack of authentic journalist wannabes. And, indeed,

> Presidents and prime ministers and putative leaders rush to appear on their programs because the hosts are presumed to be in touch with the public, as measured by Nielsen and Arbitron numbers that certify who is hot and who's not. (Kurtz 1996, 10)

From a presidential candidate playing an amazingly bad saxophone to political couples discussing the intimate details of their marriage, to an entertainment celebrity announcing his run for California's governor's office, political talk has become a cornerstone of the American political scene.

Such infotainment pressures and success stories have led some journalists to worry that such popular, tabloid versions of journalism will soon become the norm rather than the exception. Ian Jack writes: "In an unforgiving market, all of them [news organizations] perceive the need to be more popular and therefore, more dramatic, playful, and 'human.' A sort of warmth has been achieved at the expense of credibility and trust" (1998, 3). Such observations have led many to conclude that continued market pressures have led many news organizations to deliberately dumb-down their news offerings, appealing to the vulgate (Manning 2001; see chapter 4 for more on infotainment).

Another particular infotainment note is a strain of newspaper journalism best termed "literary journalism" (Coffey 1993), or the melding of fiction and journalism. During the 1960s, some journalists sought to challenge traditional approaches to their craft. Rather than sticking to the traditional method of news delivery—the relating of facts within a structured narrative—journalists sought immediacy and realism. In other words, they sought to make their news stories come alive for the news consumer. In short, such journalists wished to "infotain" their audiences by engaging in fictional techniques. Rather than stay on the sidelines, journalists wrote from the perspective of actors involved within the news events; they delved into the human psyche and the social and cultural traditions that guided "the players" in the news event. Such practice embodies the notions of Tom Wolfe (1973), an early devotee of the practice, whose writings are presented and excerpted here by Fuller (1996, 138):

> The power of novelistic [read fiction] writing in journalism, he writes, comes from four basic devices: (1) "scene by scene construction, telling the story by moving from scene to scene and resorting as little as possible to sheer historical

narrative" [original in Wolfe 1973, 31]; (2) "the recording of everyday gestures, habits, manners, customs, styles of furniture, clothing" and other details "symbolic of people's status life" [original in Wolfe 1973, 32]; (3) "realistic dialogue [that] involves the reader more completely than any other single device" [original in Wolfe 1973, 32]; and (4) "the technique of presenting every scene to the reader through the eyes of a particular character, giving the reader the feeling of being inside the character's mind and experiencing the motional reality of the scene as he experiences it" [original in Wolfe 1973, 32].

In short, such journalistic expressions presented news audiences with the opportunity to engage in what I term **news voyeurism**, the gratification of living vicariously and seemingly dangerously through the heightened lives of others very dissimilar to one's self. Journalists advocating literary journalism practices included Gary Wills, Jean Genet, Hunter Thompson, Tom Wolfe, George Plimpton, Truman Capote, Joe McGinniss, and "gonzo" journalist Hunter Thompson (Fuller 1996). The proponents of literary journalism were heavily criticized by their contemporaries, and while often wildly successful in publishing novels based on historical events, their views on the future of journalism fell out of favor. Indeed, mainstream journalism's criticism of Joe McGinniss's *Last Brother* (1993), a literary-journalism portrait of the last of the three Kennedy brothers, Senator Edward "Teddy" Kennedy, provides an excellent example of the journalistic outrage directed at literary journalism practices. The *New York Times*'s Francis X. Clines called McGinniss's work "shameless" and the literary devices utilized "licentious" (Clines 1993). Despite the status quo's rejection of literary journalism's techniques, many of these same literary practices ultimately became accepted by practicing journalists.

Ironically, however, the influence such literary journalists had on contemporary journalism often remains overlooked, according to Fuller (1996). First and foremost, today, journalists don't bother with tape recorders and frequently don't make much use of their reporter notebooks and pencils. Journalists are free to reconstruct quotes from their sources from memory. In short, they may improvise, improve, or clean up what they remember their sources to have said. And journalists have changed the manner in which they address their audiences. Journalists no longer stick to first-person or eyewitness accounts of what they or others have personally observed (e.g., "I was in our news office; the phone rang and my wife told me that the Tower had been hit. I raced to the window. The fireball was enormous. The gravity of what had happened to those people in the tower and to our nation weighed down upon me.") Often they write in second person, inviting the reader or viewer to anticipate what they themselves would have thought or done (e.g., "You would have been overwhelmed with smoke, horrible chemical smells, and the stench of death.") And, just as frequently, they write in third person, "getting inside everyone's minds" (Fuller 1996, 144) (e.g., "Overhead loudspeakers kept telling the office workers to remain calm and stay in their offices, but the firefighters knew such advice would mean inevitable death, and they raced to reach those trapped people in time, knowing as the building trembled and groaned the futility of their own efforts and the certainty of their own deaths"). Simply put, contemporary journalists engage in aspects of literary journalism every day. One only has to read *Newsweek* or *Time* or listen to CNN to find ready examples. The continued popularity of newspaper giants such as Bob Woodward, Carl Bernstein, and Sidney Blumenthal provides evidence that literary journalism still has its proponents, and infotainment lives on.

It may be said that great journalists as well as great literary authors share what Shafer (1976) has called a **tragic vision**:

> The tragic vision is expressed in a keen responsiveness to the great dilemmas, paradoxes, ambiguities, and uncertainties pervading human action and subjective experience. It manifests itself in alertness to the inescapable dangers, terrors, mysteries, and absurdities of existence. It requires one to recognize the elements of defeat in victory and of victory in defeat; the pain in pleasure and the pleasure of pain; the guilt in apparently justified action; the loss of opportunities entailed by every choice and by growth in any direction; the reversal of fortune that hovers over those who are proud or happy or worthy owing to its being in the nature of people to be inclined to reverse their own fortunes as well as to be vulnerable to accident and unforeseen consequences of their acts and the acts of others. (35)

In short, great journalists and great authors know a great story when they hear one. And they rejoice in the multifaceted dilemmas and serendipities confronting humankind, and they present these to their audiences with a variety of literary and journalistic techniques, intending to re-create other places, other times, and other people for the purposes of both entertainment and enlightenment.

In 1999, Dautrich and Hartley placed a new spin on the continuing debate surrounding journalism as a commodity. In examining voter satisfaction with presidential campaign coverage during the 1996 election cycle, they found that while voters overall were satisfied with news media performance, they shared many of the same criticisms concerning political reporting that political communication scholars have long voiced. For instance, voters were annoyed with horserace campaign reporting, and they were also disenchanted with the meta-campaign coverage, emphasizing the candidates' campaign strategies and tactics. Voters were also dissatisfied with the reporting frenzy associated with the reporting pack's discovery of a front-runner. In addition, voters expressed some frustrations that it was the reporters rather than the candidates who seemed to be determining campaign issues. While we have long known that such meta-campaign coverage increases voter cynicism (Capella and Jamieson 1997; Fallows 1997; Lawrence 2000; Patterson [1993] 1994; Valentino, Beckmann, and Buhr 2001), Dautrich and Hartley (1999) argue rather convincingly that such practices are unlikely to change, for they emphasize that such reporting is perceived by news organizations as being entertaining, attracting larger audiences, and therefore generating greater advertising revenues. And while voters may say they dislike such reporting styles, they nevertheless continue to use the same news sources. "Voters who dislike certain aspects of coverage are less likely to give the media a positive rating; but they are not less likely to use the media over the course of a few weeks or month" (Dautrich and Hartley 1999, 171). In short, Dautrich and Hartley conclude:

> As often as journalists, editors, publishers, and producers call attention to the First Amendment's protection of the independence of the news media, they point to the need of the news media to raise the revenues needed to cover their costs and satisfy their stockholders. Revenues come from advertising, and attracting advertisers depends on retaining a mass audience. If voters do not display their dissatisfaction with their feet (or their remote controls or radio dials), then news organizations do not have a powerful incentive to improve the content of the news or to improve the way they conduct themselves in elections. (1999, 171)

Journalists and their coworkers are confronted with a seemingly endless variety of potential news items; therefore, each organization must develop a means to evaluate, select, prioritize, and schedule its news items. Organizational routines are the means by which news assemblers **manage the news.** Tuchman observes:

> Governing the flow of news work, like the organization of most work, involves more than scheduling. It also involves the allocation of resources and the control of work through prediction. To cope with these tasks, newsmen distinguish among spot news, developing news, and continuing news. (1973, 119–120; see also Shoemaker and Reese 1991)

Through the years, newspeople have developed a news classification system that helps them manage the news. According to Tuchman (1973), the three categories of news are spot news, developing news, and continuing news stories. **Spot news** is the "*specifically unforeseen event-as-news*" (Tuchman 1973, 120; emphasis in original). Examples of spot news stories include wildfires, international incidents, or the death of a movie star. Spot news may well turn into developing news stories. **Developing news** stories are characterized as *"emergent situations"* (Tuchman 1973, 121; emphasis in original). In such situations, little may be known immediately, as in the case of an airline disaster, and, consequently, accounts of the event change throughout the course of the day, days, or even weeks. In other words, the airline disaster story is a developing story. An initial wildfire story (spot news) may turn into an arson investigation (developing news), eventually identifying a state fire-prevention worker as the arsonist, yet another major story component. When news organizations deal with spot news or developing news, newspeople are in a coping mode. Because the events were unexpected, reporters must scurry to determine both background and initial event information. And, because the cause(s) and/or the implications of the event have not been determined, journalists have to be prepared for the unraveling of the news story across time. On the other hand, **continuing news** facilitates smooth news coverage, because the coverage is expected, preplanned, and therefore prescheduled (Tuchman 1973). Consequently, continuing news brings some degree of sanity to the newsroom. Editors are able to predict where news reporters need to go and whom they need to interview; this provides editors with a measure of control in a business often characterized by chaos.

But it is not just in the planning of news assignments that news organizational routines affect the character and content of news reports. Editors influence reporters' news copy, for reporters are not the lone creators of news; rather, they merely submit copy to a hierarchy of editors who then delete, add, or in some fashion alter the submitted copy to suit their own preferences or the needs of the medium. Print headlines or broadcast lead-ins are written for the copy by editors, changing the perceptual environment surrounding the piece. Decisions on length and placement within the newspaper or broadcast are made not by reporters but by editors and news directors.

The influence of newspapers and television news organizations using a beat system in the assignment of reporters to specific spheres of influence, whether it is the Pentagon or the FBI, encourages the standardization of sources (see chapter 7). A **beat** is an area of inquiry that is assigned to a specific reporter for an extended period of time, whether it is education, crime, or health care. News organizations view this practice as improving the efficiency and therefore cost of news production, in that reporters become familiar with potential sources and the issues under active investigation, evaluation, and consideration. This buildup of knowledge is viewed as improving reporter performance, ultimately improving the quality of news content. Clearly, the beat system is based on economic norms supplied by the business plan of the news organization (Bennett 1996; see chapters 6 and 7).

Reciprocal Media Influence

Newspeople not only face the organizational constraints of their immediate employer, but they are also constrained by "strong reciprocal media influences among the various media in terms of developing their issue agenda for the day's or week's events" (Johnson a.k.a. Johnson-Cartee 1984, 1; see also Crouse 1972; Ehrlich 1992, 1995; McManus 1994; Noelle-Neumann 1973; Rhodebeck 1998; L. V. Sigal 1978; Scheufele 1999).

> The veteran journalists who occupy the territory at the very center of the political system—whether by virtue of their insight, contacts, or institutional positions—set the tone for what many of their colleagues say and write about politics, and thus much of what the public will hear and read about their leaders. (Lichter and Noyes 1995, 5)

Crouse (1972) found that influential national publications and wire services and the journalists who worked for them had a disproportionate influence in determining news angles and news stories among journalists on the presidential campaign trail. Particularly, journalists relied on the AP reporter when constructing news leads, because they learned that their editors back home questioned them if their news leads differed from that carried on the wire. D. Shaw (1989) has argued that CNN and computer data services have only increased the likelihood of intermedia influence. And, with the growth of Internet news services, the potential for cross-pollination is even greater.

Grossman and Kumar (1981) have argued that influential national news organizations, whom they refer to as "the majors" in the political news business, wield considerable clout among other news organizations and their representatives covering routine presidential news. Similarly, Paletz (2002) distinguishes between two highly influential media organizations, the elite and the prestige media. The **elite media**, according to Paletz,

> Tends to emphasize government and politics, employs foreign correspondents and reports their stories, strives to delve into issues and trends, and indulges in investigative journalism. Its news stories include background and explanations, often containing more than one perspective and source. It treats the news with sobriety, downplays flamboyant material, and eschews hyperbolic (but not evocative) language. (2002, 72)

Elite media are identified as "the *New York Times,* the *Washington Post, Los Angeles Times,* the *Wall Street Journal,* National Public Radio's 'All Things Considered' and 'Morning Edition' and weekend equivalents, and Public Television's 'The NewsHour With Jim Lehrer'" (Paletz 2002, 72). The elite media have disproportionate influence on other media news organizations, particularly the *New York Times*, an organization that "serves as a guide, even guru, for the rest of the press," whose "news stories set the agenda," and whose "frames are frequently adopted and adapted by other news outlets" (Paletz 2002, 72).

Prestige news organizations include the top three national newsmagazines, *Time*, *Newsweek*, and *U.S. News*. The top three commercial networks, ABC, NBC, and CBS, as well as the premier all-news network, CNN, are also considered members of the prestige press. The prestige press shares many of the same reporting practices, standards, and values with the elite media. However, the prestige news organizations do not have the resources to uniformly cover all domestic and international news events with the same degree of excellence as the elite press. In recent years, the television commercial network giants have significantly curtailed their news operations, particularly in international news. However, the prestige press exercises formidable power and influence, for when faced with a historically significant event, they depart from their survey of news practices to focus their massive resources on one single news story, for instance, the 9/11 terrorist attacks in America (Paletz 2002).

Profession-Based Conceptualizations of the Audience

In addition to professional and organizational constraints, newspeople have pictures in their heads of their audience, their readers or listeners. Audience images assist news reporters in evaluating occurrences and constructing public events (Wills 1982). Journalist Gary Wills claims that reporter-held audience images "determine what the media will say, more than do the so-called managers of the media" (1982; see also Michelson 1972). In one influential study, Grunig (1983) found that the combination of how an environmental reporter views his or her beat and how he or she, in turn, perceives the public's view of the environmental beat affects how a reporter covers the beat and the amount, depth, variety, and tone of news content. After analyzing Grunig's study, it is possible to discern four separate reporter-public situations that are useful in analyzing a wide range of news reporting:

1. *Active reporter and active public:* In this situation, the reporter is interested in all matters concerning the environment, and he or she also perceives an activist environmental public, needing and requiring environmental news concerning a wide variety of matters. This type of reporter actively engages in information seeking, processing, and story production.

2. *Active reporter and single-issue public.* Under these circumstances, the reporter has interests in a wide variety of environmental matters, but he or she perceives the public as being a single-issue public. These reporters still actively seek and process environmental information; however, they are not as likely to generate stories from that process. Rather, such reporters temper their own enthusiasms by writing only stories that also interest their public.

3. *Passive reporter and universal issues public.* Under these circumstances, the reporter is not likely to aggressively seek information; however, he or she will process what information is readily available. The reporter selects stories that involve nearly everyone, for example, the deregulation of natural gas. In this way, the reporter is assured of meeting the needs of a public who is only interested in environmental issues that affect everyone universally.

4. *Education-directed active reporter and obstinate single-issue public.* Under these circumstances, the reporter actively seeks and processes environmental information, writing a wide variety of stories in the belief that he or she knows what the public needs more so than the public. Such a reporter tends to look at the public as a single-issue public who doesn't particularly care about environmental matters outside of their immediate interest. However, while the reporter views his or her role as that of a crusading educator, he or she also recognizes that his or her efforts may well go unnoticed by an apathetic, obstinate, and perhaps lazy public.

Clearly, a reporter's orientation to his or her news beat determines to a great extent the intensity and the pervasiveness of news coverage produced. And it also suggests that different reporter-public orientations may well produce different orientation levels of negativity. Therefore, it seems reasonable that a political leader, a press secretary, a bureaucrat, and a campaign consultant, for example, should come to know reporters' reporter-public orientations in order to provide themselves with clues as to how to frame and pitch news stories to these journalists. And knowledge of the reporters' reporter-public orientations could well provide the raw material from which to predict how each will handle an upcoming event, announcement, or potential crisis.

In Conclusion

Working journalists are constrained by personal baggage, professional standards, organizational culture, and self-held audience images. News creation is truly a social construction, involving a multitude of present, past, and anticipated distant or future forces influencing the newsperson. Nowhere is this more readily apparent than in the numerous newsgathering mythologies and strategic rituals governing the practice of news writing and news reporting. We turn to a consideration of these mythologies and strategic rituals in chapter 4.

4

Newsgathering Mythologies and
Strategic Rituals

S YKES (1965, 1966, 1970) MAINTAINS THAT BUSINESSES, industries, work-
places, and even occupations develop mythologies that assist workers in
their daily jobs. These myths develop from observations of "how things are
done" or "how things should be done." In some cases, it may be that workers notice that management or supervisors reward others for acting or completing their work in a particular way. Such observations lead workers to
identify the particular behavior as the preferred means of completing a task.
Once this happens, according to Sykes, the particular behavior takes on a
"*concrete* form" (1970, 18; emphasis in original) and becomes myth—"a paradigm or model of the general situation" (Sykes, 1970, 18). Sykes (1970) explains more fully:

> The term myth will be used to mean the expression of abstract ideas in a con-
> crete form. A myth takes the form of a story that embodies certain ideas and at
> the same time offers a justification of those ideas. If the myth is to be effective it
> must be so constructed as to appeal to the emotions and enlist sympathy for the
> ideas expressed. . . . The actual truth or falsity of the story is irrelevant; what is
> important is that the story and the ideas it embodies are accepted and believed
> to be true. (17)

Thus, occupational mythologies develop over time, and as new trainees
or employees enter the field, the older members of the occupational force
see to it that they are socialized into the occupation by learning the occupational mythologies. This is true for journalism as well. Whether from

journalism lectures, on-the-job editorial directions, or personal observations, new journalists quickly learn what is expected of them, and they
adopt the field's mythologies as their own. Nimmo and Combs (1980) put
it very well; they write that ultimately, myth is "a credible, dramatic, socially constructed re-presentation of perceived realities that people accept
as permanent, fixed knowledge of reality while forgetting (if they were ever
aware of it) its tentative, imaginative, created, and perhaps fictional qualities" (16).

Myth of Professional Objectivity

In the Western world of industrialized democracies, professional journalists
and journalism educators adopted the ideal of professional objectivity during
the 1920s (see Schudson 2001; Streckfuss 1990). "Inextricably intertwined
with truth, fairness, balance, neutrality, the absence of value judgments—in
short, with the most fundamental journalistic values—objectivity is cornerstone of the professional ideology of journalists in liberal democracies"
(Lichtenberg, 1996, p. 216). The **ideal of professional objectivity** posits that
educated and experienced journalists are able to assume a professional objectivity that negates any personal subjectivity—the subjective beliefs, values,
and schemas inherent to each cognizant individual—by following "a journalistic system the [sic] subjected itself to the rigors of the scientific method"
(Streckfuss 1990, 974; see Schudson 2001). The belief in such a scientifically
based journalism practice grew out of the dissatisfaction with the often emotional and jingoistic news produced by American reporters prior to, during,
and after World War I (Schudson 2001; Streckfuss 1990). Journalists and social philosophers such as Walter Lippman and John Dewey feared the power
of propaganda machines and what they saw as the resulting emotionalism and
sensationalism apparent in newspaper copy; for this reason, they argued that
democracy must be protected by a professionally educated journalist cadre,
well versed in the scientific method, applying only the highest principles of
truth-revealing practices. Such principles were to be learned from the developing fields in social science, principally political science, economics, psychology, and sociology (Streckfuss 1990). Journalists were to be trained in
these developing sciences, ultimately yielding an individual better prepared to
analyze events and social forces operating within the world at large, consequently producing information for news consumers that would better enable
them to make rational decisions, ultimately elevating humankind. Such beliefs
are evident in Lippmann's writings; he wrote in 1920 perhaps the definitive argument for objective journalism:

With the increase of prestige must go a professional training in journalism in which the ideal of objective testimony is cardinal. The cynicism of the trade needs to be abandoned, for the true patterns of the journalistic apprentice are not the slick persons who scoop the news, but the patient and fearless men of science who have labored to see what the world really is. It does not matter that the news is not susceptible of mathematical statement. In fact, just because news is complex and slippery, good reporting requires the exercise of the highest scientific virtues. They are the habits of ascribing no more credibility to a statement than it warrants, a nice sense of the probabilities, and a keen understanding of the quantitative importance of particular facts. (63)

Despite Lippmann's best intentions in creating a far wiser and far more educated journalist cadre, he neglected to understand that social scientists also fall victim to their own subjectivities. Indeed, Thomas Kuhn's *Structure of Scientific Revolutions* (1970) provides ample evidence of this phenomenon. Kuhn argues that culturally derived rules determine the parameters of scientific research, although such socially constructed rules may not be obvious to the layperson. Indeed, often scientists themselves aren't fully cognizant of how their research methodologies are intellectually grounded. Kuhn explains that this lack of self-awareness is actually rooted in the "nature of scientific education," for, he writes, "Scientists, it should already be clear, never learn concepts, laws, and theories in the abstract and by themselves. Instead, these intellectual tools are from the start encountered in a historically and pedagogically prior unit that displays them with and through their applications" (1970, 46). Consequently, Kuhn goes on to write that while "scientists talk easily and well about the particular individual hypotheses that underlie a concrete piece of current research, they are little better than laymen at characterizing the established bases of their field, its legitimate problems and methods" (1970, 47).

Thus, the notion of humans—even a highly educated human—being objective is ludicrous, for a person's very knowledge of the world is subjectively constructed, learned, and modified through a process of experience in the context of social interactions, involving role taking, and role modeling through the course of a lifetime. Because of different levels of perceptual skills, both physical and mental, no two people perceive the world in the same way; and no two people have the same social interactions that help build social identities and the self or that organization of qualities and traits an individual attributes to him- or herself. Thus, subjectivity is the nature of humans, and no amount of professional training and experience will change that. Califano and Simons have summarized the argument against professional objectivity well; they assert:

There can be no such thing as an objective press. This is so because there is no way an editor or a publisher can squeeze the inculcation of a lifetime from a reporter or an editor. And these inculcations—parentage, regionalism, education, friends, religion, experiences, ad infinitum—subliminally shape every story and subliminally suggest what a reporter leaves in or omits from a given story. (1979, xvi)

Myth of Objective Reality

Western journalists and journalism educators promote the notion that the news media "stand as reporter-reflector-indicators of an objective reality 'out there,' consisting of knowably 'important' events of the world" (Molotch and Lester 1974, 105). This has been dubbed the "mirror model" of news (Molotch, Protess, and Gordon 1996). Introductory journalism texts define news as complete, accurate, truthful accounts of the real social world (see Altheide 1976; Ault and Emery 1965; Brooks, Kennedy, Moen, and Ranly 1999; L. R. Campbell and Wolseley 1961; Evensen 1997; Schoenbach 1983). Thus, when college professors tell their aspiring young journalists that they must develop "a nose for news," the professors are using a hunting-dog analogy to suggest that students must uncover or discover "news" much as Ol' Yeller tracked a raccoon up a tree. Other writers have used the same "nose for news" analogy to suggest that reporters through experience develop an instinct for news (Altheide and Johnson 1980; Ettema and Glasser 1998). This suggests that "news" may not always be manifest or obvious, but with an experienced reporter on its trail, it will eventually be ferreted out. And, as Tuchman (1972) observed, this assumption that the reporter is merely an "indexer" or recorder of news relieves the reporter and the news organization of any responsibility for what they report. The prevailing journalistic attitude has been that newspapers "print all the news fit to print" in the case of the *New York Times*, or that nightly news shows broadcast "objective" reality, as illustrated by Walter Cronkite's famous signoff of "and that's the way it is." Such sayings illustrate the myth of an objective reality called news. L. W. Doob (1948) humorously criticized such naïve realism as shared by journalists when he wrote:

> Of course, as any school girl knows, facts do not speak for themselves: the people who perceive the facts do the talking and what they say depends on the facts which are presented, the way in which they are presented, and their own ongoing responses at the time when the facts are perceived. Only a journalist, moreover, is credited by journalists with the ability to gather facts—a journalist is a gifted person "with newspaper experience." (271)

I believe that the educational use of this myth is unfortunately deceptive, for the myth of objective reality portrays news as a commodity such as a book or a can of soup that one may find, pick up, and take. However, this is far from the truth. Professional guidelines or news values are used in Western journalism education to assist young, would-be reporters in the crafting of their news stories. Similar to the formal education of a painter who learns art techniques and styles, leading to the expression of his or her own individual style, such professional guides assist journalists in their craft.

However, Lichtenberg (1996) has argued that we should not abandon the concept of objective reality, for if we do "abandon the concept of a reality independent of news stories we undermine the very basis on which to criticize their work" (233). Lichtenberg (1996) goes on to suggest that if we negate objective reality, then to discuss how news is socially constructed is pointless in that bias or professional objectivity cannot be determined. Ultimately, Lichtenberg (1996) argues:

> This is not to deny that the media sometimes or even often present events in a distorted, biased, or ideological way. It is rather to insist that we can only explain this fact on the assumption that there are better and worse, more and less faithful renderings of events, and that, despite our own biases, preconceptions, "conceptual schemes," we can escape our own point of view sufficiently to recognize the extent to which it imposes a structure or slant on events that could be seen differently. (232)

Myth of Reportorial News Perspective

According to Tuchman (1972), news judgment is another indicator of the mysticism and ritual surrounding the practice of journalism, for it "is the sacred knowledge, the secret ability of the newsman which differentiates him from other people" (1972, 672; see also Ettema and Glasser 1998). Successful newspeople, however unreflective, develop what Altheide and Johnson (1980) have called "a news perspective," in that they learn how to craft their stories, utilizing professional and organizationally determined desirable components.

In one particularly insightful piece, S. Hall (1973) took the profession to task for hiding behind the "news perspective" when determining the selection of news photographs suitable for publication. He wrote:

> News values' [sic] are one of the most opaque structures of meaning in modern society. All "true journalists" are supposed to possess it; few can or are willing to identify and define it. Journalists speak of "the news" as if events selected themselves. Further, they speak as if which is the "most significant" news story, and which "news angles" are most salient are divinely inspired. Yet of the millions of events which occur every day in the world, only a tiny proportion ever become visible as "potential news stories": and of this proportion, only a small fraction

are actually produced as the day's news in the news media. We appear to be dealing, then, with a "deep structure" whose function as a selective device is un-
transparent even to those who professionally most know how to operate it. (181)

In short, news reporters take into account their repertoire of storytelling tools,
regardless of where they acquired them. And it is from this repertoire that
each reporter chooses his or her news frame when preparing to construct the
day's news narrative.

Ideological Bias

Evidence for the subjective nature of journalism rests in a number of research studies that have identified ideological bias in news reporting. An ideological bias occurs when a journalist or news organization uses his or her
own political predispositions in characterizing news occurrence (Gans 1979;
Gordon and Heath 1981; Hackett 1984; MacLean 1981). In addition, Hofstetter (1976) argues that an ideological bias may also occur because of structural
biases or biased patterns in the ways news organizations gather and disseminate news or because commercial news marketing and programming concerns alter or bias the news. For instance, no one would argue that the character of local news is unaffected by sweep weeks, where ratings of local news
are determined. In Alabama, you may safely bet that during sweeps week,
news stories will focus on stripclubs, prostitution, pornography, Internet sex
sites, and sex crimes. Titillation is the name of the game during sweep weeks,
regardless of what potential significant news events occur.

Research often focuses on ideological bias found in presidential election
news. For instance, Semetko, Blumler, Gurevitch, Weaver, Barkin, and Wilhoit
(1991) found that American newspapers were far more biased than network
coverage of the 1984 presidential election: "Political philosophies were apparent in front-page story selection, amount of directly quoted material used, the
quantity and nature of the contextualizing remarks appearing in coverage
(even in straight news stories), and in the themes embedded in stories, edito-
rials, and columns" (83). They also observed:

> Because most U.S. newspapers do not have direct competition, and because
> nearly all newspapers are locally rather than nationally oriented, this means that
> they can be more partisan in their approach to election coverage if the bulk of
> their readers are similarly partisan. (Semetko et al. 1991, 84)

Similarly, M. S. Larson (1989) in a content analysis of presidential news
provided by National Public Radio's *All Things Considered* (ATC) concluded:

ATC has systematically reported the activities of conservative presidents less favorably than liberal presidents. Indeed, the ratios of time devoted to unfavorable coverage compared to favorable coverage show some remarkable differences. That is, Ford's unfavorable/favorable coverage ratio was higher than 3 to 1; Carter's was close to 1 to 1; Reagan's was close to 2 to 1. (351)

According to researchers, it should come as no surprise that journalists are biased by their own life experiences, beliefs, and values, for they are as human as any other individual (Willis 1991). In other words, journalists do not check their humanity at the door when they leave college with their bachelor of arts degrees. As David Morley (1976) so wisely noted, there is no such thing as value-free language "in which the pure facts of the world could be recorded without prejudice" (246). Indeed, evaluations have already been made and are inherent in the words used and the concepts expressed, whether from what one records or what one interprets (Morley 1976). Tuggle writes that "journalists, like most people, tend to stereotype people, issues, and situations. These stereotypes, in turn, affect the gatekeeping process, in which journalists decide what is news and in what form the news should be presented" (1998, 67; see also Willis 1991). And, more importantly, such stereotypes form labels: "They not only place and identify those events; they assign events to a context. Thereafter the use of the label is likely to mobilise *this whole referential context*, with all its associated meanings and connotations" (Hall, Critcher, Jefferson, Clarke, and Roberts 1978, 19; emphasis in original).

Ideological bias in news coverage is influenced by the operating news philosophies within a given political culture. In a survey of journalists conducted in five countries, T. E. Patterson and Donsbach (1996) found:

> There is a significant correlation between journalists' personal beliefs and their news decisions. The relationship is strongest in news systems where partisanship is an acknowledged component of daily news coverage and is more pronounced among newspaper journalists than broadcast journalists, but partisanship has a modest impact on news decisions in all arenas of daily news, even those bound by law or tradition to a policy of political neutrality. (455)

The German news system was the most partisan with the United States and Great Britain being the least partisan (T. E. Patterson and Donsbach 1996, 465). And T. E. Patterson and Donsbach (1996) concluded, "Journalists are not nonpartisan actors; they are simply more or less partisan, depending on the country and arena in which they work" (465).

Lichter and Rothman (1983) have argued that journalists from elite news organizations are substantially more liberal than other journalists and society as a whole. However, T. E. Patterson and Donsbach (1996) have questioned that finding in that their research shows a marked similarity in journalists' partisanship across all news organization levels, and their partisanship is only slightly left of center. T. E. Patterson and Donsbach (1996) describe journalists "as a mainstream group with liberal tendencies" (465; see also Gans 1979). "Journalists' opinions affect the interpretation of facts, and fairness leans to the left" (T. E. Patterson and Donsbach 1996, 466). But news bias is not always easy to detect. For, as T. E. Patterson and Donsbach (1996) write:

> Journalism escapes close scrutiny from within and outside the news profession precisely because the bias it permits is difficult to detect. Nevertheless, as journalists go about the daily business of making their news selections, their partisan predispositions affect the choices they make from the stories they select to the headlines they write. Since the influence is subtle, most of them probably do not recognize it. It flows from the way they are predisposed to see the political world. (466)

And T. E. Patterson and Donsbach (1996) observe that a perceptual gap exists "between journalists' self-image and their actions, and it leads them to reject any suggestion that they are politically biased" (466).

Despite the findings of T. E. Patterson and Donsbach (1996), other researchers have maintained through the years that journalists are inherently conservative in their presentations because of the institutional nature of news as a business. Van Dijk (1988) perhaps best represents this perspective when he writes that because of institutional and professional constraints, the news by necessity promotes elite beliefs. After all, the news media represent the business interests of either the owners or stockholders who have a vested interest in maintaining the status quo and established patterns of economic power and wealth (e.g., Cirino 1971; Gerbner, Gross, Morgan, and Signorelli 1980a; Lee and Solomon 1990; Noelle-Neumann 1993; Schiller 1992).

News bias as a field of inquiry is particularly important in that researchers, most notably M. J. Robinson and Kohut (1988), have found that most people do indeed believe what they read, see, and hear. This phenomenon is especially true for television, where people are far more likely to believe what they see (Slattery and Tiedge 1992). "Television persuades via communication techniques that are person-centered and based on the illusion of a one-to-one relationship between sender and receiver" (Tuggle 1998, 66). This illusion of a relationship, what others have called a "para-social relationship," is also made more powerfully credible because of the perceived immediacy of the action or behaviors presented in the news (Newhagen 1989; M. J. Robinson and Kohut 1988). And, as television has been the nation's primary source of news since 1964 (Roper Starch Worldwide 1995), its perceived credibility is a significant public issue, for what television news portrays as public events plays an influential role in determining public perceptions.

Researchers have not only been concerned with reportorial and organizational bias but also with **distortion**. Hackett (1984) writes: "The moment of distortion is suggested by the terms 'warped,' 'distorted,' 'indirect,' and 'stereotyped,' versus 'straightforward,' 'factual,' 'factually accurate,' and 'truthful'" (231). Yet, as Hackett so cogently observes, nondistortion or undistorted news is not always the same thing as balanced news or two sides equally presented. This is particularly true when journalists seek out expert sources with opposing sides to meet their "balance" professional norm, yet ignore whether what either expert says is grounded in sound scientific or historical facts (see the strategic ritual of balance later in this chapter). Hackett writes: "There is a tension between impartially reporting contradictory truth-claims by high-status sources, on the one hand, and independently determining the validity of such truth-claims, on the other" (1984, 231). The early success of Senator Joseph McCarthy's communist witch-hunt provides one obvious example. Such unquestioning acceptance of truth-claims from high-status sources is particularly prevalent in international news, where American interests both economic and political are paramount (Hackett 1984). Such distortion is also apparent when considering sports reporting in both local and regional news. Sports reporters do not even make the pretense of fairness or balance; rather, they openly support and often cheerlead for favorite local teams. In my hometown of Tuscaloosa, the hallowed ground of the Crimson Tide football team, reporters treat the National Collegiate Athletic Association as the rogue elephant rather than the other way around.

As mentioned previously, Hackett (1984) argues that balance in and of itself is not sufficient to avoid distortion. He writes: "The goal of avoiding distortion implies a positivistic, nonrelativist affirmation of the ultimate knowability of 'the straight fact,' whose visibility is temporarily obscured by the biased journalist" (233). Such efforts imply, according to Skirrow (1979), that simply presenting two viewpoints or more in some way approximates truth, which is erroneous. Similarly, Epstein (1973, 67) writes about the dominant news "'dialectical' model for reporting controversial issues," which presents two highly contrasting viewpoints, with the reporter wisely suggesting or implying that the "real truth" lies somehow in between these two extremes. Yet, life and life issues are not that easily solved.

Secular Strategic Rituals

Some have argued that the decline of religion in the Western world would ultimately decrease the significance of ritual in society, but as B. Anderson (1983) has discovered, this is not the case. He (1983) maintains that as society has become more complex and has, for the most part, lost its communal nature, citizens may not hope to know and be personally acquainted with the totality of a given society. Therefore, the citizen turns to the news media to present a "public community," a dramatization of the society in which citizens work and play. This dramatization of the public life of the society is what B. Anderson (1983) calls the **imagined community** or what Meyrowitz (1989a) has called the **generalized elsewhere**.

The generalized elsewhere is a natural extension of Mead's (1934) generalized other, suggesting that there are not only generalized others but also generalized localities or communities. Meyrowitz (1989a) explains his reasoning:

> The notion of the generalized other is related to media and community in two ways. First, media have extended the generalized other so that those whom we perceive as significant others are no longer only the people we experience in face-to-face interaction within the community. People from other communities and localities also serve as self-mirrors. The "mediated generalized other" weakens (but surely does not eliminate) our dependence on loyalty and on the people in it for a sense of self. Second, by giving us perspectives external to the locality, media expand our perception of "the generalized elsewhere" as a mirror in which to view and judge the locality itself. We are now more likely to understand our place, not just *as the* community but as one of many possible communities; not just as the center of all our experiences but as a place north of, west of, more liberal or conservative, than a number of other places. (327; emphasis in original)

Citizens attending to the news media perceive themselves to be participating, knowledgeable members of the imagined community. This is particularly true for television news viewers (Meyrowitz 1985, 1989b). Television does not, however, "enhance our sense of abstract knowledge about other places so much as it feeds our sense of having experienced aspects of other places" (Meyrowitz 1989a, 328; see also Meyrowitz 1985, 1989b), which, as Relph (1976) has shown, are two widely different understandings of place.

Chaney (1986) has also argued that the reliance on the news media to make sense of our world has also changed our sense of time, and in briefly quoting B. Anderson (1983), he maintains that modern society is only possible by "a shift in consciousness concerning time, 'in which simultaneity is, as it were, transverse, cross-time, marked not by prefiguring or fulfilment, but by temporal coincidence, and measured by clock and calendar'" (30). Chaney continues, arguing:

> The interdependence of time, imagination and community is displayed through the cultural form of the newspaper where heterogeneous events jostle for space grouped only by the dateline. . . . The readers of a newspaper are symbolically integrated into a public whose common concerns are shown by the narrative of the world represented. (1986, 117)

Thus, journalists recognizing the subjectivity inherent in man have created for themselves a number of **strategic rituals** that if followed ensure, they assure us, objectivity. Elliot (1980), in his examination of strategic rituals of print news media, defined strategic rituals as "rule-governed activity of a symbolic character involving mystical notions which draws the attention of participants to objects of thought and feeling which the leadership of a society or group hold to be of special significance" (147). According to Chaney (1986), news media rituals "affirm the experience of a collectivity [journalists and news organizations] which would otherwise have only an ambiguous cultural location" (116). In short, news media rituals affirm who and what journalists are in contemporary society. The performance of the ritual constitutes the categorical explanation of journalism and the professional identification of its practitioners.

S. F. Moore and Myerhoff (1977) have identified six formal characteristics of such secular rituals:

- Repetitive acts implying continuity
- The consciousness of acting, performing a meaningful behavior for others, and thus ensuring the validation of the individual performer and establishing the significance of the act for the collectivity ensuring solidarity and for those external to the collectivity who observe and recognize the acting as reflective of the collectivity and its members
- Unique behaviors or stylizations of performances that establish tradition and ultimately legitimacy
- Order and structure that create predictability and therefore familiarity and comfort
- Evocative performances, heightened or staged performances to attract other members of the collectivity and external observers or readers, and to increase their appreciation and admiration for the ritual performances of the individual performer
- Collectivity expressions within the performance ensuring the identification of the collectivity

Thus, according to Chaney (1986), "rituals are a representation of the collectivity, a collective performance in which certain significant aspects of social relationships are given symbolic form and force" (122). Elliot (1980) argues that we must come to view news media reports as yet another form of literature, recognizing its symbolic content and the process of symbolic formation that created it (171). It would be useful to examine a number of strategic rituals used in Western journalism, both to identify the rituals and to understand how they function.

Style Rituals

Journalists in the United States obsess about style, as demonstrated by the 334 pages in the *Associated Press Style Book and Libel Manual* (Goldstein 1998) and the 573 pages of the *AP Broadcast News Handbook* (Kalbfeld, 1998). L. W. Doob (1948) made this humorous observation: "Nor is the American journalist humble about journalistic style which he considers to be the finest and clearest method of writing yet devised by mortal man in any language" (272).

Journalistic style—the form, structure, and rules of journalistic writing, whether print or broadcast—is sacrosanct; and the news promoters, particularly press secretaries or media relations specialists, who forget this do so at their own peril. In other words, news promoters must be masters of print and broadcast journalism style. Ironically, news promoters need to be—have to be—better journalists than the journalists in both style and content, for in this way only will news promoters gain the respect of news assemblers and ultimately accomplish their purpose: the dissemination of needed information to desired audiences.

News scripts follow the distinctive stylistic rules associated with introductory journalism courses whether broadcast or print. Van Dijk (1988) and Pan and Kosicki (1993) have suggested that these stylistic rules define and shape news stories, serving as the **story grammar** for news accounts.

> A generic version consists of the familiar five Ws and one H in news writing: who, what, when, where, why and how. Even though they do not have to be present in every single story, these are categories of information that a reporter is expected to gather and report. (Pan and Kosicki 1993, 60)

In addition, script grammar "contains the push of our attention to drama, action, characters, and human emotions" (Pan and Kosicki 1993, 60), and as such helps contribute to news writing being presented and perceived as storytelling.

The **traditional journalism lead** or the introduction of a print news story is a critical stylistic component, for it is the lead that must successfully entice news consumers to attend to the news story. While the traditional print journalistic lead contains either five or six information components—the who, what, when, where, why, or how of the news story—the broadcast lead contains only one or two of the previously mentioned six components. In television news, J. D. Barber writes, "The first whiff of a story is a lead and a lead is like a joke. It gets its punch from the juxtaposition of incongruities, much as a comedian's one-liner is a crisp combination of elements ordinarily apart. Dog bites man will not do" (1978, 114). But "man bites dog" will do.

Rules for attribution are lengthy and cumbersome, and vary between print and broadcast journalism. The organization of information within the story follows past patterns of organization. In print journalism, the inverted pyramid is often used, where the most important information is placed first and the least important information or filler information is placed near the end. The inverted pyramid has proven to be quite controversial in recent years. While some researchers such as Graber (1994) have argued that the inverted pyramid assists the less-educated reader in understanding the news by highlighting and emphasizing the most important points first, others have suggested that often these points aren't readily understood by the less-educated reader unless presented within the contextual information necessary to evaluate the "news," which is often placed at the very end of the story without the necessary connections having been made (e.g., Eveland and Scheufele 2000).

Motive-Lead Copy

The news story itself is the reporter's choice of observed actions that demonstrate, for the reporter at least, the actor's motive for having committed the act. J. D. Barber writes, "Journalism as literature shares a reversal contrary to the common sense that motive precedes and thus explains action; rather actions are used to educe motives, and actions which fail to meet this criterion are 'irrelevant'" (1978, 116). Journalists share Sherlock Holmes's love of deducing causes from effects. Thus, the journalist's trade is an effort after discovering the symbolic; what appears as a concrete act is really symbolic of motive or character. Journalists attempt to get inside the actor in order to reveal innermost secrets for the audience; such efforts constitute a **motivational analysis**. As a result, J. D. Barber argues that "the lead must lead inside" (1978, 116), and "the story consists of actions selected to reveal character" (116). For this reason, stories focus on actors and revelations of character.

The importance of such stylistic concerns should not be overlooked. T. E. Cook observes:

> When journalists examine their work as well as that of others, they are more likely to talk about stylistic questions, such as objectivity, specificity, drama, excitement, good visuals, and the like, rather than political notions of how the world works and how the world should work. (1996b, 472; see also Altheide 1976; Gans 1979; McManus 1992, 1994)

Thus, what we would call production values or journalistic style is of supreme importance to working journalists.

The Professional Code of News Values

News is the creation of a reporter after observing or attending to an **occurrence** or a physical happening where it is evaluated or thought of in terms of the **news values** traditionally associated with the journalism profession such as conflict, proximity, size, significance, prominence, and so on; ultimately, the occurrence may be either rejected as not worthy of attention or judged as an **event** or an occurrence deemed of some significance and potentially newsworthy (see Molotch and Lester 1974). Westerståhl and Johannson (1986) have made the telling observation that Western news values have remained remarkably static: "Many of the ingredients can, for instance, be found in classic drama" (134). This observation provides additional evidence in support of thinking of news as narrative (see chapter 5).

My focus on strategic rituals, however, should not mislead you. News construction is not only characterized by the routinized, strategic rituals of the journalism field but also by the element of chance. Berkowitz (1992) writes that certainly these strategic rituals are very significant in that "the most interesting, the most important, and the easiest to cover are likely to take precedence by simple necessity," but on the other hand, "what might be news on one particular day might not be news on another, so that the actual 'odds' of entering the news mix will vary daily" (101).

Galtung and Ruge (1981), in their study of structuring and selecting news, have argued:

Events become news to the extent they satisfy the conditions of:

(F_1)	frequency
(F_2)	threshold
($F_{2.1}$)	absolute intensity
($F_{2.2}$)	intensity increase
(F_3)	unambiguity
(F_4)	meaningfulness
($F_{4.1}$)	cultural proximity
($F_{4.2}$)	relevance
(F_5)	consonance
($F_{5.1}$)	predictability
($F_{5.2}$)	demand
(F_6)	unexpectedness
($F_{6.1}$)	unpredictability
($F_{6.2}$)	scarcity
(F_7)	continuity
(F_8)	composition
(F_9)	reference to élite nations

(F$_{10}$)   reference to élite people
(F$_{11}$)   reference to persons
(F$_{12}$)   reference to something negative (60)

According to Galtung and Ruge (1981), these factors often overlap each other. And in a situation where news assemblers find all twelve news values or factors operating within a public occurrence, they predict:

(1) The more events satisfy the criteria mentioned, the more likely that they will be registered as news (*selection*).
(2) Once a news item has been selected what makes it newsworthy according to the factors will be accentuated (*distortion*).
(3) Both the process of selection and the process of distortion will take place in all steps in the chain from event to reader (*replication*). (Galtung and Ruge 1981, 60–61; emphasis in original)

Galtung and Ruge (1981) assume that these news values are shared at all levels within the news organization. As the news story passes from hand to hand within the organization, the same news values are applied and accentuated at each level, creating a cumulative distortion. They write:

We hypothesize that every link in the chain reacts to what it receives fairly much according to the same principles. The journalist scans the phenomena (in practice to a large extent by scanning other newspapers) and selects and distorts, and so does the reader when he gets the finished product, the news pages, and so do all the middlemen. (Galtung and Ruge 1981, 61)

Similarly, Noelle-Neumann (1973) suggested that there exists a set of assumptions that all newspeople have concerning the criteria for the acceptance of their stories by their audience members. This set of assumptions or this set of criteria has long been taught in skills courses that are taught in journalism and broadcast journalism programs throughout the country. For instance, Golding (1981) lists the major news values: drama, visual attractiveness, importance, size, proximity, brevity, negativity, and recency (75). More recently, Evensen (1997) listed the major news values as conflict, consequence, prominence, timeliness, proximity, and human interest (140–141). And, in 1999, Brooks, Kennedy, Moen, and Ranly provided a highly similar listing, consisting of impact, conflict, novelty, prominence, proximity, and timeliness (5–6). To the extent that journalists share similar news value criteria, journalists are apt to create a similar news product by their efforts to meet these news values.

As a result, news values "play an important role in helping to structure public opinion" (Price and Tewksbury 1997, 177). By selecting certain events and people to include in news accounts, journalists ignore other events and people, and as a result, news consumers receive an uneven presentation of the world and consequently are "rimed to interpret their social worlds in ways that reflect that set" (Price and Tewksbury 1997, 177) of news values as expressed in the people and events that are portrayed in the news. In other words, as W. A. Gamson (1992b) and Price and Tewksbury (1997) have observed:

> Journalists' sense of news values leads them to present public issues within certain frames, often reflecting broader cultural themes and narratives, that help define the fund of ideas available to citizens as they think about and talk about politics and public affairs. (177)

Conflict, Negativity, and Drama

Graber (1989), in her discussion of the criteria for news selection, establishes negativity or "natural or man-made *violence, conflict, disaster,* or *scandal*" as one of the more important ingredients in verifying newsworthiness (84–86; emphasis in original; see also Galtung and Ruge 1981). Significantly, journalists themselves are well aware of the negativity component to their stories, for the old adage "if it bleeds, it leads" is still widely accepted and followed in American journalism (Evensen 1997). And certainly negativity, conflict, or both are central to dramatization. Such emphasis on negativity is clearly seen in political campaign news coverage where news stories emphasize the conflictual nature of political campaigns with particular emphasis on the horse-race aspects of the campaign and the political strategies and tactics used by various candidates and their consultants to win the horse race (Arterton 1984; Patterson 1980). P. H. Weaver (1972) has observed that journalists consider political campaigns to be games and

> the players' principal activities are those of calculating and pursuing strategies designed to defeat competitors. . . . Public problems, policy debates, and the like . . . are noteworthy only insofar as they affect, or are used by, players in pursuit of the game's rewards. (69)

Adatto concluded from a content analysis of television news's presidential election coverage in 1988:

> The language of political reporting was filled with accounts of staging and backdrops, camera angles and scripts, sound bites and spin control, photo opportunities and media gurus. So attentive was television news to the way that campaigns constructed images for television that political reporters began to sound like theater critics, reporting more on the stagecraft than the substance of politics. (1990, 5)

The news media's **conflictual orientation** is abundantly clear to press secretaries or public relations officers. One such promoter, a political campaign manager, explains how the news media's definition of newsworthiness affects how he manages his political candidates' campaigns:

"Newsworthy" means featuring disagreement, conflict and contrast. It means painting campaign participants as heroes and villains. It means making one's point briefly, at the start of a speech, and using popular, emotionally stirring symbols. It means tailoring one's speech to the needs of the moment and capturing the audience's fancy. (Lorenz, 1978)

The end result is that "political campaigns have become little more than a series of performances calculated to attract the attention of television news cameras and their audiences" (Matthews 1978, 55). And T. E. Patterson (1991) observed that "increasingly, journalistic values rather than political values have characterized election news and have molded the process by which Americans choose their presidents" (145).

In the presidential primary arena, Matthews (1978) argues that campaign news is particularly powerful in that news accounts affect both the process of nominating a party presidential candidate and the resulting outcome of a likely presidential nominee at the end of the primary season (56; see also J. D. Barber 1978; Bartels 1988; Kendall 1995). Obviously, the news media are influential in determining who decides to run, who drops out of the preprimary race, who enters what primaries, who wins pivotal state primaries, and, consequently, who are the favored candidates going into the presidential conventions, and eventually who is the favored victor in the general election (J. D. Barber 1978; Kendall 1995; Matthews 1978).

Social Impact, Importance, Consequence, or Significance

Stories are likely to be reported that will have an **impact** on the audience. Stories are selected that will "touch" or affect the audience in some way; in other words, the stories will "connect" with audience members, establishing resonance. Thus, stories are provided that people can relate to as individuals, whether stories of airline disasters, consumer fraud, social security, or health hazards; such stories either touch our lives directly or touch someone we know and care about. As audience members, people assign **importance** or **consequence** to those things that are likely to affect their lives and their loved ones' lives either positively or negatively. And those things that are judged important are considered to be **significant**. Often such stories are personalized in order that people may relate to the specific people who have experienced, in this example, tragedies. By personalizing the story, reporters recognize that audience members are more likely to be affected, which ultimately is the reporting goal (e.g., Brooks, Kennedy, Moen, and Ranly 1999; Evensen 1997).

Size

Size is the quantification of the "largeness," "weightiness," or "frequency" of an occurrence or the quantification or estimation of the number of people, animals, places, or things affected by the size of the occurrence. Size is often a component in determining significance. Therefore, assertions of significance are normally accompanied by size estimations or quantifications. For example, the greater the number of people dead or injured, the greater the amount of dollars lost in property destruction, the more significance the news reporter will assign to the story.

Proximity

Often newspaper editors and local television news producers, when asked what the most important news value is in the construction of news, will name proximity. Proximity is the "closeness" of an occurrence to the location of the news outlet's audience.

Timeliness

The old adage "news is new" is still true. For the most part, reporters make story selections based on the recency of the action. For the daily newspaper, such news values are often interpreted as action occurring either today or yesterday. For the local television evening news team, it is far more likely to be action having occurred that day. Television seeks immediacy even more than newspapers. Newsmagazines, on the other hand, have the advantage of reporting not only the week's events but also reporting on trends or movements across time that are currently affecting society in a different or more significant way. Having a larger news hole and more time between deadlines, the weekly newsmagazines enjoy more latitude in what they report.

Novelty

Journalists prefer that which is out of the ordinary or that which is least expected or not predicted. This may be because the type of occurrence doesn't happen in the community every day; for example, the opening of the first civic center in a recently incorporated city will be considered novel by the local newspaper, radio, and television stations. Or the type of occurrence might be chosen because it is outside the normal experience of their audience members. In Miami, Florida, where the outside temperature is a balmy 78°F, the city's newspaper will likely publish an AP wire photograph showing fifteen-foot snowdrifts, towering over the roofs of ranch houses, in the outskirts of Chicago, Illinois. Such photographs bring a different world, a different way of life into people's lives.

Familiarity

Although reporters prefer the novel, the unusual, or the extraordinary, they recognize that for audience members to be attracted to the news story it must contain elements of familiarity. News stories centered around celebrities, whether sports figures, music superstars, or television and movie stars, are always popular. And, often, familiarity is added to stories by the use of **exemplars**—the personalization of an issue or occurrence by telling the story through the eyes of an individual who has dealt with this situation or problem (see exemplar discussion, chapter 8). Fundamentally people identify with other people, and they are more able to understand and remember stories that are concretized by such examples than those that are not.

Action

Reporters prize action on the part of leaders, whether they are corporate executives, governors, vice presidents, or the local sheriff. "Political actors are expected to be direct and consistent. Likewise, action is a good in and of itself; inaction is taken as a sign of incompetence, bad faith, and/or pettiness" (T. E. Cook 1996b, 47). In other words, inactivity violates the reporters' expectations, and when reporters' expectations are violated, they frequently will search for the reasons behind the violation. And it is in these circumstances that we will likely see the negativity of the news content increase (see Johnson a.k.a. Johnson-Cartee 1984). Graber (1997) notes that "important social, cultural, or technological developments" dramatized by action will receive substantial coverage (118). For example, the Million Man March by African American men during 1995 helped dramatize the plight of African American men in America, their concern for their community, and their commitment to their families.

Brevity

Journalists favor stories that are easily told; such stories are often simple and direct. And, therefore, shortness or brevity can be achieved in that the story stands by itself; it does not need to be explained, put into a larger context, or linked with previous news articles. News stories that report a local hotel kitchen fire, a high school graduation ceremony, or a new automobile tire plant's groundbreaking are all examples of stories that may easily stand alone.

Visual Attractiveness

Television news reporters and print photojournalists seek opportunities to capture objects, people, places, and so on that are visually attractive. Sunsets, desert or beach scenes, snow-covered mountaintops, attractively displayed food, babies, or beauty contestants are all favorites of the working journalist.

We will now move our attention away from news values per se and consider the strategic ritual of balance.

The Strategic Rituals of Balance

Western reporters believe that news stories should present both sides of an issue, the pro and the con, and the **presentation of both sides** should be as equal in length and treatment as possible. However, it may only appear to be both sides, for the rule of getting an **official reaction** to events such as disasters, accidents, or international events will often necessitate only one perspective as to what happened; there may not be "another" side to present (at least at initial stages of reporting). Presenting both sides is an effort to achieve balance, and as such, it has been institutionalized; it is simply required (Bennett 1996). In this way, journalists argue that they have achieved balance or fairness; and if they have achieved balance or fairness, then they must be without bias; therefore, they are objective. The argument that journalists present is circular and self-serving, presenting logical straw men that only muddle and confuse the issue. However, as Hackett has observed: "Far from being in some absolute sense neutral, news balance generally leads the media to reproduce the definitions of social reality which have achieved dominance in the electoral political arena" (1985, 256).

Journalists also suggest they have provided a balanced account (and, in their logic, acted objectively) if they allow individuals, corporations, or other entities when attacked by the government or their competitors an **opportunity to respond.** If the attacked choose not to respond, the journalists by professional training will simply report that the individual or organization "refused to comment," "declined to be interviewed," "could not be reached for comment," or "failed to respond to phone calls." The journalists believe that ensuring an opportunity for the attacked to respond relieves them of any responsibility for presenting a one-sided or biased report. In addition, when a journalist sued for libel, the news organization's having provided an opportunity to respond is received very positively by the court.

But journalists are also deceived by their own **perceptions of duality**; they identify two sides to every public controversy—good versus bad, pro versus con, or right versus wrong; and it is these voices that are heard as news sources within the news story itself. Yet rarely in the affairs of humankind may it be said that a controversial public issue has but two sides or two viewpoints expressed concerning that issue. In many situations, multiple interest groups compete with multiple versions of reality and as many recommendations for policy. Rarely are public issues so carefully drawn that one may distinguish two sole positions.

In addition, Western journalists have an extremist orientation in that journalists will often choose sources or spokespersons who represent the most extreme positions on an issue. This comes from the mistaken belief that sources from the extremities of public discussion more clearly and more effectively communicate the values and beliefs being debated. This is why representatives from the National Organization of Women (NOW), who wants no legislation altering a women's current legal right to an abortion, are pitted against such pro-life forces as Joseph Schledier and his Pro-Life Action League, who utilize nonviolent, legal means to end abortion (but who threaten violence if legal means are not sufficient); or Randall Terry and his Operation Rescue group, which promotes the harassment of medical doctors who perform abortions, their families, and their patients; or Donald Treshman and his Rescue America organization, which publicly applauds the political assassinations of doctors who perform abortions while distancing the organization from the perpetrators as individuals (see Muir 1995). Such news coverage of the abortion issue serves only to inflame the emotions of those already committed to one extremist position or another, and narcotizes or turns off those individuals who would like some closure on the issue but who prefer a resolution somewhere between the two warring factions.

However, under certain circumstances, this **extremist orientation** actually serves to reinforce the status quo and to support the continued state of non-issue-resolution. In these instances, the news report still offers two opposite perspectives, but the way in which reporters construct the story around those opposites leads the vast majority of audience members to support the **status quo orientation** or majority position (L. Danielian 1992). Shoemaker, Chang, and Brendlinger (1987) explain this phenomenon:

> Critics of the U.S. media have suggested that the media act as agents of social control, not by preventing the publication of new and different ideas, but rather

by varying their coverage of political groups according to how different the groups are from the status quo. (362)

This is easily observed when the news media deal with gay rights. News stories use radical-right leaders, usually clergy or conservative authors, as con sources who appear as average, familiar, and comfortable citizens who proselytize to gays and lesbians, urging them to undergo a sexual conversion, the rejection of their own sexual identity. And while many mainstream, conservative Americans do not appreciate the radical right's zealousness in imposing their viewpoints on others, the majority of those who do disagree would not find these leaders to be overwhelmingly alarming. On the other hand, the pro position is illustrated with images of participants in gay pride parades, those with mannerisms held to be stereotypically gay by heterosexual America, or those who publicly display their sexuality in public (as most heterosexuals do) by hugging, fondling, kissing, or holding hands; yet all three presentations are hardly the mainstream of gay life in America and do not adequately reflect the gay and lesbian communities. It's as if the news media take scenes from a gay night club in Atlanta; a gay rights parade in San Francisco; a beach scene in Pensacola, Florida, or Galveston, Texas; and street scenes in Greenwich Village in New York, and then suggest that this composite reflects the totality of gay life. Moritz (1995) observes:

> Certainly gay pride parade images will be read differently by straight, white, conservative audiences than they will be by gays and lesbians who are likely to view these events as queer performance, that is, an expression that may incorporate irony, camp, comedy, confrontation of mainstream sexual mores, exotica, erotica, and more. By showing only those gays and lesbians who most critically challenge conventional standards for public behavior and cultural expression . . . [it] implies that they represent the entire group. As many have pointed out, this is the equivalent of showing pictures of drunks during Mardi Gras to illustrate the lifestyle of white, heterosexual men. (71)

Or it is the equivalent of showing the movie *Animal House* to illustrate the college fraternity environment and the lifestyles of white, heterosexual fraternity brothers. In other words, by not depicting the more mainstream representatives of the gay world, doing the routines of life—working, shopping, cooking, cleaning, or interacting with friends and neighbors—the only portrait painted is one of unfamiliarity and a resulting discomfort. If viewers can't view depictions of such minority groups as people much like themselves, experiencing both the labors and joys of life, then they tend to marginalize the minority group as "the other," assigning negative attributes to the group.

But it also is necessary to note that the radical right, while an extreme political orientation, is not necessarily the most extreme group the media could have chosen; there are those who support the incarceration of gays and lesbians in either mental hospitals or prisons. L. Danielian (1992) explains, "Although radically dissenting opinions do gain access . . . the news media tend to exclude those issues and sources that seriously conflict with the status quo or sources that are extremely controversial and outside the mainstream of political discourse" (76–77). Thus, for the most part, the concerned, calm, religious-oriented, white, middle-class heterosexual male rather than a fire-breathing, neo-Nazi skinhead is positioned against gay men dressed in drag or lesbians dressed in chain mail and leather.

As much as anyone, journalists are the product of their cultural environment. According to Kennamer (1992), U.S. journalists frame their news stories within a status quo worldview; he writes:

> Journalists don't operate in social or cultural vacuums. They very much reflect the societies and cultures in which they operate. Thus they apply the standards and expectations of that dominant culture to everyday news stories, to provide the "framing" consistent with the standards and expectations of the dominant culture. In fact, these are the standards by which journalists and others judge their stories to be "objective." (8; see also Hackett 1985)

Salmon and Moh (1994) maintain that the news media's status quo orientation has significant ramifications for society; they write:

> The many ways in which the media portray a consonant ideology—particularly that of individualism—are subtle and veiled. By consistently structuring problems in certain ways and by accepting the inevitability of existing political and social institutions, the media contribute to the delimiting of human potential by failing to seek and legitimize alternatives for meaningful change. (159)

The Strategic Ritual of Factism

It has often been said that journalists are obsessed with uncovering, discovering, or collecting facts, for producing "facts" in their news stories legitimizes the account and establishes its objectivity. The line of *Dragnet*'s police sergeant Joe Friday when interviewing a crime witness, "Just the facts, ma'am, just the facts," is the news assembler's motto.

Public Opinion Polls

In addition to official news sources, news assemblers also emphasize public opinion polls, associating polling data and analysis with the "scientific community," yet another producer of "indisputable facts." At times, journalists, rather than quoting official sources, turn to "official" polls to demonstrate their continued objectivity. Such emphasis on facts, disconnected from explanations, creates what Crespi has called a self-fulfilling prophecy or a feedback loop in which "(1) definitions of what is news, (2) determine the content of polling, (3) affects the political process, (4) which then becomes news" (1980, 466). In other words, as an aptly titled *Progressive* magazine article, "Pox Populi," stated, "A poll suggests an issue to which there is a political response, which is then reported, and another poll is taken to determine the response to the action, beginning a sort of chain reaction" (Broh 1980, 527–528). The widespread use of political polls during campaign seasons has led Patricia Nelson Limerick to observe that "the pollsters have taken an electoral process that people once fought and died for and made it the moral equivalent of the Pepsi taste test" (1988, 6A).

Boorstin (1961) and Gollin (1980) have argued that the American news media have gone far beyond "news gathering" to "news making" in that they routinely produce "pseudo-events." Clearly, public opinion polling is a ready example. Gollin (1980) maintains that the pseudo-event is something created by the news organization "specifically in order to be reported, whose ambiguity of meaning is intrinsic to its interest, and that often has the character of a self-fulfilling prophecy" (449).

Public opinion polls—particularly political opinion polls—in the hands of a journalist often become a far different animal than what was originally intended. Political polls provide a mere superficial acquaintance with the expressed views of those sampled and questioned. "Polls are short-lived, easily misinterpreted and, unfortunately, can take on a life of their own," according to Gallup's Larry Hugick (as quoted in Kierstead 1988, 14). According to Ratzan, "There is little reflection on the validity of the data, the logical strength of such claims, but what we do have is the spitting back of statistical data generated from polling the public in place of reflective thinking, the deliberate discrimination among competing values" (1989, 452). The inclusion of such superficial analysis of polling results in news reports often leads the reporter to make sweeping generalizations, often misleading news consumers, particularly the attentive political elite. Similarly, Gollin (1980) writes that one negative criticism sees media polls "as reflecting or contributing to a serious misapprehension of the nature of the public opinion—polling's crucial legitimating concept—and its ideal or actual relationship to representative democratic institutions and policy processes" (454).

According to Traugott (1992), polls have wide-ranging influences in the political sphere that we often don't immediately think about when reviewing polling data. He writes:

Polls can influence political elites as well. Most financial contributors, for example, want to back a winner. Results from media polls, as well as private polls paid for by a campaign, are commonly used by candidates to encourage support for their efforts or to discourage contributions to an opponent who, they would argue, has little chance of winning. These effects can be especially pronounced early in the campaign, when candidates are often not well known and not rated highly in polls. (128; see also Dexter 1954)

At such times, published poll results will often influence the potential pool of campaign workers and volunteers. Traugott writes:

> Professional campaign staff workers who are trying to decide which campaign to join, and whose careers are often based on their record of working for successful campaigns, use the results to evaluate candidate's chances. . . . A poor showing in the polls can devastate a nascent candidacy, especially of someone who is qualified but relatively unknown, if it limits fund-raising possibilities and campaign staffing. (1992, 129; Dionne 1980; Hickman 1991)

An emphasis on facts as presented by news promoters and political polling reports is a dangerous practice in the construction of news, for journalists believe that they "must be able to identify 'facts,' even though some truth-claims are not readily verifiable" (Tuchman 1972, 665). Unfortunately, this results in the journalists' naïve presentation of "the statement 'X said [or reported] A' as a 'fact,' even if 'A' is false" or misleading (Tuchman 1972, 665). And, as Tuchman dryly noted in 1978, officials in the federal bureaucracy, other elite sources such as corporate executives, or the polling reports of information promoters are probably everything but objective.

Yet despite journalists' widespread use of opinion polls, they rarely conform to established AAPOR (American Association for Public Opinion Research) poll-reporting standards in their dissemination of poll results (Rollberg, Sanders, and Buffalo 1990; see textbox 4.1). For this reason, news audiences do not have the essential descriptors necessary to evaluate effectively both the validity and reliability of the poll. Paletz, Short, Baker, Campbell, Cooper, and Oeslander (1980) found in a study of poll reports on two national television networks and those published in the *New York Times* during 1973, 1975, and 1977 that poll sponsorship, one of the most significant of the poll-reporting standards, appeared in only 25 percent of the news stories. This led M. M. Miller and Hurd (1982) to write, after observing a similar paucity of poll-reporting standards in their own content analysis of three regional newspaper powerhouses, that "newspaper editors do not see the methodological details required for conformity to AAPOR reporting standards as automatically worthy of highly valued news space" (246; see textbox 4.1). Salwen (1985) found roughly a 50 percent conformity rating to

AAPOR guidelines for Detroit daily newspapers' coverage of campaign polls during a sixteen-year timeframe. And in 1990, in a content analysis of regional and national newspapers, overall conformity to AAPOR guidelines fell just below 50 percent (Rollberg, Sanders, and Buffalo 1990, 88). Newspapers, by discounting how important methodological considerations are in an individual's determination of the merits of a given poll, have ultimately worked "to trivialize the political process by failing to give the voters sufficient information to make sound judgments" (Rollberg, Sanders, and Buffalo 1990, 90).

Infographics

Because of this emphasis on facts, news researchers during the past twenty-five years have worked to discover alternative methods of presenting facts in a more user-friendly format. This area of research is called information graphics, or infographics. The findings of researchers in this area have spawned news assemblers and news promoters who are trained in the development and

---

Textbox 4.1
The AAPOR Minimal Standards for Disclosure

1. Who sponsored the survey, and who conducted it
2. The exact wording of questions asked, including the text of any preceding instruction or explanation to the interviewer or respondents that might reasonably be expected to affect the response
3. A definition of the population under study, and a description of the sampling frame used to identify this population
4. A description of the sample selection procedure, giving a clear indication of the method by which the respondents were selected by the researcher
5. Size of samples and, if applicable, completion rates and information on eligibility criteria and screening procedures
6. A discussion of the precision of the findings, including, if appropriate, estimates of sampling error and a description of any weighting or estimating procedures used
7. Which results are based on parts of the sample rather than on the total sample
8. Method, location, and dates of data collection

Source: AAPOR, March 1986, www.aapor.org/ethics/code.html (accessed February 15, 2002).

production of infographics for both print and broadcast news media. Infographics has literally transformed the means by which news agencies present the news, for more complex stories can be presented with greater clarity.

A virtual explosion in nontextual representations of information has occurred in the nation's newspapers. Both newspaper professionals and news researchers point to the twenty-year-old *USA Today* as being the primary front-runner and change agent in modernizing newspaper graphics (E. J. Smith and Hajash 1988). While information graphics per se are not new, it took the leadership of a new national newspaper to usher in the widespread use of such design tactics (Garcia 1987). Baird, Turnbull, and McDonald have described infographics as "the most spectacular development in image presentation by the mass media" (1987, 129). Similarly, Garcia (1987) suggests that the technological advances in the creation, distribution, and eventual dissemination of infographics to the public have fundamentally changed "the way newspapers convey information" (46), predicting that future advances will only bring about greater change in the newspapers' information dissemination (48).

In 1989, Hilliard found that more than 75 percent of newspapers surveyed belonged to a graphics network. Graphics networks have facilitated the increased use of infographics in newspapers in the United States. With the help of a graphics network, "Artists can retrieve graphics stored in digital form from numerous databases, alter and update them as desired, and produce graphics ready for pasteup in less than an hour" (Mintz 1986, 12–14). According to Hilliard (1989), most infographic specialists had commercial-art backgrounds, particularly in advertising graphics, and 88 percent preferred using Apple computers in their design work (Hilliard 1989). Similarly, Silverstone and Webb (1986) report that Apple computers and printers were literally revolutionizing the graphics capabilities at most newspapers. But it is not just commercial graphic artists who are changing the look of our nation's newspapers. Hilliard (1989) found that many news personnel, recognizing the growing trend in infographics, were retooling and learning the new technology. Photojournalists were most likely to retool, but reporters with an interest in infographics, such as business or economic news reporters, were also retooling.

Newspaper infographics are more likely to be used in news stories dealing with business and economics, weather, and public affairs (government, politics, and education) (E. J. Smith and Hajash 1988). "The location of graphics on the page—with large proportions in the upper left and right—implies that informational graphics, like photographs, are being used as display elements to anchor page corners" (Smith and Hajash 1988, 718).

Kelly (1993) found that "tables and graphs are more efficiently processed than text presentation of the same data" (140). Tufte (1983) argues that pie

charts displaying sections of pie, representing different quantities or percentages of the whole pie, are too difficult for readers to interpret. And he concludes (1983) that "the only worse design than a pie chart is several of them"
(178) in a composite design. D. B. Ward (1992) has argued that graphs should
be kept simple in order to improve reader comprehension. He also suggests
that a small text block within the graphic will help readers understand what
they are to look for in the graphic. Or the graphic designer might include step-
by-step instructions labeled 1, 2, 3, and so on to pull the reader through the
various points of the graph to again aid reader comprehension. Ward (1992)
found that stories that were accompanied by a sidebar (graphic with explanatory text) received the highest reader comprehension scores.

In television, a wide variety of visual techniques, some employing textual
presentations, are now used. Zettl observed as early as 1979 that television
news has been transformed through what he called "graphication"; he writes:

> Computer-generated graphics pop on the screen to give us headlines, field re-
> porters and their stories are squeeze zoomed in and out over the news anchor's
> shoulder, and fancy lettering repeats what we have heard the newscaster tell us.
> Through the magic of digital video, live scenes are frozen into still images and
> peeled off the page by page as though we were flipping through a magazine. (137)

This virtual revolution in infographics has led Schamber (1987) to urge
that news assemblers, news promoters, and news analysts develop what Foote
and Saunders (1990) have termed "the specific skills to understand visual
grammar and syntax and be able to integrate visual and verbal content at
every stage" (Schamber 1987, as summarized by Foote and Saunders 1990,
502) in the construction of news process.

Foote and Saunders have identified seven kinds of television infographics:
"1) symbols/typography; 2) illustrations; 3) map, graph, diagram; 4) film or
video [not filling entire screen]; 5) cartoons (still and animated); 6) photographs; and 7) composite, a graphic made up of two or more of the above
kinds" (1990, 503). Such infographics serve important information functions
in television news construction, for example, (1) establishing and introducing
the news story, (2) providing detailed information or explanations, (3) illustrating concepts or story themes, (4) providing background information or
historical time lines identifying key events, (5) placing multiple sources of information or information points within one framework, and (6) previewing
upcoming news items to motivate future viewing patterns (see Foote and
Saunders 1990). Foote and Saunders (1990) found that composite graphics
account for more than one-half of all televised infographics; news producers
are making use of such techniques in the presentation of otherwise complicated and difficult-to-understand news content.

Official Sources

One way that journalists assure themselves that they have collected suffi-cient "facts" is by emphasizing official sources in their news accounts. Jour-nalists believe that the use of authoritative or official sources produces "legit-imate, official facts," creating, when crafted together, "an objective news story." Journalists believe that such a practice protects them from charges of political bias. T. E. Cook (1996b) writes:

> The prime way to do so, of course, is to rely on authoritative sources to cue them into topics, stage events that can become a focus for a story, and provide quotes to inform and enliven the final product. By using authoritative sources to pro-vide value judgments, reporters can elide [sic] questions of factuality. (476)

We will consider journalism's reliance on official sources in much greater depth in chapters 6 and 7.

The Ritual of Dramatization

In an oft-cited NBC News memo, then executive producer of the evening news broadcast Reuven Frank wrote to news personnel:

> Every news story should, without any sacrifice of probity or responsibility, dis-play the attributes of fiction, of drama. It should have structure and conflict, problem and denouement, rising action and falling action, a beginning, a mid-dle, and an end. These are not only the essentials of drama; they are the essen-tials of narrative. (As quoted in Epstein 1973, 4–5)

Reuven recognized a fundamental characteristic of human narratives and news stories—drama, the evoking of story lines with good guys and bad guys struggling for dominance with exciting twists and turns in the plot and re-verses in fortune for the protagonist.

"Drama" itself is a news value and so is its counterpart, conflict. Four types of dramatic conflict are used in news stories: man versus man, man versus himself, man versus fate, and man versus nature (see Johnson a.k.a. Johnson-Cartee 1984). Political leaders are pictured as "Davids" fighting the mighty "Goliaths" of pollution, unemployment, global warming, or AIDS. However, the story rarely has a happy ending. Pollution or global warming isn't killed, and unemployment doesn't fall to the ground. AIDS lives on to kill another day. It often seems that there are no happy endings.

Nimmo and Combs (1983) believe that news, like all human communica-tion, may be characterized as storytelling (see also Bormann 1972; W. Fisher

1984; see chapter 5). These stories involve conflict and uncertainty whether man versus man, man versus himself, man versus fate, or man versus nature (Johnson a.k.a. Johnson-Cartee 1984). "When something happens that is ambiguous in meaning, provokes people's interest, and raises doubts demanding resolution, the popular urge is to represent *what really happened* in dramatic ways" (Nimmo and Combs 1983, 14; emphasis in original; see also Bennett and Edelman 1985; Darnton 1975; G. Knight and Dean 1982; Schudson 1982; Tuchman 1976). Darnton (1975) has argued that journalists are assemblers of stories who then judge their own achievements and professionalism by how well their constructed stories are "played" in the news, the prioritization of their story against other stories in the news as determined by the journalist's superiors. For this reason, journalists search for naturally occurring dramatic happenings or those occurrences deemed exceptional.

The Standardized Exceptional

Leon Sigal has observed that news is "the standardized exceptional" (1973, 66; see also Wilkins 1964). And, as Doris Graber so cogently explained:

> Each day's or week's news is like a familiar play with slight changes in the scenes and dialogue and with frequent replacements in the cast of minor players (although not of major actors). News is exceptional in the sense that it does not portray ordinary events, such as eating breakfast or washing clothes or taking the bus to work. It is standardized in the sense that it deals with the same types of topics in familiar ways and produces standardized patterns of news and entertainment throughout the country. Repeated coverage of the same familiar scenes conveys to the public the feeling that all is going according to expectations and that, even when the news is bad, there is little to worry about. It has all happened before, and people have managed to cope. (1997, 109)

As we have seen, news is routinized; however, it is the routinization of the unexpected or the exceptional. J. D. Barber (1978) wrote that the

> *story begins when one notices contrasts coinciding.* The reporter's raw material is differences—between what was and what is, expectations and events, reputations and realities, normal and exotic—and his artful eye is set to see the moment when the flow of history knocks two differences together. (1978, 114–115; emphasis in original)

What entices the reporter is the exception. For example, while reporters believed Bill Clinton to be a hopeless womanizer before he was elected president, they couldn't quite come to grips with his (1) having trysts in the Oval Office, and (2) having trysts with a student intern less than half his age. Such attention to the exceptional or that which is readily dramatized by journalists suggests a "melodramatic imperative" operating within the process of news creation (Bennett 1988; Nimmo and Combs 1983; P. H. Weaver 1976). In literary criticism, **melodrama** refers to plays:

> Based on a romantic plot and developed sensationally, with little regard for convincing motivation and with an excessive appeal to the emotions of the audience. The object is to keep the audience thrilled by the awakening, no matter how, of strong feelings of pity or horror or joy. Poetic justice is superficially secured, the characters (who are either very good or very bad) being rewarded or punished according to their deeds. Though typically a melodrama has a happy ending, tragedies which use much of the same technique are sometimes referred to as melodramatic. (Holman 1972, 312)

Soap operas and other serial television programming are contemporary examples of melodrama. However, Bennett (1988) believes that the melodramatic imperative is evident in political news as well; he writes, "Dramatized news is more melodrama than serious theatre, more soap opera than Shakespeare" (40; see also Nimmo and Combs 1983). Using a dramatic organizational structure is an efficient organizational style for the working journalist. T. E. Cook (1996b) writes:

> To be able to crank out news on a regular basis, reporters gravitate toward continuing sagas. Not only does this further routinize the news, it also fulfills the venerable news mission of indicating where things are and where they are going so that news audiences can react accordingly and intervene if need be. (474)

Although nightly news packages and news articles in daily newspapers are self-contained units, often such dramatic narratives may be viewed as episodes in a continuing saga or as the acts in a multiact play. Journalists observe and describe human behavior, placing it within dramatic frames and narratives and linking it with similar and related narratives to form sagas. T. E. Cook (1996b) explains: "For news to be produced routinely, journalists must be able to visualize events as part of a larger, broader storyline and must move the plot along from one episode to the next" (474; see also J. P. Robinson and Levy, 1986b).

All news is dramatic, but the melodramatic imperative becomes more apparent

> the farther one gets from the first page of a newspaper and the lead in a broadcast newscast. As social significance wanes and as economic considerations are

elevated, the production values of news become more important, particularly "drama, color, or vividness, or on formulaic stories that encapsulate the enduring values [of professional journalism]." (T. E. Cook 1996b, 475; see also Darnton 1975; Epstein 1973; Gans 1979)

T. E. Cook (1996b) believes that this dramatic or melodramatic imperative is so powerful that it is this force that determines more than anything else the structure and content of news. Cook asserts that it is the dramatic imperative, not journalistic norms or organizational routines, that gives news in the United States its sameness or homogeneity. T. E. Cook (1996b) writes: "I suggest that news norms are not closely connected to news content and that journalistic routines cannot explain the consensual pictures presented in the news" (469). For Cook, journalists work to "generate a predictable stream of nonfiction stories about the world . . . seeking to find ways to craft a continuing and compelling saga" (1996b, 469).

Bennett finds dramatized news troubling, in that he believes there may be hidden dangers in dramatized news:

> Because dramas are simple, easy to grasp, and offer a semblance of insight into the individual motives behind an action, they may give people a misguided sense of understanding the politics of a situation. People may think they understand an issue when, in fact, their understanding is based on a mixture of fantasy, fiction, and myth. (Bennett 1988, 40)

According to Bennett (1988), melodramatic news has severe consequences: "1) distraction from potentially important causes of problems, 2) creation of a false sense of understanding rooted in individualistic explanations, and 3) the promotion of dramatically satisfying but practically unworkable solutions" (44). As a result, "Because people hold a false understanding of the problems and opportunities in today's society, they are not able to effectively solve problems or to maximize their opportunities" (Johnson-Cartee and Copeland 1997a, 64).

Infotainment

Miller Spangler has argued that the selection of news and news presentations are based on marketing decisions made by the news assemblers. He writes:

> These decisions typically respond to fairly well known formulas as to what excites the interest and curiosity of the public rather than any assumed desire of the public to be educated in a well balanced manner. . . . Especially is this true of

events involving the drama of death, tragic economic and social consequences, courageous or faulty actions, and the need for making difficult decisions in the face of public controversy. (1986; as cited in Gorney 1992, 455)

This focus on entertaining the audience is particularly obvious during campaign seasons, when news assemblers shift their focus from discussions of policy differences to character profiles and assessments of who is likely to win—the practice of profiling and handicapping the candidates (Bennett 1996). As a result, campaigns and elections have become entertainment for the American public, rather than the serious business that our founding fathers had desired.

Today, even routine broadcast news is affected by the entertainment focus. Significant economic pressure brought about by an increasingly competitive news business, a dwindling mass audience for network news, and an increase in news organizational diversity has produced a situation where news executives stress the need to entertain audiences in order to survive financially in this changed competitive environment. Such an economic imperative clashes with the traditional socially responsible view of providing what audience members needed to know whether they recognized their needs or were oblivious (Kimball 1994; McManus 1994). But because of such strong economic pressures, Bennett (1996) recalls that it is not unusual for news executives to discuss the modern news organization's product as **infotainment**, which provides entertaining news that audience members want rather than what the journalist views as being imperative for audience members to function effectively in a democratic system. As a result, *Entertainment Tonight* (*ET*) and the ABC *Evening News* have remarkably similar formats and reporting styles; *ET* focuses on celebrities, and ABC focuses on political leaders. Bird (1992) demonstrated that even supermarket tabloid writers consider themselves to be "journalists," adhering to professional journalistic standards and strategic rituals and emphasizing particularly the reliance on expert quotes. Bennett (1996) has observed that "the narrative forms that dominate mainstream news generally contain lowest-common-denominator information that secures the daily news supply, often at the expense of topical continuity and citizen enlightenment" (383; Bennett and Edelman 1985; McManus 1994). And one of the characteristics of this lowest-common-denominator information is sensationalism, which we turn to next.

Gorney (1992) has defined **sensationalism** as "the use of anything that plays on sense perceptions and emotions to elicit a quick, intense and usually superficial interest or reaction. In brief, that which is sensational limits experience as a source of knowledge in favor of emotional or sensory stimulation" (455). While a number of researchers have identified specific types of news stories such as disasters, accidents, or crimes (Adams 1978; Hofstetter and Dozier 1986; Wulfemeyer 1982) as inherently sensational, others have suggested that sensationalism is deliberate exaggeration on the part of news assemblers in their depiction of events (Fishman 1981). However, the Media Institute of Washington, D.C., and the Public's Right to Information Task Force of the President's Commission on the Accident at Three Mile Island have both suggested that news assemblers' speculations (crystal-ball gazing, predictions, worst-case scenarios, or "what if" projections) are most indicative of sensationalism in the news (Gorney 1992). Anyone who has watched CNN immediately after an airline disaster has had significant experience in news speculations. In such occurrences, when confusion reigns and little or no authoritative information is available, CNN news assemblers fill airtime with speculation after speculation. Such speculation is indicative of sensationalism. However, sensationalism has consequences in that it often serves to create fear among the attending public. In addition, "realizing that viewers respond emotionally to the plight of people like themselves on the screen, television in particular loads its coverage with the fears and complaints of these ordinary citizens, at the expense of presumably more knowledgeable sources" (Media Institute as quoted in Gorney 1992, 457). The use of airline-crash survivors, eyewitnesses, and the loved ones of dead passengers in news accounts are all indicators of sensationalism, in that the use of such individuals does not provide the audience with any meaningful information about the event and only serves to titillate or excite the viewer.

The News Paradigm and Hegemony: Social Ramifications

Reese (1990) has argued that the myths of objective reality and professional objectivity as well as the strategic rituals practiced in journalism constitute what Kuhn (1970) has termed a **paradigm**. Paradigms are socially constructed views of the world that are constructed by those involved in specialized information-producing tasks or behaviors. In other words, in Kuhn's view, these paradigms are "firmly based upon one or more past scientific achievements, achievements that some particular scientific community acknowledges for a time as supplying the foundation for its further practices" (1970, 10). For Kuhn, the seminal works or classics of a given field of inquiry would serve as the means by which future endeavors would be designed, executed, and ultimately evaluated. According to Kuhn, this occurs because

their achievement was sufficiently unprecedented to attract an enduring group of adherents away from competing modes of scientific activity. Simultaneously, it was sufficiently open-ended to leave all sorts of problems for the redefined group of practitioners [read future practitioners] to resolve. (1970, 10)

Such paradigms and the classic works on which they were based are used by teachers, professors, or mentors in the training and socializing of future scientists or practitioners (see Kuhn 1970). "Thus, one learns the paradigm by engaging in the discipline, and the paradigm's effectiveness is not inhibited because it may be unwritten or even inarticulable [sic] by its practitioners" (Reese 1990, 392).

For Reese, what is most significant is that the news paradigm and all that it entails serve to construct our secondhand reality. Reese suggests that the paradigm, in effect, produces what has been termed "hegemony" (1990). Gitlin has written that hegemony is the "systematic (but not necessarily or even usually deliberate) engineering of mass consent to the established order" (1980, 253). Hegemony "entails moral, political, and intellectual leadership within a social system; the ruling group does not simply impose a class ideology on others but rather provides the articulating principle by which diverse ideological elements are unified into a world-view" (Reese 1990, 394). Reese goes on to suggest that the media portray the parameters of legitimate society, from normalcy to deviancy (1990). And, as Sigal (1973) so long ago suggested, the journalists' reliance on strategic mythologies, rituals, and official sources produces a rather predictable world view, one ultimately supporting the status quo.

In the words of Gaye Tuchman (1978):

News both draws upon and reproduces institutional structures. Through its arrangement of time and space as intertwined social phenomena, the news organization disperses a news net. By identifying centralized sources of information as legitimated social institutions, news organisations and newsworkers wed themselves to specific beats and bureaus. Those sites are then objectified as the appropriate sites at which information should be gathered. Additionally, those sites of news gathering are objectified as the legitimated and legitimating sources of both information and governance. Through naive empiricism, that information is transformed into objective facts—facts as a normal, natural, taken-for-granted description and constitution of a state of affairs. And through the sources identified with facts, newsworkers create and control controversy; they contain dissent. (210–211)

5

News as Narrative

██

While news may be viewed as a window on the world through which Americans learn of their institutions and their leaders, it is a window that reflects largely the media's own construction of reality.

—Turk 1985, 34

Media frames, largely unspoken and unacknowledged, organize the world both for journalists who report it and, in some degree, for us who rely on their reports.

—Gitlin 1980, 7

The Epistemology of News

IN CHAPTER 1, I ARGUED THAT KNOWLEDGE is socially constructed, and the news media, in particular, play an increasingly powerful role in the process of constructing political reality. Similarly, Lichter and Noyes observed in 1995 that

today, new media technologies, the centralization of media power, the fragmentation of American society, and the decline of political parties have combined to create a new environment where journalists have at least as much control over the public images of national leaders as the politicians have themselves. (1)

Drawing upon the early work of philosopher William James (1896), noted sociologist and former journalist Robert Park argued as early as 1940 that news should be regarded as epistemic or as a source of knowledge. For most of us, what we know about such faraway places as Afghanistan and Iraq is based on what we have read or seen in the news. "The world that we have to deal with politically is out of reach, out of sight, out of mind. It has to be explored, reported, [and] imagined" (Lippmann 1921, 284). News content helps shape our political and social reality, for such content contains the political mosaics from which we choose to construct our own personal realities.

Michael Schudson (1995) has argued that news plays a significant role in the formation of public knowledge, contributing in no small way to the widely shared beliefs about public events, places, actors, and so on. In short, Schudson argues that news contributes to what sociologists would call "culture," going so far as to suggest that news itself is "a form of culture" (1995, 3). The noted sociologist Ann Swidler (1986) has defined culture as "the publicly available symbolic forms through which people experience and express meaning," consisting "of such symbolic vehicles of meaning, including beliefs, ritual practices, art forms, and ceremonies, as well as informal cultural practices such as language, gossip, stories, and rituals of daily life" (1986, 273). And, to the extent that news contributes to our awareness and our utilization of such symbolic vehicles, then news as a social process assists in the construction of our culture and our social reality. Swidler's attention to culture contributed significantly to our understanding of the social construction of reality. According to Swidler, culture shouldn't be thought of as a passive collection of symbolic vehicles thought to represent the habits of a people, but rather as an active, ongoing process by which people make sense of their world, interact with others, and ultimately form cooperative relationships to coexist with others. In short, culture is the host of symbolic vehicles utilized by individuals in the "social processes of sharing modes of behavior and outlook within [a] community" (Hannerz 1969, 184). From Swidler's perspective, culture is the means by which we plan and conduct our behaviors or actions within our world. It is both the setting in and the process by which we construct our social reality (see chapter 1). In that vein, this chapter will present two theoretical areas that contribute to our understanding of the epistemology of news: the narrative paradigm and framing.

The Narrative Paradigm

The *Oxford Dictionary and Thesaurus* (1996) defines narrative as "a spoken or written account of connected events in order of happening," providing as synonyms "story, tale, chronicle, description, revelation, portrayal, account, report, record, history, recital, [and] statement" (990–991). And, for those who engage in narration, *Oxford* provides an equally interesting list of synonyms: "commentator, announcer, reader, reporter, storyteller, raconteur, taleteller, anecdotist, anecdotalist, relator, annalist, chronicler, [and] describer" (1996, 991). A reading of just these terms suggests to us that narration or human storytelling is a large part of everyday life.

Through the ages, humans have passed on their cultural histories, values, and norms through narratives or short stories. These narratives not only socialized successive generations but also provided an epistemic anchoring for the species. Whether formulated in songs, poetry, epics, or broadsides, humankind has passed on what it deemed important. Indeed, whether we are students of medieval literature, military history, or ethnography, we recognize again and again the power of narrative. "Man is in his actions and practice, as well as in his fictions, essentially a story-telling animal" (MacIntyre 1981, 201). Similarly, White in 1980 argued that narration is a "human universal" (6; see also Rayfield 1972; Scholes 1982; V. Turner 1982). And Bateson (1979) went so far as to maintain that humans and other minded creatures think "in terms of stories" (14).

Consequently, increasing numbers of communication scholars have studied narrative as a significant human artifact (T. E. Cook 1998). Perhaps the most widely known communication researcher in the area of narrative is Walter Fisher. In 1984, Fisher wrote:

> The idea of human beings as storytellers indicates the generic form of all symbol composition; it holds that symbols are created and communicated ultimately as stories meant to give order to human experience and to induce others to dwell in them to establish ways of living in common, in communities in which there is sanction for the story that constitutes one's life. (1984, 6)

For Fisher, narration is the means by which societies ultimately govern themselves, for these shared stories establish commonalities, promote goodness, and discourage wickedness. Narratives provide societies with their moral reasoning. This view was recognized by Johnson-Cartee and Copeland when writing:

> All short stories have a beginning, a middle, and an end. They present, either explicitly or implicitly, age-old conflicts: person versus person, person versus self, person versus fate, and person versus nature. Through conflict resolution, the short story is said to ultimately reveal truth. Indeed, James Joyce called the short story an epiphany because of the revelations that emerged through its thematic conflict resolution. (1991, 34)

In 1984, Fisher proposed the **narrative paradigm**, a "theory of symbolic actions—words and/or deeds—that have sequence and meaning for those who live, create, or interpret them" (2).

Frentz and Farrell (1976) played a significant role in Fisher's reasoning, in that they had identified symbolic acts as "verbal and/or nonverbal utterances which express intentionality" (1976, 340). For Frentz and Farrell, symbolic acts possess propositional, expressive, and consequential force (1976, 340). **Propositional force** refers roughly to the semantic meaning of the act, **expressive force** refers to a manner of delivery that contains meaning within it, and **consequential force** is the "effect the act has on another actor" (Frentz and Farrell 1976, 340).

When symbolic acts are placed within the context of an episode that is a "rule-conforming sequence of symbolic acts generated by two or more actors who are collectively oriented toward emergent goals" (Frentz and Farrell 1976, 336), then they may be said to have **episodic force**. Episodic force specifies "the communicative function of acts within the overall sequential structure of an episode" (Frentz and Farrell 1976, 340). Meaning, then, rests not within the individual symbolic acts but within the episode itself. For instance, wedding rituals within the United States might not necessarily be understood outside of the wedding ceremony as a unit. The sharing and drinking from the wedding chalice; the joint lighting of the single, large, white candle; the exchange of rings; the giving of the bride to the groom; and the promises and oaths exchanged might not be evaluated and understood if considered separately or outside the context of the wedding ritual. Taken in combination, such acts have episodic force.

Other theories such as symbolic interactionism (H. Blumer 1969) and social convergence theory (Bormann, 1985) had accounted for how people come to learn about and adopt stories that they then use in their everyday lives to guide behavior, but W. R. Fisher argued that his narrative paradigm went beyond such explanations (1985). The narrative paradigm takes the activist vision of people a step further by recognizing that men and women determine the stories or narratives they choose to use in their lives. Fisher maintained that the narrative paradigm was unique in "providing a 'logic' for assessing stories, for determining whether or not one *should* adhere to the stories one is encouraged to endorse or to accept as the basis for decisions and actions" (1985, 348; emphasis in original).

In 1984, Walter Fisher identified four presuppositions underlying his narrative paradigm:

> (1) humans are essentially storytellers; (2) the paradigmative mode of human decision-making and communication is "good reasons" which vary in form

among communication situations, genres, and media; (3) the production and practice of good reasons is ruled by matters of history, biography, culture, and character along with the kinds of forces identified in the Frentz and Farrell language action paradigm; (4) rationality is determined by the nature of persons as narrative beings—their inherent awareness of narrative probability, what constitutes a coherent story, and their constant habit of testing narrative fidelity, whether the stories they experience ring true with the stories they know to be true in their lives. (7–8)

For Fisher, the

narrative paradigm goes beyond traditional social scientific theories . . . in that [it establishes] the concept of *narrative rationality,* which provides principles— probability and fidelity—and [gives] considerations for judging the merits of stories, whether one's own or another's. (1985, 349; emphasis added)

In 1985, W. R. Fisher provided further refinements to his concepts of narrative probability and fidelity. He wrote:

Narrative probability refers to formal features of a story conceived as a discrete sequence of thought and/or action in life or literature . . . i.e., it concerns the question of whether or not a story coheres or "hangs together," whether or not the story is free of contradictions. *Narrative fidelity* concerns the "truth qualities" of the story, the degree to which it accords with the logic of good reasons: the soundness of its reasoning and the value of its values. To test soundness, one may, *when relevant,* employ standards from formal or informal logic. (W. R. Fisher 1985, 349–350; emphases added)

For Fisher, "narrative rationality . . . is an attempt to recapture Aristotle's concept of *phronesis,* 'practical wisdom'" (1985, 350). For instance, in the Christmas Eve disappearance of a pregnant Modesto, California, woman, news reports initially presented sympathetic images of the young woman's husband being supported by both sets of parents. News stories depicted a loving husband in seclusion because of his grief. Several weeks after the disappearance, news stories reported that police had received tips indicating that the husband had been involved in an extramarital affair. Both the husband and members of the extended families vehemently denied the reports. Soon after, however, a woman came forward, providing evidence of an affair. In addition, a substantial insurance policy on the life of the wife, which previously the husband had denied had existed, was brought to public scrutiny. In short, the disappearance of the pregnant wife began to take on new dimensions for its audience, for the husband's telling of the story began to have contradictions. After refusing to cooperate with police by taking a

polygraph and refusing to provide additional pieces of information re-
quested, the husband began closing down volunteer search efforts. Would a
husband who had lost an eight-month-pregnant wife whom he purportedly
loved refuse to cooperate with the police investigation? Would the husband
refuse to take a test that could clear him of suspicion in order that the investigation not waste time focusing on someone not responsible? Would he
discourage volunteer efforts to find his wife either alive or dead? The husband's actions began to be questioned by the public, the police, and news accounts in terms of the logic of good reasons. In addition, news accounts
showed the family members grieving openly, but the husband remained
calm, laughing and smiling for the television cameras. The open grief of
family members contrasted sharply with his behavior. News reports and
news talk shows such as *Larry King Live* began suggesting that the husband
might be responsible for his pregnant wife's disappearance. Several months
later, police arrested him for the murders of his pregnant wife and unborn
son. Fisher's logic of good reasons arguably sealed the man's fate in the public's eye; poll results indicated that the majority of Americans believed him
to be guilty as charged.

Walter Fisher (1984) summarized his ontological approach: "The materials
of the narrative paradigm are symbols, signs of consubstantiation, and good
reasons, the communicative expressions of social reality" (8). **Signs of consubstantiation** are the commonalities or common meanings shared by individuals in a given culture. Thus, when an individual is presented with a narrative, whether in the form of a song, play, short story, or news story, the
individual may consciously evaluate the narrative by analyzing (1) the symbols used, (2) the shared meanings associated with those symbols, (3) how the
story parts either cohere or fail to cohere, and (4) the degree to which the story
satisfies the person's formal and informal logic patterns.

For Fisher, narrators tell stories for a reason or, in some cases, for *reasons*.
Thus, a narrator has a motive in telling his or her story. "Motives are names
which essentialize the interrelations of communicator, communication, audi-
ence(s), time, and place" (W. R. Fisher 1970, 132). Such motives influence not
only the content of the narrative but the delivery as well. Fisher writes: "A
communicator perceives a rhetorical situation in terms of a motive, and that
an organic relationship exists between his perception and his response to that
circumstance; his perception determines the characteristics of his discourse
and his presentation" (1970, 132).

As listeners, we recognize the "mindedness" of narratives, and, consequently, we often ask ourselves, "Why?" and "For what reason(s) did the narrator tell me this story?" We conduct, in effect, what Walter Fisher has called a

motive analysis. According to Fisher, when we ask ourselves why a narrator is presenting his or her story to us, we are doing only what comes naturally—we are engaging in motive analysis. Schutz (1962, 1967) distinguishes between "because of" motives and "in order to" motives. **Because of motives** are variables in life that "cause" or "lead" people to act in a certain way (i.e., personality, race, religion, social class, and so forth); however, an awareness of these "causes" alone is not enough to understand people's behavior. A person is more than a set of characteristics; he or she is a minded animal. "People project their actions, plan, and anticipate meaning for those proposed actions" (Combs 1973, 54). Individuals, thus, have **in order to motives**, which create goal-seeking and goal-achieving behaviors.

Often, when we engage in motive analysis or in asking ourselves "Why?" we are analyzing the theme, thesis, or the point of the story. "What was the point of the story?" "What am I left with, now that the story is finished?" W. R. Fisher writes that a narrative "expresses a theme or thesis, an inference or judgment, which is to be preferred above any other proposition or proposal that relates to its subject matter" (1970, 131). Narratives, then, contain not only content but also an attitude about that content. Such discourse is "advisory; it says how one should think, feel, and act in a given case where certainty cannot be achieved" (W. R. Fisher 1970, 131).

However, what should be recognized is that a narrative

> is also a fiction in the sense that it is the product of and is itself an art. Created out of words, it reflects the literary ability of its author. It proceeds from an act of creative insight, reveals inventiveness of mind and imagination, demonstrates the capacity to achieve order, unity, coherence, and force in expression, and indicates the author's sensitivity to human nature as well as the time and place of his presentation. (Fisher 1970, 132)

We must emphasize, yet again, that such narratives, even though fictional, have real consequences, for if the narrative is accepted by its audience as truthfully representing what they know to be reality, the fiction becomes a **real fiction**. "The fiction is not hypothetical; its author wants and intends that it be accepted as the true and right way of conceiving of a matter; and, if he is successful, his fiction becomes one of those by which men live" (W. R. Fisher 1970, 132).

> Fiction is a generic term that encompasses in whole or in part persona, fantasy theme and rhetorical vision, social reality, political myth, and ideology. This is to say that each of these concepts is a symbolic construction that exerts persuasive force in the making of persons, community, and the nation. (W. R. Fisher 1980, 122)

As we are all narrators, we are accustomed to constructing narratives—whether we are presenting a lecture to a graduate class on symbolic interactionism or whether we are explaining to our spouses the many interconnected disasters that made up our day; we live by and through our narratives. However, each time we construct a narrative, we are not reinventing the wheel, so to speak. We take advantage of not only our knowledge of past narrative constructions but also our audience's knowledge of past narrative constructions. In other words, we develop a repertoire of narrative forms on which we construct our new narratives. For instance, one spouse believes she is unappreciated at work, often portraying her lot as being taken advantage of by coworkers or abused by superiors. Consequently, when she is communicating yet another wrong perpetuated upon her, the husband has an already well-established narrative form upon which to build. Such habits or patterns of narration are found in all social situations. Simons and Aghazarian (1986) have observed "that amid the flux and uncertainty of rhetorical action, there exist levels of stability and predictability—made so by the very nature of rhetoric as a practical, pragmatic enterprise" (45). Those predictable, oft-used narratives are important social indicators, whether of a marital relationship or of a presidential convention. Simons and Aghazarian choose to study such patterns or social indicators, for they engage in what they call the **sociology of rhetorical choice**, making "sense of the actions of persuaders, as opposed to the reactions of their audiences" (1986, 45). According to Simons and Aghazarian, the sociology of rhetorical choice has great utility, for with it we are in a better position to evaluate performances, guide future performances, and predict future performances. The sociology of rhetorical choice is "rules-oriented," for through observation, it attempts to make generalizations of the "'as a rule' variety that is intended to cover types of practices, namely, genres rather than specific acts" (Simons and Aghazarian 1986, 46; see also Cushman 1977; Shimanoff 1980). In other words, observations are made, characterizations of what is observed are established, and narrative types or narrative rule types are predicted. For instance, presidential inaugural addresses contain language marking the end of partisan competition and the beginning of a reinvigorated national unity. Healing rhetoric is used to calm those still bitter after their defeat. The president of the United States, although elected through a partisan contest, is expected to be the president of all the people; the inaugural address begins the transformation from partisan contender to the president of the people. Presidential speechwriters, news reporters, and the public all recognize the significance of this transformation for the health and welfare of the nation. Consequently, it is expected and, in effect, demanded of the president to perform this ritual. And presidential speechwriters and the president comply; reporters comment on the president's satisfactory completion of the transformation, and the people feel reassured, convinced that although the election was divisive, the nation is back again on an even keel, with all represented by the president.

However, while rules are helpful in our understanding of the narrator, persuader, or communicator, it should be noted that, as in all human behavior, rules "are expressions of human choice, and can thus be violated" (Simons and Aghazarian 1986, 46). We're not always as predictable as we might believe. For instance, it is traditional in the United States for a bride to wear either white or off-white when getting married. The colors are said to indicate virginity or maidenhood. However, one bride known to me chose to wear black to her wedding. While this may have been interpreted by the audience as either being indicative of the state or lack thereof of the bride's virginity or indicative of the bride's rejection of societal traditions, the bride chose the wedding dress to make her appear svelte on this important day.

Simons and Aghazarian (1986, 46) have argued that in most rhetorical situations, two types of rules exist: **descriptive rules** and **prescriptive rules**. Descriptive rules are acquired by observing narrators performing various roles in various social situations and are "givens" in terms of how narrators most often operate. Prescriptive rules are acquired by studying various social situations and judging what is "appropriate or efficacious" in a given situation, even when such actions might not be deemed "wise or just" at some future date (Simons and Aghazarian 1986, 46). For instance, the president might urge the nation to take a smallpox vaccine (intended to protect against a naturally occurring virus) even though, at the time, there might not be any evidence that the vaccination protects against a weapons-grade smallpox contaminant.

According to Tilly 1979, an analysis of rhetorical patterns, the discovery of rules,

> implies that the standard forms are learned, limited in number and scope, slowly changing and peculiarly adapted to their settings. . . . [The execution of the choices—i.e., the performances—are not] necessarily frozen, regimented and stereotypical. . . . Nevertheless, a limited repertoire sets serious constraints on when, where and how effectively a group of actors can act. (26, as quoted in Simons and Aghazarian 1986, 56)

In the example given above, the president is constrained by the public's expectations of presidential activism (Fenno 1975; P. Hall 1977; Kumar and Grossman 1982; Neustadt 1980). In the U.S. political culture, it is better for a political leader to appear decisive and active than to be indecisive and inactive. Americans not only expect but also demand decisiveness and activism from their political leaders, particularly their president. Presidents who have failed to heed this cultural expectation have met with widespread criticism and rejection. During the Iranian hostage crisis, President Jimmy Carter refused to present himself to the news media and to the public; instead, he remained within the White House, hidden from view, a practice that reporters dubbed pejoratively "the Rose Garden strategy." Political rhetoricians have their own name for Carter's behavior—"a strategic silence"—and they have argued that within the American political tradition such a strategy is often counterproductive, if not deadly, to the political future and popularity of the leader so unwise as to utilize such an approach (Brummett 1980; Edelman 1964; Kumar and Grossman 1982). In politics, political talk establishes and maintains political relationships. Silence is the temporary denial of these relationships. And, according to Brummett, this denial creates a situation in which "mystery, uncertainty, passivity, and relinquishment" rule the day (1980, 297). Leaders who refuse to talk create an air of mystery surrounding their actions. The people are not sure what to expect, breeding tension and anxiety. Because the leader is not sharing his or her plans or actions with the people, the leader appears passive. And, in the worst instance, he or she may appear to have relinquished control to some other individual(s) or group(s). Such political behavior is dangerous in America. "Americans are accustomed to admir[ing] men who get things done, men who radiate faith and confidence. Americans are not inclined toward doubt; they like to be all for or all against something, right away if possible" (Roper 1957, 219–220). And as for the fate of the president in the Rose Garden, Jimmy Carter, he went down to an ignominious defeat in his next election—a defeat many attributed to his handling of the Iranian hostage crisis.

As narrators operating within groups, societies, or cultures, we develop a repertoire of narratives we typically utilize when we are performing certain roles in certain social situations. As members of a society, we are also able to recognize social situations where particular narratives are likely to be more efficacious or appropriate than others.

News as Narrative

While journalists routinely refer to their news copy as "news stories," they appear rather uncomfortable when academicians or social critics refer to their communication products as either stories or narratives (Bird and Dardenne 1988; Schudson 1991). Yet Gary Woodward argues that the use of the term "news stories" by either journalists or academicians provides significant insight into the news process; he writes:

The word *story* is such a basic descriptor of a news event that we tend to forget that it defines a unique way for organizing ideas. Storytelling involves the organization of facts and human motives in a definite sequence of stages. To tell a story is to set up a general structure for organizing a set of actors and events in ways that meet certain prior expectations. The story format defines actors moving through a sequence of events filled (usually) with victims, villains, and heroes. Conflict generates our interest, and sets up the search for a final or at least temporary resolution. The story format exists in most general news reporting because it is an efficient structure for reducing complexity to a minimum, and for collapsing a long time frame into a short and interesting summary. (1997, 76–77; emphasis in original)

For the most part, journalists still hold to the notion that they simply reflect reality in their news accounts, "that every news story springs anew from the facts of the event being recorded" (Bird and Dardenne 1988, 66). Journalists will argue time and again that they simply report the facts, nothing but the facts, maintaining that they are mere recorders of human events.

McNair (1998) incorporates these notions in his definition of journalism or news; he writes that journalism is "any *authored* text, in written, audio, or visual form, which claims to be (i.e., is presented to its audience as) a *truthful* statement about, or record of, some *hitherto unknown* (new) feature of the *actual, social* world" (4, emphasis in original). McNair argues that journalists stand on the "truthfulness and accuracy" of their reporting, yet they fail to recognize that in their selection of facts (whether stock market share prices or inches of snow fallen) and in their contextualizing of those facts, journalists create news by giving such facts "meaning and context—when they are transformed into a story or narrative—by an author" (McNair 1998, 5). Journalists, in effect, by denying the narrative quality of news are also denying their own authorship of news. By portraying themselves as mere purveyors of information, they negate the act of authorship. Authorship is of paramount importance to McNair, who writes: "No story can be told, no account of events given, without contextualization around a set of assumptions, beliefs, and values. This is in the nature of storytelling" (1998, 5; see also Schudson, 1982). Such contextualizations are the key to understanding the significance of authorship in that they are an ideological expression. McNair writes:

Journalism, therefore, like any other narrative which is the work of human agency, is essentially *ideological*—a communicative vehicle for the transmission to an audience (intentionally or otherwise) not just of facts but of the assumptions, attitudes, beliefs and values of its maker(s), drawn from and expressive of a particular world-view. (1998, 6; emphasis in original)

Here it is fruitful to consider the historian Hayden White's observations about the writing of history. Events happen. A chronology of events is observed. But these events are not history; they are merely potential story or narrative elements (see White 1987).

The events are *made* into a story by the suppression or subordination of certain of them and the highlighting of others, by characterization, motific repetition, variation of tone and point of view, alternative descriptive strategies, and the like—in short, all of the techniques that we would normally expect to find in the employment of a novel or play. (White 1978, 84; emphasis in original)

In their narration of historical chronology, historians ultimately create what is viewed as an authoritative account. And, through the years, this may come to be thought of as what in "reality" happened. However, it should also be remembered that other interpretations of the same historical events, other narrations telling the stories of history, could also be produced. Consider the number of different academic accounts purporting to examine the "causes" of the Civil War. From economic competition to slavery, a wide range of explanations or historical realities has been presented (e.g., Rozwenc [1961] 1972). The narration or the historical story is in the eye of the beholder, the author. To negate authorship is a deliberate obfuscation of the ideological dimensions of news. Such a practice not only separates the journalist from the news story, but it also hides the source of and expression of values, beliefs, and world views presented within the news story. In short, such a practice deceives.

Similarly, W. A. Gamson (1989), in writing about news, argues:

Facts have no intrinsic meaning. They take on their meaning by being embedded in a frame or story line that organizes them and gives them coherence, selecting certain ones to emphasize while ignoring others. Think of news as telling stories about the world rather than as presenting "information," even though the stories, of course, include factual elements. (157)

And it is the journalist, of course, who creates the story line. Consequently, news researchers, such as Tuchman (1976) and Schudson (1991), find the notion that journalists, in their day-to-day work, construct news narratives as being patently obvious and not in the least controversial. Schudson explains:

Journalists write the words that turn up in the papers or on the screen as stories. Not government officials, not cultural forces, not "reality" magically transforming itself into alphabetic signs, but flesh-and-blood journalists literally compose the stories we call news. (1991, 141)

Consequently, "a reporter writing a news story is not that much different from a storyteller or a novelist writing a fictional story" (Pan and Kosicki 1993, 60). And, "A story's quality is judged by the 'play' it receives in the news, which presumably is both an indicator and a predictor of the ascendancy of the reporter's career" (T. E. Cook 1996b, 473).

Yet journalists often justify their "mirror on reality" perspective by arguing that "if you put six journalists in a news event, all six will produce the same news story"; they offer this as proof of their objectivity and their mirroring of reality (Chibnall 1981). But researchers find such evidence not indicative of either journalistic objectivity or their mirroring reality; rather, they find the sameness in news products to be evidence of "formulaic narrative construction" (Bird and Dardenne 1988, 67). In other words, journalists have in their reporting repertoire a set of previously determined narrative structures or, if you will, **narrative frames** (Bateson 1972; Goffman 1974) on which they hang the "facts" of their stories. For purposes of clarification, then, a narrative is the fully developed, fully fleshed-out story with characters, scene descriptions, conflict(s), actions with motives, and, ultimately, resolution(s). The narrative frame, on the other hand, is the basic organization of the structural components used in the story. It helps, perhaps, to think of the narrative as a package with an internal structure, as W. Gamson and Modigliani (1989) have suggested. And "at its core is a central organizing idea, or frame, for making sense of relevant events, suggesting what is at issue" (W. Gamson and Modigliani 1989, 3). For instance, we are all familiar with Shakespeare's play *Romeo and Juliet*, a fully fleshed-out story if ever one was told. But, if we examine the structural components—star-crossed young lovers, warring families, well-intended but faulty communication, and ultimately tragedy and death—we may recognize the narrative frame again and again in other stories—such as *West Side Story*, originally a Broadway musical and then a Hollywood movie.

Such narrative frames occur regardless of the form of journalism product. McNair identifies five basic forms of journalistic output:

- the *news report*, which aims simply to inform us about what is happening of importance and, of course, is in some sense *new* in the world around us;
- the *feature article*, which presents more in-depth reportage and analysis of a particular subject, and its broadcasting equivalent, the documentary and current affairs programme;
- the *commentary* or *column*, in which a journalist presents his or her readers with an (assumed to be) authoritative viewpoint on a particular issue, and its equivalent in broadcasting, the output of the specialist pundit;

- the *interview*, probing the views and policies of those in the news, especially politicians and celebrities;
- the *editorial*, in which a newspaper or periodical "speaks out" in its "public voice." (1998, 9–10; emphasis in original)

Such journalism products are merely discursive types with "distinctive rhetorical styles, aesthetic conventions, and communicative functions" (McNair 1998, 10). All five types may be analyzed by the narrative frames utilized within.

The Framing Paradigm

The concept of framing in communication research is based on a multidisciplinary theoretical construct that Tannen (1993) has called, for simplicity's sake, "structures of expectation" (15). For Tannen, these **structures of expectation** constitute frames. In an intensive review of a variety of academic and professional disciplines, Tannen has found evidence for a mutual regard for expectations. Tannen explains her fascination with expectations:

> In order to function in the world, people cannot treat each new person, object, or event as unique and separate. The only way we can make sense of the world is to see the connections between things, and between present things and things we have experienced before or heard about. These vital connections are learned as we grow up and live in a given culture. As soon as we measure a new perception against what we know of the world from prior experience, we are dealing with expectations. (1993, 14–15)

The study of human frames has produced significant works in multiple academic disciplines such as psychology, psychiatry, sociology, anthropology, epistemology, ethnography, and linguistics and communication (Tannen 1993). Consequently, we have different academic terms representing the same intellectual construct in both scholarly and professional writings. For instance, Bird and Dardenne's "formulaic narrative constructions" (1988, 67) represent what Tannen (1993) would call the journalist's structure of narrative expectation or what we call frames. Similarly, psychologists, psychiatrists, and some linguists utilize a "framing construct" called the **schema** (Bartlett 1932; Chafe 1977a, 1977b; Head 1920). Other linguists, however, prefer the construct **prototype** instead (Fillmore 1975). Social and political behaviorists have coined the term **script** (Abelson 1975; Schank and Abelson 1975, 1977). And these are just a few of the many "labels" available for framing, or the structures of expectation (Tannen 1993).

What various academic researchers call a theoretical construct is not the issue. What is important are the shared versions of reality of the human communication dynamic. Tannen eloquently summarizes the commonalities:

> What unifies all these branches of research is the realization that people approach the world not as naïve, blank-slate receptacles who take in stimuli as they exist in some independent and objective way, but rather as experienced and sophisticated veterans of perception who have stored their prior experiences as "an organized mass," and who see events and objects in the world in relation to each other and in relation to their prior experience. This prior experience or organized knowledge then takes the form of expectations about the world, and [in] the vast majority of cases, the world, being a systematic place, confirms these expectations, saving the individual the trouble of figuring things out anew all the time. (1993, 20–21)

Accordingly, Tannen's (1993) structures of expectation provide four significant implications for human communication: (1) the meaning of words is learned through such social interaction, and concomitantly language itself is acquired; (2) individuals store social interactions as a series of frames to be accessed in the future as a tool to help them better comprehend and respond to other social situations; (3) individuals in the course of their lives develop a substantial repertoire of frames to assist them in re-creating appropriate behavioral responses in their daily lives and social interactions; and, (4) just as significantly, these same individuals, in turn, call upon this repertoire to help them create stories or personal narratives about their own social experiences to establish commonalities or relationships with others. In short, people share their personal meanings through narrative.

News Writing as Framing

Journalism students learn the patterns of previously written news stories through their news classes. As they begin their professional life and as they develop their craft, news reporters continue to accumulate such news frames into a "*repertoire* of examples, images, understandings, and actions" (Schön 1983, 138, emphasis in original). Journalists take incoming information or fast-breaking facts and assemble these items, fitting them into already existing news frames (Wolfsfeld 1997). In other words, journalists judge the "narrative fit" of incoming information (Reese 2001). Often, news reporters have specialized theoretical knowledge of the issue area on which they are reporting. Thus, news reporters will utilize not only professional experience but also social theory when constructing news accounts. Schön (1983) has argued: "If anything, the effective use of specialized knowledge depends on a prior restructuring of situations that are complex and uncertain" (19). In other words, the successful practitioner applies theoretical knowledge to news frames within his or her repertoire, enriching and perhaps altering the frame repertoire. Similarly, Ettema and Glasser (1998) have suggested that the key to becoming a master reporter is in the art of learning to "frame" the story:

> Professionals may select the frame for the problem from among those used successfully in past practice, but that initial choice may be only the beginning of a process of framing and reframing in which practitioners search for meaning and coherence in the situation at hand. (21)

Reporters involved in the process of news framing are engaged in what Schön has called "the logic of affirmation" (1983, 155). In their efforts to define the situation, select a news frame, and then build upon that news frame, reporters seek evidence, whether in the form of expert testimony, written reports, public records, or eyewitness accounts, that affirms their approach to the story. They ask themselves, "Is my evaluation of the situation supported by available evidence?" Master reporters, according to Schudson, establish a "mature journalistic subjectivity" where they challenge social conventions or status quo evaluations. They are compelled to ask themselves if they have considered all the possibilities and "Have I investigated alternative means of analyzing this situation?" Such reporters look beyond the obvious. They develop the confidence in their own abilities to demonstrate "tolerance of uncertainty, and acceptance of risk and commitment to caring for truth" (Schudson 1978, 194). Similarly, W. A. Gamson (1992b) and later Wolfsfeld (1997) distinguished between older and newer frames. Some frames may be viewed as "deep" or longstanding, widely shared, and taken for granted, while others are relatively new or "shallow," utilized in a very specific context, recently constructed, and emerging in public consciousness (W. A. Gamson 1992a, 1992b; Wolfsfeld 1997). Such characterizations help illustrate how a reporter's repertoire of news frames is refined and expanded through his or her professional years.

Despite a plethora of articles, book chapters, and even books on the topic, an operational definition of framing is difficult to find. "As a concept, it seems both indispensable and elusive" (W. A. Gamson, Croteau, Hoynes, and Sasson 1992, 384), for despite framing's omnipresence in the academic news literature, political news scholars have only "casually" (Entman 1993, 52) defined the concept within their own writings (see, for instance, Cappella and Jamieson 1997). Entman writes:

> Framing essentially involves *selection* and *salience*. To frame is to *select some aspects of a perceived reality and make them more salient in a communicating text, in such a way as to promote a particular problem definition, causal interpretation,*

moral evaluation, and/or treatment recommendation for the term described. (1993, 52; emphasis in original)

Similarly, Kahneman and Tversky (1984) also emphasize the structuring of information in such a way as to increase the significance or salience of individual elements within the news story for news consumers.

Iyengar (1989) found support for such conceptualizations of framing. In addition, by examining how people understand news accounts, he isolated another important component in news framing, **the assignment of responsibility**. Recognizing that researchers have found little or modest connections between specific issue positions and abstract universals such as liberalism-conservatism, Republican-Democrat, socioeconomic status, or perceived self-interest–group-interest (Kinder 1983; Kinder and Sears 1985; Luskin 1987), Iyengar examined a more idiosyncratic conceptualization of public opinion. Drawing from the work of Brady and Sniderman (1985) and Hurwitz and Peffley (1987), Iyengar argued that specific issue opinions are based on "domain-specific" items that individuals perceive as being particularly relevant to a given issue. Specifically, Iyengar argued that "the primary consideration that governs any issue opinion is the assignment of *responsibility* for the issue in question" (1989, 879; emphasis added). Research has shown that individuals routinely assign responsibility when confronting social problems (Nisbett and Ross 1980; Iyengar 1987), even when the social problem is the result of a random event such as a natural disaster (Langer 1975; Wortman 1976). And such "attributions of responsibility powerfully influence attitudes toward the self, interpersonal evaluations, and emotional arousal" (Iyengar 1989, 879; see also Bettman and Weitz 1983; Fiske and Taylor, 1984; Folkes, 1984; Pettigrew, 1979; D. J. Schneider, Hastorf, and Ellsworth, 1979). Drawing upon the work of Fincham and Jaspars (1980) and Brickman, Rabinowitz, Keruza, Coates, Cohn, and Kidder (1982), Iyengar (1989) operationalized issue responsibility as falling into two categories: **causal responsibility**, or the emphasis on the origin of the social problem; and **treatment responsibility**, or the emphasis on who or what has the means to resolve the social problem, whether by solving the social problem, alleviating the social problem, or perpetuating the social problem. In a laboratory experiment, Iyengar's (1989) participants read news stories covering four social issues (crime, terrorism, poverty, and social inequality) and then answered lengthy questions about the issues presented within the stories. Iyengar concluded:

> The results indicate that for all four issues attributions of responsibility significantly affect issue opinions independently of partisanship, liberal-conservative orientation, information, and socioeconomic status. In general, agents of causal responsibility are viewed negatively while agents of treatment responsibility are viewed positively. (1989, 878)

In a later study, Iyengar (1991) found that the news media were far more likely to present news from an *episodic perspective* rather than a *thematic perspective*. Instead of providing the historical background of a given issue and the related social, cultural, and political forces affecting the issue (a thematic perspective), the news reporter is likely to focus on a recent alarming or attention-earning event that highlights an individual's or group's plight through personal illustrations (an episodic perspective). Gitlin (1980) has observed that journalists evaluate newsworthiness according to "traditional assumptions in news treatment: news concerns the *event*, not the underlying condition; the *person*, not the group; *conflict*, not consensus; the fact that '*advances the story*,' not the one that explains it" (28; emphasis in original). Consequently, Iyengar (1991) has argued that when people view news accounts from an episodic perspective, they are far more likely to attribute responsibility for social problems to individuals (people choose poverty) not systemic attributions, such as poverty is caused by cultural deprivation, educational and job inequalities, drug addiction, or discrimination. "The lack of historical and social context creates a discursive space where readers are less likely to fully appreciate, understand or interpret the implications of events and issues" (Greenberg 2002, 194). Television news is far more likely to be devoted to episodic framing because of its obvious time and commercial constraints (Iyengar and Simon 1993). For example, Iyengar and Simon (1993) found that two-thirds of all stories about poverty on television news for a period of six years were stories about a particular poor person, and 74 percent of all news stories during that same time period concerning terrorism were live reports highlighting a specific terrorist act, victim, or event. Weimann and Brosius (1991) also found that media selection and coverage of terrorist acts were influenced by "the level of victimization, the type of action, the identity of the perpetrators, and an attributable responsibility" (333).

Pan and Kosicki (1993) have argued that the frame of a news story is the same thing as the theme of the news story. "A theme is an idea that connects different semantic elements of a story (e.g., descriptions of an action or an actor, quotes of sources, and background information) into a coherent whole" (Pan and Kosicki 1993, 59). The theme is related to meaning—the residue of meaning left with the individual after attending to the news story. For Reese (2001), "Frames are *organizing principles* that are socially *shared* and *persistent* over time, that work *symbolically* to *structure* the social world" (11; emphasis in original).

It is helpful to consider such conceptualizations while analyzing a real-world news story. For illustration purposes, we choose one episode within a high-profile scandal involving the Roman Catholic Church in the United

States. In December 2002, after more than one year of repetitive disclosures of pedophilia and other sexual misconduct among the nation's Catholic priests, the powerful Cardinal Bernard Law of Boston resigned his position while visiting the Vatican. And *Newsweek* ran a headline saying, "A Cardinal Offense" (Adler 2002, 50). The subhead read: "After a year of controversy over his handling of sex-abuse cases, Bernard Law quit. How it happened. What it means" (Adler 2002, 50–51). We chose first to examine the head and subhead, because Teun van Dijk (1991) has reported that headlines, in particular, are often used to frame stories. Headlines serve to lure or to entice readers to read the story, and at the same time they often provide readers with a snapshot of the reporter's handling of the story. In this case, the head and subhead provide the entire frame of the story; we only have to read the story itself to flesh out the narrative. Using Entman's (1993) four-pronged outline of most news story accounts, we identified the following information components contained within "A Cardinal Offense":

1. *Define problems*: Bernard Law, first as archbishop and later as cardinal of the archdiocese of Boston, repeatedly forgave priests engaged in repeated acts of sexual misconduct, primarily involving child sexual abuse, and protected them from either scandal or prosecution. Eventually, a large contingent of lay Catholics and their priests called for his resignation and, after consulting with the Holy Father, Law resigned.

2. *Diagnose causes*: The Roman Catholic Church operates in a realm of secrecy and separateness from host governments even within the United States. The loyalty of the church's leadership has always been to the Roman Catholic Church as an institution and to the Vatican and, ultimately, to the ruling pope. Consequently, the leadership structurally, philosophically, and morally answers only to Rome, not to parishioners. Thus, when sexual abuse charges surfaced, church officials predictably showed little if any concern for the victims but instead sought to shield the church from scandal and sought spiritual renewal for the perpetrators.

3. *Make moral judgments*: As a check on the secrecy and traditional absolutism among the church's leadership, American parishioners must be involved in church decision making, and church leaders must be held accountable for both their personal behavior and their participation in church decision making. In short, the Roman Catholic leaders in the United States must be accountable not only to their parishioners but also to U.S. and state law. No priest, no archbishop, no cardinal is above the rule of law in the United States; to allow anything else is morally wrong and un-American.

4. *Suggest remedies*: The Vatican must accept reformation in the Church within the United States. Church laypersons and lower-level church leaders must be empowered, and the church's traditional totalitarianism must be altered. The institutional structure of the Church must be altered to reflect a greater openness and ownership by its members. Some are calling for either noncelibate women or men to be allowed to serve as clergy as a means to remedy the shortage of priests and lay clergy in America, to reduce the strength and secrecy of what many see to be a increasingly gay-clergy culture, and to increase the sensitivity and empathy shown to both sex abuse victims and church laypersons. Above all, people in positions of power must be held accountable, whatever their title, gender, sexual preference, celibacy, or marital status. (Words in italics taken from Entman's discussion of framing components; 1993, 52)

Entman's four framing components are but one way to analyze news stories; we will turn to alternative methods in the next section.

Framing and Issue Cultures

W. A. Gamson and Lasch (1983) have suggested that within a given political culture, a repertoire of idea elements surround a given political issue, ultimately producing an issue culture. These idea elements are symbolic devices, which are "grouped into more or less harmonious clusters or interpretive packages" (398). Framing, then, deals "with the gestalt or pattern-organizing nature of the political culture" (W. A. Gamson and Lasch 1983, 398). For any given issue culture, numerous interpretive packages may emerge. In the area of welfare policy, for instance, W. A. Gamson and Lasch (1983) point to four main interpretive packages: welfare freeloaders, working poor, poverty trap, and regulating the poor (410–411). Each interpretive package has its own symbolic devices associated with its use within the political arena. Symbolic devices are the "words, actions, body movements, and visual cues that stand for ideas and objects and to which members of a culture attach similar meanings" (Perucci and Knudsen 1983, 77). For instance, when politicians use the expression "family values," Johnson-Cartee and Copeland (1997b) have argued:

> They are speaking to the conservative strain of American politics that glorifies the America of yesteryear, a time that may never have been, but one that is now held up as an ideal nevertheless. As a campaign platform, "family values" evoked the idea of perfect families living in houses with picket fences, with Pa gainfully employed and Ma making cookies in the family kitchen. As a background for this picture is the tableau of a small town with the little white church down the street

and the neighborhood school where the children are all alike and eager to learn. Divorce, drugs, abortion, unemployment, welfare, domestic violence, racial divisiveness, and delinquency are not part of this picture. (64)

As one can see from the previous example, the idea elements as expressed in symbolic devices reinforce each other within each interpretive package. Often these interpretive packages become so widely utilized and recognized by political officials, political activists, and political journalists that when a news consumer hears or reads about one prominent idea element (within a known package), it conjures up the totality of the package. For instance, when one reads the phrase "deserving poor" within a news story, the entire meta-debate surrounding the welfare and workfare system in the United States comes to mind. In effect, the phrase "deserving poor" cues the entire interpretive package. According to W. A. Gamson and Lasch (1983), these interpretive packages may be divided into two components: (1) the framing or the "pattern-organizing nature" of the issue culture and (2) the "reasoning and justifications for positions" verbalized within each issue culture (398).

Each interpretive package has a symbolic **signature**—a cluster of condensational symbols used to suggest not only its frame but also its reasoning and justifications. A **condensational symbol** "is a highly condensed form of substitutive behavior for direct expression, allowing for the ready release of emotional tension in conscious or unconscious form" (Sapir 1934, 493; see also Edelman 1964, 1971, 1977). In other words, condensational symbols are a shorthand means by which large numbers of beliefs, feelings, values, and perhaps world views are telegraphed to others sharing a similar culture. The example of "family values" is just such a condensation symbol. Conservatives using the phrase "family values" *evoke* a wealth of positive cognitions, attitudes, and past behaviors among those similar to themselves. Consequently, it is perhaps more appropriate to say that condensational symbols evoke stored meanings already residing within the minds of individuals sharing a given political culture. When such condensational symbols are said to be salient across large numbers of members of a given culture, they are also said to be **significant symbols** (Mead 1934).

In 1989, W. A. Gamson warned that in analyzing news content for the frames being presented, it is essential to consider both manifest and latent content. Freud (1952) originally drew two distinctions when considering significant symbols (Mead 1934) or condensational symbols that are "commonly salient across individuals" (Cobb and Elder 1972, 80). For Freud, **manifest content** was that which is obvious, readily perceived, or on the surface of the content (see Johnson-Cartee and Copeland 1991). **Latent content** was the underlying meaning, present but not obvious, or hidden. To ensure a full accounting of both the manifest and latent content of news frames, it is important to consider the "social and linguistic context in which they exist" (Johnson-Cartee and Copeland 1991, 64). Leymore (1975), Nimmo and Felsberg (1986), and Graber (1976) have all emphasized the importance of such contextual analysis. As political communication analysts, we must examine the "total societal context in which communication occurred, an evaluation of each of the communicators and of their interactions, and judgments concerning the long-term and short-term objectives of the communication" (Graber 1976, 101). As Breen and Corcoran (1982) explained, "The story is often made meaningful only when its manner of encoding interlocks with the perceptual process supplied by the viewer [the perceived situational context], which is itself culturally mediated" (128). Cobb and Elder (1972) have explained it in this manner:

> Because individual symbolic orientations are necessarily a function of an individual's socialization and life experiences, differences in symbolic orientations are likely to cluster in either an additive or interactive way along standard demographic dimensions which provide indices of common socialization, life experiences, and patterns of signification. (85)

In *Negative Political Advertising: Coming of Age*, Johnson-Cartee and Copeland used George Wallace, a longtime governor of Alabama and frequent presidential candidate, and his political rhetoric to illustrate the importance of contextual analyses that reveal both manifest and latent content. I will borrow from this earlier work here (1991, 65): Wallace frequently used the symbolic phrase "states' rights" in his public appearances, writings, and political advertising; however, "states' rights" meant more to Wallace and Wallace supporters than the political construct that states should maintain their individual sovereignty when functioning as a part of a federation of states. "States' rights" was a euphemism for segregation. Wallace and his supporters were fighting the federal-court-mandated integration of schools, buses, neighborhoods, restaurants, and so on. According to Makay (1970), the Alabama governor "spoke in kind of code" (172); that is, Wallace used latent political symbols. Makay recounted a statement that was supposed to have been said by an Alabama state senator: Wallace "can use all other issues—law and order, running your own schools, protecting property rights—and never mention race. But people will know he is telling them 'a nigger's trying to move into your neighborhood'" (172).

Because Wallace spoke in code, voters in midwestern and northern states often didn't understand why many liberal southerners found him so offensive. States' rights didn't mean segregation to them, just as Wallace's use of the phrase "the Alabama tradition" didn't evoke negative press coverage in the North. Northern voters thought of magnolias, mint juleps, and women in hoop skirts when he used the phrase, but southerners knew that when Wallace used that phrase, he was promising not only segregation but also the permanent disenfranchisement of blacks and the permanent positioning of them as second-class citizens in Alabama, if not the entire United States. This illustration emphasizes what W. A. Gamson argued in 1989: that the "etiology of content does not lie entirely in these political, economic, and organizational factors; part of it must be explained at the cultural level. The frames for a given story are frequently drawn from shared cultural narratives and myths" (161). And these myths may be shared at various levels of organization in society (see Johnson-Cartee and Copeland 2004).

The condensational symbols used in the construction of these interpretive packages may be categorized as pertaining to the frame or to the reasons and justifications. Those associated with the frame are "metaphors, exemplars, catchphrases, depictions, and visual images" (W. A. Gamson and Lasch 1983, 399). A **metaphor** is "the application of a name or descriptive term or phrase to an object or action to which it is imaginatively but not literally applicable" (*Oxford Dictionary and Thesaurus* 1996, 940). When describing the impact of the U.S. Department of Agriculture's discovery that a cow with bovine spongiform encephalopathy (BSE, or mad cow disease) had entered the U.S. beef supply in four states, *Newsweek* compared the impact to when one cow "kicked over a lantern and burned down most of Chicago" (Adler 2004, 45). A metaphor has two halves: the individual, party, object, action, or issue being characterized (the true subject), and the attributes and/or relationship characteristics of an associated individual, party, object, action, or issue used to characterize the true subject. When only one attribute of an associated subject is used, it is said to be a single-valued metaphor, and when two or more attributes of an associated subject are used, it is termed a dynamic metaphor (see W. A. Gamson and Lasch 1983). W. A. Gamson and Lasch (1983) present a cartoon illustrating a metaphor associated with the welfare interpretive package of welfare freeloaders. The cartoon shows "a gluttonous bureaucrat sharing a generous meal with a well-fed welfare bum at public expense" (410).

Exemplars are the dramatized accounts of real events, whether produced by witnesses, politicians, political activists, or journalists, which are then used to represent abstract forces, issues, or entities (see chapter 8). For instance, American journalists head to the ghettos when portraying American families on welfare, where inevitably they will interview an African American woman with numerous children—all whom were fathered by different men now missing from their lives. This classic news item has been described pejoratively by both political leaders and journalists as the "welfare queen" story. Exemplars may also be single-valued or dynamic. The example provided is a dynamic exemplar. **Catchphrases** are "attempted summary statements about the principal subject" (W. A. Gamson and Lasch 1983, 399–400) whether in the form of taglines, slogans, or catchy themes. Walter Mondale's oft-cited "Where's the beef?" in response to Ronald Reagan's vacuous handling of debate questions provides a ready example. In a series of television ads comparing two hamburger franchises, a quarrelsome little old lady had yelled at her companion, "Where's the beef?" Americans were well aware that the catchphrase suggested someone was getting shortchanged. **Depictions** are routine characterizations of the principal subject. For instance, George W. Bush has called those responsible for the September 11, 2001, terrorist attacks "evildoers," and since then, he has referred to Iran, Iraq, and North Korea as the "Axis of Evil." And, in his State of the Union Address on January 28, 2003, Bush described Saddam Hussein's use of chemical weapons and torture on his own subjects, and he observed, "If this is not evil, then evil has no meaning" (Stevenson and Sanger 2003, A12). **Visual images** are routine visual characterizations used in illustrating the issue cluster's interpretive package. For instance, a flag-draped coffin leaving a military airplane brings a gripping, cold reality to any discussion of war, which is why the George W. Bush administration prohibited journalists from photographing coffins returning from Iraq.

The condensation symbols used in presenting the reasons or justifications for a particular policy position on an issue are "roots, consequences, and appeals to principle" (W. A. Gamson and Lasch 1983, 399). **Roots** are the condensational symbols that provide the historical, often multifaceted, "causative dynamics" underlying the issue in question. In his 1996 Republican National Convention speech, Bob Dole argued that current social decay had its roots in a civil war against American values; he told his audience:

> After decades of assault upon what made America great, upon supposedly obsolete values, what have we reaped, what have we created, what do we have? What we have, in the opinion of millions of Americans, is crime, drugs, illegitimacy, abortion, the abdication of duty, and the abandonment of children. (1996, August 15, televised speech)

Consequences are the condensational symbols that project various outcomes associated with different policy decisions. Sometimes both short-term and long-term consequences are presented. At times, a cost-benefit analysis is presented as well. During his State of the Union Address on January 28, 2003, President George W. Bush, for instance, explained why he was willing for the United States to "go it alone" against Iraq, if need be: "We will consult, but let there be no misunderstanding: If Saddam Hussein does not fully disarm, for the safety of our people, and for the peace of the world, we will lead a coalition to disarm him" (Stevenson and Sanger 2003, A1).

Appeals to principle are condensational symbols evoking moral values, sometimes religious values, and general societal and cultural self-images to generate enthusiasm for particular policy choices. During the 1996 Republican National Convention, vice-presidential nominee Jack Kemp appealed to all Americans to reembrace the work ethic, arguing that the seeking of material success was a seed planted by God in every American. He said:

> Not just the hope of wealth, but the hope of justice. When we look into the face of poverty, we see pain and need. But above all, in every face, we must see the image of God. The Creator of All has planted the seed of creativity in us all, the desire within ourselves to work and build and improve our lot in life, and that of our families and those we love. (Kemp 1996, August 15, televised speech)

Ball-Rokeach, Power, Guthrie, and Waring (1990) and Shah, Domke, and Wackman (1996) have shown that the news media utilize value-framing issues, emphasizing "particular values—for example, honesty, equality, or competence—in treating issues and public figures and that this form of media emphasis can powerfully shape public understanding" (Price, Tewksbury, and Powers 1997, 483). Because these researchers see values as being at "the hub of individual belief systems," they believe that "the value-framing concept points to the criteria that determine what is relevant to issue formation and resolution" (Ball-Rokeach and Rokeach 1987, 184; see also Shah 2001).

Signature Matrix

In their analysis, W. A. Gamson and Lasch (1983) note that issue cultures often contain multiple issue clusters or interpretive packages. They suggest that to undercover the full realm of an issue culture, one should draft a **signature matrix**, consisting of rows representing the interpretive packages and columns representing the eight condensational symbolic devices (metaphors, exemplars, catchphrases, depictions, visual images, roots, consequences, and appeals to principle). The words of political leaders, activists, and journalists serve as the raw materials from which to draw representative expressions of the condensation symbols. Gamson and Lasch (1983) recommend a content analysis of news content taking into account the national prominence and the popularity of the media outlet. Such an analysis provides significant insights not only to the student of political news but also to working journalists, policy advocates, and political leaders. They have suggested that measuring the quantity of competing interpretive packages provides an individual with a means of assessing how successful a particular frame has become.

Not all news is about issues, however. Nimmo and Johnson (a.k.a. Johnson-Cartee, 1980) have utilized a similar procedure to analyze political campaign news stories. During the opening days of January 2004, the mainstream news media seemed to sing the same tune about front-runner Democratic presidential contender Howard Dean: "Dangerous Dean." CNN and network news shows ran stories about how "Washington insiders" and "major Democrats" feared Dean and his meteoric rise to the head of the Democratic pack. *Time* magazine ran a six-page news story, with the headline "Inside the Mind of HOWARD DEAN" (Tumulty 2004, 25; capitalization in original). And visual images presented showed Dean first in a full-page photo of his face partially obscured by shadows, second in a shot with Dean gritting his teeth and shaking his fist, and third with him laughing like a hyena. The message: Dean is unknown, but what we do know is that he is mercurial. *Newsweek* ran a ten-page story with the headline "The Dean Dilemma" (Fineman 2004), and the first visual image presented showed Dean in a full-page photo taken from the side, where he looked disgruntled. The second showed Dean in a lineup for a debate; and the third photo had him talking on the phone and looking at his watch.

Time magazine used a belittling depiction of Dean, referring to him as "the quirky doctor who was an ex-governor of a small New England state" (Tumulty 2004, 25), and after summarizing some of his campaign gaffes, the newsmagazine asked "What is he thinking?" Interestingly, *Time* decided to list the "charges" against Dean in subheads throughout the article:

He is an accident waiting to happen
He is just not likeable
He is too liberal
He is just not electable (Tumulty 2004, 25–29)

And, while *Time* in some ways discounted these "charges," it nevertheless had given voice to them. *Newsweek,* during the same week, told its readers that even Dean's own supporters were worried about "Dean's confrontational personality" (Fineman 2004, 18), and they quoted worrisome comments that were posted on a forum on Dean's official website. One "Deanie," as *Newsweek* described Dean's supporters, posted this comment on the site: "Dean is portrayed as a man who, rather than share a beer in a local hangout, will fight you for yours," (Fineman 2004, 20), and they used a shortened version of this quote in enlarged type at the bottom of page 27. The magazine quoted Bill Clinton's right-hand man, political adviser James Carville, as saying, "I think the guy has mad-mouth disease," a metaphor utilizing the nation's mad-cow disease scare (Fineman 2004, 21). But perhaps what was most damning was the magazine's evaluation of Dean's chances if he proved to be the Democratic Party's nominee. With a historical analogy, *Newsweek* smeared Dean's chances:

> The occasional whispers on his blog [website] are amplified to a deafening roar elsewhere—by rivals on the campaign trail who are honing strategies (and sometimes plotting with each other) to stop him; by Beltway insiders, especially Clinton loyalists, who fear (correctly) that Dean represents a changing of the guard, and by Republicans in and out of the White House who cannot wait to get their hands on a man they—and many Democrats—see as a composite reincarnation of big-time losers such as George McGovern, Walter Mondale and Michael Dukakis. (Fineman 2004, 20)

And, if Fineman hadn't made his point perfectly clear, he turns to a football metaphor later in article, suggesting that Dean's campaign performance thus far had placed his campaign manager in an uncomfortable position, writing, "Dean's campaign manager, Joe Trippi, sounds like a football coach praying for a first down that will allow his team to run out the clock" (Fineman 2004, 25). While not all the elements of the signature matrix will be utilized for such nonissue news stories, the ingredients for "reading between the lines" are there to decipher campaign news stories.

J. W. Tankard (2001) has developed a list of "framing mechanisms, or focal points for identifying frames" (101) that greatly assists anyone interested in discovering news frames utilized by various news organizations:

1. Headlines and kickers (small headlines over the main headlines)
2. Subheads
3. Photographs
4. Photo captions
5. Leads (the beginning of news stories)
6. Selection of sources or affiliations
7. Selection of quotes
8. Pull quotes (quotes that are blown up in size for emphasis)
9. Logos (graphic identification of the particular series an article belongs to)
10. Statistics, charts, and graphs
11. Concluding statements or paragraphs of articles (J. W. Tankard 2001, 101)

For J. W. Tankard (2001), analyzing such structural devices ultimately reveals news framing.

News Archetypes

According to Price, Tewksbury, and Powers (1997), news "frames often reflect broader cultural themes and narratives, and they supply citizens with a basic tool kit of ideas they use in thinking about and talking about politics" (482). Political news does more than chronicle or list events of the day; rather, the news is presented in familiar formulaic stories, which have been built on previously conceived narrative frames (see Frayn 1981; Galtung and Ruge 1965; V. Turner 1982; Rock 1981). Whether reporting crime stories, house fires, or international summits, reporters have in their repertoire narrative frames that fit the occasion. These narrative frames are learned by journalists first as news consumers, for many narrative frames are **archetypal**, ideal types that fit various occasions within human existence (S. Hall 1984; Herrnstein Smith 1981). Bereavement stories, rags-to-riches stories, wicked stepmother stories, rugged individualism stories, and so on are cultural archetypes that journalists through their own early socialization learn as acceptable, understandable, and efficacious narratives. Through educational and on-the-job training, such archetypes get reinforced by positive feedback first from professors and later from employers. The journalist's narrative frame repertoire provides him or her with a ready-made set of tools from which he or she crafts or creates products or news accounts. Bird and Dardenne (1988) write:

> In practical terms, news values, rules, and formulas are essential for journalists to do their jobs. Reporters may have to write many stories in a week, or they may have to move to a different community and start writing about it immediately. They can comfortably do this with all the story-telling tools at their disposal, giving them a skeleton on which to hang the flesh of the news story. (73)

While the number of archetypal narrative frames may grow and vary within each reporter's repertoire, the familiarity and cultural similarity remain consistent (see Darnton 1975; S. Hall 1984; Herrnstein Smith 1981). A **reportorial consonance** results, in that separate, discrete events, with significant differences and widely different effects, are often reported utilizing the same narrative frame (see Berkman and Kitch 1986; Galtung and Ruge 1965; Graber 1980). For instance, as American soldiers continued to be killed in Iraq after President George W. Bush had told the nation that we had won the war, reporters began reporting news of the occupation of Iraq in the same news frames as they had reported the quagmire of our "peacekeeping" missions in Vietnam thirty years earlier.

Considering the Consequences of News Narratives

Cultural Hegemony

Reporters are as immersed in American culture as those who are in their audience. They were politically socialized by their schools, churches, and families in the same way that millions of Americans have been since the beginning of the Republic. For this reason, it should be understood that the vast majority of reporters are operating from within a purely American ideological perspective and that their news stories will necessarily reflect that perspective. And, for the most part, the views, beliefs, and ideas expressed in news accounts will reflect the dominant ideology operating in the United States at that particular time in history. Thus, it is to be expected that our news narratives have cultural origins. This has been called **cultural hegemony** by media critics.

Enduring Values in the News

In 1979, Gans (1979) identified what he called the **enduring values in the news,** which are expressed again and again by news reporters in their news accounts. Gans wrote:

> Enduring values . . . are values which can be found in many different types of news stories over a long period of time; often, they affect what events become news, for some are part and parcel of the definition of news. Enduring values are not timeless, and they may change somewhat over the years; moreover, they also help to shape opinions, and many times, opinions are only specifications of enduring values. (41)

We think it helps to understand enduring values by thinking of them as reoccurring **cultural themes.** After reading a news story, what does the reader retain? What meaning is residual? Gans (1979) identifies six clusters of enduring values: small-town pastoralism, ethnocentricism, individualism, moderatism, altruistic democracy, and responsible capitalism (see also W. A. Gamson and Lasch 1983). We will consider each in turn.

Small-Town Pastoralism

Johnson-Cartee and Copeland (1997b) defined small-town pastoralism as "the Jeffersonian myth that places special value on rural, pastoral America"

(77). However, as a news value, it should be recognized that small-town pastoralism means more than just the veneration of picket fences, main streets, and the local general store. It is a veneration "both of nature and of smallness per se" (Gans 1979, 49). And, correspondingly, the negation and rejection of all things big: "for in the news, Big Government, Big Labor, and Big Business rarely have virtues. Bigness is feared, among other things, as impersonal and inhuman" (Gans 1979, 49). In an earlier example, we analyzed a news story about a recent scandal involving the Boston archdiocese. Perhaps the reader is already recognizing the similarities between the enduring value of small-town pastoralism and those expressed within the Adler article (2002). The Roman Catholic Church is monolithic; and, more importantly, it operates as an institution—hierarchical, bureaucratic, and impersonal. Some would say in light of recent events that the church is also uncaring. Today, more than twenty years after Gans wrote *Deciding What's News*, we return to this noted author's words, and one passage in particular stands out: "The fear of bigness also reflects a fear of control, of privacy and individual freedom being ground under by organizations too large to notice, much less to value, the individual" (1979, 49). Adler's *Newsweek* article (2002) certainly illustrates this enduring value of small-town pastoralism; in this instance, the tale is particularly poignant, for of all institutions, it is the Roman Catholic Church that has publicly dedicated itself to the caretaking and shepherding of humankind.

Ethnocentrism

While most Americans do not like to think of themselves as ethnocentric, the truth remains that we, for the most part, very much are. And, in many respects, the fault rests with our public education system. From the earliest grades, we are taught that the United States is the greatest, most moral, most successful country in the world. We are told that our form of government and our economic system are superior to all others. Most Americans grow up with little or no appreciation for other countries, cultures, and religions. Indeed, many of you reading this will unthinkingly agree with those evaluations, without considering for a moment what such a belief means in our attitudes about other countries, peoples, and societies. Gans writes:

> American news values its own nation above all. . . . This ethnocentricism comes through most explicitly in foreign news, which judges other countries by the extent to which they live up to or imitate American practices and values, but it also underlies domestic news. Obviously, the news contains many stories that are critical of domestic conditions, but these conditions are almost always treated as deviant cases, with the implication that American ideals, at least, remain viable. (1979, 42)

For instance, during the Iranian hostage crisis, network news anchors and foreign affairs reporters repeatedly described the Ayatollah Khomeini as a religious fanatic, a madman. More importantly, governmental spokespersons and television commentators repeatedly criticized the Iranian leader for not following Western negotiating principles. Because Ayatollah Khomeini refused to play by our rules, we saw this as additional evidence of his "madness" or insanity. News accounts did not provide the necessary information to understand the historical, political, economic, and social background for this fundamentalist Islamic movement. We could not comprehend that a governmental leader would not put human rights above all else. And we could not comprehend young men and women willing to die for what they saw to be a cultural and religious insult. Our leaders and political commentators failed to recognize that the ayatollah saw the hostage crisis in absolute, religious terms; he could and would not compromise his religious principles (see Johnson a.k.a. Johnson-Cartee and Nimmo 1986; Kissinger 1966). Nor as a society were we aware of our own responsibility in providing the shah of Iran with modern weaponry used to put down revolts within his own borders. We failed to appreciate the Iranian people's hatred of the American government for aiding, in their eyes, their oppressor. Therefore, Khomeini wanted all his demands to be met, or nothing would be done. Our nation was at a stalemate for more than one year, because our leaders could not grasp that not all foreign leaders would conform to our standards and principles of international negotiation.

Other nations and their leaders often find Americans and their governmental representatives arrogant. When teaching or guest lecturing in other nations besides my own, I am frequently asked, "Why do Americans believe that they have the right to tell other countries what to do?" Similarly, one year after September 11, an English couple, visiting America for the sixth time and enduring both CNN reports and southern cocktail parties, observed:

> We Brits really don't have anything in common with you Americans at all. We thought we knew Americans, but we don't really. Your opinions you speak with such certainty; your orders for the rest of the world are so arrogant. What gives you the right?

Elliott (2002) provided an unusually introspective view of American leadership in the twentieth and twenty-first centuries when he wrote:

> Perhaps above all, the President thought big; he had grand, expansive ideas of how the world might be ordered to increase human security and happiness, and he cast these thoughts not in terms of some narrow set of American interests but as universal truths applicable to all nations and all problems. In international affairs,

he lived by a clear identification of what was good and what was evil and he believed in inclining American policy so that it supported the former; he was a great believer in moral clarity.

All of which, to many of those who had to deal with him, made him a royal pain. The British Prime Minister thought the President behaved like a heathen come to rescue the missionaries. The French Prime Minister, exasperated by the President's airs, said that talking to him was like talking to Jesus Christ. Europeans found the President ignorant; he was, said the leading public intellectual of the time, not just "ill-informed" but "slow and unadaptable." The central problem, this observer believed, was that the President's "thought and his temperament were essentially theological not intellectual, with all the strength and the weakness of that manner of thought, feeling and expression." (108)

Elliott was not writing of George W. Bush, but of Woodrow Wilson, who sought to impose his views on the world after World War I. And Wilson failed miserably, in part because he did not understand that other world leaders did not and would not share his beliefs and values. Today, Elliott observes that our nation is involved in "a sort of muscular Wilsonianism," finding its voice in President George W. Bush (2002, 108). Elliot writes:

> In a series of speeches since Sept. 11, 2001, the President has shaped a "Bush doctrine" that commits the U.S. to do everything it can—including unilateral, preemptive military action—to eradicate international terrorism, reform the nations that support it and neutralize rogue states that seek to possess weapons of mass destruction. (2002, 108–109)

Perhaps it is best to hear and to understand our "native" ethnocentricism by reading the president's own words:

> "Our nation's cause has always been larger than our nation's defense. We fight for a just peace—a peace that favors human liberty. We will defend the peace against threats from terrorists and tyrants. We will preserve the peace by building good relations among the great powers. And we will extend the peace by encouraging free and open societies on every continent." (Elliott 2002, 109)

And, as Americans, we have heard such sentiments expressed so often by our political leaders that we don't critically analyze what is being said, nor do we stop to think what other world leaders and other peoples might make of what is being said. When President Ronald Reagan invaded Grenada, when he bombed Khadaffi's home, or when, out of the blue, President Bill Clinton bombed Afghanistan, we, for the most part, remained silent, placing our enduring trust in our leaders and the rightness of American vision.

Individualism

As a relatively new nation, we regard our early settlers and frontiersmen with high esteem. And we venerate those who display traits associated with "rugged individualism" or "the self-made man." As a culture, we value the "ferocity of spirit that is associated with the lonesome, noble brow of the pioneer" (Johnson-Cartee and Copeland 1997b). We watch news reports detailing the actions of men and women who become heroes and heroines when confronted with disaster. News reporters treat mountain climbers, astronauts, and Olympic athletes with awe, characterizing them as exemplifying the very best in the American spirit. In our culture, "the ideal individual struggles against adversity and overcomes more powerful forces" (Gans 1979, 50). We are proud that a young, poor orphan boy who chopped firewood and read by fuelight grew up to be president of the United States. We found comfort in presidential candidate Bill Clinton's Democratic national presidential convention video, "A Man from Hope," which told of a fatherless boy, growing up in a poor family, struggling to finance his education, and ultimately serving his state through elected offices and finally his nation by seeking national office. Such emphasis on rugged individualism should come as no surprise to a nation of moviegoers fascinated with movies such as *Rocky* and *Rambo* and their many permutations (see Combs and Nimmo 1993).

Moderatism

As a country, we discourage extremism. "Lack of moderation is wrong, whether it involves excess or abstention" (Gans 1979, 51). News reports condemn both obesity and anorexia nervosa. And conspicuous consumers such as the yuppies in the 1980s are vilified as much as the naturalists or survivalists who forsake normal society for a life of spartan hardship. But nowhere is moderation so valued as in its application to politics. Gans (1979) writes:

> Political ideologists are suspect, but so are unprincipled politicians. The totally self-seeking are thought to be consumed by excessive ambition, but the complete do-gooders are not to be believed. . . . Those who regularly follow party lines are viewed as hacks, and those who never do are called mavericks or loners— although these terms are pejorative only for the politically unsuccessful; the effective loner becomes a hero. (52)

Historically, those presidential candidates labeled extremist, whether on the far right such as Barry Goldwater or on the far left such as George McGovern, have met with overwhelming defeats.

Altruistic Democracy

News reporters expect and demand that all matters associated with the political process and American government should be held to the highest standards. In short, all political processes, whether informal or institutionalized, "should follow a course based on the public interest and public service" (Gans 1979, 43). Honesty, efficiency, and frugality are valued above all else. Corruption, red tape, and waste are disparaged as being un-American. But it is not only the political elite who are held to such high standards; ordinary citizens are also expected to participate in grassroots politics, solving problems for themselves and their communities.

Significantly, the American news media, however, keep economic news disassociated from the political process. While economic indicators are watched and discussed as predictors of presidential evaluations and ultimately electoral successes, concrete connectors often remain missing. For the American news media, "the polity and the economy are separate and independent of each other" (Gans 1979, 45). Gans observes:

> Of course, the news is aware of candidates who are millionaires or who obtain substantial amounts of corporate or union campaign money, but it is less conscious of the relationship between poverty and powerlessness, or even of the difficulty that Americans of median income have in obtaining political access. (1979, 45)

News provides us with stories about crime, about poverty, and about the permanent underclass. But rarely are the issues connected meaningfully. As a society, we want "to be tough on crime," and we're willing to spend between $18,000 and $30,000 per criminal per year to warehouse them across the nation. But we are unwilling as a society to invest in public education, continuing education, and cultural interventions that would alter or eradicate the forces within communities that breed crime. As a people, we haven't made the intellectual connection between a culture forged in poverty, ignorance, and hopelessness and a culture consumed with crime.

Responsible Capitalism

Our liberal democratic tradition manifests a strong belief in the sanctity of the marketplace of ideas and the nobleness of those who participate in that marketplace. Thus, to engage in competition within the marketplace of ideas is a notion that is carried over into the economic marketplace as well. Gans writes: "In the good society, businessmen and women will compete with each other in order to create increased prosperity for all, but . . . they will refrain from unreasonable profits and gross exploitation of workers or customers" (1979, 46). However, in keeping with the enduring value of small-town pastoralism, small businesses are preferred and big businesses are suspect. Any deviations from responsible capitalism, such as excessive profits, monopolizing business practices, or unethical stockbrokers, are aberrations involving individuals failing to perform in the American way.

Often, however, news consumers are not cognizant of the enduring values expressed in the news. The attendant public is unaware, for the most part, when reading or listening to the news, of the frames used in its production and the resulting consequences this reporting choice has on news consumers' political perceptions. Gitlin (1980) writes: "Media frames, largely unspoken and unacknowledged, organize the world both for journalists who report it and, in some important degree, for us who rely on their reports" (7).

Yet such media frames are readily understood by the audience, because they are perceived as being so familiar that they are taken into account, talked about and perhaps altered, and then perhaps are acted upon in similar ways because of the very nature of the narrative frame chosen by the reporter to tell the story (Bennett and Edelman 1985; Chibnall 1985; Darnton 1975; Nimmo and Combs 1980, 1983). Ultimately, what we know as our "political reality" is truly a product of this multilayered and multidirectional process, which Nimmo and Combs (1983) called our **mediated political reality.**

6

Actors in the Social Construction of News

M OLOTCH AND LESTER (1974) were the first to argue that news was the result of a social construction, and they identified three major news stages
that affect the construction of news—news promoters, news assemblers, and
news consumers. News promoters and news assemblers are both goal-driven
participants who produce communication products with a given public or
target audience in mind. News consumers are those who attend to and talk
about mass-mediated news reports.

News promoters are those individuals or groups who draw attention to occurrences, naming and identifying these occurrences as significant for others.
In other words, news promoters shape happenings or occurrences into "public events" by their actions. News promoters may be presidential press secretaries, vice presidents of public relations, directors of corporate affairs, directors of public information, or any other individual desiring to promote an
occurrence as a public event. Molotch and Lester (1974) deliberately chose the
then unfamiliar term of news promoter in their discussion of the social construction of news, rather than the more conventional journalistic terminology
of a news source, to emphasize the strategic and tactical dimensions associated
with news promotion. "News source" sounds passive, while "news promoter"
indicates activism.

News assemblers, "working from the materials provided by the promoters, transform a perceived finite set of promoted occurrences into public
events through publication or broadcast" (Molotch and Lester 1974, 104).
These news assemblers may be reporters, assignment editors, producers,
copy editors, page or section editors, or even editors in chief. The social

construction of news involves multiple assemblers, each contributing to the eventual production and dissemination of the public event.

In other words, news assemblers with the assistance of news promoters create "public events," introducing such socially constructed events to their audiences in the form of a news story. Public events should be distinguished from mere happenings or occurrences, for a public event is widely noticed, often discussed, and ultimately shaped or understood through such discussions. Once the news story is disseminated, news consumers interpret the news story, talk about the news story elements with others, alter their perceptions of the news story as a result of these discussions, and ultimately form their own versions of reality. **News consumers** are all those who attend to the news, whether as Internet users, radio listeners, television watchers, or newspaper or newsmagazine readers. In short, news promoters, news assemblers, and news consumers contribute to and create public knowledge about political happenings, for they are involved in the ongoing social construction of reality.

As Nimmo and Combs (1983) observed:

> Humans are not passive creatures. The things that reach them in their everyday lives—whether through direct, firsthand experience or indirectly by way of groups and mass media—have no inherent meaning. People must take such messages, interpret them, and act. Some things impress people, others they forget, others they avoid. People are active mediators, or interpreters, of their worlds. They are a part of a communication process that creates realities. (5)

As we go about our lives, we "define situations, problems, and the means of coping with difficulties—it simply makes living together possible" (Nimmo and Combs 1983, 5). Indeed, the only way we make sense of world is through communication. And as Nimmo and Combs (1983, 4) have observed:

> Even when we are directly involved in things, we do not apprehend them directly. Instead, media of communication intervene, media in the form of language, customs, symbols, stories, and so forth. That very intervention is a process that creates and re-creates (constructs and reconstructs) our realities of the moment and over the proverbial long haul. Communication does more than report, describe, explain—it creates. In this sense all realities—even those emerging out of direct, firsthand experience with things—are mediated.

As we have indicated previously, consumers attend to the news media with collective images of their past experiences, future expectations, and current or present evaluation of news media content and public occurrences. They interact with other members of their social network: friends, family members, and coworkers. Consumers attend to additional sources of news; they think about, talk about, or debate public issues with others. The sum totality of that process constitutes their political reality. But the available number of authoritative sources and media outlets is limited for the average citizen, and the information available is necessarily "truncated" by the newsgathering practices of media outlets and their reporters (Molotch and Lester, 1974, 106). And the average news consumer has neither the resources nor the power to propagate personal opinions to those outside of his or her immediate social circle; in this, news consumers differ substantially from either news promoters or news assemblers.

The journalist and social commentator Walter Lippmann understood that news was produced through a social process involving multiple actors working from often different perspectives or even motives. Consequently, in his classic work, *Public Opinion*, Lippmann ([1922] 1965) made a very important distinction between news and truth; he wrote: "The function of news is to signalize an event, the function of truth is to bring to light the hidden facts, to set them into relation with each other, and make a picture of reality on which men can act" (358). Or, to perhaps explain this in yet another way, news accounts are similar to the products of historians. In this day and time, we no longer consider historical accounts as objective; rather, we recognize that historians view public events subjectively, recounting their significance for future generations based on their own world view (Ricoeur 1981). News assemblers work in much the same manner, producing narratives that place actors and their actions into some meaningful web of social experiences based on the news assemblers' own world views. Bird and Dardenne (1988) write:

> Considering news as narrative does not negate the value of considering news as corresponding with outside reality, as affecting or being affected by society, as being a product of journalists or of bureaucratic organization, but it does introduce another dimension to news, one in which the stories of news transcend their traditional functions of informing and explaining. . . . The facts, names, and details change almost daily, but the framework into which they fit—the symbolic system—is more enduring. And it could be argued that the totality of news as an enduring symbolic system "teaches" audiences more than any of its component parts, no matter whether these parts are intended to inform, irritate, or entertain. (69)

Jamieson and Waldeman (2003) note that "the reports that journalists offer their readers, listeners, and viewers are not called 'stories' by accident. By arranging information into structures with antagonists, central conflicts, and narrative progression, journalists deliver the world to citizens in a comprehensible form" (1; see chapter 4) And they go on to warn that "the stories that journalists tell and the lenses that color their interpretation of events can sometimes dull their fact-finding and investigative instincts" (Jamieson and Waldeman 2003, 1). The researchers also point out the similarities between news assemblers or journalists and the news promoters or political leaders who spin the news, explaining:

> Politicians cast the world in stories, too. Political actors argue through the use of narrative for a number of reasons. First, they understand that narrative has persuasive power; when arguments are arranged into stories, they are more readily recalled and more easily believed. Second, they understand the reporter's preference for good stories around which news can be built. (Jamieson and Waldeman 2003, 1)

Ultimately, what people know or what constitutes their knowledge of the world is myth or what is believed to be true by those involved in the social construction of reality. And as Bird and Dardenne so eloquently argue, socially constructed news accounts are mythical narratives in that news accounts reassure the audience "by telling tales that explain baffling or frightening phenomena and provide acceptable answers; myth does not necessarily reflect an objective reality, but builds a world of its own" (1988, 70). While Drummond (1984) was writing about movies and myths, his definition of myth sounds amazingly like news stories; for Drummond, "Myth is primarily a metaphorical device for telling people about themselves, about other people, and about the complex world of natural and mechanical objects which they inhabit" (27; emphasis in original). Mythical narratives are comfortable much like old shoes, for the narrative forms are familiar, readily understood, and easily digested. Rock (1981) makes the point that news accounts are "eternal recurrences" in that new people, places, activities, forces, and so on are placed into familiar news structures. Rock (1981) writes: "The content may change, but the forms will be enduring. Much news is, in fact, ritual. It conveys an impression of endlessly repeated drama whose themes are familiar and well understood" (68; see chapters 1, 4, and 5).

Today, the social construction of news is widely accepted among news scholars (Entman 1989a, 1989b; W. A. Gamson 1988b; W. A. Gamson, Croteau, Hoynes, and Sasson 1992; Graber 1982; Johnson-Cartee and Copeland 1997b; McNair 1998; Neuman 1982; see chapter 1). While Molotch and Lester used "news stages" as a discussion point, I find it more useful to think of them as three separate active actors who participate to varying degrees in the news construction process.

News Promoters and News Assemblers: A Symbiotic Relationship

News assemblers begin the process of news creation by evaluating a public occurrence and the promoter's publicity surrounding it, and by comparing the public occurrence's attributes with the needs and news values of professional journalism. As Molotch and Lester (1974) have indicated:

> The nature of the media as formal organization, as routines for getting work done in newsrooms, as career mobility patterns for a group of professionals, as profit-making institutions, all become inextricably and reflexively tied to the content of published news. (105)

It should be obvious by now that the event needs of the promoter may well differ from the event needs of the media organization. This natural tension involving conflicting or dissimilar information needs among news promoters and news assemblers is often the subject of professional humor. For example, President Reagan's press secretary Larry Speakes kept a plaque on his White House desk: "You don't tell us how to stage the news, and we won't tell you how to cover it" (T. E. Cook 1996b, 470). This often cited "tension" between news assemblers and news promoters is said to demonstrate the media's independence in the news construction process, for the news assemblers may well choose not to describe an occurrence as an event and not disseminate information about the occurrence to news consumers. Therefore, the occurrence will never achieve a status in "public time," or in the public's eyes, and will never have a widely held public character.

Although the media have the final say in which occurrences are deemed newsworthy, seemingly demonstrating their independence in the news process, the reality is really quite different. Media organizations are inherently a part of the community where they exist, and for this reason they are subject to community influences, particularly powerful influentials and their needs (Kuypers 2002). In one example, a daily newspaper refused to take an editorial stand on a referendum determining whether alcohol could be served within the city limits. Alcohol was available over the county line, and research indicated that the city was losing nearly $2 million in potential alcohol consumption and sales taxes a year to the neighboring county. The newspaper covered the referendum as a "news event," carefully balancing coverage between proponents and opponents of the measure. Grocery store owners, restaurants, and service stations supported alcohol sales, while the Baptist churches in the community opposed the referendum. Although increased sales-tax revenues and alcohol-consumption taxes would have brought funds for needed salary increases and equipment purchases for the police and fire departments, the newspaper chose not to support the passage of the referendum, because the editor and publisher feared the local churches would boycott advertising in the newspaper. Local church announcements generated significant revenue for the newspaper on both Wednesday and Sunday. In this instance, the newspaper feared the perceived power of the local Baptist churches and their impact on the newspaper's revenue base. Despite the fact that the churches had no alternative media outlet, the editor and publisher chose to avoid alienating a powerful interest group, ultimately protecting the newspaper's profitable bottom line.

When news promoters and news assemblers' interests clash, as in the pro-wet (pro-alcohol) forces and the daily newspaper, the news promoters themselves may threaten an advertising boycott or engineer a negative letter-writing campaign to the editor when news policies are perceived as hurting the needs of the promoter. However, such threats ultimately will damage the relationship the promoter has with the media outlet. It should be remembered that the relationship between promoters and assemblers is a symbiotic one; each uses the other one for its own benefit. And, ultimately, both the newspaper personnel and the news promoters work to protect that relationship. In this circumstance, the newspaper gave the pro-wet forces more flexible advertising-copy deadline times than other advertisers enjoyed. Indeed, both news promoters and news assemblers work to enhance their working relationships.

According to Gandy (1982), assemblers "favor bureaucratic sources who can provide a regular, credible and ultimately usable flow of information, insight and imagery with which to construct the news" (13). And elites or news promoters work to provide information subsidies—readily understood and easily utilized information with the air of authenticity and with the appropriate news values—helping to ensure that news assemblers will use these information subsidies in their construction of news stories, ultimately reaching the desired target audiences (see Turk 1986a, 1986b). According to Pan and Kosicki (2001), elites or news promoters strategically craft a "'web of subsidies' to privilege the dissemination and packaging of information to their advantage" (44). They argue:

> Strategic framing involves both weaving and mobilizing such webs of subsidies. Issue entrepreneurs may subsidize public deliberation through three routes. First, they may subsidize the news media, thus influencing media discourse, by (a) lowering the cost of information gathering and (b) generating cultural resonance of their frame with the news values held by journalists. Second, they may subsidize the policymakers, thus influencing the elite discourse, by (a) reducing the cost for policymakers to garner and process information and (b) reducing

the (perceived) political risks for policymakers to take a stand on an issue. Third, issue entrepreneurs may subsidize the public, thus influencing public opinion, by (a) creating ideologically toned and emotionally charged catchphrases, labels (e.g., pro-life vs. pro-choice) or exemplars and (b) linking a position to a political icon, figure, or group. (Pan and Kozicki 2001, 46)

Bureaucratic sources need to get information out to the public, elected officials, and other agencies. And news reporters need the information to fill their news hole. In short, the framing of a news story "is a reciprocal process between political elites and journalists" (Kuypers 2002, 11; Nelson, Oxley, and Clawson 1997). W. Gamson and Stuart (1992) suggest that journalists are dependent on their official sources to provide them with much-needed information, and, as a result over time, relationships develop based on mutual trust. And "with any beat, there is a tendency to adopt the frames of one's sources, which increases with sustained contact" (W. Gamson and Stuart 1992, 57). Furthermore, news organizations fail to realize that by assigning reporters to beats, by identifying and prioritizing societal arenas and issues for coverage, by including some and excluding others, the news organization has committed an ideological act, promoting a single world view (see Eliasoph 1988). Determining who and what is to be covered and covered routinely is an ideological determination.

Similarly, Bennett, Gressett, and Halton (1985) argue that news beats, news sources, and newspeople exist in a symbiotic relationship with each other, using each other for the purposes of their own survival. By centering the news on news beats, newspeople focus on official actions and reactions by governmental actors; this focus yields a "popular myth that the pronouncements of government officials and institutional elites somehow represent the reality in which the majority of people live" (Bennett, Gressett, and Halton 1985, 51). Such a presentation has significant consequences in that this popular myth serves to legitimize the government and governmental actors. Because "the press frames virtually all important stories around the actions and reactions of institutional officials, the key institutions of polity, economy, and society appear to be responsive to all legitimate issues and interests" (Bennett, Gressett, and Halton 1985, 51). Thus, the media portray the government as responding to the needs of the citizenry, legitimizing the government's actions.

News beats institutionalize the symbiotic relationship between bureaucratic news sources and newspeople; the frequency and routinization of interactions builds familiarity and creates interpersonal relationships that affect the news process (B. C. Cohen 1963; Gans 1979; Lawrence 1996; Sigal 1973). Indeed, official news sources are "coparticipants with the media in the creation of standardized news themes" (Bennett, Gressett, and Halton 1985, 50; see also Bennett 1983; Darnton 1975; Fishman 1980; Molotch and Lester 1974; Sigal 1973; Tuchman 1978a). Thus, it may be argued that newspeople and news sources depend on each other to achieve their own personal, political, and/or institutional agenda. Nelson, Oxley, and Clawson (1997) have explained that "frames serve as bridges between elite discourse about a problem or issue and popular comprehension of that issue" (224). Consequently, political elites from campaign spin doctors to congressional committee chairpersons "devote considerable effort toward influencing not only *what* information gets on the air but *how* it is presented" (Nelson, Oxley, and Clawson 1997, 224; emphasis in original). Political elites provide the news media with a rich menu of pithy sound bites, analogies, metaphors, slogans, one-liners, and exemplars constructed to entice working journalists to use them (Nelson, Oxley, and Clawson, 1997). And these rhetorical devices often make their way into the nation's news stories in whole or in part, portraying the issue to the advantage of the political elite who initially constructed them.

Elites have also learned that the more inflammatory, the more anti-oppositional, the more controversial their remarks, the more likely their comments will be picked up by both print and broadcast reporters (Hallin 1992a, 1992b). Nelson, Oxley, and Clawson (1997) have observed:

> Elites seem to have learned that it may be more profitable in such an environment to try to frame issues in advantageous ways than to try to change public beliefs by offering evidence or logical argumentation. Journalist's [sic] reliance on elite sources for material means that even if they dispute the source's assumptions or conclusions, they still construct the story in terms established by that source. This dynamic interplay between political elites and mass media practitioners is a far cry from the more simplified portrayal of source parameters in standard persuasion studies. (1997, 238)

According to Kuyper, political elites or news promoters have greater influence over news frames when journalists are facing a new event-specific situation than when journalists are facing an often reported, familiar news situation (2002). The advertising recession and accompanying economic constraints during the 1980s and after produced a greater willingness on the part of news assemblers to utilize governmental and nonprofit press releases to fill the news hole, particularly if they were well written and conformed to journalistic style (Curtin 1999).

However, some researchers have questioned the symbiotic hypothesis of journalist-source interactions (Berkowitz 1992), suggesting, in effect, that the process of news construction is far more complicated than I have now presented it to be. For instance, Berkowitz (1992) suggests that we must understand the functioning of journalist-source interactions as a by-product of their perceived roles within their individual, organizational, professional, and societal spheres. Each actor, then, has multiple, often competing roles within and among role spheres. Berkowitz views the way journalists or sources view "their jobs" as "the result of several levels of forces in constant interaction. Further, this interaction is dynamic, so that each level—individual, organizational, professional, societal—might be more or less influential at any particular instance" (1992, 95). I find no conflict with Berkowitz's analysis, although I find it to be far from a repudiation of the symbiosis hypothesis in that it appears to be a restatement of the basic symbiosis principles, with an increased emphasis on the variability of power within the relationship. Such a perspective resembles the earlier work of Johnson-Cartee and Copeland (Johnson a.k.a. Johnson-Cartee 1984; Johnson-Cartee and Copeland 1997a). I see the source-journalist interaction as dynamic, circular, negotiated, evolving, and in flux (see also Reese 1991).

Berkowitz's notion of a negotiated order or a shared culture of role expectations is an important addition to the literature. Berkowitz emphasizes that a shared culture of role expectations is built up over time through repeated journalist-source interactions. Berkowitz (1992) writes:

> In essence, this shared culture becomes an unofficial set of ground rules for journalist-source interaction. Although both parties might not be fully satisfied by the constraints and obligations related to their role prescriptions, they nonetheless learn that meeting expectations of these externally prescribed roles is crucial to effectiveness and success within their respective organizations. (95)

Knowledge of this shared culture has important implications for policymakers and other news promoters in that:

> As policymakers [and other news promoters] attempt to place news stories, not all news favorable to a policymaker's interests will meet the expectations of the shared culture. In these cases, policymakers who understand the rules of the culture the best will be most capable of transforming a news item's appearance to conform more closely to the culture's current news definitions. When policymakers do so, journalists can cover the news item and still remain within the boundaries of their internal role-expectations. In this way, more powerful policymakers will have a greater degree of agenda influence, if not the exact news story that they want. (Berkowitz 1992, 97–98)

According to Molotch, Protess, and Gordon (1996), journalists and their sources have "by virtue of their differential skills and status positions, varying degrees of access to participate. Because they so continuously anticipate each other's moves, their activities are, as a matter of course, mutually constrained"

(59). They describe journalists and their sources as being involved in an evolving "ecology of games" or an "ecology of dance" (Molotch, Protess, and Gordon 1996, 59). And as the news promoter's and the news assembler's relative positions, skills, and expertise vary within the ecology of dance, on some occasions the journalist does the leading; yet, on others, it is the source who does the leading.

In a related argument, Molotch, Protess, and Gordon (1996) have argued that as scholars of the media, we should cease focusing on the content of the message or its effects and instead focus on the functioning of this shared culture and the revelations and ramifications therein. They write:

> The critical issue is not so much the technical and substantive nature of a given message (although such things do matter), but how that message relates or fails to relate to the practical purposes—at that time point—of actors in a number of other significant realms. Media "effects" on policy (as on anything else) come from the capacity of journalists to play a role (delimited, but omnipresent) in this larger ecology of individual and institutional practices. (Molotch, Protess, and Gordon 1996, 59)

Ultimately, this symbiotic relationship between news promoters and news assemblers may be characterized as series of maneuvers on both their parts to gain control of the news (T. E. Cook 1998). Ericson, Baranek, and Chan (1989) provide an interesting perspective when considering the role of news promoters operating in society, for they view news promoters as staking out "knowledge" (or their version of it) for news reporters and, if accepted by these news assemblers, ultimately for the public as well. Similarly, Roscho (1975) argued that news promoters

> are continually deciding whether certain information should be revealed, which details should be highlighted or discarded, when the story should be offered to the press. Every such decision, which makes some data visible to the press and relegates other data to invisibility, is an act of news management. (84–85)

The trick for the news promoter "is to appear to be disclosing more while actually enclosing on what is publicized" (Ericson, Baranek, and Chan 1989, 383). In other words, the news promoter must always appear to be open, accessible, and fully disclosing, yet at the same time, in reality, the news promoter must be carefully controlling what is released.

Frequently, according to Ericson, Baranek, and Chan (1989), multiple news promoters or what they call "knowledge stakers" are competing against each other, vying for what version of reality, what "knowledge" or version of knowledge, will be accepted and reported. They focused on multiple knowledge stakers participating in the criminal justice system, each with a different agenda, a different desired slant or take on the possible news story. And, as Leigh has explained:

> Knowledge is, of course, power. So to discuss the way information is shared out in society is to talk about the politics of information gathering. The relationship between journalists, private citizens and government organisations in the criminal justice system—police, courts, and prisons—is a particularly interesting one, because three ideas about information collide—sometimes nastily—in this arena. These are the concepts of publicity, privacy, and secrecy. (1982, 74)

Leigh and Ericson, Baranek, and Chan recognize that all players, whether the police, the courts, or the prisons, come to the table with their own agenda, their own values, and their own version of reality. And all players want to influence the working journalist to accept their own definition of reality, their own truths, or what they find to be knowledge. Such exchanges among news promoters and news assemblers are efforts to control the news or what has been termed "negotiations for control" of the news (Ericson, Baranek, and Chan 1989). Such negotiations are carried out on three different playing fields: the physical, or the setting of the process of gathering and collecting the news; the social, or the social relationships existing among news promoters and news assemblers; and the cultural, or the professional or societal beliefs, values, and expectations held by the news promoters and news assemblers (T. E. Cook 1998; Ericson, Baranek, and Chan 1989).

Tuchman has emphasized how **news beats**, or "the routine round of institutions and persons to be contacted at scheduled intervals for knowledge of events" (1978b, 144; see also Manoff 1987), significantly impact the construction of news. Reporters and their sources develop significant professional relationships through the established patterns of these news beats. Fishman (1980) found the degree of symbiosis present among Forestry Service bureaucrats and local news reporters to be remarkable; he wrote, "When it turned out that even rocks, trees, and squirrels are made available to the newspaper through official agencies, then it is no exaggeration to say that the world is bureaucratically organized for journalists" (51).

Frequently, organizations will provide office space and facilities for working journalists; this proximity to their organizational sources encourages their socialization into the social and cultural spheres of the organization, developing shared values and beliefs over time. Fishman wrote: "Even though the reporter takes . . . the beat as the object of reporting, reporters are part of that object. They participate in the activities that they report" (1980, 30). Consequently, researchers have emphasized the symbiotic relationship between journalists and their sources.

In short, journalists assigned to news beats practice what Strentz (1989) has called "rolodex journalism" in that they spin through their Rolodex of established and trusted news sources for comments on developing stories. Soley (1994) pointed out that print journalists enjoy a far larger Rolodex of sources because they don't have to worry whether their sources are capable of producing concise eight- or nine-second sound bites, and they don't have to worry about their sources appearing attractive or likable.

Behavioral patterns emerge for both news promoters and news assemblers; one such behavioral pattern is the handling of "back-region disclosures," or conversations and written materials understood to be "off the record" by both the news promoters and the assemblers (Ericson and Baranek 1982; Ericson, Baranek, and Chan 1989; Fishman 1980). Tacit understanding exists that such information is not to be reported to news consumers. Such back-region disclosures are viewed by news promoters as a means to allow news assemblers a

Textbox 6.1

News Promoters' Goals

To build support for their organization, cause, policy, or position, enhancing or maintaining a positive public image

To build support for either an existing policy or program or a newly introduced program

To negate support for an existing policy or program they wish to transform or to eliminate

To neutralize or negate support for an existing program or newly proposed program promoted by others

To support a new or existing program promoted by a policy confederate, maintaining and enhancing policy coalitions

To neutralize or attack perceived organizational, policy, or programmatic enemies or rivals

To achieve personal publicity, enhancing or maintaining an existing positive public image

To dramatize personal power; to maintain or enhance perceptions of power among other insiders, the news media, and the public

To repair or to rehabilitate a negative personal public image

To inoculate against potential negative attacks on the promoter, policy, program, or organization (Johnson-Cartee and Copeland 1997a)

To announce occurrences, providing neutral information for the purpose of stimulating awareness

To secure news media support for policies, programs, or organizational authority by encouraging positive editorial reviews glimpse at how decisions are made; this is believed to increase not only the news assemblers' understanding of the process but also the reporters' approval or sympathetic acceptance of what transpires. Such tacit understandings build social relations between reporters and news promoters and build shared cultural orientations involving not only organizational decision making but also operating norms between reporters and news promoters. Over the years, such negotiations of control yield **news cultures**, where news promoters and news assemblers know and follow the unwritten rules of conduct.

The Agenda of News Promoters

News promoters are goal-seeking individuals not only for themselves personally but also for the organization they represent. News promoters view news assemblers as one possible means of reaching desirable goal states. They utilize the news media under a variety of circumstances; see textbox 6.1.

To promote a positive public image and a positive momentum assessment among attentive publics

To highlight problems, potential negative threats, or both to the organization, policy, or program by alerting political activists likely to assist the promoters

To test attentive publics, news media, interest groups, and insider reactions to potential solutions to identified problems

To highlight opportunities or potentially advantageous trends affecting the organization, policies, or programs by alerting political activists who are willing to assist

To test attentive publics, news media, interest groups, and insider reactions to possible policy actions capitalizing on such opportunities

To provide the appearance of informing the public and seeking the attentive public's support for organizational and programmatic legitimacy

To showcase policy deliberations to encourage the attentive public's acceptance of the policy process

To showcase policy deliberators as operating in the public interest

To maintain or build relationships with reporters by providing information or copy that they need in order to mine that relationship in the future

To reward cooperative reporters for their support or efforts in the past by giving exclusives

To deny access to information; to punish uncooperative, obstructionist, or unduly negative reporters for their past behaviors

To buy time until either more is known or more is forgotten (see Dunn 1969)

News promoters who are government officials utilize news reporters as a primary linkage with others in their political environment. It is the reporter, not the news promoter, who often presents the news promoter's public political face to the world. Indeed, because political power is often based on public perceptions rather than on objective realities, "an official's relations with the press are likely to be one of his preeminent concerns" (Dunn 1969, 171). In addition, news promoters utilize respected journalists as their own sources of information. When confronted with new policies or new decision-making arenas, news promoters seek to gather as much information as possible, often turning to journalists who often have related issue experience in covering past news stories. Such related issue experience provides important frames of reference for government officials dealing with a newly introduced issue on the policy agenda (see Dunn 1969).

News Promoters' Communication Practices

News promoters have a wide variety of communication tools at their disposal when interacting with news assemblers; they provide information to the news media through:

Press releases or information subsidies: Whether print, radio/television release scripts, or video news releases, whether as stand-alones or as provided in media kits, which are delivered via e-mail, fax, telegram, delivery service, radio/actuality lines, U.S. mail, Federal Express, or United Parcel Service. Also given as a handout before a press conference or speech. Written in a news story format with pertinent facts and positions included (Dunn 1969).

Media fact sheets: The who-what-when-where-how-why staccato listing of routine announcements, either stand-alone or as provided in media kits.

Backgrounders: Detailed analysis of an issue area, potential positions on the issue, potential supporters and opponents for each position, internal and external impact assessments for both short and long term; only provided to the most trusted journalists on a not-for-attribution basis (Mack 1997).

Options papers: Basic information related to an issue, key provisions of recommended positions, arguments pro and con, potential supporters and opponents, probable impact internal and external for the short and long term, possible adjustments in the recommended positions (Mack 1997).

Position papers: Description of an issue, an organization's position on an issue, research justifying the position, impact analysis (Mack 1997).

White papers: More detailed, more research-based position papers (Mack 1997).

Speeches: Speeches delivered during legislative sessions, committee investigations (B. C. Cohen 1963; Matthews 1960), association meetings, annual stockholders meetings, or party conventions.

Press conferences: Following major announcements or publicized speeches, often followed by question-and-answer sessions.

Question-and-answer sessions: Little or no preliminary talk, simply an opportunity for reporters to obtain needed information, frequently seen after press conferences or as follow-ups involving ongoing stories.

Special events: Conferences, meetings, or tours allowing for formal and informal thematic interchange between news sources and journalists (Dunn 1969).

Pseudo-events: Activities that ordinarily would not have taken place except for the news media covering them (Boorstin 1961, 1971; Shoemaker and Reese 1991; Wolfsfeld 1984), for example, protests, demonstrations, ribbon cuttings, groundbreaking ceremonies, or photo opportunities (Baudrillard 1988).

Corporate board meetings: Regularly scheduled "news-generating" meetings, routinely covered by news people (Dunn, 1969).

Editorial board meetings: Officials meet one-on-one with editorial news staff, typically providing written remarks to the news staff and entertaining questions put before them (Dunn 1969).

Personal contact: Telephone or personal interview with journalist(s).

News Promoter Values

Successful news promoters have a keen understanding of the news organizations' and the news assemblers' news values in order that the promoters may construct or create newsworthy activities or stories that the journalist is likely to judge as worthy of attention, development, and ultimate dissemination. McCamy (1939) and Dunn (1969) have termed such a practice the **cultivation** of reporters or the process by which news promoters go about discovering reporters' "interests and needs and then fulfilling them as well as possible" (Dunn 1969, 139). According to Wallack, Woodruff, Dorfman, and Diaz (1999), the golden rule for successful news promoters or what they call news advocates is to "understand the conventions and values that drive journalists" (40). It is little wonder, then, that the news judgments of public relations practitioners and the news values of journalists have been found to be remarkably similar (Kopenhaver, Martinson, and Ryan 1984).

When comparing and contrasting the news values presented in academic journalism writings (see chapter 4) with those presented in public relations academic writings, we find remarkable similarity. For instance, PR writers Wallack, Woodruff, Dorfman, and Diaz (1999) list eleven newsworthy elements: controversy/conflict, broad interest, injustice, irony, local peg, personal angle, breakthrough, anniversary peg, seasonal peg, celebrity, and visuals (43–51). For the uninitiated, a "news peg" is a narrative angle from which the reporter is able to develop a story. Similarly, PR writer J. Salzman (1998) provides characteristics of both newsworthy and unnewsworthy events. He writes:

> There are a number of characteristics commonly associated with a "news" story. The more of these characteristics connected with an event, the more coverage it will likely get:
>
> Novelty
> Shock
> Conflict
> New data
> Simplicity
> Kids
> Social issues or a prominent public figure involved
> Humor
> Outdoor location
> Action
> Bright props and images
> News stories about the event published in advance
> Local impact
> A symbol of a trend
> Holidays, anniversaries
>
> Following are some characteristics of an event that will keep many journalists away:
>
> Indoor location
> People reading scripts
> A private, profit-oriented goal
> Complexity
> Unknown participants
> Bad timing or remote location
>
> A story with credible, new data about a timely subject will often interest a print reporter but not necessarily interest a television reporter, who needs visual imagery. If you've got new information and a visual to go along with it, you've got the strongest story for the widest variety of journalists. (Salzman 1998, 16–17)

Clearly, then, news promoters have a vested interest in learning the news business from the inside out. The better able promoters are to craft newsworthy stories, the more likely their objectives in gaining favorable news media attention will be reached. Journalists are far more likely to utilize information provided to them in a news form that is consonant with their own professional, organizational, and personal values (see chapters 3 and 4).

News Promoter Framing

News promoters seek to influence news assemblers to accept desirable definitions of situations involving their organization or cause (Nelson and Oxley 1999). They construct information that promotes their preferred version of reality; in other words, they construct narrative frames, selecting "*some aspects of perceived reality and mak[ing] them more salient in the communicating text, in such a way as to promote a particular problem definition, causal interpretation, moral evaluation and/or treatment recommendation*" for the issue at hand (Entman 1993, 55; emphasis in original). As we saw in chapters 1 and 5, framing theory and analysis have become a significant part of the news analysis tradition during the past twenty years. However, framing theory is just as important for those engaged in news promotion, social influence, or social influence research (such as public relations practitioners, advertising consultants, marketing experts, and political communicators) (Bodtker and Jameson 1997; Culbert and McDonough 1990; Duhé and Zoch 1994; Gray 1997; Hallahan 1999; M. G. Knight 1999; Putnam and Holmer 1992; Wallack, Woodruff, Dorfman, and Diaz 1999). News promoters, seeking to influence journalists and ultimately the public, construct frames to influence perceptions of themselves, their organizations, or the policies, programs, or causes with which they are involved (see, e.g., Halloway 2000).

While news promoters may operate with various occupational titles, it is helpful to think of their activities directed at the news media as a form of public relations. And framing is an essential part of public relations practice. Hallahan writes:

> Public relations professionals fundamentally operate as frame strategists, who strive to determine how situations, attributes, choices, actions, issues, and responsibility should be posed to achieve favorable outcomes for clients. Framing decisions are perhaps the most important strategic choices made in a public relations effort. It is out of strategic framing that public relations communicators develop specific themes (i.e., key messages or arguments that might be considered by publics in the discussion of topics of mutual concern). Framing also provides the foundation for choosing images and other framing devices that can be

used to dramatize and reinforce key ideas. Finally, framing provides the basis for how people should be asked to evaluate information, make choices, or take action. (1999, 224)

Individuals observe situations, comparing them to past situations and seeking commonalities in order to project both societal roles and rules that govern human interactions. Such situational framing allows individuals to "locate, perceive, identify and label" (Goffman 1974, 21; see also W. A. Gamson 1985). Individuals recall past situations and interactions to bring understanding to present situations. For instance, news promoters may recall historical episodes, relating past behaviors and decision making to present circumstances in order to encourage news assemblers to draw similar conclusions. A president seeking to justify a declaration of war may compare the present circumstances to those faced at an earlier time, when entering a war was widely approved. During the days after September 11, 2001, political leaders as well as journalists compared the day's events to those at Pearl Harbor on December 7, 1941.

News promoters will frame attributes associated with the people, organizations, issues, policies, or positions in negative or positive terms. Such characterizations influence how others will evaluate the subjects. For example, if someone says a heart surgical procedure has a 60 percent success rate, it evokes different meanings than if the individual says the surgical procedure has a 40 percent failure rate. Research has shown "that positive framing of attributes consistently leads to more favorable evaluations of objects and attributes than negative framing" (Hallahan 1999, 213; Levin 1987; Levin, Schneider, and Gaeth 1998). Ericson, Baranek, and Chan (1989) argue that news promoters frequently utilize "hurrah words" when speaking to journalists; hurrah words are significant symbols evoked to portray legitimacy of governmental agencies and agency decision making. For instance, news promoters will argue that decisions have been made in the "interest of national security." Or they may argue that a particular piece of legislation assists in the renewal of "community" in America. Or they may justify legislative action by arguing that "American public opinion would not have it any other way."

When decision-makers are analyzing a variety of choices within a given policy domain, they are facing uncertainty and potential risk. Kahneman and Tversky (1979) have investigated the framing of choices, finding that decision-makers discuss such matters as "the acts, outcomes, and contingencies associated with a particular choice" (263; see also Kahneman and Tversky 1984). They discovered that individuals are far more concerned with loss prevention than they are with gains. "People tend to avoid risks when a choice is stated in terms of gains but will take greater risks when choices are stated in terms of losses" (Hallahan 1999, 214). This finding, which is now known as **prospect theory**, has held true through a variety of research environments. For instance, "mediators have been found to favor bargainers who frame issues in terms of losses rather than gains" (Hallahan 1999, 215).

On a practical level, companies seeking new customers have to overcome their prospective customers' comfort with maintaining the status quo by offering significant positive gains to those who switch. Recently, AT&T offered potential customers $50.00 to switch to their long-distance service, and it undercut the competition's service prices. Companies that already enjoy a positive relationship with their customers but recognize that their customers are receiving seductive lures to change to other companies will likely warn customers of the dangers of switching services. Digital telephone carriers frequently warn their customers that other carriers have dead service areas, fewer towers, or no international presence. Such negatives encourage customers to stay with the familiar.

Decision-makers often must frame actions in such a way that their audience chooses to comply with performing specific desired behaviors. For instance, a furniture store finances its own credit purchases. If customers pay off their bills within six months, they receive their loan interest back in full. If customers do not pay off their bills within the six-month time period, the interest they have paid the furniture company is lost to them. "Positive action (goal) framing involves focusing attention on obtaining a positive consequence (gain), whereas the negative frame focuses attention on avoiding the negative consequences (loss) resulting from not taking a particular action" (Hallahan 1999, 216). Studies have shown that "framing of actions in terms of negative consequences appears to have greater persuasive impact than framing that emphasizes positive consequences or gains" (Hallahan 1999, 216; see also Block and Keller 1995; Ganzach and Karahi 1995).

News promoters engage in issue framing to influence when and how policy decisions are made. Consider the distinction being made when groups describe themselves as pro-choice rather than pro-abortion. Pro-choice has a more positive spin than does pro-abortion. Campaigns geared at promoting sympathy for AIDS sufferers have different levels of success, depending on which AIDS groups are identified. People react differently to calls to help hemophiliacs than they do to calls to help intravenous drug users (Hallahan 1999). Similarly, when proponents of an education tax increase target the elderly, tax supporters will often find them more receptive if they emphasize educating children to keep them off the welfare rolls and out of the prison system rather than if they emphasize improvements in education for improvement's sake.

When assigning credit or blame, news promoters are framing responsibility. Who caused the problem? And who is responsible for fixing the problem? Government investigations may reveal that a particular industry is guilty of polluting the environment with a given toxic substance. Governmental leaders may then argue that the industry must be responsible for cleaning up the environment. In this way, governmental leaders appear both reasonable and fair.

Promoter Operating Philosophies

News promoters have operating philosophies that guide their interactions with news reporters. In other words, those involved in public relations activities are well aware of operating principles that assist them in their efforts to gain control over the news.

Scholars have often emphasized the importance of news promoters developing "cordial personal relations" (Dunn 1969) with journalists likely to cover their organization or cause. Being accessible to journalists, returning phone calls from journalists, and answering e-mails from journalists are just the first steps in earning working journalists' respect. News promoters willing to provide background information or research materials to a journalist covering a story will likely earn brownie points with the journalist, because the journalist doesn't have to take the time to do it. While it assists the journalist, it also works in favor of the news promoter. The background or research given to the journalist is from the perspective of the news promoter, improving the likelihood that the news story eventually generated will be consistent with the news promoter's position. In addition, this gives the news promoter

> an opportunity to present his version of the truth, to explain his position privately, and perhaps to elucidate candidly his motivations and his interpretation of the motivations of the opposition—factors he might not discuss in press releases, press conferences, or speeches. (Dunn 1969, 140)

Given the significance of the relationship between promoters and assemblers for the successful achievement of promoters' goals, smart promoters utilize impression-management strategies to build credibility especially with news assemblers and to avoid antagonizing them. Recognizing that reporters are their access points or contacts to other news assemblers in the news organization (e.g., editors or news producers) makes the promoters' relationships with reporters critical to the achievement of promotional goals. Promoters need their information used by reporters; therefore, they work to establish a reputation of fairness, building their credibility within the news community.

On the other hand, reporters count on promoters to notify them of potentially newsworthy occurrences and to provide them with background information, facts, public interest angles, other sources, photographs, videos, or other needed materials. In other words, promoters do much of the legwork or information gathering for news stories. They make the journalist's job far easier, and if a positive relationship is established between the promoter and the news assembler, it is far more likely that the promoter's event needs will be met, because the journalist recognizes that by fulfilling the promoter's event needs, his or her own event needs in terms of so many paragraphs of copy or so many minutes of video will also be met. In addition, news promoters often reward a news assembler by assigning the reporter "a most favored status." The news promoter may give an initial exclusive interview to a favored reporter when a story is breaking. Or a public relations director may arrange for a high-ranking corporate officer to be available for a public statement. A press secretary for a U.S. senator may make sure that the senator is available for a one-on-one interview with a favored reporter during a particularly hectic legislative day. In addition, a news release provided exclusively to a most favored media outlet is a substantial reward when the news release is concerning a truly significant occurrence. Or, in other cases, special news releases, which may go to multiple but noncompeting outlets, reward reporters who are cooperative. Promoters may also choose to leak information not for attribution to their favorite news assemblers.

In addition, promoters work to impression manage their personal relationship with news assemblers; they often will use ingratiation to secure a more positive working relationship, causing some researchers to characterize these professional interactions as "sweetheart relationships" (Molotch, Protess, and Gordon 1996; Johnstone, Slawski, and Bowman 1976). For instance, promoters often provide journalists with invitations to charitable dinner dances, with the tickets paid for by the sponsoring company.

Promoters may write thank-you notes to individual reporters or send glowing letters to their supervising editors, praising their work in covering an occurrence. In some situations, promoters may nominate news assemblers for prestigious journalism awards.

In addition, promoters often use other impression-management strategies to achieve their objectives. When releasing bad news such as a company shutdown, employee layoffs, or a poor financial rating, promoters may schedule press conferences for late Friday afternoons, when the regularly assigned reporters or beat reporters will find it difficult to cover it. If beat reporters are unable to attend, those whom the news organizations do send are likely to be at an informational disadvantage, in that they will not have any historical background on either the organization or its players. In addition, press conferences are often held so late in the day that even though beat reporters will be able to attend, there will be no time or opportunity for follow-up questions if news assemblers are to make publication or broadcast deadlines. And while news assemblers may recognize that they are being manipulated, they do not evaluate this tactical manipulation with the same degree of umbrage as they would a promoter deliberately misleading or deceiving them. For news assemblers, such maneuvers are merely the professional routines of the promoter.

Recently, some researchers have suggested that within this symbiotic relationship, it is the news promoter, especially in high-level political circles, who has the upper hand. Graber (1997) suggests that in such cases, reporters often fall victim to what she calls political pressures; she explains:

> Intensive, frequent contacts and the desire to keep associations cordial may lead to cozy relationships, which make critical detachment unlikely. The ability to woo reporters and elicit favorable media coverage is the mark of the astute politician. Reporters can rarely resist the blandishments of politicians for fear of alienating powerful and important news sources. (103)

Having said all that, it should be reiterated that successful relationships involving news assemblers and news promoters are fundamentally based on the development of mutual trust and respect. When either side violates the unwritten rules of their symbiotic relationship, serious organizational and personal consequences result. News promoters who lie or mislead news assemblers are either ignored or treated negatively in future news accounts. And news reporters who publish off-the-record information or who treat a source or organization unfairly will often find themselves "frozen out" of future news stories, for their sources will have dried up as a consequence of their unethical behavior (see Ericson, Baranek, and Chan 1989).

Frequently, news promoters assist journalists by making story suggestions (Cater 1959; Dunn 1969). News promoters will often point out emerging issues to their news assembler friends. Promoters provide information, anecdotes, or basic research to assist the journalist in evaluating the story idea. Often, promoters provide journalists with the names of experts or other news sources willing to assist in the development of the news story. These experts and news sources are selected by the promoter because he or she recognizes them as being sympathetic to the promoter's cause or position. Indeed, Wallack, Woodrugg, Dorfman and Diaz (1999) have argued that news promoters are far more successful when they "pitch stories, not issues" (43), for by pitching stories, they avoid appearing too overly self-interested. When news promoters pitch an issue, news reporters perceive them as having an ax to grind or a bias toward an issue position. However, when news promoters pitch stories, reporters perceive this as being more balanced, fitting their requirements for two sides in a news account and fulfilling their need for constructed news narratives.

News promoters anxious to preserve not only their own positive public image but also their organization's are far more likely to exercise information-flow control, controlling what information is released and by whom. Chief executives or agency heads often order subordinates not to speak with reporters, for if such executives or heads are going to be held accountable for what is said to the press, they are far more likely to want to be the ones speaking with the journalists.

And if an organization speaks with one voice, it is far more likely to be consistent. Journalists value consistency in working with news sources, for consistent presentations, in the eyes of working journalists, give the "impression of authenticity" (J. E. Combs 1980, 98). Furthermore, news sources who are consistent make it easier for journalists to "stereotype" them; stereotyping is "basically a process of definition based upon past experiences" (O'Hara 1961, 170). O'Hara explains:

> We first, define, and then we "see," that is we "see" things not as they are but as what our definition tells us they should be. And our definition reflects the sum total of our experiences with the thing being defined, which is brought to bear at the moment of perception. (1961, 170)

Stereotyping "enables the mass communicator to frame his message with the least amount of lost motion, and it enables the receiver to comprehend what is being communicated with equal speed and facility" (O'Hara 1961, 194; see also Gans 1979; Lippmann [1922] 1965).

At other times, news promoters will often exclude or withhold information from news assemblers, or they may discount or discredit information, facts, or contextual circumstances when discussing potential news items with news assemblers. Brown, Bybee, Wearden, and Straughan (1987) observed that "true power lies not only in the decision-making arena, but, perhaps most importantly, with those who can determine which issues will be debated" (54). Similarly, Schattschneider (1960) observed that "some issues are organized into politics while some issues are organized out" (18). But this information-flow control often involves more than just withholding either written or spoken words; such control may also include the restricting or even withholding of visual communication. For instance, broadcast journalist Daniel Schorr observed that at least for television news, the opportunity or lack thereof for taped footage illustrating the news story determines in no small way what becomes known to the general public. Schorr writes:

> Denying "picture opportunities" becomes the objective of those wishing to keep a story out of the public eye—almost literally—and creating such opportunities becomes the need of those who want the story told. In that sense, television becomes not merely the witness to a contest, but the arena for the contest, and perhaps the arbiter. (1977, 17; see also Altheide 1976; Epstein 1973)

Information control is also used to disguise backroom political behaviors. The wheeling and dealing often associated with legislative action and bureaucratic wrangling often dictate that the private culture of an organization be maintained. Such machinations, if exposed, might fuel public sentiment that governmental leaders are less than honorable. The news promoter's ability to keep things under wrap or secret is true power, for, as Tuchman (1977) has observed, "The power to keep an occurrence out of the news is power over the news" (53).

Sometimes "cordial personal relationships" turn into friendly personal relationships. While many reporters as well as news promoters will often warn against becoming social friends with each other (Blau 2001; Strentz 1989), the reality is that it does happen. Senator Ted Kennedy and his family have been longtime friends with veteran broadcast journalist Roger Mudd and his family, often vacationing together. And legendary CBS news anchor (and now print columnist) Walter Cronkite and his wife have been close personal friends with a long list of Democratic heavy hitters, including former president Bill Clinton and his wife, Hillary. Such friendships are rarely publicly acknowledged. However, such friendships and the recognition of such friendships are important in understanding the social construction of news. In a network news special, Roger Mudd queried Ted Kennedy about his marriage, his family problems, and the Chappaquiddick scandal when Kennedy decided to challenge incumbent president Jimmy Carter for the Democratic nomination for president. The news special was intended to put an end to the speculations and rumors surrounding Kennedy's controversial personal life. However, the well-intended Mudd couldn't protect Kennedy from his own self-destruction. Ironically, the interview was seen by political pundits as severely harming Kennedy's run for the nomination and as cementing Mudd's reputation as a hard-hitting journalist and a consummate interviewer. Kennedy's aloof, self-important, and often insensitive responses were further highlighted by his inappropriate attire, a navy blue blazer with a gold anchor embroidered on the pocket and leather Docksiders without socks. His nautical attire turned off many viewers, reminding them of his role in Mary Jo Kopechne's death off Martha's Vineyard years earlier.

News Consumers

While news assemblers and news promoters play important roles in the social construction of news, we cannot forget the importance of the news consumer in this process. News consumers select from mass media presentations, evaluate their selections, and ultimately decide to retain or ignore what was presented. Simply put, then, what consumers know about occurrences comes from the news assemblers' construction and dissemination of a crafted public event. News assemblers provide the mosaics of meanings with which news consumers ultimately craft their own public meanings. News consumers are the readers, viewers, or listeners of media outlets. However, the process of news construction does not end with dissemination; news consumers are active agents in the process as well. As we noted previously, consumers think about public events; they evaluate what they have learned through their own images of the world based upon their past experiences, present experiences, and future expectations. Consumers may seek out additional information, or they may choose to talk with others about the news. They may engage in arguments or debates with others concerning the meaning of the news. Through this process, consumers alter or redefine the public event through their interactions, ultimately negotiating the meaning they individually assign to the public event.

Consumer News Values

For the purposes of this work, however, the emphasis on the news consumer will be with regard to their perceived influence on the communication behaviors of both news promoters and news assemblers. What is judged to be relevant or suitable for inclusion in news narratives is "associated with audience expectations and . . . legitimated in terms of audience desires" (Chibnall 1981, 87). After all, news is a business, and news stories are products; if no one wanted to buy the product, then there would be no news. Consequently, news narratives are constructed with the news consumer in mind.

Successful news assemblers and their organizations take into account the desires of their audiences. News values in no small way mirror what news assemblers believe to be desired by the news audience. If audiences enjoy conflict, they get conflict. If they enjoy sex, they get sex. "News values distill what people find interesting and important to know about" (Shoemaker and Reese 1991, 90). P. Schlesinger writes:

> Production routines embody assumptions about audiences. . . . When it comes
> to thinking about the kind of news most relevant to "the audience," newsmen

exercise their news judgement rather than going out and seeking specific information about the composition, wants or tastes of those who are being addressed. (1978, 115–116)

Similarly, successful news promoters must determine if the information
they hold and wish to disseminate does in fact have "values consonant with
the needs of the mass media audience" (Gieber 1960–1961, 77). In other
words, if the relevant information that a promoter holds is salient or important to the news media's audience, then the news promoter will seek access to
news assemblers, with the likelihood of news assemblers' interest in the topic
being high. If, however, a news promoter recognizes that the information is
only important to the promoter's own personal, organizational, or political
goals, the strategic news promoter will first use advertorials or advocacy advertising to disseminate the desired information, recognizing that news assemblers will have little or no interest in disseminating the information. Typically such advocacy tactics become the fodder of news reporters exploring
why the organization devoted resources to advertising organizational viewpoints, achievements, or policies. In this way, the news media's reporting
about the advocacy advertising expands the sphere of those knowledgeable
about the organization's information needs; thus the news promoter ultimately achieves his or her objectives, even though it had to be done through
a more circuitous and expensive route than routine news generation.

Consumers' Prospective and Retrospective Potential
Uses of News Content

News promoters must be highly strategic in their selection of information
to be made public, for they must consider both the "prospective and retrospective potential uses" of their promotions (Molotch and Lester 1974, 104).
In other words, news promoters must consider how various promotional
strategies will play with both the news assemblers and the news consumers.
When considering various promotional strategies, news promoters analyze
their own goals and objectives and what the execution of the promotions
would likely achieve or what information environment would be created. For
example, a public information campaign director for the Centers for Disease
Control might choose to hold a press conference to release information about
a public health issue. The information presented will disclose a particular
health danger or threat, as well as the means by which the public may avoid
failing victim to this danger. Thus, the conference is held with the assumption
that new information about negative health issues will be considered newsworthy and will therefore be covered by the news media, creating the social

multiplier effect once their coverage is disseminated. The director assumes that consumers will attend to the coverage out of self-interest, and that as rational decision-makers they will alter their behavior in order to avoid known health risks. In another situation, an organized group decides to hold a protest march around city hall to dramatize its displeasure over the routing of a major thoroughfare near a residential neighborhood and community school. The march is selected by the group because its leaders recognize that the disruption of the routine around city hall will generate media interest, whereas simply stating their displeasure would likely draw very little, if any. In this way, the group's social disruption of societal routines expands the range of consumers exposed to their story.

Promoters, in deciding how to promote their needs or interests, identify "what-will-be-made-of-it and what-it-really-was-all along" for each potential promotional activity (Molotch and Lester 1974, 104). In other words, what will news assemblers and consumers make of it? And what needs or interests will the promotional effort likely fulfill for the promoter? The necessity of such considerations is illustrated by the Nixon administration's public behavior during the Vietnam War. The White House press secretary or a Pentagon spokesperson would announce bombing missions in Vietnam, describing them as "limited" and directed at "select" military targets. But news reporters in the field, observing firsthand the bombing, reported "indiscriminate massive bombing" (Molotch and Lester 1974, 104). Such public inconsistencies ultimately created a significant credibility problem for the Nixon administration. Promoters, at times, may well publicize the activities of others, particularly when the promotion of those activities presents the promoter in a positive light. For example, hospitals may promote or sponsor health fairs or fundraising events for charitable organizations devoted to health issues. While the hospital does not directly benefit from the charitable organization's activity, the promotion indirectly aids the hospital by spreading goodwill among community members and with officers of the charitable organization.

Corporate philanthropy, sponsorships, and other outreach promotions are designed to improve the public image of the promoter while directly benefiting others. In Atlanta, Georgia, during breast cancer awareness month, one hospital formed a sponsoring partnership with a popular television news show to promote breast self-examinations for women. Such a partnership benefits both the hospital and the television station, ensuring the social multiplier effect without additional media costs. An elected official will often donate time to charitable events not only to help a worthy cause but also to promote him- or herself as a civic-minded person. And, because charitable events attract media attention, the elected official benefits from publicity generated by the charity and disseminated by the news media.

In other situations, promoters may expose the corrupt or dangerous practices of competitors, making such practices "public events" and shaping the public's knowledge of the competitor. This practice elevates the promoter in the eyes of the public, because the promoter is perceived as being a guardian or protector of the public, and the credibility and public appraisal of the competitor is significantly reduced, ultimately benefiting the promoter (see Molotch and Lester 1974, 104–105). In an Alabama congressional race, the Democratic primary challenger, Artur Davis, publicized the Democratic incumbent's introduction of a bill in Congress to forgive nations either condoning or sponsoring terrorism after the September 11 attacks. Alabamians were in no mood to forgive the likes of Libya, Iraq, and Afghanistan, especially with the Alabama National Guard and Alabama military reservists fighting prominently in the War on Terror. And, as a consequence, Davis defeated the incumbent, Earl Hilliard.

Molotch and Lester's Typology of Public Events

Molotch and Lester (1974) also developed a typology of public events: routine events, accidents, scandals, and serendipity. This typology proves useful in understanding why happenings become events, how news promoters and assemblers interact, and how various occurrences are evaluated and framed differently by news assemblers.

For Molotch and Lester, **routine events** are typified by happenings that "are purposive accomplishments and by the fact that the people who undertake the happening (whom we call 'effectors') are identical with those who promote them into events" (1974, 106). A mayoral press conference or a public address at the local auditorium is such a routine event. However, happenings such as a public address do not necessarily become public events unless the news assemblers define or judge the happening as being newsworthy and therefore potentially "a news story." Promoters of happenings must have access to news assemblers, or the second stage of news construction, before the happenings can be shaped into public events. Molotch and Lester (1974) have identified three subtypes of routine events by their accessibility to the news assemblers:

(a) those where the event promoters have habitual access to news assemblers;
(b) those where the event promoters are seeking to disrupt the routine access of others to assemblers in order to make events of their own; and
(c) those where the access is afforded by the fact that the promoters and news assemblers are identical. (107)

Some individuals or groups do indeed enjoy habitual access to the news media in that their mere presence attracts news assemblers by virtue of who or what they are. Government officials such as the president, the Speaker of the House, or the Senate majority leader have habitual access by virtue of the office or position they hold. Major corporate figures such as Bill Gates of Microsoft or Steve Jobs of Apple Computers also have habitual access. And certainly Ross Perot and Donald Trump, by virtue of their corporate clout, enormous wealth, and flamboyant personalities, easily obtain news media access. Celebrities such as Oprah Winfrey, Puff Daddy, Michael Jackson, and Madonna are able to command habitual access as well, because the news assemblers recognize that the public has an insatiable appetite for news concerning currently "hot" or popular entertainers.

On occasion, those who have habitual access to the news media will have to compete with others who also have habitual access. Or those with habitual access will have to compete with those groups who figuratively explode onto the media scene either by accidents or by deliberate disruptions. The news hole for any day is limited by what the news organization is able to effectively cover. But, as Molotch and Lester indicate:

> Intra- or inter-group competitions withstanding, habitual access is generally found among those with extreme wealth or other institutionally-based sources of power. Indeed, this power is both a result of the habitual access and a continuing cause of such access. Routine access is one of the important sources and sustainers of existing power relationships. (1974, 107)

Often access is granted to public officials because of their position, with little or no consideration as to the newsworthiness of the happening. Often such precipitating occurrences are pseudo-events or media events, which are happenings created by promoters for the sole purpose of being reported in the news media. Frequently such pseudo-events are symbolic gestures by public officials to reassure the public that the government is both conscientious and effective in managing "the people's business." When presidents or first ladies visit the sites of tornadoes or flood-devastated areas, the happening is judged as newsworthy because of their position or status. Such happenings have symbolic importance, however trivial we might sometimes consider them to be.

Very few individuals or groups are able to maintain habitual access to the news media "across time and issue," for the news assemblers' evaluation of individuals or groups will change across time. Certainly, the president of the United States has habitual access; however, even the president at times has been denied access to network broadcast time for a presidential address, because network executives after examining the text of the president's remarks judged them to be unnewsworthy. Ironically, the news executives' refusal to disrupt prime-time programming became a news story because of the news organizations' shared assessment of the address as mere presidential self-promotion. Other groups such as environmental organizations, women's rights, or gun-control lobbyists will enjoy habitual access at some points in time, but their access to news assemblers will, in Molotch and Lester's words, "ebb and flow over time and place" (1974, 108). "For this reason, the ideal typical routine event is taken to be the generating of a public experience by those in positions to have continual access to asserting the importance and factual status of 'their' occurrences" (Molotch and Lester 1974, 108).

In addition to persons of wealth and power, other individuals and groups will generate access to the news assemblers by their disruptive acts, characterized by their violence, shock value, or inconvenience to others. "Thus, the relatively powerless disrupt the social world to disrupt the habitual forms of event-making" (Molotch and Lester 1974, 108; see also M. E. McCombs and Shaw 1977). The Montgomery bus boycott or the Tuskegee shop boycott are two examples from the civil rights movement when African Americans in those Alabama cities refused to ride buses or shop in local stores, resulting in economic disruption or hardship on white bus and shop owners. And for this reason, the news media gave access to civil rights leaders who had organized the boycotts. In Danville, Virginia, civil rights protesters assembled in the city hall, lying down in the corridors and refusing either to leave or to stand up, thus disrupting routine governmental services and ultimately generating media access (see chapter 7).

Unfortunately some groups use violence such as bombings to generate news media attention to their cause. The Oklahoma City, Oklahoma, federal building bombing; the Atlanta, Georgia, Olympics Park bombing; and the Birmingham, Alabama, abortion clinic bombing were all eventually recognized as issue-related protests or domestic terrorism. Gay rights activists who drenched themselves with ketchup or animal blood to graphically demonstrate the urgent need for federal dollars for HIV research and an eventual cure for the autoimmune disorder crafted such events to shock others, thus gaining access to the news media. And animals rights activists who throw paint on women who wear fur coats or leather suits, destroying the garments in the process, creating economic loss and inconvenience, use such incidents to gain media access for their cause. Such occurrences are "antiroutine" and, therefore, groups who commit these happenings temporarily gain access to the news media. "This 'obvious' disruption of normal functioning and its challenge to the received social world prompts the coverage of the mass media. The disruptive occurrence becomes an event because it is a problem for the relatively powerful" (Molotch and Lester 1974, 108; see also Myerhoff 1972).

However, unless such disruptive occurrences have identifiable organizers or leaders, the disruption and how the police, National Guard, or other relevant authority groups handle the disruption will be the news story (see Bennett 1983; Tuchman 1981b). Unless groups have identifiable "leaders," the news assemblers will not recognize them as "news sources" or promoters, and the protest group will not have "a voice" in the news content (Molotch and Lester 1974; Sale 1973). For example, until Martin Luther King Jr. and Malcolm X emerged as two civil rights leaders representing two distinct constituencies, it was rare that news stories contained any reasons for civil rights demonstrations, for the news assemblers presented such happenings as disruptions and the societal response to the disruptions rather than as a reasoned happening to highlight social injustices. Similarly, few student activists who protested the Vietnam War were ever given a substantive voice in the nation's news media (Sale 1973).

In some circumstances, the news media will ignore disruptive activities for fear of their coverage precipitating additional disruptions or copycat acts. In effect, news organizations exercise self-censorship in that while the happening fits the journalistic definition of news, they choose not to report it because of what they see to be potentially significant negative societal effects. "The purposiveness underlying all routine events can be selectively perceived at appropriate moments to justify canceling a story because it is viewed as promoted precisely for its media effects" (Molotch and Lester 1974, 108). During the 1960s, campus protests were often ignored by the news media for fear of promoting such behavior. And, Molotch and Lester conclude, "When important people see a potential event as too costly, given their purposes at hand, there are various resources for eliminating it" (1974, 109). For example in 1998, the U.S. Congress launched an investigation into crime on college and university campuses across the country and into the college and university compliance with the Student "Right to Know" and the Campus Security Act of 1990, which required the publishing of crime statistics by school officials. This investigatory action was precipitated by the pressure put on legislators by their constituents who were concerned by their college-age children's victimization while attending college. The eventual congressional report exposed that colleges and universities either were, as a matter of policy, not releasing crime statistics for their campuses or deliberately misrepresenting or incorrectly reporting those crime statistics that were released; or were, in collusion with the local news media, choosing not to make such information public, for fear of negatively affecting student recruitment, continued enrollment, and the resulting generation of dollars for both the institution of higher learning and the community. In short, it became apparent that economic interests had prevailed over safety interests in college and university locales across the nation. Because of these findings, Congress moved to expand the original 1990 act, renaming it the Jeanne Clery Act after the Lehigh University student who was raped and murdered in her dormitory in 1986. The revised act requires not only campus police but also other administrative personnel to publicly report crime statistics of which they are aware; for example, disciplinary boards or committees must also now report crime statistics such as alcohol or drug abuse and weapons violations. It took not one but two congressional efforts to effectively force colleges and universities to accurately report crime statistics and make them available to the public through either published news reports or other means.

Under some circumstances, news assemblers themselves generate news ideas. In this situation, they serve as both promoters and assemblers. They are one and the same. A reporter who decides to do a feature story on a woman who weaves pine straw into baskets is an example of direct access (Molotch and Lester 1974). Or a reporter may choose to investigate something that seems odd to his or her everyday knowledge of the world and may uncover criminal acts or corruption. In such a situation, the reporter again serves as both promoter and assembler.

Molotch and Lester (1974) distinguish between routine events and accidents in that for **accidents**, "(1) the underlying happening is not intentional, and (2) those who promote it as a public event are different from those whose activity brought the happening about" (109). For instance, a train engineer continues on his normal route unaware of a broken railroad spur up ahead; the train derails, causing severe damage to the train and killing or injuring a number of passengers and crew members. Although the engineer was purposefully running the train, he did not intend for it to derail. Thus, the train derailment was unintentional. And it is not the train engineer who brings it to the attention of the news media through promotional efforts. Rather, it is the police, medical personnel, firefighters, rescue workers, or the corporation who owns the train who promotes the event. Or the promoter might be a retired lady who lives next to the train tracks where the train derailed, and she witnessed the happening and called the news media.

Accidents will often have consequences far greater than the initial happening, or what I call accident fallout. For example, beyond the news story concerning the train wreck, the loss of life and personal injuries, and the economic loss to the corporation is the larger story of the general disrepair of the railroads in the state of X or perhaps in the overall U.S. rail system. Thus, in Molotch and Lester's words, accidents have a way of fostering "revelations which are otherwise deliberately obfuscated by those with the resources to create routine events" (1974, 109). In our example, both the railroad company that owns the railways and the government agency that inspects them are exposed for either their wrongdoing or negligence, two behaviors the organizations are very unlikely to promote themselves. In some circumstances, an accident may bring to light personal attributes or behaviors otherwise not known or recognized by the public. Ted Kennedy's Chappaquiddick car accident provided an opportunity for the news media to explore dimensions of his character, lifestyle, marital relationship, and behavior that otherwise would never have emerged. When such accidents occur, people who have power will exercise it in order to remove the accident from the public eye. They will try to "define the accident out of public politics" (Molotch and Lester 1974, 109). When accidents occur, elite groups relevant to the accident are often caught unprepared to publicly deal with the accident. And at such times, such groups often present contradictory versions of reality before eventually settling on a public stance. For example, when an airline loses a plane at sea, the Federal Aviation Administration, the Coast Guard, the Federal Bureau of Investigation, the National Transportation Safety Board, the airline itself, air traffic controllers, the maker of the plane, the governor of the state of origin, and so on will all be contributing to the public dialogue, resulting in chaos, misinformation, and ultimately public confusion. In such times, powerful groups or actors begin to try to make sense of what happened and then fashion that information in a manner by impression-management strategies that best serve their own interests. Often such actors begin assigning fault for the accident in order to avoid negative evaluations of their own domain and activities. The actors try to "restore traditional meanings" or images of themselves that were previously held by the public before the accident (Molotch and Lester 1974, 109). For example, in one recent airplane disaster, it was suggested that it wasn't either the airline's fault or the airplane maker's fault; rather, these powerful corporate actors presented the accident to the public as the result of a copilot's suicide, despite a lack of evidence of depression or problems normally associated with suicide such as economic hardships, alcohol or drug dependency, or career setbacks. Thus the airline and the airplane manufacturer engaged in impression-management behavior to shift blame from themselves. However, as Molotch and Lester (1974) have observed:

> In their realization as events, accidents are far less contingent than are routine events on the event needs of the powerful. Given the inherent drama, sensation, and typicality of accidents, it is difficult to deny their existence; and typically nonimportant groups can more easily hold sway in the temporal demarcation process. (109–110)

For instance, an eyewitness who sees a plane exploding in midair and subsequently talks with news reporters will have a significant role in the telling of the story.

However, not all accidents are created equal. Hirsch (1969) has shown that an incident involving the accidental emission of deadly nerve gas into the air at the Dugway Proving Ground (in Utah) received little news coverage. Yet an oil spill off the coast of California received a huge amount of media attention (Lester 1971). The difference—the nerve gas accident did not have powerful visuals, and it was the U.S. government that was the culprit in the nerve gas incident—further illustrates the impact of the powerful. It is also important to note that accidents closer to the news organization's market will receive far more news attention than accidents that occur far away in another country. A plane that crashes in the United States receives far more news media attention in the United States than one that occurs in China. Yet a plane crash in another country resulting from terrorist activities will generate significant news coverage in the United States. Or a plane crash in another country with powerful people on board, particularly if they are American, will also receive significant news coverage in the United States. And, as Molotch and Lester (1974) have observed, "All this attests to the fact that all events are socially constructed and their 'newsworthiness' is not contained in their objective features" (110).

The third type of public event, **scandals**, "involves an occurrence which becomes an event through the intentional activity of individuals (we call them 'informers') who for one reason or another do not share the event-making strategies of the occurrence effectors" (Molotch and Lester 1974, 110). Frequently, the publication or broadcasting of the event surprises the original effectors. In order for a scandal to occur, an individual with some degree of credibility, legitimacy, and power derived from either occupying an influential position in the organization or having firsthand experience, or from hearing eyewitness accounts or effector revelations, comes forward. Or, in other situations, informers are privy to memos, letters, tapes, videos, or other forms of permanently recorded communication artifacts detailing the behavior of the effector because they occupy a position within an organization that guarantees access to such information, for example, an executive assistant or secretary (see Molotch and Lester 1974). Linda Tripp, the White House secretary who revealed President Clinton's affair with a White House intern, is a good example.

It should be noted, however, that accidents and scandals provide a unique opportunity for not only news reporters but their consumers as well, for it is only during such events that reporters are able to "transcend" routine news work, "allowing access to information which is directly hostile to those groups who typically manage public event making" (Molotch and Lester 1974, 111).

Similarly, Bachrach and Baratz (1962) and Edelman (1964) have suggested that only under these rare conditions can one truly observe the "second face of power" or the real power dynamics (Molotch and Lester 1974, 111). Observing the news coverage of Monica Lewinsky before she presented herself to the public in a one-hour Barbara Walters special, it is easy to see President Clinton's foes and allies scrambling to redefine her story and her to their own advantage. She was depicted in a wide variety of ways by news sources, sometimes as a lovesick teenager who worshiped the president, sometimes as a sexually precocious but innocently naïve young woman, and at other times as either a psycho-stalker or a promiscuous sexual predator who was "after" the president.

Molotch and Lester (1974) identify a fourth type of event called a **serendipity** that shares some of the same properties as their accident and routine categories. "The serendipity event has an underlying happening which is unplanned (as with accidents) but is promoted by the effector himself (as with routine events)" (Molotch and Lester 1974, 110). For instance, hypothetically, if the Alpine Hospital Chain, a twenty-four-site hospital chain operating in three Rocky Mountain states, decides to fund the National Head Injury Association's (NHIA) fundraising events for a three-year period, the resulting publicity and favorable public commentary will naturally benefit the image of the Alpine Hospital Chain, in addition to improving the awareness of brain injury as a societal problem and of the brain-injured among the residents of the three-state area. The fundraising events provide opportunities for the disabled and the able-bodied to participate in supervised winter snow sports and spring and summer horseback riding with the accompaniment and attention of caring instructors and health care professionals. News accounts of these events highlight that with new drugs and innovative rescue and resuscitation procedures, more and more of the brain-injured are surviving. As a result of these modern medical practices, many experience a full recovery; others, however, need months or years of physical and occupational therapy; and for those most seriously injured survivors, around-the-clock, full-time health care workers will be required.

A couple (an eighty- and a seventy-eight-year-old) watch the news coverage of the first Alpine-NHIA Winter Snow Spectacular, and they are moved by the scenes of disabled children creating snow angels as they play. The man and his wife learn of the wondrous medical strides that benefited so many, eventually returning them to productive lives; but, ironically, such advances have saved others only to leave them in a comatose or near-comatose state. Forty years ago, the couple's only daughter was brain-injured and within a matter of hours died from an automobile accident. The plight of the brain-injured and their families is all too real for the couple. After talking about the

NHIA-Alpine alliance, the couple decides to leave their estate, which is estimated to be worth $7.5 million, to the NHIA on the condition the money is to be used to construct a national research center and brain rehabilitation center at one of the centrally located Alpine Hospitals. This would be a serendipity. And it is very likely that both Alpine and the NHIA would publicize such an occurrence.

In Summary

Molotch and Lester (1974) write that news, rather than depicting or reflecting an objective world, merely showcases "the practices of those having the power to determine the experience of others" (111). Their critical analysis of the news process, as well as my own is not intended to ridicule the practicing journalist or journalism as a vocation, but rather is intended to present the reader with the tools not only to understand the news but also to see how the news product comes to be shaped and presented as it is, and—even more importantly—why. To understand these three things is political empowerment, for the reader is able to read between the lines, identifying the currents and forces necessarily operating to have brought a particular news product's existence about. Molotch and Lester (1974) recommend "examining media for the event needs and the methods through which those with access come to determine the experience of the publics" (111). Perhaps our attention, then, should not always be on the "objective world" but on the "purposes which underlie the strategies of creating one reality instead of another," for such an analysis is likely to reveal far more than our own observations of physical or social occurrences (Molotch and Lester 1974, 111).

7

Standardization in Framing

Source Standardization

SOURCE STANDARDIZATION REFERS TO THE PRACTICE of journalists using the same group of informants or interviewees over and over again. In effect, journalists often share a common dependency on a select group of informants (Entman 1981). Because journalists seek out "experts" or "qualified informants," they depend on the "centralization of information in bureaucracies and the generation of facts by bureaucrats" (Tuchman 1981a, 88; Entman 1981; Noelle-Neumann 1973).

News beats also invite journalists to use formulaic metaphors or ritualized metaphors in crafting their stories. T. E. Cook (1996b) observed that presidents order, judges rule, scientists make breakthroughs, Congress legislates, and doctors cure—all of these are routine narrative structures often provided to the journalist through source-promoted events. But it is not just "people act" frames that journalists use; rather, they provide the audience with complete, self-sustaining narratives. Danielian (1992) writes:

> Because competitive organizational and economic imperatives necessitate stories that can maintain large audiences, newsmakers believe that images should be easily consumed, and this emphasis leads to stories that best fit into traditional and easily recognized narrative plot lines. The resulting coverage tends to focus on the event rather than on the issues and the underlying conditions involved, the individual rather than the group, conflict rather than consensus, and the facts that advance the story line rather than those that explain the situation. (77; see also Epstein 1973; Gitlin 1980; Nimmo and Combs 1983)

Reliance on Elites and Officialdom

Consequently, journalists rely on elites who meet journalistic norms for source selection. First, elites satisfy the availability criterion in that they tend to be geographically close and socially similar to working journalists; and elites have the power and resources necessary to attract and sometimes command journalistic attention. In addition, elites often speak officially for large organizations, constraining subordinates and exercising information flow control to the news media (see Brown, Bybee, Wearden, and Straughan 1987; Gans 1979; Stempel and Culbertson 1984). And elites meet the journalistic norms for source selection in that they meet the suitability criterion. Elites occupy power positions within organizations and are more likely to meet the "standard definitions of reliability, trustworthiness, authoritativeness and articulateness" (Brown, Bybee, Wearden, and Straughan 1987, 46; see also Gans 1979). Consequently, the news media "favor high prestige sources" (Lasorsa and Reese 1990, 60). "Those with economic or political power are more likely to influence news reports than those who lack power" (Shoemaker and Reese 1991, 151). Journalists view these bureaucratic sources as legitimate, because the "facts produced by centralized bureaucratic sources are assumed to be essentially correct and disinterested" (Tuchman 1981a, 89). Nowhere is source standardization more evident than in the use and misuse of what Soley (1992) has called the news shapers.

News Shapers

In 1992, Lawrence Soley published his enlightening work, *The News Shapers: The Sources Who Explain the News.* News shapers should be distinguished from newsmakers, according to Soley. "News makers, such as government officials, are individuals who are the legitimate focus of the news. They are distinguishable from news shapers, who provide background or analyses for viewers but are not the focus of the news" (Soley 1992, 14; see also Nimmo and Combs 1992; Nimmo and Newsome 1997). They are often described by news organizations as "a leading political scientist," "an acknowledged expert," or "a noted foreign policy observer and scholar." In short, news organizations bestow upon these chosen news shapers the air of objectivity and detachment and, thus, legitimacy. Soley writes:

> They are presented as nonpartisan, even if they have long histories of partisanship. Some news shapers are former government officials; some are former politicians. Despite this, they are frequently described with impartial titles. . . . Their sole function is to provide commentary or analysis, although their statements are never described as such. (1992, 2)

David Gergen is a prime example of a news shaper. A popular visitor on network news and on CNN, "David Gergen is the quintessential news shaper, because he attended and taught at a private, Ivy League university, was associated with a former Republican administration, worked at a conservative Washington, D.C., 'think tank,' and carries the mantle of journalist" for serving as the editor for both *Public Opinion* magazine and *U.S. News & World Report* magazine (Soley 1992, 2–3). In fact, Gergen worked under three Republican administrations (Nixon, Ford, and Reagan), and he served as campaign adviser to George H. W. Bush. After Bush lost his bid for a second term, Gergen went to work for the troubled Democratic administration of Bill Clinton, who faced a recalcitrant Congress and sagging popularity ratings. Interestingly, Gergen's willingness to work for a Democratic administration further endeared him to the American news media, for they took his willingness to work for a Democrat as evidence of his objectivity.

Page, Shapiro, and Dempsey (1987) found that news shapers, or so-called experts' commentary significantly influence public opinion shifts among network television viewers. "They shape the news that is delivered to a politically immobilized public. Experts provide citizens with a superficial knowledge about events, and this knowledge becomes a substitute for political involvement" (Soley 1992, 27). And such news presentations soothe the news consumer, for they are comforted that these so-called experts are on top of things, demonstrating their "commanding knowledge about social problems and processes" (Soley 1992, 27). If they are on the job, then an ordinary citizen need not get involved. The use of news shapers on television news increased threefold in the 1980s, the presence of news shapers doubled in newspaper stories during the same time period, and their use appears not to be abating (Soley 1994).

This is troubling in that many of these news shapers are deemed expert simply because other news organizations at one time or another have used them (Soley 1992). Since the terrorist attacks of September 11, 2001, news consumers have frequently been treated to commentary on political terrorism provided by Ronald Payne. Payne, a former Fleet Street reporter, has authored a number of paperback books on terrorism; however, none of his books are peer reviewed, nor do they have footnotes or documentation as to his sources or his purported evidence. In short, Payne wrote paperback books asserting that he knew a great deal about political terrorism, and he was picked up by news organizations needing a news shaper to talk about terrorism (Soley 1992).

According to Soley (1992), Washington reporters are members of what C. Wright Mills (1956) called the **power elite**. The power elite is multiple interlocking networks "whose members know one another, see one another socially and at business, and so, in making decisions, take one another into account" (Mills 1956, 11). As recently as 2002, Moore, Sobieraj, Whitt, Mayorova, and Beaulieu in an analysis of interlocking elites found in corporate, government, and nonprofit sectors reaffirmed the existence of a power elite in America.

According to Soley, prestige reporters or those working for the top news outlets attended the same elite, private, or Ivy League colleges and universities (or other highly prestigious institutions of higher learning such as Stanford University, University of Virginia, and so on) as did the very top of the political elite in Washington. Family ties explain much of the influence patterns found in Washington, D.C., but even if reporters were not born into the "first families," they can earn their way into the upper echelons by the prominence of their alma mater or by the sponsorship of someone already a member of the power elite. For example, Henry Kissinger, a working-class electrician, became the favorite of McGeorge Bundy after Kissinger entered Harvard; and it was Bundy who secured Kissinger's place in power circles after his graduation. Domhoff (1970) has shown that such prestige reporters establish the journalistic standards for those working for less prestigious news organizations. Consequently, the prestige reporters' selection of certain news shapers is noticed and picked up by less prestigious journalists.

"The news shapers, like the reporters who use them, are members of the power elite" (Soley 1992, 143). They work together and play together. Consequently, prestige reporters seek out the views of other members of the power elite, whether they are current or past government officials, Ivy League professors, corporate executives, top military or intelligence leaders, or the directors of think tanks. And, to complicate matters further, a power elite revolving door exists in Washington, D.C., where it becomes quite difficult to type the players at any one point in time. "Reporters become think tank analysts, government officials, or professors, government officials become think tank analysts, professors, and reporters, and think tank analysts become reporters, professors, and government officials" (Soley 1992, 143; Domhoff 1990). The likes of a David Gergen or a Bill Schneider (CNN commentator) provide ample evidence of this revolving-door career path. While many prestige reporters may individually be liberal (Lichter, Rothman, and Lichter 1986), they are submerged in a power elite where conventional wisdom rules. And conventional wisdom favors the status quo, reinforcing a conservative approach to government and to policy making (Hoynes and Croteau 1989; Whitney, Fritzler, Jones, Mazzarella, and Rakow 1989). And news shapers, as members of the status quo power elite, will naturally dominate political discourse whether it occurs on television newscasts, during congressional hearings, in Ivy League lecture halls, or in think tank publications (Soley 1992). Soley (1994) found that newspaper journalists who are members of the prestige press not only prefer Ivy League experts, but they also prefer those with administrative authority, using deans or center directors rather than mere professors.

Bennett (1996) observes that U.S. reporters' overwhelming emphasis on public officials is at least partially explained by the reporters' understanding that the American government is a representative democracy where "power is transferred from the people to public officials" (375). And, thus, the news media feel a social responsibility to keep the public informed about their political leaders' actions in order that people might fully exercise their constitutional right to reject political leaders who fail to adequately represent their viewpoints in governmental affairs.

In addition, reporters focus on "official voices" in order to avoid charges of personal bias. Sigal (1973) wrote:

> Even when the journalist is in a position to observe an event directly, he remains reluctant to offer interpretations of his own, preferring instead to rely on his news sources. For the reporter, in short, news is not what has happened, but what someone says has happened. (69)

In addition to avoiding charges of personal bias, journalists are often placed in the position of reporting about matters that they know little or absolutely nothing about. Therefore, in order to avoid looking ignorant in the eyes of their editor and their readers, journalists rely on official sources or experts to tell the story. David Halberstam (1979) recalled foreign policy reporters' reliance on official sources during the Vietnam War:

> If after their arrival in Washington they wrote stories about foreign policy, they did not dare inject their own viewpoints, of which they had none, or their own expertise, of which they also had none. Rather they relied almost exclusively on what some American or possibly British official told them at a briefing or at lunch. The closer journalists came to great issues, the more vulnerable they felt. (517–518)

But it is not just in foreign affairs that reporters are often at a disadvantage. After one victorious congressional primary, I, as the political consultant, was, along with the candidate, his wife, and campaign manager, meeting and greeting celebrants as they entered the campaign headquarters. A broadcast journalist who had interviewed me several times for political commentary spotted me as he came through the door, and he moved past the others, ignoring their outstretched hands to get to me. In a series of rapid-fire declarations and questions, the reporter illustrated the dangers of ignorance in domestic politics: "Hi. I know I'm supposed to be here. My assignment editor sent me. Who is the candidate and did he win? What is he running for?" On another occasion, a television news program arranged through the university's press office to interview me for a campaign story involving false and misleading political advertising by religious groups. The press officer told me to meet the reporter at a specific spot on the university's quad. Seated on a stone bench, I watched the reporter arrive, dragging a camera case and a light kit to the arranged interview. Between his teeth, he had a yellow pencil and a reporter's notebook. Setting down the camera and the light, he spat out the pencil and notebook, asking, "Look, I don't know why I'm here. You must be someone important. Who are you? And what is it that you know?" After listening to my rather halting explanation, he then queried, "So I'm supposed to be asking you stuff about false ads?" It is little wonder that journalists (particularly local reporters with extremely limited resources) rely on their sources. Zaller and Chiu have concluded that "dependence on sources goes beyond the need to have someone to quote; it is one of the most ingrained features of modern journalism" (1996, 386; Althaus, Edy, and Phalen 1994).

Negrine (1996) has observed that this reliance on official sources, who often have their own ax to grind in their public comments, has severely limited the critical debate of public issues. He notes that journalists are not seeking information but sources, and this orientation has led to their ignoring less exciting but often illuminating government documents or academic research. By routinely avoiding the tedious, the difficult to find and digest, the news organizations artificially reduce the readily available pool of information, filter whatever information they do collect through their professional judgment screens as to newsworthiness, and subsequently cull the newsworthy from the unnewsworthy (but often "providing adequate explanatory frameworks"). The news media are ultimately unable, unwilling, and often unprepared "to confront and make sense of the complexity of causes and effects which surround events and happenings in the contemporary world" (Negrine 1996, 16). And the news media's preference for exciting, often inflammatory sources may also prove to work against the news organization's or reporter's credibility. Rouner, Slater, and Buddenbaum (1999) report that audience members often do not distinguish between news story bias and source bias. Rather, if they perceive a news source as being biased, they assume that because a journalist chose the source, then the journalist is guilty of manipulating the content of the news story in the selection of sources.

News reporters assigned to the same beat in the nation's capital, for instance, tend to rely on the same types of people or even the exact same people for information (Manoff 1987). Tuchman explains that the working journalist is "enmeshed in . . . bureaucratized and routinized interactions between and among workers in legitimated institutions" (Tuchman 1981a,

88). Zoch and Turk (1998) found that newspapers, whether those on the national level or those on the local level (which are heavily influenced by wire services), primarily use male elites or men in executive positions as their sources (Brown, Bybee, Wearden, and Straughan 1987; Bybee 1990; Hansen, Ward, Connors, and Neuzil 1994; Hernandez 1995). In short, male sources far outweigh female sources even in areas considered traditionally female domains such as education (Zoch and Turk 1998). Zoch and Turk (1998) concluded that the world view presented by the nation's media "would have audiences and consumers believe that women are virtually without power and thus have no access to information that would be of use to the public" (771). Even within the context of candidates for political office, early research indicated that women were disadvantaged by gender-based media patterns (Kahn 1992, 1994; Kahn and Goldenberg 1991; Leeper 1991; Sapiro 1982). However, in the mid- to late 1990s, researchers began to report that at least in this arena, the news media were beginning to cover male and female candidates similarly (Berke 1994; K. B. Smith 1997; Wilcox 1994).

Presidentialization of National News

Since the 1970s, roughly 25 percent or more of domestic news concerns presidents or presidential candidates (Entman 1981). This is in no small part because the president is a lone individual; it is impossible for the national news to consider each congressional member with the same intensity as it does the president. Greider writes that "the President is so close to us, he seems larger than life. . . . He is a living presence; the others are dim figures" (1976, C1; see also Miroff 1982). The president's domination of public attention has led Miroff (1978) to define American politics as "a presidential drama" (219). And, more importantly, "presidential drama is *expected* to fill up the public space; presidential dominance over visible publication is now as much demanded by the media as it is sought by the President" (Miroff 1978, 5, emphasis in original; see also Ceasar, Thurow, Tulis, and Bessette, 1982). The presidential dominance of news has ramifications not only for a president's political agenda but also for the American political system. As early as 1965, Cornwell was able to conclude:

A process of interaction between the developing media of communication and their generalized impact, on the one hand, and growing presidential use of them, on the other, has altered both the center of gravity of the national governmental system, and the frame of reference of the public in viewing government. Progressively, during this century . . . the President has become the source of initiative and stimulus for action. He has done so by exploiting his unequaled platform for popular leadership. This fact, with a powerful assist from the burgeoning commercial media, has virtually transformed the White House occupant into the personification of the national government. (5)

This is all the more remarkable in that, as Cornwell has observed, the president's power is "'hortatory' rather than 'determinative'" (1965, 5), in that the president does not have the constitutional power to demand specific policy changes. The president "must persuade, bargain, exhort, and on occasion, bribe. Above all he must win and channel public support" (Cornwell 1965, 6).

"The American presidency's power is essentially 'plebiscitary' in its basis" (Cornwell 1976, 55–56). And any "leverage the President has acquired in the lawmaking process has been indirect, based on use of the arts of persuasion, and ultimately grounded in the popular support he can claim or mobilize" (Cornwell 1965, 4; G. Edwards 1976). The president is able to attract news coverage through virtue of the office and personal charisma. The media capitalize on the presidency as an easily simplified, readily personalized, and optimally dramatizable news commodity. Similarly, Hess (1986) found that most stories originating from Washington, D.C., flow from what he calls the "golden triangle" of news origin: the White House, the Pentagon, and the State Department (all most likely to be pro-administration sources; 1983). Similarly, Foote and Steele (1986) found support for Hess's golden triangle. Eight of the most visible news correspondents originated their leads and stories from the golden triangle. And these same correspondents frequently "piggybacked" onto international news stories even when their news stories were only marginally related to the foreign correspondents' news packages (Foote and Steele 1986); in this way, correspondents increased not only their own prestige in linking top presidential administration sources with foreign leaders in one story, but also that of the office of the president. Moreover, Foote and Steele (1986) observed that congressional reporters rarely appeared in these news accounts to comment on White House statements and those of the other likely pro-administration sources at the State Department and the Pentagon; therefore, the president and his administration dominated national network news coverage of the nation's capital. Although at times the news content was critical of the administration, it still left the impression that it was the White House that exercises both power and action. This positions the Congress of the United States as an afterthought and weakens the public's perception of its contributions to the domestic and international agenda (Foote and Steele 1986).

Print versus Broadcast News Sources

In unexpected events involving massive complexities, organizational imperatives will often yield clues as to what types of news sources news assemblers will select. And those news sources may well be different for each medium but remarkably similar within each medium outlet. In a study of the 1987 stock market crash, Lasorsa and Reese (1990) found that the print media focused on Wall Street sources who primarily emphasized the effects of the crash on other economic and political matters. And network news focused primarily on governmental sources who blamed the stock market crash on the staggering national debt (Lasorsa and Reese 1990). Because television news focuses on sound bites from prominent people who are able to explain the situation in easy-to-understand, simplistic terms, government sources are the obvious choice. On the other hand, the print news media worked to provide a more comprehensive news story, one that not only detailed what happened but also what was likely to happen now that the crash had occurred. Both observed news orientations are representative of the two different media's approaches to news (see Lasorsa and Reese 1990). But what must be emphasized is that the news source used by a news reporter determines to a large degree what the news consumer is exposed to and thus considers, which has a significant impact on that news consumer's political reality. Lasorsa and Reese (1990) write that "the use of different sources resulted in distinctly different slants. Public views of the crash would have been shaped as much by the sources cited as [the] medium read/viewed" (60).

Reliance on Official but Faceless Sources

Often journalists may not have all the facts needed for an assigned news story, or they may not be able to find anyone willing to provide information for attribution. It is then that journalists turn to what we call "faceless sources" in validating their stories. Brown, Bybee, Wearden, and Straughan (1987) found in their study of national and local newspapers that more than one-half of newspaper sources were unidentified. Yet the attribution of a source with an indicator of why that person is being used by the reporter (eyewitness, expert, officeholder, victim, and so on) serves an important information function for any audience member attending to the news. Lasorsa and Reese (1990) write that attribution "alerts the reader [listener or viewer] both to the expertise and the motives of the source. When critical readers 'consider the source,' they essentially make judgments about both the source's capacity to offer evidence and motivation in presenting it" (Lasorsa and Reese 1990, 60).

Therefore, Brown, Bybee, Wearden, and Straughan (1987) suggest that this practice of using unidentified or faceless sources distorts the political reality of most Americans, who rely primarily, if not exclusively, on the mass media to provide information about the world immediately outside their personal sphere. They conclude: "Continued condoned anonymity of sources in all but a few cases perpetuates the invisibility of the truly powerful" (Brown, Bybee, Wearden, and Straughan 1987, 54). Parenti (1970) has argued that the true power is evidenced not by winning a political tug-of-war contest but the ability to predetermine the terms of the struggle, the issues at stake, the naming of the contest, and whether the struggle even materializes. Thus, anonymous power brokers who play a significant role in assisting the media in determining the media agenda are often hidden from view, faceless and therefore unaccountable to the American people.

The significance of this finding should not be underestimated. Even the politically powerful, such as high-level appointees and bureaucrats, are influenced sometimes unknowingly or sometimes consciously by their own personal ideological predispositions, which often are unacknowledged in their contacts with news reporters (Gitlin 1980). And if reporters are blissfully unaware of these ideological predispositions, routinely using anonymous power brokers without identifying caveats of ideological leanings, then we are left with an information situation where we cannot hope to understand or evaluate how or why "conceptions of necessities, possibilities, or strategies" (Gaventa 1980, 15) have been identified, organized, and presented for our news consumption. Thus, we are left without knowledge of who the impression managers are, what their goals or objectives are, what benefits they seek, who they wish to punish or reward, and what persuasive tools they have used in their efforts to impression manage what the news reporters receive as information subsidies, from which news reports are constructed (see Gaventa 1980).

As news consumers, we are all way too familiar with faceless sources, whether in our newsmagazines, nightly network newscasts, or national newspapers. L. W. Doob, as early as 1948, warned news consumers about the hidden power of those faceless sources, and he provided us with a list of faceless attributions to watch out for when considering or evaluating the news:

According to official sources
According to unofficial sources
According to usually reliable sources
According to well-informed sources
According to unconfirmed reports
According to best available information (271)

In addition to these faceless attributions, journalists will sometimes use the "Mr. Ubiquitous It" as the attributable authority (L. W. Doob 1948, 272). L. W. Doob again provides a number of examples:

It was learned
It appears
It is reported
It is unconfirmed
It is known
It is suspected
It is thought (1948, 272)

However, these same faceless sources appear simultaneously in competing news organizations' copy, making it likely for Washington insiders to guess the unnamed source who briefed the press but did not want to be quoted (Johnson a.k.a. Johnson-Cartee 1984). A point should be made that at least these faceless individuals got their viewpoints heard, even if the audience members did not necessarily know how to evaluate what was said because of the anonymity of the source.

News Convergence

While Entman's original conceptualization of source standardization meant that journalists use the same group of informants over and over (1981), for the purposes of this work, a concept of "standardization" will be used to include other factors creating standardized news. For instance, normative organizational practices have produced a consonance or standardization in the nation's news even though news reports originate from a wide variety of media outlets. According to Lasorsa and Reese (1990), mediated news convergence is the "tendency for all the media to focus on the same story at the same time" (62). T. L. Patterson (1992), in his study of five democratic nations, found that while the American press enjoyed the most press freedoms in terms of news content, American journalists produced more consonant or more standardized news stories and news judgments than the other four democratic nations' news media. But it is important to note that the other four did demonstrate a strong degree of consonance—just not as much as the United States (see also Bennett 1988; Gans 1979; Graber 1997; Nimmo and Combs, 1983). In an analysis of candidate and news media campaign agendas in Great Britain and the United States, Semetko, Blumler, Gurevitch, Weaver, Barkin, and Wilhoit (1991) found that newspaper and television agendas in both countries were highly similar in subject content. Interestingly, the research documented significant differences between candidate and media agendas. While the candidates emphasized issues and qualifications for office, the media concentrated on the horserace aspects of the political campaign, emphasizing public opinion polls and the "behind-the-scenes" activities of campaign operatives.

Bennett (1996) has presented five rules of political coverage observed by journalists that promote such news standardization or news convergence. I have excerpted Bennett's rules in the following section:

> "*The first and most extensively researched rule of political reporting, then is the imperative to build a story line—whenever possible—upon official or at least authoritative viewpoints.*" (376)
>
> "*This second rule of political reporting is that sources and viewpoints are 'indexed' (admitted through the news gates) according to the magnitude and content of conflicts among key government decision makers or other players with the power (as perceived by journalistic insiders) to affect the development of a story.*" (377)
>
> "*The development of a story beyond normal institutions and news beats suggests a third representation rule for journalists pursuing a complex developing story: follow the trail of power.*" (378)
>
> "*The areas of politics represented in the news by familiar cultural metaphors and rituals indicate a fourth broad rule followed by journalists: observe, narrate, and, when necessary, adjudicate the themes and customs of the political culture.*" (379)
>
> "*Events that contain credible (i.e., spontaneous, empirically convincing) images that challenge existing policies or official definitions of situations may become news icons. Such icons may license journalists to move challenging or politically marginalized ideas into the center of news coverage. However, the emergence of conditions that trigger the application of rules 1–4 may reintroduce familiar official or cultural themes into the news as the story develops.*" (380–381; emphasis in original)

The Role of the Elite Press

In addition to Bennett's (1996) analysis of factors leading to news convergence, Graber (1997) has also offered some interesting ideas. For Graber, the overshadowing influence of the elite press necessitates convergence. According to Graber, the elite press, physically located along the northeastern seaboard and accounting for only 8 percent of practicing journalists, serves as "generative" media in that the elite press produces or generates the news that the "derivative" media then adopt and disseminate throughout the United States (1997, 97). And of added significance is the fact that the elite newspapers, for the most part, cover the same powerful sources simultaneously (Reese and Danielian 1989). Furthermore, an analysis of four network news programs revealed that the same elite sources were used within and across programs, forming an elite "insiders'" group of sources (Reese and Danielian 1994, 84). Thus, whether the derivative media get their news agenda from the *Washington Post*, the *New York Times*, or another member of the elite press, for the most part the derivative media will be attending to the same powerful sources conducting the same type of activities regardless of the newspaper. McCombs and Shaw (1972) and Lasorsa and Wanta (1988) found substantial agreements among the news mixes and news agendas of various multilevel, multimedia newspaper and print publications.

Graber (1997) provides an alternative listing for her "generative media" to Grossman and Kumar's (1981) listing of "media majors," but Graber's study considered more than political news stories. Graber investigated the influence of a variety of publications oriented toward various aspects of American life. Graber maintains that television, whether local or national, is valued far less highly as an information source by news assemblers than are national print publications such as "*New York Times*, the *Wall Street Journal*, *USA Today*, and the *Washington Post*; and major news magazines such as *Newsweek*, *Time*, and *U.S. News & World Report*; and major magazines such as *National Geographic* and *Sports Illustrated*" (1997, 97).

Similarly, Lasorsa and Reese report that "the elite serve an important role in coordinating and policing elite opinion. The differences in functions are suggested by the readership of the elite press" (1990, 70). For Washington insiders, the *Washington Post* serves as their primary source of news. The *Wall Street Journal* serves Wall Street and the financial community. On the other hand, the *New York Times* is the newspaper of record for all institutional elites (Lasorsa and Reese 1990, 70).

Another factor underlying the news convergence process is "the *herd mentality* of the mainstream media as they look to each other for guidance" (Lasorsa and Reese 1990, 62, emphasis added; see also Reese and Danielian 1988). National desk editors, regional and local newspaper editors, television network news assignment editors, and news service reporters will start their work day by reading the *New York Times*, the newspaper of record in the United States. Such reliance on the *New York Times* sets an agenda of news coverage for most of America.

A third factor that leads to news convergence is the routine practice of **pack journalism** or the habit of journalists to share angles on routine stories and for younger reporters or those from less prestigious news organizations to follow the lead of senior reporters from more prestigious news organizations on what is important, what should be included or discarded, and the angle or theme of the day's news stories (see Crouse 1972). In addition to the herd mentality of news assemblers and the routinized practice of pack journalism is the newsmagazine's use of **group journalism**—the practice of using, in one story, the inputs of multiple authors who are physically separated, unknown to each other, and reporting on disparate occurrences. Both *Time* and *Newsweek* magazines "see their role as weekly summarizers and explainers, putting the news of the week into historical, political, or scientific perspective, to express the meaning in the news" (Hiebert, Ungurait, and Bohn 1982, 444). And, for this reason, the magazines' headquarters serve as clearinghouses for facts sent from multiple news reporters around the country, working on related occurrences, as evaluated and characterized as such by the news editor. News editors and their staffs design thematic structures in their dramatization of the news story; facts that fit within those socially determined thematic structures are used, and those that don't fit comfortably are discarded. Hiebert, Ungurait, and Bohn (1982) provide us with a glimpse of what goes on behind the doors of *Time* magazine:

> *Time* especially has perfected the technique of "group journalism," where facts are sent to New York headquarters from many different persons and many different angles on a given story. These facts are chewed over and digested at the Olympian heights by editors and specialists, who then put together a final summary, synthesizing, interpreting, and analyzing the facts in some perspective. (444)

In addition, journalists' **reliance on elites** and officials often produces a marked similarity or parallelism in their news accounts of the same occurrence; such parallelism is often called **consonance** or homogeneity (Bennett 1988; Fishman 1978; Tuchman 1973). Fishman (1978) went so far as to suggest that trends in news accounts such as reported crime waves are really ideological manifestations of the way in which news reporters go about their work; he writes:

> The business of news is embedded in a configuration of institutions. These include a community of news organizations from which journalists derive a sense of "what's news now," and governmental agencies upon which journalists depend for their raw materials. Through their interactions and reliance on official sources, news organizations both invoke and reproduce prevailing conceptions of "serious crime." (1978, 532)

And Lasorsa and Reese (1990) have observed that powerful sources often have an influence on observed news convergence. They explain that when "national leaders speak, they often are able to amplify their voices through the tendency of the elite newspapers to cover them simultaneously" (Lasorsa and Reese 1990, 62). Frequently, the exact same unattributed quote will appear in news stories in the *Washington Post*, the *New York Times*, *Time*, and *Newsweek*. Thus, elite newspapers define the prominence of news sources in similar, if not identical, ways, resulting in the covering of prominent news sources and their self-dramatized activities created for public and media consumption. To provide an illustrative issue, I examine in depth the 1986 drug war and media convergence in the appendix.

As early as 1949, Stanley Bigman concluded that the news media were "rivals in conformity." Graber, in her analysis of news stories provided by local television evening news, national television evening news, and local newspapers in Chicago, Illinois, found that her analysis produced

> striking evidence that the same kinds of stories and story types—although not necessarily identical stories—are reported by all news outlets. When the proportions of various types of news are compared, the similarities are greatest among the members of each of the three types of media. National television patterns show heavier proportionate emphases on stories about the national government and international news and proportionate de-emphases of sports news. Thanks to more available space, newspapers carry more nonpolitical news. (1997, 109)

In an analysis of network television news, Lemert (1974) found that 70 percent of the stories found in network newscasts during a two-week period were used by at least two networks, and the more newsworthy the network news directors thought the stories, the closer to the front of the newscast they were located. Interestingly, Epstein (1973) found that network news executives consistently watch their competition daily, with particular attention to lead stories, and often evaluate their own newscast performance on their choice of leads and other stories as compared to their competition's. This is why television newsrooms have multiple television sets tuned to competing news programs.

In an international study of democracies, Galtung and Ruge (1970) observed that Western democracies by and large had news organizations that followed identifiable news values:

> The more the event concerns elite nations, . . . the more the event concerns elite people, . . . the more the event can be seen in personal terms, as due to the action of specific individuals, . . . the more negative the event is in its consequences, the more probable that it will become a news item. (265)

Marginalization of Groups

Other individuals, groups, or movements are not as lucky as American officials and elites in gaining access to the news media, and the result is marginalization within American society. To understand marginalization, we must
first consider what appearing in the news means to most Americans. We turn
to the work of Lazarsfeld and Merton ([1948] 1960), who identified what they
called the **status conferral function** of the mass media. For the average person,
simply the appearance in the news of a person, object, or public act is enough
to lead to the conclusion that the person, object, or public act must be important. And, in short-circuited reasoning, if a news consumer sees a person
considered important by the media, then that same person must also be legitimate or be legitimate in their representation of like-others. Thus, the news
media confer both status and legitimacy on people, groups, issues, and objects. But what is absent or missing in the news is just as important as what is
contained in the news. When people, groups, issues, or objects are ignored or
left out of news media coverage, they do not exist in the public sphere; and,
therefore, they have no status or legitimacy. Tuchman (1981b) has called this
symbolic annihilation. People, places, objects, products, causes, or groups are
marginalized because who they are, what position they hold, or what private
or public acts are exercised are not deemed newsworthy by journalists. They
simply, according to journalists, do not make the grade when evaluated by
professional news values.

While researchers take note of the types of Washington insiders and power
elite members who appear in television newscasts and within prestige newspapers' copy, they also report on who wasn't there: labor union spokespersons,
minority spokespersons, environmental spokespersons, and leaders of grassroots political organizations (Hoynes and Croteau 1989; Soley 1992; Whitney
et al. 1989). Soley (1992) explains that such groups aren't members of the
power elite, and therefore they are for the most part invisible in our national
news. P. Schlesinger and Tumber (1994), D. Miller (1994), and Manning (1998)
have argued that noninstitutional and resource-poor groups rarely have more
than a fleeting presence on the national scene. Elite sources have greater legitimacy in the eyes of journalists, who judge authority and power on the basis of
news routines that reflect the dominant ideology of officialdom.

Grassroots Ambivalence

Journalists routinely demonstrate a preference to use sources and to cover
stories within the three largest media capitals. Dominick (1977) found that
roughly two-thirds of network broadcasts originated from Washington,

D.C., Los Angeles, and New York City, all three of which were at the time recognized as media capitals in the United States. And more than one-half of these broadcast news accounts originated from Washington, D.C. The dominant preference to interview the powerful, the elite, and the official leads to grassroots ambivalence or the reluctance of news reporters to cover policy or other political views from actors in what they consider the hinterlands (Bennett 1996). Thus, news accounts overwhelmingly depict the two coasts of the United States.

When international news is presented, the reports are overwhelmingly from developed nations; thus, in terms of the world's population, the vast majority of people are unrepresented in U.S. news accounts (Larson 1984). When they do appear in network newscasts, they are likely to be depicted as the victims of natural disasters. The ease with which networks can arrange for news coverage of events in foreign countries determines to a great extent what is covered; and it is only when natural disasters occur that the networks will send news crews to those areas less hospitable in terms of travel and newsgathering conditions.

Clearly, then, the national news media are ambivalent about the utilization of sources outside of their primary media domains. And even in terms of domestic news, interest groups, protest groups, and social movements vying for media access that are outside the media capitals are carefully screened for legitimacy by news assemblers. Such evaluations indicate that the existence of such groups is not an indicator of legitimacy as are the positions of officials and elites. Some additional attribute must be present as part of the group's profile that news assemblers consider newsworthy before the news media treat such groups as serious contenders for news access.

But "even when particular [grassroots] viewpoints are admitted into the pool of recognized sources for a story, those views are further contextualized with symbolic cues that color their credibility and salience for news audiences" (Bennett 1996, 374; see also Entman and Rojecki 1993; Gitlin 1980). Tuchman suggests that such **condemnations** or **trivializations** are further evidence of symbolic annihilation (1981a). Danielian (1992) reports that in local news, the depictions of action groups are particularly affected by power relationships existing in the community; he writes, "In small communities, groups use the press as a device for defining problems and for creating awareness about issues for the community at large in order to affect decision-making" (73). But the newspapers' coverage of the group and its associated issue(s) becomes part of the public controversy in that "the community media tend to back the winners in conflicts, rather than less powerful citizen interest groups" (Danielian 1992, 73; see also Tichenor, Donohue, and Olien 1980). For the national news media, those groups outside the main media capitals and particularly those outside Washington, D.C., are considered suspect; such sources do not receive the same respect as insiders and are often discounted by the manner or context within which they are presented.

Unconventional News Sources

Tuchman (1978) and Soley (1992) have made the argument that the routine use of "official sources" has meant that what journalists view as "objective reporting" is the mere perpetuation of the status quo. "'Objective reporting' perpetuates the status quo because it does not criticize the existing social order and because it relies heavily upon sources from legitimated institutions, such as businesses, government, trade groups, and professional associations" (Soley 1992, 23). With the advent of electronic information technologies, some observers (see, e.g., Ward and Hansen 1993) predicted that journalists would finally be free of their reliance on bureaucratic and official sources; however, Hansen, Ward, Conners, and Neuzil (1994) found that the new technologies only increased the number of bureaucratic and official sources that were consulted. In short, reporters' reliance on traditional news sources remained. Official sources are viewed as "conventional sources" (Strentz 1989), and those that offer anti–status quo perspectives are viewed as "unconventional" (Soley 1992). Reporters who want to get stories published or aired and who want to get along with their superiors in the news organization avoid selecting unconventional sources for their stories (Tuchman 1972; Soley 1992). For instance, probusiness sources are routinely used but consumer activists rarely.

Furthermore, research has shown that news coverage of social protests and the resulting audience evaluations of those social protests are directly related to the level of status quo support expressed in the news. McLeod and Detender (1999) report:

> Status quo support had significant effects on viewers, leading them to be more critical of, and less likely to identify with, the protesters; less critical of the police, and less likely to support the protesters' expressive rights. Status quo support also produced lower estimates of the protest's effectiveness, public support, and perceptions of newsworthiness. (3)

All too often in the United States, a social protest narrative is presented as a violent crime narrative by the reporting organization's reliance on official, status quo sources (McLeod and Detender 1999; McLeod and Hertog 1992, 1998). In short, protest news and the efforts of those involved in social protest are frequently the victims of "delegitimization, marginalization, and demonization" (McLeod and Detender 1999, 5; see also Gitlin 1980; McLeod and Hertog 1998).

Other groups face the double bind of being not only anti–status quo but also prebureaucratized. The civil rights and Vietnam War protest movements during the early 1960s were viewed as little more than masses of protesters. Because these social movements were in the prebureaucratic stages of development, reporters discounted the significance of movement-related protests. And because such protesters offered information contrary to that supplied by the journalists' preferred sources, the officials and elites making up the accepted establishment in America, reporters simply ignored them or pejoratively described them (Bennett 1983; Tuchman 1981a). The result was that few Americans were exposed to the protest movements' perspectives or demands, and few understood why people were even protesting until the latter half of the 1960s. Indeed, both social movements were originally portrayed as threats to the established order and rule of law (Bennett 1983; Tuchman 1981a).

However, the government's position on social protest must at least be credible. For three days, April 29 through May 1, 1992, the streets of Los Angeles were ablaze. Lawlessness ruled in the city. These social protests followed the acquittal of five policemen for beating an African American man, Rodney King. What made this case unusual was that the beating had been captured on videotape by a bystander. The excessive brutality was aired on television newscasts for months. Americans had seen for themselves what had occurred, and while the vast majority condemned the resulting riots, they also condemned the court system that allowed these policemen to go free. On May 4, 1992, Marlin Fitzwater, George Bush's White House spokesman, told the news media that the three days of Los Angeles riots were the result of failed social welfare policies. Fitzwater's account simply wasn't credible, and the majority of the nation's news reporters ridiculed his words (Page 1995). Such contrived explanations wouldn't work when the American voters had seen with their own eyes what had transpired. "By better than a two-to-one margin, Americans blamed Reagan-Bush neglect rather than Great Society programs for the riots" (Page 1995, 247).

Interestingly, news coverage of social protests in other countries corresponds with our government's "foreign policy toward both the foreign government and protest movements" (Wittebols 1996, 345). If our government supports a foreign government, the protests are ignored and dismissed. If our government doesn't support a foreign government, the protests are highlighted and praised by the reporter.

Such prebureaucratized interest groups rarely have direct access to political leaders. Thus, these groups must find an alternative route in their search for public recognition. According to Cobb and Elder (1983), "For an item or an issue [or an interest group or social movement] to acquire public recognition, its supporters must have either access to the mass media or the resources necessary to reach people" (86). Goldenberg (1975) has identified seventeen political resources instrumental in reaching people and six key political resources in gaining access to the news media:

Group Political Resources

1. money and credit
2. control over jobs
3. control over the information of others
4. status
5. knowledge and expertness
6. popularity, esteem, charisma
7. legality, constitutionality, officiality
8. cohesion
9. the right to vote
10. overlapping memberships with targets
11. size
12. feelings of political efficacy
13. location
14. legitimacy in the eyes of public, target, third parties—brought about by the group image as representative and moral
15. credibility (of claims and threats)—whether at the polls or in the streets—brought about by attitudes expressed by members and leaders, past behavior, lack of other options, public declaration and commitment
16. visibility
17. intensity of feeling (Goldenberg 1975, 33)

Key Resources to Gain Access to the News Media

1. status/officiality
2. location
3. information/knowledge
4. money
5. size/legitimacy/intensity
6. credibility (Goldenberg 1975, 40)

Because most prebureaucratized interest groups have few, if any, political resources, the mass media often become their only hope to attain the policy agenda. This is true although the newsgathering "source standardization process" is biased against them. According to Goldenberg (1975):

The media are often involved in indirect attempts to influence policy. They are key access points to public officials for all groups. Through the media, issues are frequently brought to the attention of the public and of government officials. News coverage is used by groups in gaining status and visibility, in expanding the scope of conflict, in reinforcing attitudes, in activating third parties on their behalf, and in gaining a hearing in the political process. (1)

Often at the prebureaucratized stage, the only resource the group has is "intensity of feeling" (Goldenberg 1975, 33). And, for this reason, such groups often participate in some socially unacceptable behaviors that impede the natural order of day-to-day living. The media label such behaviors as deviant or outside the traditionally recognized realm of legitimate political behavior (Molotch and Lester 1974). Tuchman (1981a) has argued that for prebureaucratized groups to be recognized by the news media, they must be "in the wrong place at the wrong time to do the wrong thing" (90; see also Molotch and Lester 1974). "The more a group's political goals deviate from prevailing social norms, the more likely the group is to gain access to the press, other things being equal" (Goldenberg 1975, 28–29; see also Bennett 1988). Because the mass media will judge their behavior as **violating the status quo**, established order, or the recognized routine, news journalists will display these negatively evaluated acts prominently in news stories. Thus, negativity assessments make the news.

The development of the activist interest group Mothers against Drunk Driving (MADD) provides a good example of this violating the status quo phenomenon. On October 25, 1982, President Reagan signed into law the Alcohol Traffic Safety Programs Act (Public Law 97-364), which required that in order for a state to receive federal highway funds it must first raise its drinking age to twenty-one. MADD has been credited with securing the passage of this act just two years after the birth of the organization.

In 1980, Candy Lightner started MADD after her thirteen-year-old daughter was killed by an intoxicated driver as the teenager walked to church. Although Lightner was a political neophyte, she recognized quickly that she couldn't get the media's attention by writing or telephoning news journalists. Lightner and her supporters decided to pursue a "get in your face" strategy by carrying photographs of lost loved ones killed in alcohol-related automobile accidents to the nation's newsrooms, courtrooms, judicial chambers, and state legislative corridors, and to the halls of Congress. By using the force of insistent, loud, if not obnoxious, interpersonal persuasion and by violating the personal physical comfort zone of journalists and political/judicial figures, MADD forced the issue into the nation's agenda. Crushed automobiles were prominently displayed at major crossroads with MADD posters showcasing photos of the dead. By providing heart-wrenching, personal background stories and alarming statistics, the news media adopted MADD's message that drunk driving was no longer politically or socially acceptable, and it was time for the government to act. The nation came to know Candy Lightner's story—a story of personal tragedy, and her story and that of her daughter came to represent the drunk driving issue in the United States. By 1984, MADD had more than 320 chapters in the United States and 600,000 volunteers and donors.

Marginalized Minority Groups

In some situations, causes may develop bureaucratic structures with organizational officers, membership rolls, bank accounts, and physical headquarters or offices. Yet these groups may still find it difficult to obtain media attention. In some situations, it is the news reporters' view of market forces that influences their decision to ignore marginalized groups rather than the journalists' own personal evaluation as to either the newsworthiness of the group or the worthiness of the group's cause (see Gieber 1960–1961). Reporters and other news assemblers fear alienating the "dominant culture" by drawing attention to marginalized segments of society. In the past, such marginalized groups have been minority political groups, religious groups, the poor, or gays and lesbians. To the extent that the news media virtually ignore such groups, viewing these groups as being outside the desired public sphere of their audience, it may be said that such groups simply do not have a public existence. To the extent that such marginalized groups are covered by the news media as challengers to or violators of the status quo, news consumers are likely to assign such groups a deviant public image. For the most part, marginalized groups do not exist for the average American, for they are, in effect, **functionally invisible** to mainstream America. When the existence of such a group becomes known, however, the average American is likely to classify the group as a **deviant** group (Danielian 1992).

For example, it was not until the late 1980s that gays and lesbians were considered worthy of news coverage. But, even then, coverage of events was often spotty at best. "In 1987, to cite one notorious case, both *Time* and *Newsweek* ignored the gay rights march in Washington, D.C., the largest civil rights demonstration in the capital since 1969" (Moritz 1995, 65; see also Freiburg 1993). When gays and lesbians finally made it into mainstream news organizations' news reports, it was because of AIDS. Overwhelmingly, news accounts dwelt on what reporters considered to be their "promiscuous and abnormal" sexual behavior and lifestyle. . . . A common media frame was to distinguish between the "innocent" victims of AIDS, those who did not acquire the virus from gay sexual contact, and, implicitly, the "guilty" victims of AIDS, those who did. (Fejes and Petrich 1993, 403–404)

Shoemaker (1984) found that newspaper editors' images of marginalized groups are reflected in their newspapers' coverage of those groups, for groups considered deviant by the editor received unfavorable news coverage that portrayed these marginalized groups as illegal and socially nonviable. In an earlier study of news coverage of marginalized groups, Shoemaker (1982) found that news portrayals affect how audience members evaluate the groups' legitimacy. Those presented as eccentric, weird, or deviant were seen to be far less legitimate than those presented without such depictions.

Many marginalized-group members do not perceive themselves as "political activists" or, as the news assemblers might view them, as members of "fringe groups." Rather, they see themselves as educators who have both information gain and persuasion as their societal goals (see Gieber 1960–1961). Gieber (1960–1961), in his early examination of civil rights groups and their relationships with news media personnel, provided interesting insights in that marginalized groups, despite their stated objectives, often operate in manners inconsistent with their stated goal of achieving public recognition, for marginalized-group leaders often misunderstand how to interest and gain access to news assemblers. Gieber (1960–1961) identified a number of self-defeating mind-sets and behaviors shared by marginalized group leaders and their members, which in practice eliminate or reduce their access to news assemblers; he writes that marginalized groups:

1. Often misperceive the mass audience.
2. Tend to perceive their relevant publics in terms of a hostile governing elite versus their own members and likely sympathizers. This naive duality is further exacerbated in that these two factions are perceived as being diametrically opposed to each other, creating an US versus THEM scenario.
3. Tend to discuss issues in the abstract without "concretizing" their issues with specifics and personalities which would attract news assemblers and their organizations.
4. Tend to phrase their messages with symbols common to their own internal group members but not necessarily understood by either the mass audience or the news assemblers and the organization.
5. Often hesitant to publicize grievances or wrongs perpetuated against their group for fear of copycat perpetuators repeating the wrongs. Often such wrongs do not

become public events unless these instances sometimes reach a court or judicial phase in their resolution. [However, forty years after Gieber's writing, this may have well changed in that while still fearing retaliation or copycat acts, marginalized groups may recognize that public outrage over their mistreatment might well prove to be their only means to successfully seek and find relief from injustices.]

6. Tend to be suspicious of the news media. Often tending to "preach" or "educate" reporters which is met with hostility. In some circumstances, group leaders may be openly hostile to the news media, further hindering their access to the news media and to the governing elites. And most importantly, "They do not perceive the representatives of the press as their *first* audience." (Gieber 1960–1961, 83; emphasis in original)

In addition, Gieber (1960–1961) identified a number of newsmaking procedures that discouraged the coverage of such marginalized groups:

1. Reporters focus on the politics of the newsroom, not necessarily the interests of the community.

2. Reporters are concerned with obtaining information, organizing the material according to professional stylistic criteria, and crafting moving and memorable symbols to dramatize the account. Gieber writes: "Although the product of his craft often has serious consequences to society, the reporter is not concerned over the fate of his story after it has left his hands" (1960–1961, 80). And he goes on to explain, "The reporter is no different from any skilled person involved in symbolic manipulation who is employed in a bureaucratic structure; his frustrations are focused within the newsroom, not the community" (1960–1961, 80).

3. News organizations impose their own definitions of news on news reporters; and, while useful for the reporter in that he or she understands the news policy of the organization and therefore increases reporting efficiency, the policy also "dictates to a reporter how he should manipulate his facts and what kinds of news and names are interdicted" (Gieber 1960–1961, 80). Gieber (1960–1961) observes that the coverage of civil liberty stories is "not determined by the needs of the community or the mass media audience but by the demands of the reference group of which the communicator is a member or employee" (83).

4. News assemblers' orientation to constructing news utilizes criteria that emphasize pertinence, human interest, humor, shared symbolic events, conflict, and prominence. Clearly, this definition of what constitutes news does not reflect the marginalized group's definition of news, which tends to emphasize their cause and their belief that it is the media's job

to inform the public as a measure of their social responsibility (see also Berkowitz 1992).

Gieber (1960–1961) concludes his observations by underscoring that just as marginal groups have a distorted view of news assemblers, they also have a distorted view of the mass audience. Moreover, Gieber (1960–1961) argues that the needs and preferences of mass audiences are only dimly understood by either the news media or marginal groups, implying then that the needs of the mass audience are ill served.

Framing Prescriptions for Marginalized Groups

As scholarly interest has developed in news framing, a corresponding emphasis on issue groups', activist groups', or marginalized groups' framing of their issues and concerns for distribution to news assemblers and the public has also developed (e.g., Ryan 1991). Framing is viewed as an essential part of deliberative democracy, recognizing the strategic actions of multiple actors engaged in social influence (Pan and Kosicki 2001) and characterizing a process of ideological conflict and political battles. Indeed, the literature indicates that to be successful, social movements or interest groups must pay particular attention to how they frame their goals and activities. "Which frame to sponsor, how to sponsor it, and how to expand its appeal are strategic issues to participants [in social movements, interest groups, or other grassroots organizations]" (Pan and Kosicki 2001, 39; see also Ryan 1991). M. M. Miller and Riechert (2001) have argued that a "spiral of opportunity" exists when stakeholders engage in issue framing; they write:

> Attempts to frame issues interacts with fundamental human values in ways that affect the relative attractiveness of policy options to the public and policymakers. Stakeholders articulate their positions and then monitor public responses to those articulations. If a stakeholder's articulation resonates positively with the public, then that group will intensify its efforts. On the other hand when an articulation resonates negatively, the stakeholder group will change its articulation or withdraw from debate. (M. M. Miller and Riechert 2001, 108–109; see also Shah 2001)

And, as Gerhards and Rucht have concluded:

> Framing processes play a decisive role in mobilization campaigns. The best chance for protestors to influence society consists in their capacity to make their definition into a public definition of the problem, to convince as many groups

and people as possible by their framing of the situation, to create support for their cause, and to motivate others to participate in the process. (1992, 572; see also Klandermans 1988)

Snow and Benford suggest that for any interest group or social movement to be successful in garnering support, whether from members, potential participants, or the interest of the news media, it must perform three fundamental framing tasks:

> (1) a diagnosis of some event or aspect of social life as problematic and in need of alteration; (2) a proposed solution to the diagnosed problem that specifies what needs to be done; and (3) a call to arms or rationale for engaging in ameliorative or corrective action. The diagnostic and prognostic framing tasks are directed toward achieving consensus mobilization. The latter task, which concerns action mobilization, provides the motivational impetus for participation. (1988, 199)

And Snow and Benford argue that the "more the tasks are robust or richly developed and interconnected, the more successful the mobilization effort, *ceteris paribus*" (1988, 199). Gerhards and Rucht (1992) have argued, however, that diagnostic framing is far more important for protest and social movement campaigns than prognostic framing:

> In contrast to political parties, social movements and protest groups do not compete to occupy administrative positions in order to propose and implement solutions to problems. Therefore, protest groups, unlike parties, are not usually expected to offer solutions to the defined problems. (582)

A. Schneider and Ingram's (1993) research on the social construction of target populations has important ramifications for those involved in social change movements. "The social construction of target populations refers to the cultural characterizations or popular images of the persons or groups whose behavior and well being are affected by public policy" (A. Schneider and Ingram 1993, 334). In effect, the researchers argue that the way in which a target population is defined by those involved in influencing public policy determines to no small degree what is politically possible to achieve. For instance, when discussing Aid to Families with Dependent Children, different public perceptions are evoked when a protest group uses the term "welfare queen" rather than "welfare mothers." Such utterances have real policy implications. "There are strong pressures for public officials to provide beneficial policy to powerful, positively constructed target populations and to devise punitive, punishment-oriented policy for negatively constructed groups" (A. Schneider and Ingram 1993, 334). Consequently, when social change or protest groups identify social wrongs, it is important that they frame those who are victimized by those social wrongs in ways that promote a sympathetic, positive public image.

Terkildsen and Schnell (1997) have suggested that "political movements or interest groups who wish to mobilize broad electoral support would do well to package their issues to appeal to the most commonly held societal values and avoid appeals to economic rights or group-specific legislation" (893). Similarly, A. Davis (2000) argued that noninstitutional groups such as unions enjoy a modicum of success when they wage complete public relations campaigns directed at generating "media-friendly lines of argument" and at dividing oppositional coalitions by hounding their leaders with questions of impropriety and dishonesty. Particularly if they eliminate threats to the status quo or business-as-usual crowd by removing union strikes as viable alternatives in industrial-union conflicts, then the unions are far more likely to receive neutral, if not positive, coverage by the press.

In their study examining the framing of the women's movement during five decades, Terkildsen and Schnell (1997) found that once the movement sought specific benefits such as equal pay, an immediate negative reaction occurred, particularly among men. They argued that when interest groups ask for something for themselves, those outside the group perceive the group as a threat and react negatively toward the group. They suggest that the suffragist movement was successful, in part, because it utilized universal values. In short, the threat activation for those outside the group was not triggered. However, Terkildsen and Schnell (1997) also warn that this strategy may well alienate group members or those likely to be sympathetic to the cause, because such individuals may view the emphasis on widely held societal values and the avoidance of demands for the members' rights as a form of selling out to the status quo. In addition, the news media's interest in conflict makes appeals to universal rights a hard sell.

On another front, it is important for social movements or interest groups when diagnosing social ills or injustices to do so in a way that leaves room for hope. If a societal ill is presented "cataclysmically and hopelessly," then frequently those outside the movement or group will perceive that there is no use trying to improve or change the intolerable situation, for it can't be changed, or it can't be improved (Snow and Benford 1988, 203). The framing of social ills must leave room for "ameliorative action" (Snow and Benford 1988, 203).

Snow, Rochford, Worden, and Benford (1986) focused on the role of social psychological and structural/organizational considerations in influencing support for and participation in social movements. In their examination of a variety of social movements, the researchers suggested that frame alignment was the linkage between social psychological consideration and structural/organizational considerations. And they believed that social movements and individual behaviors toward them could be explained by examining four frame alignment processes: "frame bridging, frame amplification, frame extension, and frame transformation" (464). I include a discussion of their groundbreaking work here, because these same frame alignment processes engineered to secure movement supporters may also be utilized in attracting news assemblers' interest.

Frame alignment is the degree to which an individual's interests, values, beliefs, and goal states are congruent with the social movement's stated ideology, objectives, and activities. In other words, an individual's world view and the social movement's stated world view need to be complementary for the individual to be supportive of the social movement's agenda. Clearly, "Frame alignment is a necessary condition for movement participation, whatever its nature or intensity" (Snow, Rochford, Worden, and Benford 1986, 464). For frame alignment to be established and maintained, a process of communication interactions must be created; this process the authors call **micromobilization**. In other words, social movement members, news assemblers, and members of the general public must have the opportunity to engage in repeated communication interactions. Such social interactions, either real or para-social, provide opportunities for all involved to recognize the similarities in beliefs and values. Only through repeated interactions is frame alignment possible. Micromobilization comprises the many discrete and diverse communicative acts leading to frame alignment.

Frame bridging is when individuals or social movements recognize that they hold mutual or congruent ideological positions in different issue arenas, and they join together to seek common goals. For example, one women's group is concerned with universal child-care legislation. Another women's group is concerned with universal elder care. Both groups believe it is the rightful role of the government to provide social services to assist those needing help functioning in their everyday lives. One emphasizes governmental assistance for those caring for children, and the other emphasizes governmental assistance for those caring for the elderly. Individuals or social movements may recognize the ideological similarities and join forces to successfully achieve their goals. However, for this frame bridging to take place, specific communication tasks and events must occur or the process of micromobilization must be activated. "This bridging is effected primarily by organizational outreach and information diffusion through interpersonal or intergrouop [sic] networks, the mass media, the telephone, and direct mail" (Snow, Rochford, Worden, and Benford 1986, 468). For instance, Richard Viguerie, the famed Christian Right direct-mail king, has successfully utilized computerized mailing lists and targeted mail appeals to raise hundreds of millions of dollars for Christian Right causes. Snow, Rochford, Worden, and Benford (1986) explain:

> For Viguerie and other new right leaders, the utility of direct mail as a key bridging mechanism rests on the presumption of the existence of ideologically congruent but untapped and unorganized sentiment pools. Computer scanning and name culling provide the lists of prospective constituents; direct mail provides the key to frame bridging. (468)

According to Snow, Rochford, Worden, and Benford (1986), successful social movements must stay vigilant in reenergizing their members and attracting new members by redefining and reinvigorating the interpretive frames utilized by their movements. They call this invigoration of a social movement's interpretive frame the process of **frame amplification**. Frame amplification may take two forms: value amplification and belief amplification (Snow, Rochford, Worden, and Benford 1986).

"Value amplification refers to the identification, idealization, and elevation of one or more values presumed basic to prospective constituents but which have not inspired collective action for any number of reasons" (Snow, Rochford, Worden, and Benford 1986, 469). For instance, neighborhood associations or movements may have different goals during their life cycle. They may want a neighborhood crime watch, they may want less trash in their streets, they may want to preserve their cultural heritage by holding neighborhood celebrations, and so on. Depending on their goals, they may emphasize in their communication products the appropriate value to mobilize support for the desired goal state. For instance, if they want to preserve their cultural heritage, they might emphasize family, neighborhood integrity, or ethnicity. If they want to eliminate trash on their streets, they might emphasize property values and neighborhood pride values.

Belief amplification is the process by which two separate ideational elements are linked together by a social movement in order to mobilize support for something or against something. Snow, Rochford, Worden, and Benford (1986) provide the example of a neighborhood association working to prevent a Salvation Army facility from locating to their neighborhood. Recognizing that the Salvation Army was well associated in the minds of their members and prospective members with Christian charity and good works, the neighborhood association instead attacked the types of people likely to frequent the facility, particularly undesirable male transients who might be a perceived threat to the neighborhood's women and children. In short, while they couldn't link the Salvation Army directly with negative associations, they acknowledged that "everybody can agree to spit at sort of half-alcoholic, twenty to twenty-eight-year-old, unshaven men" (Snow, Rochford, Worden, and Benford 1986, 470).

Under certain conditions, social movements may "promote programs or causes in terms of values and beliefs that may not be especially salient or readily apparent to potential constituents and supporters" (Snow, Rochford, Worden, and Benford 1986, 472) in order to attract new members. When this happens, a **frame extension** has been made; and "the micromobilization task in such cases is the identification of individual or aggregate level values and interests and the alignment of them with participation in movement activities" (Snow, Rochford, Worden, and Benford 1986, 4). For instance, a women's resource center was originally organized and funded to support victims of domestic violence and sexual assault or abuse. However, the organization found that after its initial success at recruiting volunteers and funding, it was not able to secure additional volunteers or money to assist in the expansion of its services. The center decided to expand its mission statement to include language that the center opposed any discrimination against gays, lesbians, or transgendered individuals and any discrimination against ethnic, racial, or religious minorities. Through this frame extension, the group was able to significantly increase its volunteer pool and its funding.

On other occasions, social movements may find themselves promoting ideas and values that are antithetical to accepted lifestyles, beliefs, and values found within a given culture. To be successful, the social movement must engage in what Snow, Rochford, Worden, and Benford (1986) have called **frame transformation**. "New values may have to be planted and nurtured, old meanings or understandings jettisoned, and erroneous beliefs . . . reframed in order to garner support and secure participation" (Snow, Rochford, Worden, and Benford 1986, 473). Frame transformation may occur at two levels: domain-specific and global interpretive frames. When utilizing frame transformations on either level, social movements must dramatize that an existing condition or state that has long been lamented but tolerated is in fact no longer tolerable; the condition or the state is fundamentally unjust. In addition, the responsibility or the assignment of blame for the existence of the intolerable and unjust condition must shift. For example, the civil rights movement in the United States was successful, in part, because the movement identified social forces that had previously been tolerated and labeled them as intolerable and unjust, and they argued that the inferior economic, political, and social standing of the American Negro was caused by the U.S. government; a government pledged to recognize that "all men are created equal" was in fact creating a legal atmosphere that did exactly the opposite. Domain-specific frame transformations "seek dramatic changes in the status, treatment, or activity of a category of people" (Snow, Rochford, Worden, and Benford 1986, 474). Mothers against Drunk Driving transformed deadly traffic accidents involving alcohol abuse from what once was thought of as an unfortunate accident to an inexcusable tragedy; and, at the same time, MADD redefined drunk driving and the legal and social penalties associated with it (Snow, Rochford, Worden, and Benford 1986). Speaker of the House Newt Gingrich made an unsuccessful frame transformation when he tried to influence the federal government to move away from aid to dependent children to warehousing poor children in orphanages (Asen 1996). On the other hand, global interpretive frame transformations are far larger in the degree of the change in frames held, for global transformations are shifts in world views—the fundamental shifting of how one views the world. Religious conversions or religious unconversions may be viewed in this light.

Gramsci (1971) recognized that for social movements to be successful, they must frame their arguments from within the dominant ideology of the culture. In other words, to develop a counter-ideology, the group must utilize existing belief systems within the ruling class hegemony or dominant culture. In order to bring about frame transformation, the counter-ideology must be grounded in the culture's "stock of folk ideas and beliefs" accepted as givens within the dominant culture (Snow and Benford 1988, 204; see also Gramsci 1971; Rude 1980; Swidler 1986). In other words, the framing transformations are only successful when frames have **resonance** (Snow and Benford 1988). In short, the transformative frames must evoke that which is already believed, valued, and respected. And the transformative frame must be judged as relevant as demonstrated by (1)"empirical credibility, (2) experiential commensurability, and (3) narrative fidelity" (Snow and Benford 1988, 208). **Empirical credibility** means that the frame lends itself to testing. Evidence exists that supports the diagnostic, prognostic, and motivational claims made within the social movement. And the frame must have **experiential commensurability** in that it suggests "answers and solutions to troublesome events and situations which harmonize with the ways in which these conditions have been or are currently experienced." (Snow and Benford 1988, 208). In short, is the frame commensurate with the audience's life experiences? And does the frame have **narrative fidelity** (see discussion of W. Fisher 1984 in chapter 5), striking "a responsive chord in that it rings true with existing cultural narrations" (Snow and Benford 1988, 210)? Does the frame fit with other cultural stories, myths, or narratives? For example, when trying to change people's minds about recognizing gay unions, it is often helpful to provide an example of two cohabiting, unmarried heterosexuals. One of the partners dies, and he leaves his estate to his girlfriend. However, his mother challenges the will, arguing that under Georgia law the girlfriend cannot inherit money or benefit financially from an illegal act. Under Georgia law, the girlfriend is denied her boyfriend's estate because they had an illegal sexual relationship outside of marriage. After hearing such a story, people normally get enraged, even the most conservative and the most religious. And rarely does their indignation over such injustice and unfairness change when the moderator tells them that this happens all the time to gay couples.

W. A. Gamson (1988a) has argued, however, that social movements have greater flexibility within a given culture than many have previously suggested. He argues that scholars should investigate "cultural themes" or "the frames and related symbols that transcend specific issues and suggest larger world views" (W. A. Gamson 1988a, 220). For Gamson, cultural themes represent the ideology, values, and belief systems of a given culture. However, such cultural themes must be viewed dialectically. As Burke (1966) has argued, humankind is the "animal inventor of the negative" (16). In other words, when contemplating a belief, a value, or a societal proscription, we, at the same time, are capable of contemplating the opposite. In his observation, it should be recognized that

> We construct our rules and regulations based on our symbolic knowledge of the world. We know good and bad, right and wrong, just and unjust. We deal with these polarized symbols or positive-negative dichotomies in our political negotiations. . . . These positive-negative dichotomies in some strange way comfort us, for we believe that the world is knowable, that our life tasks are do-able. We can make sense out of the complexities of life, and thus we can in some small way manage and control the world around us. (Johnson-Cartee and Copeland 1991, 1–2)

Similarly, W. A. Gamson has observed: "There is no theme without a countertheme. The theme is conventional and normative; the countertheme is adversarial and contentious. But both have their own cultural roots and both can be important in assessing any specific symbolic struggle" (1988a, 221; see also Tankard 2001; Tankard, Hendrickson, Silberman, Bliss, and Ghanem 1991). He provides us with a noteworthy case in point. American society has long been obsessed with progress and technological advances. Indeed, efficiency, expediency, and innovation are all highly praised values in our culture. Yet, at the same time, a cultural tension has existed between progress on the one hand and nature on the other. W. A. Gamson writes:

> American culture, however, also contains a countertheme, skeptical of, or even hostile to, technology. . . . Our technology must be appropriate and in proper scale. There is an ecosystem to maintain and the more we try to control nature through our technology, the more we disrupt its natural order and threaten the quality of our lives. Thoreau at Walden Pond is also part of American culture. (1988a, 221)

Gamson suggests that these counterthemes or counterframes provide an opportunity for those seeking social change, for while governmental and institutional forces exploit cultural themes for their own purposes, they are also evoking in the minds of their audience the possibility of the opposite or the negative. In short, when they call for progress, they invoke the costs of progress or the negative displacement of nature. By championing the cultural theme, authorities make "the countertheme relevant as well, and therein may lie opportunity" (W. A. Gamson 1988a, 221).

In chapter 5, we noted that in analyzing public issues, we may observe an issue culture or the sum total of all the interpretive packages competing to define the issue for the public (see also Simon and Xenos 2000). Each interpretive package has its own symbolic devices associated with its use. However, for an interpretive package to remain in serious contention for defining the political issue, the package must be capable of adapting to changes in the environment, whether new facts, new events, or new actors. For illustration, Gamson presents us with an interpretive package about the role of nuclear power to generate electricity for the masses, which he labels *Faith in Progress*:

> If the electric chair had been invented before the electric light, would we still be using kerosene lamps? There has always been resistance to technological progress by nervous nellies who see only the problems and ignore the benefits. Resistance to nuclear energy development is the latest version of this irrational fear of progress and change. Of course nuclear energy development is not free of problems, but problems can be solved as the history of technological progress shows. The failure to develop nuclear power will retard our economic growth and renege on our obligation to the poor and to future generations. If we do not move ahead now with nuclear energy, the next generation is likely to be sitting around in the dark blaming the utilities for not doing something this generation's officials would not let them do. (W. A. Gamson 1988a, 222)

For this interpretive package to remain viable, those who propagated this interpretive package would have to successfully react to the Three Mile Island (TMI) and Chernobyl nuclear incidents. In the case of Chernobyl, perhaps they would offer that this nuclear disaster was the result of an inferior Russian design further hampered by shoddy Communist workmanship. And, for the TMI incident, the *Faith in Progress* proponents might use a multitude of interpretations: (1) TMI was the result of faulty sensors, (2) TMI's significance was overblown by the media, and (3) existing safeguards worked, and we avoided a nuclear catastrophe. In short, the interpretive package must interpret new events by "providing them with a meaning that is plausible and consistent with the frame" (W. A. Gamson 1988a, 223).

Within public debate, competing interpretive packages battle for public acceptance (e.g., Hornig 1992). When considering the rise and fall of social movements or issue publics, it is helpful to keep in mind that it is the propagation of interpretive packages and the resulting clashes between interpretive packages that mobilize public support or condemnation. It is within this competitive arena of interpretive packages that "consensus mobilization" occurs (Klandermans 1986). How well these interpretive packages are presented, what symbols are utilized, and what cultural themes and counterthemes are explicated determines in large part how successful challengers or those involved in social change movements are likely to be (W. A. Gamson 1988). Nelson and Oxley (1999) have suggested that strategic political communicators would do well to study belief importance when preparing to frame issues, for, ultimately, the successful communicator is the one who correctly identifies what "beliefs, concerns, values, and goals take precedence over others" (1,061). And, for the most part, the arena or battleground over interpretive packages is the nation's newspapers, broadcast newscasts, cable newscasts, and websites "on which various social groups, institutions, and ideologies struggle over the definition and construction of social reality" (Gurevitch and Levy 1985, 19).

The importance of promoting public acceptance of a protest or social movement's interpretive package defining an issue arena should not be underestimated, for, according to Gerhards and Rucht (1992), it is the "key factor" in determining if a protest or social movement is to be successful (572). "Protest movements usually have no other resources or only small amounts of them (money, power, connections to decision makers) at their disposal" (Gerhards and Rucht 1992, 572–573; see also Neidhardt and Rucht 1991).

Ironically, individuals will also emerge in the news media for brief periods of time simply for conducting themselves in ways that are unexpected. Couldry (2000) reports incidents where a single individual became a short-time celebrity by daring to tape the inhuman circumstances surrounding animal slaughterhouses and markets; by doing the unexpected and by exposing the underbelly of meat manufacturing through videotape, one individual became the temporary poster child for animal rights. But it is important to recognize that this individual successfully dramatized the situation, making herself an essential ingredient in the action. Such presentations are fodder for news organizations, because they meet the news organizations' definition of news. When such dramatizations occur, individuals may emerge as the national exemplar of a cause or social group. Dramatized individuals are far more likely to gain access to the contemporary media than their social groups or organizations (Manning 2001).

In Summary

Chibnall (1981) has observed that the operation of journalistic rules and news typifications or rituals "ensures that large segments of the social world are systematically excluded from representation and discussion in the media, and thus public knowledge of those segments if effectively impoverished" (87). However, social protest movements and their activists may gain access to the news media if they craft their news promotion frames in ways acceptable to both the news assemblers and news consumers. Knowledge of framing research is critical to the success of a political activist.

8

Personalized and Confrontational
News Framing

Personalization of News

NEWS STORIES ARE NOT TOLD from the standpoint of political institutions, economic forces, or laws and bureaucratic regulations; rather, news stories involve people, individuals engaged in conflict and seeking resolution of disputes. Galtung and Ruge (1970) have argued that this personalization of the news might be related to our Western culture in that as a society, we believe that as individuals we are responsible for our own destinies. Through our free will, we create the world in which we live. In order for news narratives to be effective or understandable, news reporters believe that the audience must somehow relate to the story; in other words, the audience must identify with the players in the narrative. And, because reporters believe that their audience members understand human motives and human greed, their stories often focus on the behind-the-scene manipulations and governmental officials' political motives (see Galtung and Ruge 1970).

For Woodward (1997), it is the narrative format or story format that produces the personalization of news. Woodward explains:

> Storytelling is a dramatic form that typically places responsibility for an individual's condition squarely on the human participants involved. To a large extent, therefore, stories tend to underestimate the hard-to-dramatize structural causes of human actions in favor of the drama of individual combat. (1997, 77)

According to T. E. Cook (1996b),

> The *sine qua non* of news is not conflict in and of itself, but an endless series of conflicts and momentary resolutions. Conflict may be one of the few cross-cultural characteristics of news, but without resolution, it is not newsworthy, because it does not move the narrative along. (474; see also A. A. Cohen, Adoni, and Bantz 1990)

In other words, we may read or view a story involving individuals engaged in drug trafficking, but the stories are pitched as drug lords fighting the Drug Enforcement Agency or the local or state police. In some instances, the stories may be about rival drug lords involved in a turf war. However, we don't learn how these people think. We don't learn what happened in their lives to lead them to take this course of action. We don't know about the cultural, economic, or political factors that contributed to the situation. We learn only the most superficial personal characterizations of individuals engaged in a war frame.

Implications for Motive Presentations

Carey (1986) has observed that journalists focus on motive in trying to explain political events. Similarly, Woodward has argued that "in the framework of storytelling, events do not simply occur, to be observed on their own terms. Events are the result of specific human agents with honorable or dishonorable motives" (1997, 78). Journalists believe that political leaders are motivated in what they do by the achievement and maintenance of political power. As such, a leader's motivations, following a journalist's reasoning, explain the leader's political behaviors. Thus, a seemingly complicated series of events is readily understandable by first examining and then presenting the leaders' motivations. As we have mentioned earlier, motive analysis is not unique to journalists; as individuals, we conduct our own motive analysis when confronted with new people or new narratives. However, when we as individuals conduct such motive analysis, the ramifications are usually limited to the people involved in the narrative exchange. We certainly do not expect our own motive analysis to affect the political views of the entire Western world. Yet, when journalists engage in motive analysis, the potential exists for just such an effect. Cappella and Jamieson write:

> By supplanting the what of politics with the why, we have interiorized the process, making it about the psyche and self of individual politicians rather than about policies and their outcomes on the lives of the citizenry. By answering the question Why? through the assumption of self-interest in conflict with public interest, we risk casting everyone in political life as a venal schemer. (1997, 27–28)

Because journalists are consumed with motives, they are also consumed with political strategies or the plans devised by politicians to achieve desired political goals. A focus on strategy has led journalists to approach the political process as little more than a game.

Politics as Gaming or Political Competition

During the past sixty years, the news media have increasingly portrayed the political process as individual leaders involved in hotly contested games, where strategy is king (e.g., Arterton 1984; Carey 1976; Clancey and Robinson 1985; Jamieson 1992; Kerbel 1997; Orren and Polsby 1987). Reporters depict political leaders as "scheming" manipulators intent on winning at any cost; however, their efforts to win aren't based on any high-minded public service ideals. Rather, they are shown to be in it for their own aggrandizement and their greed for ever-increasing political capital (Fallows 1997). Cappella and Jamieson (1997) have labeled this approach to political reporting "the strategy frame," while Patterson ([1993] 1994) has called it the "game schema." Fallows (1997) and T. E. Cook (1996a) view this **gaming frame** as the consequences of the reporters' definition of news; if conflict reigns supreme in reporters' news values, then naturally the conflict involving political actors will be a primary focus.

Tedesco (2001) found that candidates who recognize the news media's interest in game framing and who frame their public pronouncements and press releases on voting, political advertising, and campaign polling will receive more favorable and more extensive news coverage. He (2001) argues that John McCain's meteoric rise in public popularity during the 2000 presidential primary was because of the news media's acceptance of McCain's strategy and process framing of the presidential primary season.

Lawrence (2000) has suggested that the gaming frame is far more likely to be used when it involves national news stories, where the individuals involved are far removed from the everyday lives of the news audience. And she has also found that the gaming frame is far more likely to be used when presenting news accounts concerning the legislative branch rather than in stories about the governmental bureaucracy and the implementation phase of governmental policy making. Congressional leaders, in the eyes of reporters, are scheming, manipulative, master sportsmen, while bureaucrats are simply drudges following regulatory procedures.

Cappella and Jamieson (1997) have argued that the strategy frame increases cynicism among voters, often provoking hostile responses (Jamieson 1992; Lawrence 2000; Patterson [1993] 1994). "The reaction of individuals exposed to such frames is to mistrust the intentions of political elites and, perhaps, reinterpret and recoil against their perspectives" (Shah, Watts, Domke, and Fan 2002, 345; see also Rhee 1997).

Nowhere is this gaming frame more apparent than in presidential campaigns. Patterson ([1993] 1994) has documented the meteoric rise of game frames in presidential campaign news. In 1960, less than 10 percent of national campaign news stories utilized the game frame; however, by 1992, nearly 80 percent of national campaign news stories were casting the presidential campaign as a game. The game frame as used by national journalists has five components:

1. Winning and losing as the central concern
2. Emphasis on strategies and tactics
3. The language of wars, games, and competition
4. A story with performers, critics, and audience (voters)
5. Heavy weighing of polls and the candidates' standing in them

The game frame, as entertaining as it may seem, has significant consequences, for voters are turned off by the game frame. They do not like to think of presidential contenders as dirty political strategists. Valentino, Beckmann, and Buhr (2001) found that voters recognize the difference between news stories framed as games and those framed as policy news frames. Policy news frames, or what they have called "sincere" news frames, emphasize problems that confront everyday citizens, present meaningful analysis of those problems, and evaluate a range of proposed solutions. Contrary to journalists' expectations, voters prefer sincere or policy news frames rather than game frames.

Researchers believe that the game frame has had serious consequences in our political system as well (Cappella and Jamieson 1997; T. E. Cook 1996a; Fallows 1997; Lawrence 2000; Patterson [1993] 1994; Valentino, Beckmann, and Buhr 2001). Numerous research studies have found that with the increase in game framing in campaign news coverage, numerous corresponding consequences have resulted:

1. Decline in civic participation at all levels of political activity
2. Decline in voting
3. Increased cynicism toward the government
4. Depressed political engagement or interest
5. Increased political alienation
6. Suppressed information retention about public issues and political campaigns

Journalists view a presidential debate as a "newsworthy event that fits within the game motif" (Wayne 2000, 233). Journalists depict candidates as modern-day gladiators warring against their competitors, satisfying the journalists' need to entertain news consumers (Wayne 2000). Candidates, for the most part, view presidential debates as an opportunity to dramatize their political leadership abilities (Hinck 1993). After reviewing the literature on presidential debates, Jamieson and Adasiewicz (2000) have concluded that debates

> are more likely to reinforce a voter's perceptions than alter them; that debates teach voters both about the candidates' stands on issues and character; and that debates forecast the issue agenda of the future president as well as his communicative competence and habits of mind. (25)

And, for this reason, debate performances are carefully planned and rehearsed in much the same manner as a made-for-TV movie (Schroeder 2000). Journalists engage in predebate prognostications, labeling likely winners and losers. "With assistance from their campaign sources, reporters fix a conventional wisdom that departs from the standard journalistic mission of factual storytelling; in turn, this predebate 'morning line' becomes the yardstick by which postdebate judgments are rendered" (Schroeder 2000, 79). And political pundits "cram the airwaves, spouting predictions, analyzing strategy, and revisiting debates past" (Schroeder 2000, 80). Political campaign spin doctors work before the debates to ensure that their candidates receive favorable predebate and postdebate assessments. If a candidate is perceived as being far better than other debaters, campaigns will often downplay his predebate advantage; in this way, when the candidate does win the debate, it is still news. And candidates who aren't expected to win debates and who perform respectably in the debates send their spin doctors out to tell the world about their candidate's unexpected winning performance. Tom Brokaw remarked after the 1988 vice presidential debate, "There was so much spinning going on here tonight it's a wonder that the Omaha Civic Auditorium didn't lift off into orbit" (as quoted by Schroeder 2000, 184). Candidates and their campaign consultants recognize the power of postdebate reports. "Postdebate press reports can alter the public's sense of who 'won' and 'lost' a debate and focus viewers and readers on tactical assessments rather than on a debate's substance" (Jamieson and Adasiewicz 2000, 25). Lemert, Elliott, Bernstein, Rosenberg, and Nestvold (1988) found strong evidence to suggest that news verdicts on who won or lost expressed in postdebate reports do influence public perceptions of debate performance, and this evidence "still holds *after* controlling for partisan predispositions and demographic variables"

(255; emphasis in original). They conclude that exposure to postdebate analysis emerges as the strongest debate-related influence on performance impressions, a composite presidential candidate image measure, and voting intentions" (Lemert, Elliott, Bernstein, Rosenberg, and Nestvold 1988, 256).

Adwatches

The strategy frame is accentuated by the news media's focus on political advertising. Since the presidential campaign of 1988, adwatches or "media critiques of candidate ads" (Tedesco, McKinnon, and Kaid 1996, 76) have become an important part of campaign news coverage. The 1988 presidential election campaign was noteworthy in "that for the first time in the television age, ads for one major party presidential candidate lied blatantly" (Jamieson and Waldman 2000, 106). In response to journalists' disgust with the Republican political consultant Roger Ailes's stretching of the truth in campaign ads, adwatches "designed to inform the public about truthful and misleading advertising claims" (Kaid, Tedesco, and McKinnon 1996, 297) became a favored campaign reporting tool. West (1993) has offered a similar definition, writing that adwatches "review the content of prominent commercials and discuss their accuracy and effectiveness" (68).

By 1999, Kaid, McKinney, Tedesco, and Gaddie observed that adwatches were utilized by both print and broadcast journalists at all levels of media outlets to cover presidential campaigns but that candidate advertising below the presidential level received far less attention. And when adwatches were used in campaign coverage below the presidential level, they were for the most part descriptive in that journalists failed to provide the careful scrutiny necessary to judge the claims and evidence presented in the ads; Kaid, McKinney, Tedesco, and Gaddie suggested:

> The failure to provide in-depth analysis may leave voters confused by competing and often contradictory, claims that go unexplained or clarified. Such journalistic coverage of ads was most apparent in local television newscasts, as campaign reporting would often feature candidates' response ads as a convenient way to develop the narrative of a negative or nasty campaign, while ignoring the actual claims made in the ads. (1999, 288)

Only one-third of television news adwatches provided any in-depth analysis, and less than one-half of newspaper adwatches presented such an analysis (Kaid, McKinney, Tedesco, and Gaddie 1999). And despite widespread use of technological manipulations in political advertisements such as "special effects, video editing, digital alterations, color or shaded video, altered sound effects or any other technique that might be designed to mislead or create false impressions for viewers," only one in seven adwatches made any mention of these techniques (Kaid, McKinney, Tedesco, and Gaddie 1999, 289). Tedesco, Kaid, and McKinnon (2000) found this to be true of network evening news adwatches during the 1996 presidential primary and general election campaign as well.

Negative ads, or ads attacking a candidate or comparing a candidate unfavorably with another, are far more likely to be the focus of adwatches (Tedesco, McKinnon, and Kaid 1996; Tedesco, Kaid, and McKinnon 2000) for negative ads fit journalism's definition of news by being negative. "The failure of the media to scrutinize the messages candidates provide in positive ads not only contributes to the public impression of negative campaigning but also leaves politicians free to make undetected false and misleading claims in positive ads" (Tedesco, Kaid, and McKinnon 2000, 550). In a study of ABC, NBC, and CBS evening network news's use of adwatches during the 1996 presidential campaign, Tedesco, Kaid, and McKinnon (2000) found that the coverage tone was either neutral or negative. "When a slant was presented within all network adwatches, it was overwhelmingly negative (30 percent during the primaries and 21 percent during the general election). Not a single adwatch presented the spots in a most favorable light" (Tedesco, Kaid, and McKinnon 2000, 548–549).

Johnson-Cartee and Copeland (1997a), when surveying existing research on the effects of adwatches on voters, found:

> Some research has indicated that media criticism of political advertising may actually create an undesirable effect as less-educated voters and female viewers may interpret the criticism as being in support of the targeted ad, and when this occurs, the influence of the ad goes up (Cappella & Jamieson, 1994; Jamieson, 1992; Pfau & Louden, 1994). And perhaps most important, research has shown for well-educated viewers, media criticism may have the desired effect in terms of "punishing" the sponsor of the questionable ad; however, such criticism of the sponsor has not been shown to salvage the damaged reputation of the candidate who was attacked (Capella & Jamieson, 1994). (204)

What is clear from the body of research examining adwatches is that news consumers attending to these news stories are more likely to perceive the candidates as self-serving, backstabbing liars intent on only one thing—winning the game.

Horserace Frame

Closely aligned with the game frame is the horserace frame, which treats political candidates at all levels as horses racing against each other as they rush toward the finish line of Election Day. Consequently, stories focus on who is perceived as winning and which candidates are losing. In fact, the horserace frame is the most emphasized aspect of modern-day campaign reporting; it permeates all campaign news (Lichter and Noyes 1995). Jamieson (1992) explains:

> The language through which the press reports on politics assumes that the American electorate selects a president through a process called a "campaign" seen as a "game" or "war" between a "frontrunner" and an "underdog" in which each candidate's goal is "winning." Candidate's words and actions are seen as their choice of what they presumably envision as a means to victory. So enmeshed is the vocabulary of horse race and war in our thoughts about politics that we are not conscious that the "race" is a metaphor and "spectatorship" an inappropriate role for the electorate. (165)

Campaign journalists treat the presidential contenders as horses competing in the Kentucky Derby. As soon as a presidential candidate surfaces, announcing his or her candidacy, the political handicapping begins. Journalists lay odds on who will win and who will lose. But, starting with the Iowa caucus and the New Hampshire primary, the handicapping gets deadly serious, for this is when a majority of the politically interested begin to pay close attention to the nomination portion of the presidential race. Consequently, campaign journalists place a great deal of emphasis on **political polling**, reporting who is ahead and who is behind (Fletcher 1996; Mann and Orren 1992; Lavrakas and Holley 1991; Paletz 1996). By 1988, close to one-third of campaign stories on network newscasts and in national newspapers contained poll reports (Fletcher 1996, 303).

As each caucus reports and as each primary contest's results are announced, the journalists have another horserace finish to declare, reporting who placed first, second, and third. And journalists then tell us what these finishes mean for the next primary or the next caucus battle, and who is likely to win and lose there. As a result, "The electorate can know who is ahead, why, and what strategies are necessary for each to win without knowing what problems face the country and which candidate can better address them in office" (Jamieson 1992, 186).

According to Lichter and Noyes (1995), campaign journalists focus on two dimensions in their horserace handicapping: "what kind of people they are, and how likely they are to win" (16). And, frequently as we will see, these judgments are blended together. Good people win; bad people lose. It's simplistic, but it is the cornerstone of presidential campaign reporting. Lichter and Noyes (1995) put it this way:

If the candidate is seen as winning, journalists will attempt to illustrate that by presenting favorable comments about that candidate's chances from voters or political experts. If a candidate commits a gaffe, subsequent news stories will probably not convey any hint that the candidate enjoys strong support on a variety of other issues. (16)

During the nomination phase of the presidential campaign process, journalists also assess candidates' **viability** or electability; and they use a variety of indicators in their analysis: poll results (Lichter and Noyes 1995), local and state news coverage, state political leaders' assessments, money raised (Lichter and Noyes 1995), the media placements' sophistication, campaign workers' sophistication levels, volunteers' enthusiasm, campaign manager's sophistication, political advertising's sophistication, spin doctors' sophistication, national name recognition, political machine size, campaign coalitions, political spectrum positioning, regional appeal, candidate appearance, candidate charisma, and contest results.

The journalists' assessments of candidate viability are critical for the success of a presidential campaign, because research has found that voters often take into account journalists' viability assessments when making their voting decisions (Abramson, Aldrich, Paolino, and Rhode 1992). Voters don't like the idea of voting for a known loser; they often vote for those they think most likely to win.

Ironically, Dautrich and Hartley (1999) found that voters said the news media presented too much information about the 1996 presidential candidates' personal lives and about horserace aspects of the campaign. And "more than three-quarters (77%) of voters reported being very interested in candidate issue positions and in how the election outcome might affect them" (Dautrich and Hartley 1999, 121). Clearly, what news reporters think makes for good news is not what the voters say they want and need to make informed voting decisions.

Prognostications: Forecasting or Manipulating?

Much has been made of the seemingly partisan news coverage of the 1992 presidential campaign. After independent candidate Ross Perot bailed out—albeit temporarily—of the race, the news media turned their attention to the Democratic nominee, Bill Clinton, forecasting him as the frontrunner in the election. Uniformly, Clinton received far more favorable news coverage than the incumbent George Bush (Lichter and Noyes 1995). Seventy-nine percent of all the news coverage concerning the Bush reelection campaign was negative (Lichter and Noyes 1995, 214). Over and over again, the national news organizations hammered Bush on the state of the economy. Despite widespread evidence to the contrary, reporters continued to lament the dismal state of the economy, emphasizing that the country was in a recession. Lichter and Noyes observe:

> The economy was growing rapidly at precisely the time the public was processing the frequent media reports to the contrary. The recession, which was relatively mild and brief in historical terms, ended after the first quarter of 1991. By the third quarter of 1992, the GDP was growing at the robust rate of nearly 4% in real terms. (1995, 217)

Reporters' dismal projections about the future of the economy may well have turned the tide in the election, for Americans are well known to vote on their perceptions of the national economy (Feldman 1982; Kinder, Adams, and Gronke 1989; Lewis-Beck 1988). When Americans asked themselves, "Are we better off today than we were four years ago?" many of them answered with a resounding "NO!" in no small part because of the stream of negativity provided by the news media (Joslyn and Ceccoli 1994; Lichter and Noyes 1995).

While some news scholars lamented the open partisanship of the campaign news coverage, Lichter and Noyes (1995) perceived the tone and content of the news to be less a display of partisanship and more the result of the reporters' efforts to tell a good tale. News reports frequently "reduce candidates to caricatures" (Lichter and Noyes 1995, 219), and the

> reporters who resort to them are motivated not by partisanship, but by their professional incentive to tell a good story. The biases such rhetorical devices introduce are inadvertent, the result of journalists following their own professional dictates without regard to the larger consequences. (Lichter and Noyes 1995, 219)

Whatever the reason for the distorted depiction of the economy and the negative evaluations of George Bush, we would do well to remember:

> The stories that the journalists tell of the candidates are not harmless little tales that mix fact and fiction. They are narratives with real consequences, because they affect the images that voters acquire of the candidates. The press is the message. (Patterson [1993] 1994, 170)

And American voters are just as disturbed by campaign news accounts perceiving them as biased. Dautrich and Hartley (1999) found that 65 percent of Americans believe that the news media provide biased accounts of campaign news. Republicans were far more likely to perceive the news media as biased.

By election day [1996], only 37 percent of conservatives said coverage was balanced, compared to 68 percent of moderates and 73 percent of liberals. Not surprisingly, those conservatives who sensed a bias were much more likely to say there was a liberal bias (55%) rather than a conservative one (4%). (Dautrich and Hartley 1999, 105)

On the other hand, only 18 percent of Democratic voters perceived a bias in the 1996 election campaign coverage (Dautrich and Hartley 1999, 105).

Ironically, political communication research investigating the news media's interest in presidential campaigning serves to exaggerate both the public's and journalism's interest in lower-level elections. Clarke and Evans (1983) have found that congressional elections create very little interest among likely voters or the journalists covering the political campaigns. Indeed, perhaps one of the best-known adages among political consultants working for congressional candidates is that their employers will only make the newspaper twice during the political campaign season: once when they announce, and the second time either when they give their concession speech or when they declare victory on election night (Trent and Friedenberg 1995; Shea and Burton 2001).

Personalistic Encapsulations

The journalists' emphases on individual leaders and their struggles in resolving issues among themselves produce what have been called personalistic encapsulations (see Pool 1965; Bennett 1996). Such routine encapsulations produce significant consequences not only for the character of the news product but also for the ultimate definition or knowledge of public events. According to Entman (1981), in the process of applying the personality orientation to news stories, news reporters neglect the "historical or structural explanations by concentrating on individuals whose deliberate choices cause events" (81–82). In this way, according to W. A. Gamson (1992a), issues tend to be "concretized" around particular political actors and specific interest groups operating within predictable interaction patterns. For instance, Jerry Falwell, the once titular head of the "Silent Majority" and the founder of Liberty Baptist Church, will be front and center, arguing against Kim Gandy, the president and spokesperson for the National Organization of Women. Whether it is equal pay, overtime pay, abortion, birth control methods or other issues identified as "women's issues," the predictable players will be Falwell and Gandy. Similarly, in an analysis of how political parties are portrayed in the news media, Kerbel (1998) found that news stories "defined parties in terms of specific actors—candidates and a few elected officials—who could serve as 'talking head' party symbols"

(247). Seventy-eight percent of television news stories and 66 percent of newspaper stories defined political parties in terms of specific actors (Kerbel 1998, 247).

In my analysis of president-elect news coverage during transitions (Johnson a.k.a. Johnson-Cartee 1984), I found that issues were clearly associated with individual leaders, "and in many ways, the issue and the personality merged as one [each symbolizing the other]" in news reports (213). I found not only issue/personality association but also a gross oversimplification of the president-elect's platforms: "'Law and Order' was Richard Nixon. 'Human Rights' was Jimmy Carter, and 'A Strong Defense' was Ronald Reagan" (1984, 213). In this overly simplistic way, reporters use individual politicians to shape and define political issues for news consumers.

Phillips (1976) has observed that the news construction process has led to the development of a **logic of the concrete** in that journalists turn to people, their plans, and their motives—not "social forces, or 'natural' processes which are unseeable, anonymous, or abstract" (88). For instance, while the news media focus on drug use and drug-related crime, they rarely examine the economic, social, and educational forces that produce an environment where illegal drug trafficking is considered a viable profession. Consequently, news reports often mask what real issues and what real power brokers are involved in the decision making within government. We don't see the lobbyist or the corporate executive, representing a multinational, multimillion-dollar industry, who influences or even crafts the wording of legislative bills that directly benefit his or her company. We don't see the web of congressional researchers who study various issues, develop background papers, craft potential issue options, and ultimately craft their bosses' position papers. Reliance on only official faces distorts the newsgathering process. Bennett (1996) observed that "the rule that officials will dominate news representations of politics is bent toward news narratives based on personal power struggles rather than thematic analyses of institutions and the social and economic foundations of power in policy situations" (383; see also Paletz and Entman, 1981).

Not surprisingly, Just, Buhr, and Crigler (2000) found that "candidates focus on policy issues, while journalists emphasize campaign strategy and the horse race" (127; see also B. Buchanan 1996). Policy issues dominated all candidate communications, and only presidential convention speeches contained any significant amounts of information concerning either a candidate's personal or political background (Just, Buhr, and Crigler 2000). "Candidate communications try to convince voters to choose particular candidates over their opponents. To persuade citizens, candidates offer various kinds of evidence— past successes, proposed actions if elected, and demonstrations of leadership qualities" (Just, Buhr, and Crigler 2000, 123). Just the things that democratic theorists would argue would improve public deliberations surrounding political campaigns. However, candidates often fall short of the ideal in the delivery of these campaign missives:

> Candidates can be faulted for engaging in symbolic politics—making emotional appeals with little substance or relevance to policy issues facing the country. To make the best case, candidates tend to put their records in the most flattering light, to embrace issues where their positions are most popular with the electorate, and to avoid issues that are unpopular. The result can be an unjoined debate in which each candidate talks about a different set of issues. The resulting campaign discourse makes it difficult to compare candidates. (Just, Buhr, and Crigler 2000, 123–124)

Consequently, politicians are frequently blamed for the shallowness of issue discussion in contemporary politics. Patterson (1980) argued that politicians' rhetoric is most characterized by what he calls **diffuse issue presentations**, which are broad, fuzzy policy proposals, angering and alienating no one (see also Alger 1994). Such diffuse issues constitute a wish list of desirable situations such as "peace in our time," "a chicken in every pot," "a healthy economy," or "improved educational opportunities." On the other hand, journalists want **clear-cut, divisive issues** that "rest on principle rather than complex detail or relationships" to spice up their copy (Patterson 1980, 31–33; see also Seymour-Ure 1974). If Patterson's argument is correct, this leaves us with the politically nebulous issue positions of politicians and the equally ill-defined but hotly debated issue presentations of news reporters. Yet Patterson doesn't appear to find this troubling; he argues that such divisive news presentations are far better in educating voters, arguing that issues such as abortion, euthanasia, and the legalization of drugs attract audiences, and such news exposure is highly correlated with issue awareness (1980).

However, I (Johnson a.k.a. Johnson-Cartee 1984) have questioned Patterson's analysis of this process. I maintained that issue awareness should be distinguished from actual knowledge about an issue. In the literature, issue awareness has traditionally been defined as a respondent being able to "name" or "label" an issue. Thus, we might expect that people who watch a fair amount of television news will be able to name issues that are currently being discussed either by television news personnel or by national political leaders. However, just because viewers are capable of naming issues (such as gun control, abortion, or juvenile violence and crime statistics) does not mean that news consumers have any real knowledge about those issues. Drawing from Park's 1940 article that treated news as a form of knowledge, I (Johnson a.k.a. Johnson-Cartee 1984) argued that respondents' naming of issues is little more than demonstrating what Park (1940) called "acquaintance with events." Park distinguished between two "fundamental" types of knowledge—"acquaintance with" and "knowledge about" (Park 1940, 669; see also James 1896). The former is concrete and descriptive, emphasizing facts and frequently gained through personal experience. "Knowledge about" something, in contrast, is abstract, analytical, and conceptual (see Roscho 1975). For Park, the news orients people within the political world by naming issues and public acts that the news assemblers consider significant. Most often, the significance assigned to these issues and public acts is determined by reporters based on the degree of controversy surrounding them (1940). I concluded:

> For this reason, an individual is more likely to remember a controversial "naming" such as abortion [a clear-cut issue] than the more nebulous [diffuse] issue of peace. News provides very little opportunity for "formal knowledge" to be acquired from its content. (Johnson a.k.a. Johnson-Cartee 1984, 215)

Along the same lines, Roscho (1975), in his critique of contemporary journalism, argued that the construction of the news process needed to be altered in order to provide "knowledge-about" events, for he wrote: "News if not enhanced by knowledge-about, provides only superficial understanding of what is being reported" (14).

In recent years, the discussion of whether the media present enough issue coverage in the course of a presidential campaign has grown even more complicated. Lichter and Noyes (1995) have found historically that issue frames only account for between one-fifth and one-third of all presidential campaign news coverage. The remainder is devoted to candidate (personality, experience, and so on) issues and horserace frames (see also B. Buchanan 1996). "This accounts for the rising scholarly criticism of campaign coverage since the 1970s, as studies repeatedly documented that the media fail to provide coherent presentations about the policy preferences of presidential candidates" (Lichter and Noyes 1995, 79). Yet candidates do stress policy proposals in their campaign messages. But because candidates avoid controversial positions during campaigns in order to avoid alienating potential voters, their speeches and position papers tend to be more educational, offering diffuse issue presentations. Therefore, such campaign messages do not fit the journalists' definition of news; they aren't conflictual, and they aren't particularly revolutionary. Thus, journalists ignore them in their campaign news reports (Lichter and Noyes 1995). Lichter and Noyes (1995) found in their content analysis of network newscasts' and national newspapers' 1992 presidential campaign coverage that "*only 9% of all references to the candidates' issues were reasonably extensive, detailed, and contextually meaningful presentations of their records and proposals*" (95; emphasis in original). Less than one-third of issue presentations in newscasts were initiated by reporters; but in newspapers nearly one-half were the result of reporter-initiated investigations. The majority of news coverage simply followed the candidates' leads (Lichter and Noyes 1995). However, when news stories presented issue frames, the coverage in the majority of cases failed to offer "either the solutions the candidates were proposing or their past records in dealing with them" (Lichter and Noyes 1995, 99). In other words, the news stories didn't contain the information necessary for voters to distinguish between candidates. Lichter and Noyes (1995) found that although the 1992 news coverage had improved substantively over that of the 1988 presidential campaign,

> when covering the candidates, the dominant paradigm in 1992 was still the horse race and candidate mistakes (as in '88 and earlier campaigns). The issues that were most often covered were seldom linked with the candidates. Even when they were, the details were often lacking. This was primarily the result of journalists' choices, not the candidates' failures. Their speeches contained far more substance than the news accounts conveyed; they provided the raw material for any number of substantive pieces that were never written or broadcast. (127)

In their study, candidates were found to be "three times more likely than journalists to discuss the issues" (Lichter and Noyes 1995, 128).

Whether journalists' distaste for political issues or their own courting of celebrity status has created the current trend in presidential campaign news, it appears that candidate voices are shrinking. Campaign news coverage has become increasingly "journalist centered" rather than candidate centered (Hallin 1992a, 1992b; Steele and Barnhurst 1996; Wayne 2000). "The length of the average sound bite [of a candidate speaking] has been shrinking— from more than 40 seconds in 1968 to less than 10 seconds in the 1980s" (Hallin 1992b, 5). This finding indicates "a more fundamental change in the structure of the news story and the role of the journalist in putting it together: modern TV news is much more *mediated* than the TV news of the 1960s and 1970s" (Hallin 1992b, 9; emphasis in original). By the 1988 presidential campaign, journalists dedicated the lion's share of their activity to "providing and seeking interpretations and judgments about the campaign" (Steele and Barnhurst 1996, 204). By focusing on personal opinions and emotions, TV journalists now serve more as entertainers than as passionless transmitters of campaign news (Adatto 1990; Kendall 1995; Steele and Barnhurst 1996; Wayne 2000). While these studies focused on changes in television news coverage of presidential campaigns, Barnhurst and Mutz (1995) found a similar phenomenon in national newspaper coverage of presidential campaigns during the same time frame, 1968–1988. Indeed, opinion, interpretation, and analysis significantly increased, and columnists and investigative reporters became the equivalent of the TV news celebrities covering the campaigns. Consequently, today's news consumers no longer have the luxury of hearing significant portions of candidates' campaign addresses; more than ever, what news consumers know about candidates' positions is information gleaned from what Steele and Barnhurst have termed the "journalism of opinion" (1996, 187).

Exemplification

Another manifestation of personalization is the reporters' introduction of dramatized accounts of individuals, families, or homogeneous groups who are then used to represent, symbolize, or reflect a social problem or social issue. By using a personality orientation, reporters "simplify otherwise complex situations by focusing on one individual's situation as typical rather than trying to describe the general situation with all of its variations and implications" (Goldenberg 1975, 30). The process of constructing such "representative" accounts is called **exemplification** or the process of creating **exemplars**, the dramatized accounts reporters use to "represent" a social issue (see Gibson and Zillmann 1994a; Zillmann and Brosius 2000; Zillmann, Gibson, Sundar, and Perkins 1994; Zillmann, Perkins, and Sundar 1992). Such exemplification dramatizes individual, familial, or group experiences as related to some social issue, which is then framed in terms of a widely shared political or cultural mythology. According to Neuman, Just, and Crigler (1992), news reporters utilize exemplars to provide frames of reference to their viewers or readers. After analyzing news accounts, Gibson and Zillmann (1994a) found that news content may be divided into two types of information: "(a) base rate information detailing the number or proportion of people or things involved in a given social phenomenon and (b) exemplifying information, or exemplars, about individuals whose circumstances illustrate the phenomenon under review" (603–604).

Base rate information may be very specific, for instance, the use of statistics— frequencies, modes, median, ratios, or percentages. Or base rate information may be far more general, using words like *a great deal more than expected, a few, many, a majority,* or *a near-majority.* And sometimes reporters use comparisons that most audience members would not understand except that it is really, really a lot or it is really, really quite small. This is true even when the comparison is based on legitimate estimates. For instance, reporters might say that "if you were to stack one-hundred-dollar bills on top of each other, it would take a stack that reached from the earth to the moon to pay off the national debt." Now, most Americans would have no clue as to how much money that actually refers to, but the analogy makes the point that it is a huge amount.

Exemplars, on the other hand, are not chosen scientifically or systematically; rather, they are chosen because of their ease of availability and their perceived typicality (Gibson and Zillmann 1994a). For example, when reporters want to interview a welfare mother, they go to the public housing projects. In the South, this means that they typically interview a black female. Yet large numbers of white people also live in public housing, but they live in rental houses paid for by the same government programs that fund public housing projects. In an interview with the Tuscaloosa County assistant director of public housing, Willie James Forte, he told me that white people won't live in the projects because they believe it stigmatizes them as poor. That is why they are in the federal rental program. Reporters would not necessarily know this racial profile in public housing; therefore, by only interviewing black females, news reports distort the nature of the welfare rolls, giving the false impression that only blacks are on welfare. Despite their frequent lack of typicality, such exemplifications impact the public's perception of social issues (Gibson and Zillmann 1994a; Zillmann, Perkins, and Sundar 1992; Zillmann, Gibson, Sundar, and Perkins 1994).

A number of journalistic routines determine the character of exemplars presented. For example, if the exemplar has entertaining or sensational qualities, the reporter is far more likely to use it (Bogart 1980; Haskins 1981). And often exemplars are chosen from the reporter's memory of past stories covering similar or related occurrences or situations, which the reporter now believes represent the issue or phenomenon he or she is now assigned to cover. In other instances, the reporter may call a news source such as a social worker, a prison warden, a district attorney, a medical doctor, or a government bureaucrat for information, leading to an individual who will exemplify the issue or phenomenon under investigation or analysis. These individuals make recommendations, and the reporter follows through by interviewing prospective exemplars for willingness to be used as a dramatized news source. At other times, enterprising news promoters will include information about exemplars in news releases or media kits, encouraging reporters to follow up on the names provided as possible people through which the reporter tells her story.

While reporters do not use the academic term "exemplar" in relation to what they do, by routinely selecting people to represent or illustrate their stories, it may be argued that as story-makers or writers they are well aware of the need to do so. Recently broadcast news consultants have advised station news managers to monitor their **RPs** in news stories, ultimately crafting an **RP index** for newscasts. Individual incidences of **real people** appearing in news stories, personally explaining their situation to the camera, are called **RPs**. The higher the number of RPs, the better the news consultant evaluates the story. The higher the total number of RPs used during the newscast (the RP index

computed for the newscast), the better the newscast is evaluated by the consultant. Exemplars or RPs are considered to be an essential element in the construction of news stories. For example, a local reporter during this season's flu
epidemic was told to get a flu story from the regional medical center. However,
the reporter was told that it wasn't enough to show crowded waiting rooms or
medical personnel attending to the ill with a reporter's voice-over or stand-up.
Moreover, it wasn't good enough for the reporter to interview the emergency
room attending physician for her slant on the flu epidemic. The reporter was
told to find a sick person willing to talk about his or her experiences with the
flu virus. The reporter contacted the medical center's PR executive to assist in
the identifying of a cooperative flu patient. This was no easy task. The reporter
and the PR expert had a difficult time finding someone who was willing to appear on camera with the flu, looking like death (personal conversation, Brad
Fisher, January 13, 2000).

Broadcast news assemblers clearly recognize the need for exemplars or RPs
in news accounts. They recognize that research indicates that audience members have difficulty following and understanding detailed information such as
frequencies, ratios, and percentages (Robinson and Levy 1986a, 1986b; Tversky and Kahneman 1973). On the other hand, reporters recognize that
dramatic presentations of personal stories are far more likely to attract an audience and are more persuasive and more memorable, and that audience
members are far more likely to be able to recall dramatic exemplars than
quantitative measures (Gibson and Zillmann 1994a, 605; Newhagen and
Reeves 1992; Paivio 1971). This is true even though "concrete anecdotal . . .
[are] usually less valid and reliable information" than base rate information
(Zillmann, Gibson, Sundar, and Perkins 1996, 429). Research indicates that
exemplars that are vivid, emotionally engaging, and attention inviting will
have superior accessibility or memorability (see Bower and Cohen 1982; Nisbett and Ross 1980). Recently, "Studies varying the number and distribution
of exemplars have shown that, independent of base rate data, respondents
show a tendency to form perceptions and judgments on the basis of the information, presented in exemplars" (Gibson and Zillmann 1994a, 608; see
Brosius and Bathelt 1994; Zillmann, Gibson, Sundar, and Perkins 1994; Zillmann, Perkins, and Sundar 1992). Brosius and Bethelt (1994) found that
"base-rate information had almost no impact whereas exemplars had a strong
effect on the perceived distribution of public opinion about story problems"
(48).

While researchers have investigated the power of various exemplars, both
representative and nonrepresentative of issues, Gibson and Zillmann (1994a)
were the first to investigate the consequences of audience members' perceptions of social reality as the result of being exposed to inflated or exaggerated

individual exemplars in relation to the real-world phenomenon. They found that the "degree of distortion in news report exemplification does influence the formation of impressions about social phenomena" (Gibson and Zillmann 1994a, 619). And the greater the exaggeration of the exemplification presented to audience members, the greater their overestimation of the occurrence and significance of the phenomena. And the study found that this overestimation effect only increases with time; thus, the compelling, vivid, sensationalized accounts exerted greater influence on an individual's perceptions of social reality as time passed (Gibson and Zillmann 1994a, 620). In addition, exposure to the exaggerated exemplars had a cueing effect in that audience members either sought out information about similar stories or paid more attention to such stories (Gibson and Zillmann 1994a).

Interestingly, however, the researchers noted that despite the very distorted exemplars used, the respondents were uncritical of the presented news reports, accepting the veracity and generalizability of what they had witnessed (Gibson and Zillmann 1994a). Others have documented the public's tendency to accept news as representing social reality and the public's failure to critically evaluate what they are exposed to in the way of news reports (Gibson and Zillmann 1994b; Gunter 1987). "A relatively small percentage of news consumers attend to news reports with great care and interpret the presented information either critically or cautiously" (Gibson and Zillmann 1994a, 604; see also Gibson and Zillmann 1994b; Gunter 1987; Nimmo and Combs 1983).

Despite their inflated perceptions of the social phenomena or social problem presented (as a result of the exaggerated exemplification), respondents did not increase their personal apprehensiveness of how such phenomena might affect their own lives (Gibson and Zillmann 1994). This finding is not surprising, in that many people, especially the young, do not believe in and are resistant to indications or predictions that they might fall victim to some social problem (Johnson and Tversky 1983; Perloff 1983; Perloff and Fetzer 1986). Many people perceive themselves as personally invincible; the recklessness with which people, especially the young, have unprotected sex with a variety of partners is representative of this phenomenon even in this age of AIDS.

In a related study, Zillmann, Gibson, Sundar, and Perkins (1996) investigated the use of "selective exemplars" in news stories concerning the plight of American family farmers. Distinguishing between representative and selective exemplifications, "selective exemplification featured only histories of failing farms, representative exemplification a distribution of histories of failing and successful farm proportional to their occurrence" (Zillmann, Gibson, Sundar, and Perkins 1996, 427). Because atypical exemplars are often selected because of their dramatic and readily understood messages, the more extreme cases are often selected by reporters. This again demonstrates the extremist orientation of reporters in choosing news sources and exemplars. For example, most carjacking stories use exemplars where the victim is killed or brutally beaten; yet, in the majority of carjacking occurrences, the driver and passengers are not physically harmed (Gibson and Zillmann 1994a). The problem of overrepresenting extremism is common, particularly when the news media are dealing with ill-defined or unorganized groups in society.

Zillmann, Gibson, Sundar, and Perkins (1996) provided evidence that perceptions of social reality are based more "strongly on exemplification of individual cases in a population of events than on general description of properties of that population," and that these perceptions are relatively stable across time (440–441). However, if audience members hold strong prior beliefs, such as, in this case, the daughter or son of a farmer, an initial change in perceptions will occur, but their perceptions will revert back to their prior beliefs because of their personal experience with the issue.

Exemplars are often used selectively in this way to **nationalize** a problem (Linsky 1986). One story on a toxic waste situation in a given community will come to represent all potential and existing toxic waste situations across the country; this elevates the issue of toxic waste from the initial local political agenda to the national political agenda. And national policy-makers respond by focusing their attention on the issue, removing it from the domain of state and local governments (Kennamer 1992).

Zillmann, Gibson, Sundar, and Perkins (1996) address how their research should affect journalism education:

> News writers must be made aware of the implications of exemplification, especially of those concerning selective, distorting exemplification. Cognizance of glaring inappropriate exemplification should correct the practice of highly selective exemplification to some degree. . . . News writers must be appraised [sic] of the fact that pallid general information is likely to fail as a corrective for distorting exemplification. Efforts must be directed at presenting much needed base-rate information more compellingly than is commonly done. (441)

One such improvement for the delivery of base rate information is infographics (see chapter 4).

Exemplars often become narrative icons, the dramatized stories used by reporters to not only reflect a social issue but also place this issue within a widely shared public mythology that has moral and prescriptive overtones. Bennett and Lawrence (1995) and Bennett (1996) have argued that journalists create icons or dramatized symbols or myths that feature real-life people coping with the problems and travails of an identified social problem. These **narrative icons** come to represent, in the eyes of the people, a complex societal problem. Such icons are used again and again to present complex issues in a simplistic and empathetic manner; by using icons, the news media provide ordinary people the opportunity to vicariously experience the social problem, often leading to an empathetic response, and creating a sentiment that something should be done by the government about the social problem. These narrative icons are framed in widely shared political or cultural mythologies that provide the news consumer with not only an understanding of the event but also a culturally recommended prescription for human behavior and the optimal resolution of the issue. In short, myths are, according to Jack Lule (2001), "*archetypal stories that play crucial social roles*" (15; emphasis in original). Lule writes:

> They are models of social life and models for social life. Myth draws upon archetypal figures and forms to offer exemplary models that represent shared values, confirm core beliefs, deny other beliefs, and help people engage with, appreciate and understand the complex joys and sorrows of human life. (2001, 15; see chapter 4 for myth discussion)

Such icons are accompanied by what Gans (1979) has termed the "enduring values" of modern journalism—such as altruism and responsible capitalism—which provide significant insights into the mythological framework of the icon.

Confrontational News

Clearly, the news media's emphasis on conflict and its accompanying negativity deserve special mention here because of its significance in determining the character of news. Sabato (1991) has argued that during the past thirty years, the news media's emphases on the sensational, the dramatic, the titillating, and the trivial have led to increased negativity in the nation's news content. Organizational constraints and reciprocal media influences such as the competitive pressures and the nature of pack journalism have exacerbated the negativity. And, since Watergate, the United States has again and again been disillusioned by a series of political scandals involving its presidents (1970–2000). If the voters were disillusioned, so was the national news corps; from this disillusionment grew a new breed of investigatory journalism utilizing what Sabato (1991) has called an interrogating reporting style. Veteran journalist Joseph Kraft observed:

> Since [Watergate] there had been no holding us. The more august the person the hotter the chase. The more secret the agency the more undiscriminating the attack.

The general assumption of most of my colleagues, and I do not suppose I am much of an exception, is that behind every story there is a secret, and behind every secret there is a dirty secret. (1981, 36–37)

And, as a consequence, the public image of a crusading, swashbuckling reporter ferreting out evil and political misdeeds was both revered and romanticized. Consequently, several generations of reporters were raised on the interrogation style popularized by the political coverage of the time.

Similarly, Westerståhl and Johansson (1986) have argued that investigative journalism has evolved into what they call confrontational or critical journalism. Confrontational journalism may be understood as a general attitude or modus operandi as well as a specific reporting act. "The attitude implies that the journalist should not take any message for granted without forming a judgement about the credibility of the source, and, if necessary, should check the source's accuracy" (Westerståhl and Johansson 1986, 146: see also, Patterson 1996). Frequently, such high-energy, time-consuming reporting is not possible when working on a deadline; consequently, many reporters settle for what they view to be the next best thing—seek out the political opposition's viewpoints on the issue discussed. "Instead of straight news, they prefer, on supposedly professional grounds, to report a controversy" (Westerståhl and Johansson 1986, 146). Westerståhl and Johansson (1986) view this practice as a further "degeneration" of confrontational journalism, saying this oppositional journalism or controversial reporting accounts for the large increase in news negativity in modern times.

Subtext Framing

Such interrogating or confrontational reporting practices emphasize the character issue and the **subtext** in American politics. Sabato (1991) explained:

Frequently, a near consensus (accurate or not) forms around a politician's personality and faults, and each pol is typecast with shorthand labeling of various sorts. This set of preconceived images and stereotypes becomes the candidate's sub-text—that is, the between-the-lines character sketch that guides and sets the tone for press coverage. Journalists are always on the lookout for circumstances that fit the common perceptions and preconceptions about a candidate, especially his or her shortcomings. A major incident that validates the sub-text (and therefore the press's own judgment) has a good chance of being magnified and becoming a feeding frenzy. (71)

Gitlin (1990) has observed that such an insider's view of politics has led news consumers "backstage, behind the horse race, into the paddock, the stables, the clubhouse, and the bookie joints" (19). For Bennett, this is especially troubling; he writes: "The ironic result of media attempts to 'deconstruct' candidate images and expose the techniques of news control may be to reinforce public cynicism about the whole process" (1988, 34).

Subtext reporting has real consequences. In 1988, presidential hopeful Joe Biden fell victim to the media's subtext. Biden was a Democratic presidential candidate whom reporters had pegged as an intellectual lightweight who was good at giving speeches. When reporters uncovered that Biden had plagiarized or "cribbed" certain speech passages from a British politician, they immediately went on a feeding frenzy (Sabato 1991). Similarly, during the 1999 preprimary campaign season, Republican presidential hopeful George W. Bush had earned a reputation as an upbeat, laid-back, accessible candidate, but some in the media and within his own political party found his "carefree air . . . incompatible with the serious responsibilities of the office" (Burka 2000, 103). On a television interview show, he was asked to name the leaders of Chechnya, India, Pakistan, and Taiwan; however, he was only able to name the Taiwan leader. The news media made much of George W's inability to name leaders in what they judged to be "hotspots" around the world, and he became the butt of jokes on late-night talk shows, political cartoons, and cable television's political talk (and shout) shows (see Burka 2000, 114). This feeding frenzy makes a lasting impression on people's perceptions of political candidates.

Edelman (1988) has argued that such emphasis on subtext or character is grounded in the economic priorities of the news business. News organizations recognize that scandals or character-attack sagas will attract large audiences; in other words, they recognize the value of political spectacle (Edelman 1988). Taking a different view, Lichter and Noyes (1995) view the negativity of the national news as a by-product of the Washington, D.C., political culture; they write:

> The attitudes that differentiate the Washington, D.C., political culture—a fascination with power and process, attitudes of paternalism, arrogance, and casual cynicism—permeate both the Washington press corps and their dispatches from the capital. Journalists are less captives of their news sources (as some critics have argued) than co-conspirators with them. (5)

In Lichter and Noyes's view, the national news reporters and their news sources have all fallen prey to Potomac fever.

However, the nation's news watchers don't always respond to subtext frames the way that journalists expect. National reporters were puzzled, and some even appeared to be outraged, when President Clinton's approval ratings remained high despite revelations about his extramarital affair with a White House intern. Political scientist John Zaller (1998) suggested that Americans didn't care about an affair when they were pleased by so many of the Clinton administration's successes, a strong economy, and moderate fiscal policies. However, Shah, Watts, Domke, and Fan (2002) suggest that the American voters' reaction to the scandal is best understood by thinking of this episode in American history as one of competing issue regimes, "common classes of coverage [that] provide the basic standards citizens use to form and adjust their evaluations of politicians" (341). According to Shah, Watts, Domke, and Fan (2002), when an issue regime emerges, the following occurs:

> (1) particular *frames* (organizing devices used to construct news stories) and *cues* (labels and terms used to identify aspects of the news) become shared by political elites and journalists and grow commonplace in news coverage and (2) these components of news discourse become particularly likely to be adopted by the mass public informing their evaluations of politicians, fundamentally shifting the basis of judgment. (341–342)

Three frames emerged during the Clinton scandal regime: (1) the Clinton behavior frame, which focused on the sexual nature of his behavior; (2) the conservative attack frame, which emphasized the actions of conservatives in a partisan movement to remove Clinton from office; and, (3) the liberal response frame, which said the scandal was an orchestrated attempt by conservatives to destroy a popular Democratic president. Ironically, the conservative attack coverage actually helped Clinton, for it provided evidence to support the liberal response frame, creating "a backlash, moving opinion in the direction opposite the expected effect of the manifest news content" (Shah, Watts, Domke, and Fan 2002, 345). And, as a result, Americans "recoiled" against Republican Party leaders, and their approval ratings sank (Shah, Watts, Domke, and Fan 2002).

Interestingly, such negativity frames often bring charges of bias against the media, for members of the public often feel that their party or politician has been negatively and unfairly portrayed by a news outlet, and they will call upon the news outlet to alter its coverage or retract the story. Ironically such charges of bias, rather than angering or dismaying practicing journalists, often have an unintended effect on the individual reporter and the news organization. Altheide writes:

> Journalists often interpret charges of bias to be an indication of objective reporting—especially when liberals and conservatives make the charges simulta-

neously. Journalists argue that being attacked by both sides is evidence that their coverage is fair. (1976, 19)

Thus, in another circular chain of reasoning, journalists are freed from charges of bias by their nearly uniform negativity.

Hart, Smith-Howell, and Llewellyn (1990) have argued that the American news media from 1945 to 1985 portrayed the American presidency "as an increasingly besieged institution—socially, politically, and psychologically" (213). But in their analysis, they provide a discordant view of *Time* magazine's contemporary functioning as a news organization. The group reports that the magazine is increasingly taking a bureaucratic and political orientation in that news stories focus on "governmental institutions themselves, about complex patterns of wheeling and dealing, and about political deception and intrigue" (225). Rather than focusing on the individual psychology of the president as the magazine has done in the past, coverage delves into relational psychology or what they term "the psychodrama of the nation's capital" (Hart, Smith-Howell, and Llewellyn 1990, 225). Hart, Smith-Howell, and Llewellyn observe:

> *Time* now describes a government up-for-grabs, a far cry from the Great Man Politics that so long dominated it. Gone is the spectacle of the president on a white steed dominating a panoramic battle scene. In its place is Washington politics as guerrilla warfare—hand-to-hand combat, snipers along Connecticut Avenue. (1990, 227)

For Hart, Smith-Howell, and Llewellyn (1990), this signals a coming of age for *Time* magazine in that they consider a focus on institutional politics to be superior to an emphasis on an individual president. They write:

> By nudging the president offstage a bit, the magazine throws the spotlight on all that remains—congressional bargaining, White House infighting, the influence of political professionals (party officials, media personnel, political consultants, and so forth), the tortuous process by which legislation is passed, and the thousand other things that make executive politics so complicated and yet so intriguing. Ironically, *Time*'s institutional concerns fly in the face of the electronic media's corresponding personalization of politics. (228)

However, I feel compelled to ask if this observed change in the magazine's manner of operation is more reflective of the news media's obsession with subtext as described by Sabato (1991) than it is an improved, more mature reportorial style. If so, an emphasis on hidden political intrigue may only exacerbate the negativity felt by many Americans when considering their government operations (see also Patterson 1996).

Campaign Journalists as Armchair Psychologists

Jamieson and Waldman (2003) have reported that during presidential political campaigns, journalists have expanded their "watchdog" function by "vetting candidates, examining individuals instead of institutions to reveal corrupting influences and impulses" (24). They continue, arguing that "in campaigns reporters too often become amateur psychologists, probing the psyches of the candidates but largely failing to describe how what they find there relates to the job one of their outpatients will assume" (Jamieson and Waldman 2003, 24). Much has been made, for instance, of former vice president Al Gore's tendency for self-aggrandizement, focusing on his written and public statements concerning global warming. Frequently, news reporters, when discussing the horserace aspects of the campaign, explain front-runners' performances in terms of their personality characteristics; people simply like them. And, if a candidate is lagging behind, then the candidate has serious personality flaws that the voters are rejecting (Jamieson and Waldeman 2003). As a people, we are consumed with distinguishing the outside from the inside, appearances from realities, the true from the false. Nimmo (1989) writes:

> Politicians tamper with what TV newscasters think they should monopolize—the selection, control, and profit from pictures and content of campaigns. Newscasters tamper with what politicians think they should monopolize—the selection, control, and profit from episodes and incidents in the campaign. That in poaching in each other's turf they claim one another to be princes of darkness is beside the point. Neither provides the steady light to make situations intelligible for public choice. (477)

Ironically, this leeriness of image making or impression management has produced a situation where only those most adept at symbol creating and symbol maintaining are judged to be adequate leaders (Schram 1991). In a volume of his own essays for *Harper's*, Lewis Lapham includes a passage written about the presidential candidate Bill Clinton, providing a ready example:

> He defines himself as a man desperately eager to please, and the voraciousness of his appetite—for more friends, more speeches, more food and drink, more time onstage, more hands to shake, more hugs—suggests the emptiness of a soul that knows itself only by the names of what it seizes or consumes. (2000, 82)

Later on, during his last term in office, when Clinton's reported womanizing was finally confirmed, reporters returned to this explanation, frequently reporting that Clinton was neglected by his mother as a child, when she moved by herself to continue her nursing education. Their explanation for

Clinton's womanizing was that he was desperately seeking a mother figure—someone to love him.

During the 2000 presidential campaign, the news media's analysis of presidential candidates' psyches was reduced to short stereotypes: George W. Bush was stupid, and Al Gore was a liar (Jamieson and Waldeman 2003). Both depictions were harsh condemnations for men vying for the American presidency. Yet, on the whole, Jamieson and Waldeman (2003) believed that Gore got the worse end of news coverage, writing:

> Gore's flaw was reduced to trustworthiness, while Bush's was reduced to lack of knowledge, translated ultimately as inexperience. Inexperience can be remedied by experience or by marshaling a cabinet and selecting a vice president with experience. A lack of trust, on the other hand, is much harder to remedy. In addition, surveys of journalists have shown that honesty is the most important quality reporters believe a presidential candidate should have. (41–42)

And what is even more important is that voters judge honesty as the single most important characteristic for candidates running for office (Nimmo and Savage 1976).

Confrontational Politicians

Because political leaders have recognized the increasingly confrontational nature of the American news media, they have changed their behavior accordingly. Westerståhl and Johansson (1985) found that political leaders recognize the nastier they are in their public statements, the more likely they will be featured in news stories. And, consequently, officials deliberately provide heated, attack-oriented statements. Such controversy-oriented newsgathering procedures have had another consequence as well. Westerståhl and Johansson (1986) explain:

> In traditional reporting, critical statements were normally presented only when they constituted a central part of the statement, and in observance of the position of the critic. In the modern hunt for dissenting views, other standards apply. Not the weight, but rather the accessibility, the tone of the voice and, in some cases, the bias of the reporter are decisive. One result of this is that organized, special interests—always prepared to state their position—are constantly favored. (147–148)

In short, Westerståhl and Johansson (1986) believe that the general public's interests are seriously compromised by the inflated reporting of the lambasting special interests, for the general interests are never heard. And, while they do not champion the status quo, they do wonder what price to the tenor of democracy this practice has cost us as a people.

In their studies of political campaign news, Clancey and Robinson (1985) and Dewitt (1997) have found that even when candidates presented issue or public policy frames in their public speeches, the statements contained opposition attack statements, creating an even more negative campaign news presence. In this context, Clancey and Robinson (1985) have called these "candidate issues." Lichter and Noyes (1995) have argued, "While the content of such candidate news occasionally yields useful insights into an aspirant's character and personality, the preoccupation with personal questions often leaves viewers and readers ill-informed about the candidate's qualifications and policies" (79).

Presidential Transitions: A Not So Special Case

Even presidential transitions are not immune. Presidential transitions are often considered to be a "honeymoon period," a time when the news media refrain from criticizing the president-elect during the eleven weeks between Election Day and the inauguration. During this time, "A winning campaign organization must be turned into a successful governing organization, and similarly, a winning presidential candidate must turn miraculously into an effective president. The drama of an election campaign is evolving into the drama of governing" (Johnson a.k.a. Johnson-Cartee 1984, 1). This political evolution has been described as "a governing hiatus" (Blair and Savage 1980, 1), "the weakest hour of American democracy" (Benedict 1961, 16), or even more dramatically "the crisis of transition" (Benedict 1961, 16). It has been long suggested that because news media organizations recognize the uncertainty and anxiety created by presidential transitions, news assemblers voluntarily restrain themselves from criticizing the president-elect (see Grossman and Kumar 1981; Locander 1979; Manheim 1979). However, Manheim (1979) and Johnson (a.k.a. Johnson-Cartee 1985) found that the honeymoon period is a gross oversimplification and somewhat faulty explanation for what occurs. In short, the news during this time is not free from the subtext of the politics frame. Reporters use the transition to test the president-elect, and, being aware of the so-called honeymoon phenomenon, they may even overcompensate by taking a more aggressive stance than commonly expected (Manheim 1979). Much of transition reporting is covering routine announcements of staff and cabinet appointments and plans for the inauguration. The opposition virtually disappears from the radar screen of partisan commentary. However, this does not mean that such benign coverage is not littered with negativities (Johnson a.k.a. Johnson-Cartee 1985). I collected the following examples during a research project:

The slow pace of Reagan's Cabinet-Making was only part of the trouble his transition faced. Overstaffed and over its budget, the transition team has become a parody of Reagan's promise of efficient government, and Washington veterans are wondering whether the chaotic operation may foreshadow the Administration to come.

—*Newsweek*, December 29, 1980, 10

In the aftermath, it was easy for the most loyal Democrats to ascribe Bill Clinton's victory to anybody or anything but Bill Clinton. . . . Clinton? It couldn't have been he. He was neither beloved as a leader or trusted as a man; his first term had generated scandals enough to shadow his second before it had begun; his fellow Democrats avoided using his likeness in advertising; his average grade as president in a nonpartisan Pew Research Center Poll was a merely passable C.

—*Newsweek*, November 18, 1996, 126

Pervasive Negativity

Overwhelmingly, journalistic accounts of the political process are negative. "In the current era, political news is generally bad news. Journalists appear to be following the rule that if something is working in government and politics, it isn't worth reporting" (Owen 1997, 207). However, the news reporters aren't negative toward the system or the Congress as a whole; rather, they focus their negativity on individuals engaged in the political contest. "They focus blame on the individual rather than on the system, thereby protecting the legitimacy of the status quo" (McLeod and Detender 1999, 5). In 1995, Donohue, Tichenor, and Olien suggested that news scholars should rethink their conceptualization of the news media as watchdog (see chapter 3), arguing that in their unquestioning support of governmental institutions, the U.S. Constitution, and long-standing power configurations, the news media act more as a "guard dog." News reporters do more than simply "watch" and report facts about the government to their audiences. Rather, they will frequently take a bite out of those they are covering. According to Donohue, Tichenor, and Olien (1995), these guard dogs will turn on individuals, taking a bite out of political actors involved in public debate. Rozell (1994) has argued that Congress bashing, for instance, is a national pastime in no small part because of the consistent negative portrayal of the institution as well as individual congresspersons.

The exception to the guard dog analogy is when elites are not in conflict, especially in times of international conflict or war (McLeod and Detender 1999). During such times, the news media appear to "rally around the flag" and "rally around the president" as the commander in chief (Erikson, Luttbeg, and Tedin 1991). "In times of crisis reporters abandon irony, cynicism, and occasionally even skepticism to see the world through a nationalistic and patriotic lens. The lens focuses on some stories and frames that are substantially different from press practices as usual" (Jamieson and Waldeman 2003, 130–131). For example, the early news coverage of the 2003 Iraq war contrasted sharply with the news coverage during the American occupation of Iraq.

Disdaining the News

Reporters sometimes telegraph their disdain for news stories or news sources by the manner in which they write news copy and, in the case of broadcast journalism, the manner in which the copy is delivered. Patterson (1996) has argued: "Ingrained cynicism rather than knee-jerk liberalism is the media's real bias. Reporters have a decidedly low opinion of politics and politicians, and it slants their coverage of Republicans and Democrats alike" (17). Levy (1981) calls this "disdaining the news" (24). Cynicism is so widespread among reporters than even reporters whose specialty is news criticism fail to escape its pervasive influence; for example, Phillip Seib (1994) wrote in his book *Campaigns and Conscience: The Ethics of Political Journalism*:

> A related responsibility for the reporter is to recognize, and to avoid being victimized by, the unending con-game politicians run as they try to manipulate coverage. . . . As gatekeeper governing the flow of news to the public, the journalist should not let a politician's self-serving propaganda reach voters unless accompanied by substantiation. (28–29)

Disdaining the news is the process by which journalists demonstrate a consciousness of the problematic nature of covering a tainted social phenomenon by engaging in professional role-distancing behaviors that exhibit "aversion, contempt, insolence, or indifference toward a phenomenon on the part of the newsworker" (Levy 1981, 27). Levy (1981) argues that disdaining the news is a defensive professional measure protecting "the newsworker by rhetorically distancing him or her from the tainted phenomenon and by informing possible critics of the difficulty being confronted—all in the hope that news can be made while criticism is averted" (28). Goffman (1961) identified role-distancing behaviors as efforts to impression manage situations that dictate performances that violate central expectations of role behaviors for an individual.

According to Levy (1981), there are some social phenomena where competitive pressures necessarily dictate that the phenomena be covered; however, the working journalist may believe that the social phenomena are "tainted" and therefore not worthy of coverage. For Levy (1981), a social phenomenon is tainted, first, to the degree that newsworkers perceive it as deviating from or conflicting with those considerations or decision-making rules which govern story availability and suitability choices. These considerations include rules about news sources, the substantive importance of phenomena, media styles and formats, and media organizational goals. Also included among story considerations are those enduring socio-political values, opinions, and reality judgments which collectively make up the para-ideology of journalism. Second, a phenomenon is tainted to the extent that newsworkers believe that other journalists and audiences share their perception of deviance or conflict. (24–25)

Tainted social phenomena, in the eyes of the journalist, might include presidential conventions, political campaign events, pseudo-events, celebrities, and highly publicized happenings such as the Oscars (Levy 1981). Levy (1981) provides an example of such disdaining of the news by *Washington Post* reporter Nicholas Leman in 1979, during the Florida presidential caucuses. Leman wrote:

The press is here in vast numbers because the politicians are here. The politicians are here because the press is. Many headlines and much TV news will follow. . . . But not a single delegate will be chosen. . . . The Florida caucuses have elevated the media event to a whole new level. . . . This story is in the nature of warning to consumers of news, an attempt to explain how the Florida caucuses became such a big deal. (1979, 1)

Levy (1981) argues that disdaining the news is a conservative behavior in that it reinforces the status quo and the operating procedures of the news organization. And he argues that incidents of disdaining the news are likely to increase as news promoters seek to manipulate the news media into covering "tainted" events. But what remains unclear is the impact of such cynicism on audience members when it is directed at public figures, political party institutionalized activities, corporate activities, and so on. Will the cynicism spread to audience members, or will they consider the disdainful commentary to be the personal opinion of a lone individual without consequence? Research suggests that cynicism will only increase as news exposure increases. Miller, Goldenberg, and Erbring (1979) were able to explain levels of inefficacy as "a result of accumulating distrust, where policy dissatisfaction, rather than dislike of incumbent leaders, acts as the main determinant of cynicism" (67). They conclude that media criticism affects political malaise by affecting the levels of trust that audience members have in their government, which eventually leads to policy dissatisfaction and ultimately cynicism and malaise (Miller, Goldenberg, and Erbring 1979, 67). Similarly, Fuller (1996) has argued that news reporters all too often follow the political philosophy expressed in Robert Penn Warren's *All the King's Men*: "Man is conceived in sin and born in corruption and he passeth from the stink of the didie to the stench of the shroud. There is always something" ([1946] 1953, 203). Consequently, journalists have little faith in human nature, suspecting the worst, and finding it. Fuller writes:

> But this view has grave consequences. When they write this assumption into their news reports, they suggest the extremely simpleminded view that all social problems could be solved if the people wrestling with them were honest. Worse, to the potential voter, if all politicians are the same, then why bother knowing their names, let alone keeping up with them in the paper? (1996, 192)

In recent times, our nation's news stories are ones where men and women appear out of nowhere, only to rise to great fame and fortune; then, after a time, a hubris act, a fall from grace, a public lynching, and ultimately obscurity once again. Fuller (1996) writes:

> Journalism has become the means by which, like people of primitive myth, we anoint and then kill our kings. It isn't only presidents who receive this treatment. Very nearly anybody whom journalists help to raise high, they can be counted on to try to bring down. (192)

Is it any wonder, then, that American news consumers are cynical? For this condition to improve, Fuller warns that journalists must learn to bridle their cynical impulses, "to exercise more self-control over their own darkest habits of thought" (1996, 192).

Gorney has defined sensationalism as "the use of anything that plays on sense perceptions and emotions to elicit a quick, intense and usually superficial interest or reaction. In brief, that which is sensational limits experience as a source of knowledge in favor of emotional or sensory stimulation" (1992, 455). While a number of researchers have identified specific types of news stories such as disasters, accidents, and crimes as inherently sensational (Adams 1978; Hofstetter and Dozier 1986; Wulfemeyer 1982), others have suggested that sensationalism is deliberate exaggeration on the part of news assemblers in their depiction of events (Fishman 1981). However, the Media Institute of Washington, D.C., and the Public's Right to Information Task Force of the President's Commission on the Accident at Three Mile Island have both suggested that news assemblers' speculations (crystal ball gazing, predictions, worst-case scenarios, or "what if" projections) are most indicative of sensationalism in the news (Gorney 1992, 456–457).

Brosius and Eps (1995) argue that journalists respond to unfamiliar but alarming events in such a way as to cast them as "key events." Key events are regarded as exceptional events such as societal catastrophes and cataclysmic accidents. For instance, in their analysis of German news coverage, Brosius and Eps found four key events associated with what was perceived to be growing right-wing radicalism. They argue that initially journalists try to make sense of the situation by talking with other reporters, reading other news accounts, or contacting leading experts. This search focuses their attention not only on one particular key event but on any others similar to it as well. Correspondingly, this means that journalists then have their priorities structured to find similar key events, assigning meaning to them in familiar ways. Brosius and Eps (1995) suggest that a key event such as a racially motivated hate crime becomes a prototype that transforms "an abstract scheme into a concrete image of an object, person or an event. More than that, they are also recognized faster than other objects and are retrieved easier from memory" (396). The key event comes to stand for the presence of the radical right wing in German national life. Consequently, journalists are in fact "primed" to discover other key events; key events shape journalists' perceptions of reality and "create or change a frame of reference for subsequent news coverage" (Brosius and Eps 1995, 394). Such priming may "elicit disproportional attention from journalists and hence more frequent media reporting of subsequent events that have similar qualities to the key event. The quality of the event might suggest a certain type of evaluation" (Brosius and Eps 1995, 408). Terrorist acts with unexpected amounts of violence and damage often produce a lasting change in news coverage and subsequently a lasting change among political actors' and the public's discourse.

But it is not just the depictions of political intrigue or the negative evaluations of our political leaders and our policy apparatus that should concern us. The news media's negativity toward government and all those who either work there or who attempt to influence those who do has far-reaching effects on how U.S. businesses and business leaders are portrayed as well. The negativity orientation affects not only how various governmental levels are depicted interacting with the business community, but also how business, business leaders, and corporate America in general are portrayed. Corporate America shares with government the readily distinguishable "news" facilitators, the size, the formally structured organization, and the easily identifiable elite officials. We have only to consider the recent news feeding frenzy surrounding the collapse of Enron, which even placed the reporting on the War on Terror on the back burner. Therefore, both corporations and their executives fall under the scrutiny of the news media. When an American corporation makes the news, it is usually for one of the following reasons:

Plants opening or closing
Downsizing or employee layoffs; terminations

Labor and management conflicts
Contract disputes
Introduction of new products or discontinuation of old products
Notification of product dangers; recalls
Acquisitions, mergers
Bankruptcy and reorganizations
Unfair and illegal workplace activities
Unfair and illegal marketplace activities
Accidents involving loss of life or limb
Profit and loss statements, annual reports
Stock reports and stock earnings; stock splits
Executive hirings and firings
Executive salary and compensation packages
Environmental problems, pollution, contamination
Civil lawsuits against
Federal investigations and lawsuits

An examination of this listing reveals that the majority of individual news appearances by members of the nation's business, corporate, or industrial communities are precipitated by the members' actions, either current or impending, which news assemblers have judged as negative.

This news frame of negativity has received widespread criticism from the American business community. "In brief, accusations have been made that the news media are antibusiness, overemphasizing stories of consumer fraud, unethical practices, shoddy products and so forth" (Peterson, Kozmetsky, and Cunningham 1982, 57). Business executives often perceive the news media in ways that breed a natural antagonism; Banks (1978) explained:

> It is possible more or less to pinpoint three distinct levels of antagonism. The first involves everyday operational relationships, i.e., the specific reactions to specific encounters in which the business executive or his company has been involved. The second is attitudinal: a businessman's conviction that the great power of the media is used selectively to sour the body politic on corporate product profit and practice. The third is societal: a gut feeling that behind a facade of constitutional righteousness, First Amendment guarantees are being misused at the expense of other institutional rights no less basic, with a new loss to the American system. (241)

According to Peterson, Albaum, Kozmetsky, and Cunningham (1984), the antagonism is mutual. Both institutions resent and distrust the other. This mutual antagonism between business and the media is the product of both institutions viewing themselves "as competing adversaries for influence in

American society. Not only does each believe the other is too influential, but each wants to have the most influence and at the same time neutralize the influence of the other" (57). And Peterson et al. (1984) observe that this antagonistic relationship between business and the media has significant impact on American society, in that it is the expression of this antagonism within mass-communicated news reports that colors the public's perceptions of business (57).

During the last thirty years, the American public has shown decreasing levels of confidence and trust in most American institutions including business, government, and labor (Peterson, Albaum, Kozmetsky, and Cunningham 1984), whom they perceive as being primarily motivated out of greed or self-interest. "In particular, there is resentment of big business, and concentration of power in the hands of the self-interested is viewed as inherently dangerous and untrustworthy" (Peterson, Albaum, Kozmetsky, and Cunningham 1984, 57).

Yet there is little consensus among the public about media bias toward business. In a national mail survey, 61 percent of the respondents thought the media to be biased toward the media, but of those respondents, roughly one-half thought the media were biased in favor of business, and one-half thought the media were biased against business (Peterson, Kozmetsky, and Cunningham, 1982, 462). Yet distinct differences were observed among those who either perceived the media as probusiness or viewed the media as antibusiness. "Respondents intuitively favorable toward business—respondents characterizing themselves as Republicans, politically or socially conservative, or being in a household where the head is a manager—tended to perceive the media as biased against business" (Peterson, Kozmetsky, and Cunningham 1982, 464). In 1980, Robert Stevenson and Mark Greene made an astute observation about a similar analysis of data, when they observed that "news bias is less a function of reporters' accuracy or fairness and more a function of what readers and viewers think the situation is or ought to be" (121).

Similarly, in a study comparing newspaper business editors with the general public, two-thirds of the business editors thought the media were unbiased in their presentations of business news; however, less than four out of ten general public respondents shared this view. And of those business editors who did perceive a bias, 71 percent thought the media were biased against business; yet, among the general public who initially reported bias, the sample was roughly split between those who saw a positivity bias and those who saw a negativity bias (see Peterson, Albaum, Kozmetsky, and Cunningham 1984, 59). Interestingly, the study also found that business editors have far more confidence in the American economic system than do members of the general public. Eighty percent of the business editors express confidence in capitalism, while only 61 percent of the general public felt that way (Peterson, Albaum, Kozmetsky, and Cunningham 1984, 60). Perhaps the negative frames influence the news consumers far more than those who construct them.

Reese, Daly, and Hardy (1987) found, as Rubin did in a 1981 study of network news, that "television news does 'politicize' economic stories . . . and that politicization is primarily 'executivization.' The president and his branch are mentioned 81% of the time any government actor is mentioned" (Reese, Daly, and Hardy 1987, 144). In a study of national network newscasts for a ten-year period, Randall (1987) found that 40 percent of newscasts had at least one news story concerning corporate crime. This is significant, according to Randall, in that "any information conveyed to the public about corporate misconduct may result in a public demand for more stringent government regulation, and public officials, seeking to be responsive to the public, may increase regulatory controls over corporations" (1987, 150; see also Clinard and Yeager 1980).

Although the majority of public criticism is leveled at the news media for what is perceived as an antibusiness bias, it is also true that, at least for some news critics, "the news media are pro-business, catering to the desires of advertisers and public relations personnel" (Peterson, Kozmetsky, and Cunningham 1982, 461; Frankel 2000).

In a commentary by Max Frankel in the *New York Times Magazine*, January 9, 2000, Frankel decried what he perceived to be the increasingly cozy relationship between business and the news media. He argued that because of economic forces

> Many managers of media enterprises put stockholders ahead of readers or listeners. By giving priority to stock values and profit margins, they slighted their obligations to the public. Indeed, they have shown themselves ignorant or contemptuous of the ethical standards so long and painstakingly erected to protect the credibility of their news operations. (24)

Newsmagazines that accept advertorials, television news shows that hype future programming on the network or that hype celebrity movies or television shows as a result of their interview appearances, and newspapers that promise an "advertising friendly environment" appropriate to the company or the company's product are all examples of blurring the lines between news and commerce in the United States, according to Frankel (2000). Frankel is dismayed about this blurring of the lines, believing in fact that the traditional wall between the two societal forces has now crumbled; he writes:

> A wall is needed to insulate the gathering of news, which should be a selfless public service, from the pursuit of profit, which is needed to guarantee the inde-

pendence of the business. Journalism, in other words, is a costly and paradoxical enterprise: it can flourish only when profitable, but it is most suspect when it seeks a profit at all costs. (2000, 25)

Frankel's commentary was in response to the revelations concerning Chairman Mark Willes of Times Mirror, owner of the *Los Angeles Times*, who involved himself in the day-to-day news functions of the newspaper by requiring that all reporters and editors submit a business plan designed to produce greater newspaper and advertising sales.

One thing led to another, and it was suddenly revealed that the *Los Angeles Times* has been a secret partner in the building of a new sports arena; Frankel (2000) writes that the newspaper

> had agreed to divide the profits of an issue of its Sunday magazine devoted entirely to benign coverage of the project. Indeed, the arena encouraged its contractors and patrons to advertise in the magazine, which an independent newspaper might well have questioned as a kickback scheme. (25)

Not only the *Times* news staff but also working journalists everywhere were outraged. Chairman Willes eventually confessed and apologized, leaving Frankel to comment that Willes should have heeded the advice of William F. Thomas, a legendary *Times* editor, who said, "When you take down a wall, you'd better understand why it was there in the first place" (Frankel 2000, 25).

Negative Effects

Some critics do not believe that the news presents enough coverage on business affairs for either the public or the business community to make informed financial and economic decisions (Hynds 1980; Peterson, Kozmetsky, and Cunningham 1982) others argue that what economic news the news media does present is far too simplified to be considered meaningful in terms of positively affecting an individual's knowledge base in business- or economics-related decision-making processes (Adoni and Cohen 1978). And, in what at first seems a contradictory position, others have argued that "economic information is often very abstract, sophisticated and difficult to comprehend by large segments of the population even in its popularized form" (Adoni and Cohen 1978, 61) Most, if not all, economic news, though simplified, is well over the heads of most of the audience. Adoni and Cohen (1978) found that despite a widespread belief among economic news consumers that the news media fulfill their economic information needs, resulting in their "subjective feeling of understanding" (62) current economic news, economic news consumers had "a very low level of objective knowledge" about economic concepts (64). Because the news consumers are exposed to economic news, they often develop a

"vicarious sense of knowledge and understanding." They do not *really* understand, but their massive exposure to the facts and explanations given by the economic reporters and experts creates for them a false impression that the media help them understand the economic situation. (Adoni and Cohen 1978, 68; emphasis in original)

Adoni and Cohen further observe:

A striking fact in the data presented is that a large proportion of the public has very poor knowledge and understanding of basic economic concepts, used and repeatedly endlessly by the different mass media, and that the level of knowledge is lowest among two social subgroups: women and people from the lower socioeconomic strata. Moreover, the subjective evaluation of the respondent's level of understanding supports the objective test of concept definition and economic terms: more than one-third of the sample report they do not understand what is happening in the economic realm of society and another half only partly understands. (1978, 68)

Negativity's Lasting Consequences

A daily diet of negative news, whether about politicians, business leaders, or societal ills, has serious consequences on how news consumers react to their social, economic, and political environment. Such negative information seems to influence people more than positive information does (Taylor 1986). Negative information is weighted more heavily than positive information, is more persuasive, and is easier to remember. This is called the negativity effect (see Kellerman 1984; Lau 1980, 1982, 1985).

K. A. Smith (1987) found that newspaper coverage of community issues increases public concern about these issues and ultimately produces poorer evaluations or more negative evaluations of local governmental services involved or implicated in the newspaper coverage. Birgersson (1977) and Sohn (1978) noted that in communities where individuals were more likely to discuss news coverage of local community services, public issues, and their concerns about involved governmental services with friends, families, and coworkers, dissatisfaction was greatest concerning those involved community services. Thus, even though large urban communities have far more governmental services, it is the small community that has the highest levels of public dissatisfaction concerning governmental services because of the greater interactions among residents and the heavier reliance on the local newspaper

(Birgersson 1977). The more individuals discuss their concerns about governmental services, the greater their dissatisfaction with those services (Birgersson 1977; Sohn 1978).

Some research indicates that negative information will usually provide "immediate shifts in belief structures, attitudes and behaviors; in other cases, it has been argued that negativity may persist in the form of affect even after a complete invalidation of its original cognitive base" (Weinberger, Allen, and Dillon 1984, 287). In other words, even when respondents were told by an authoritative source that the previous assertion of wrongdoing was absolutely false, audience members persisted in their negative assessments of attacked individuals (see also Zajonc 1980).

In the early 1970s, Wamsley and Pride (1972) and Robinson (1976a, 1976b) warned that an emphasis on the negative aspects of politics and governmental processes in news media accounts could prove denigrative of the political system. Because contemporary news stories rarely have happy endings, our political leaders often appear ineffectual, failing to solve problems or to resolve issues (Schram 1991). Other researchers have maintained that media dependency breeds political malaise and negative assessments of government (O'Keefe 1980; Becker and Whitney, 1980), for such reports increase our distrust and disaffection with the government and governmental leaders because of the overwhelmingly negative content in mass-mediated news reports.

Miller, Goldenberg, and Erbring (1979) have provided substantial evidence to support the hypothesis that media dependency breeds dissatisfaction with government, producing distrust and cynicism, and culminating in a predominant political malaise among citizens. Their study combined

> survey data from the 1974 American National Election Study with the front-page content of 94 newspapers in an investigation of the relationship between the degree of negative political criticism found in newspapers and their readers' feelings of trust in government and a sense of their own political effectiveness. (67)

Their analysis presents an intriguing picture of America in 1974. Miller, Goldenberg, and Erbring (1979) characterize the majority of Americans in 1974 as being disaffected with their government (see textbox 8.1). Yet they found that American disaffection was not a rejection of governmental institutions; they write that

> even as these negative sentiments are directed at institutional norms, they do not reflect a desire to replace our system of government with a different set of political arrangements, but represent at this point a decided discontent with the *mal-functioning* of the government. (Miller, Goldenberg, and Erbring 1979, 81; emphasis in original)

Textbox 8.1

Mediated Discontent Terminology

Cynicism "indicates a negative evaluation of government and reflects the belief that the government is not functioning in accordance with individual expectations of efficiency, honesty, competence and equity" (Miller, Goldenberg, and Erbring 1979, 67).

Political efficacy "denotes the feeling that an individual and the public can have an impact on the political process because government institutions will respond to their needs. The lack of efficacy or the feeling of *inefficacy* indicates the belief that the public cannot influence political outcomes because government leaders and institutions are unresponsive to their needs" (Miller, Goldenberg, and Erbring 1979, 67; emphasis added).

Political disaffection is the state of discontent when individuals find governmental institutions unresponsive to their needs or demands and express their distrust of government and governmental leaders (see Miller, Goldenberg, and Erbring 1979, 73).

Political malaise is accumulated disaffection, resulting in individuals perceiving their government as responsible for what they view as widespread political, economic, and social decline. Political malaise is often accompanied by increased anxiety in that individuals have lost their faith in the government's ability to satisfy growing public demands.

And Miller, Goldenberg, and Erbring observed that Americans did indeed have a lot to be unhappy about in 1974: the political scandals of the Nixon administration, the social turmoil of the 1960s, the unpopularity of the Vietnam War, and the widespread but general disapproval of governmental policy performance left many Americans disaffected. In addition, the researchers observed that highly critical news media coverage also contributed to this growing malaise in America (1979; see textbox 8.1).

Miller, Goldenberg, and Erbring (1979) found that readers of highly critical newspapers were found to be far more distrustful of the government than readers of less critical newspapers. In the study, critical news accounts' effects on political efficacy were modest; however, Miller, Goldenberg, and Erbring (1979) suggested that perhaps this modest association was because of the rather limited time frame under analysis. And they proposed a **model of mediated discontent** that depicts political inefficacy as the result of accumulating distrust in government. They write:

As discontent with government accumulates over time, we would expect, eventually an erosion of citizens' beliefs about political institutions. The belief that institutions are not responsive to the needs of the people may, therefore, develop directly out of a pervasive sense of distrust of authorities; it would be influenced only indirectly by dissatisfaction with the incumbent administration and government policies or media criticism. (Miller, Goldenberg, and Erbring 1979, 79)

In concluding their study, Miller, Goldenberg, and Erbring (1979) observe:

Contrary to previous writing, distrust of government does not primarily reflect disaffection from current incumbents, but denotes instead dissatisfaction with governmental policy performance and the direct impact of criticism in the media; it would thus appear to be an early indicator of accumulating diffuse discontent directed first at authorities and policies and only later at institutions or regime norms. . . . Apparently, the public's evaluations of government performance flow rather directly from the image of the political process as seen through the prism of newspaper reporting. Evaluations of the political system and its institutions, however, are less directly attributable to media effects; they depend on the degree of attitudinal buffering surrounding people's beliefs in prevailing regime norms. Only through its influence on a general political distrust of authorities does the media have an indirect influence on evaluations of institutional responsiveness. Nevertheless, even among politically sophisticated citizens, cynicism due to continued and frequent exposure to newspaper articles critical of political leaders eventually accumulates into dissatisfaction with the responsiveness of institutions. Ultimately, therefore, media effects can be understood as reactions to relevant, if "mediated" political realities. (81–82)

Indirectly Negative, but Negative Nonetheless

Media portrayals do not have to be directly negative about public figures, corporations, or celebrities to ultimately have a negative effect on society. If ordinary people are routinely depicted as helpless, rather pathetic creatures waiting for their political leaders to rescue them, this portrayal could result in reduced levels of political efficacy among those attending to the media. For this reason, we will now consider two indirect negative effects: the power and efficacy effect, and the aprocessual and ahistorical effect.

Significantly, the people in the news are usually powerful political figures who are cast as either heroes or villains shaping the political realities of our times. Gans (1979) found that 70–85 percent of news stories deal with what he called the "knowns," or the publicly recognized players such as corporate heads, interest group leaders, elected officials, or political candidates (8–13). And the "unknowns," or people who are not public figures, appeared in around 20 percent of all news stories (Gans 1979, 13–15). The unknowns were the victims of crimes, perpetrators of crimes, freaks (people who are engaged in bizarre activities), survey respondents, strikers, or protesters (Gans 1979, 8–13; Lasorsa and Reese 1990). The knowns were depicted as being in mortal combat with other "knowns" or with reified social and economic forces (Gans 1979, 8–15; Tuchman 1981a, 1981b). Just as issues are depicted in terms of personality struggles, so too are social and economic forces that have been reified. Such **reification**, or the giving of concrete characteristics to abstract concepts, is common in mass-communicated news reports.

Gans (1979) found news reports presented the "unknowns" as being dependent on the "knowns" for survival, or, in other words, the news reports showed the unknowns as ineffectual while the knowns were portrayed as both powerful and effective. Similarly, Dahlgreen (1981) made the point that whether political leaders are pitted in ferocious battles against other political figures or reified social forces, the results are the same for the audience. In short, the public is presented as inefficacious (Dahlgreen 1981, 105), unable to exercise power, and ineffective in seeking solutions to either private or public dilemmas. Thus, this creates an artificial image of contemporary life where modern humans are extremely dependent on the knowns—for the most part, their own political leaders (Dahlgreen 1981, 108)—which ultimately distorts the social and political realities of our time, resulting in increased levels of inefficacy and eventually political malaise.

Similar to the news media's reification of social and economic forces, news assemblers also portrayed even collectivities, nations, or institutions in anthropomorphic terms—providing groups, populations, or organizations with personlike attributes and features (Gans 1979, 19–21). This ensures the continuing worship of the cult of personality. The United States is often depicted much like Job of the Bible, an individual repeatedly tested by God to withstand great punishments and ill luck. And even in such a diverse nation, the news often reports public opinion as a "national will" or suggests that "Americans" believe this or that or do this or act that way, as if we were "one."

However, it should be noted that while focusing on the powerful is an important journalistic strategic ritual, it should also be remembered that for the most part the power that is depicted is **formal power**. Power is equated in news stories with legalistic or institutional definitions; people have power because of their titles or the positions they occupy within the organization (Golding 1981). Informal power, or the power based on an individual and his or her impression management skills in interacting with others, is often ignored (Golding 1981). However, in my study of three presidential transitions (Johnson a.k.a. Johnson-Cartee 1984), I found a marked increase in attention to informal power. I suggested that this has probably occurred for a number of reasons: "the president's increased reliance on a personal staff; the growing fragmented nature of American politics; and, the growing consciousness of political intrigue and wrongdoings since the mid-1960s" (216). Despite this increased coverage of informal power, I noted that:

> The accounts did little to explain the processes of government. Rather it distorted the nature of politics. For a rather peculiar distinction is made: (1) the job description is a legitimate power source (institutional power, formal power), and (2) an individual's personal power (informal power) is an illegitimate power source. The word "politics" has been defined as informal power; and, for that reason, many journalists picture [or depict] political persuasion, negotiations, and compromise as a corrupt process. In many ways, to suggest that someone is political has come to suggest that someone is evil, corrupt. (Johnson a.k.a. Johnson-Cartee 1984, 216; see also Crick 1972, 15–34)

Similarly, Semetko, Blumler, Gurevitch, Weaver, Barkin, and Wilhoit (1991) in their study of political campaign news observed:

> Whether because of the greater "openness" of the American political system compared to the British, or because of the high visibility of the links between American politicians and money, with its potentially corruptible effects (which made the term *the sleaze factor* part of the American political vocabulary), or perhaps because of the apparently pragmatic, nonideological character of American politics, public perceptions of American politicians seem to be characterized more by suspicion of political activity and of those who engage in it than by respect for it. (5)

I have argued that contemporary journalists write as if they do not understand the role of power and politics in a democratic society; I explained, "Like a young child observing adults playing bridge, journalists watch the shuffling maneuvers, the feinting, the mind-reading gambits, but they do not know the rules of the game" (Johnson a.k.a. Johnson-Cartee 1984, 217).

Similar to their difficulty in addressing power, the news media often obscure the nature of political process. News speaks only to the immediate present. Events are written about in a succession. Rarely are news stories connected with similar news stories across time to form patterns or to establish the processes of history. For the most part, then, we may say that news is both aprocessual and ahistorical (Dahlgreen 1981; Golding 1981). Because of this, the audience does not see the "interconnectedness" of events; it does not see the evolution of problems, issues, or events. And, for this reason, audience members at times may feel overwhelmed by the litany of apparently unrelated and immediate problems presented by the news media, and at the same time, they may feel discouraged as problems emerge only to remain unresolved. This too breeds dissatisfaction with government and governmental actors.

Recently, researchers have focused on another disturbing consequence of negative news—compassion fatigue. In other words, news consumers are so inundated with bad news about social problems that they "burn out" or lose the ability to empathize with those in need or with those who are suffering, a phenomenon that Kinnick, Krugman, and Cameron (1996) have called the **compassion fatigue syndrome**. Such burnout is associated with a feeling of powerlessness: "'It's hopeless; you can't change things; it's bigger than all of us, so why bother trying?'" (Maslach 1982, 146). This is particularly troubling in light of the media's tendency to focus on the bad. Kinnick, Krugman, and Cameron (1996) write:

> The desire to attract media consumers has fueled a preference for conflict, violence, and crises over chronic—but perhaps more profound problems, and for social problems which are visually dramatic and consequential for a large number of people. Thus, the media tend to sensationalize social problems as crises of large and overwhelming proportions. (690)

And news reports frequently do not provide recommendations for solutions to social problems, or they fail to provide information on how audience members might act to assist or to help others experiencing the social problem. This increases feelings of inefficacy. And, often, news reports negatively portray institutions such as the mental-health-care system as being incapable of solving social problems through ineptness, lack of funding, or the sheer magnitude of the problem—a portrayal that Robinson has called "journalistic Naderism" (1976b, 420; see also Kinnick, Krugman, and Cameron 1996). Compassion fatigue is "associated with lowered interest, emotional arousal, and information-seeking toward these social problems" (Kinnick, Krugman, and Cameron 1996, 702). Kinnick, Krugman, and Cameron (1996) found evidence that compassion fatigue is common among the general population, and that mass-communicated news reports significantly influence the development of this phenomenon; they write:

> The media contribute to compassion fatigue toward social problems in two primary ways: by providing content that serves as aversive stimuli, prompting avoidance strategies; and by fostering desensitization to social problems through redundant and predominately negative messages which reach the point of saturation. Respondents blamed their desensitization and avoidance strategies on the nature and content of television news reports, and local news in particular. (703)

In Summary

News framing that personalizes politics often distorts the true nature of the political process, for the political world is far more complicated than two lone combatants attacking one another. Complex social problems should not be reduced to trivial political contests, because such presentations disguise the complexities involved in policy making and produce unrealistic expectations for quick and easy solutions. Confrontational news frames heighten news consumers' anxiety about the character and efficacy of their political leaders. Such news frames stress the malfunctions of government rather than the successes of governmental policy and, as a result, news consumers are often left feeling hopeless about the future of our democracy.

Appendix

The 1986 Drug War and Media Convergence

IN 1974, AS THE RESULT OF THE EFFORTS of the White House Special Action Office for Drug Abuse Prevention, the National Institute on Drug Abuse (NIDA) was formed to combat illegal drug use in the United States by decreasing the demand for drugs within our borders (Lachter and Forman 1989). In 1982, NIDA developed and disseminated a "Just Say No" campaign designed to reach junior high school students with the message that drug use was unhealthy and, more importantly, that a drug-free life was the preferred, dominant healthy norm for young people (Lachter and Forman 1989). This campaign is widely associated with former first lady Nancy Reagan, who made numerous public appearances supporting the "Just Say No" theme (Forman and Lachter 1989). In 1986, NIDA launched a multimedia campaign targeted at eighteen- to thirty-five-year-olds. The campaign was called "Cocaine, The Big Lie," delivering the message "Cocaine is extremely addictive and causes severe social, medical, and psychiatric problems" (Forman and Lachter 1989, 17).

Research conducted by NIDA indicated that cocaine was a substantial problem in the United States, affecting all income and class groups. Between 20 and 24 million Americans had used cocaine at least once in their lives (Forman and Lachter 1989, 13–14). A series of events accentuated the problem of cocaine use in the United States during 1985 and 1986: the assassination of two Drug Enforcement Agents in Mexico in 1985; the emergence and rapid distribution of a particularly addictive form of cocaine, with the street name of "crack," during the same year; and the overdose death of University of Maryland basketball star Len Bias during early 1986.

Reese and Danielian's research indicated that crack became a problem on the streets of New York City months before it was recognized as such in other major U.S. cities; however, because crack was a problem in New York, one of our top media cities, crack use became a problem for all Americans by virtue of the *New York Times*'s coverage of the issue (1989, 30). Such intermedia convergence on issues has been called "media hype" or "media exaggeration" (Reese and Danielian 1989, 31). The death of Len Bias in February 1986 "brought together the political and human aspects of drug abuse" (Merriam 1989, 25; see also Reese and Danielian 1989), and the proximity of Washington, D.C., to the University of Maryland gave the *Washington Post* the opportunity to dramatize the cocaine issue with the death of a well-known, well-liked sports figure (Reese and Danielian, 1989). The *Los Angeles Times* quickly followed their lead, emphasizing cocaine use in California. However, although all three national newspapers devoted a significant amount of their news hole to the cocaine story, it was the *New York Times* that clearly set the agenda for the television networks (Reese and Danielian 1989). Reese and Danielian's research clearly demonstrates that the news media do indeed "cover issues in a similar fashion and at roughly the same time" (1989, 42).

NIDA's increased public information campaign efforts as well as the deaths of prominent national figures prompted heightened news coverage of the cocaine issue, culminating in a peak of news media interest during the summer of 1986, which has come to be known as "cocaine summer" among news media personnel. Yet research funded by the federal government indicated that cocaine use had leveled off during the past decade (Baker 1986; Danielian and Reese 1989; Diamond, Accosta, and Thornton 1987; P. Kerr 1986). Reese and Danielian have argued that "lacking any objective evidence of a drug epidemic or crisis, we must look to the media themselves to determine why the drug issue received such a concentrated amount of coverage in such a short time" (1989, 30). Clearly, news convergence had occurred, but why and how had this happened?

For Danielian and Reese (1989), the answer rested with intermedia agenda setting; they wrote:

> We see the drug issue in 1985 and 1986 as having more to do with intermedia agenda-setting than with the structure of society, real-world indicators, or even spectacular news events, although of course these factors play some role in most news stories. (47)

Their research documents what they describe as a "reciprocal, back-and-forth attention cycle" among the news media—national newspapers, network news, and national newsmagazines (Danielian and Reese 1989, 55). While the *New York Times* did lead the other media in cocaine coverage and provided the longest and most consistent coverage during 1985 and 1986, Danielian and Reese (1989) observed:

> The news magazines and other influential dailies also played a part in keeping the issue before the public. There were some weeks where media coverage seemed to converge, whereas in others the media appeared to alternate covering cocaine from week to week, first one medium and then another giving the issue heavy play, until all joined in. (56)

And the researchers concluded that "the intermedia agenda setting process is more like a square dance than a force[d] march—the patterns and partners continually change as both external events and the media 'dancers' themselves call the steps" (Danielian and Reese 1989, 57). A textual analysis of their data revealed a great deal about news media convergence. Danielian and Reese observed:

> Weekly convergence on a story exists when a story is breaking, when coverage is at its peak, and when the story comes from a national or international source. When the newspapers all go in on a breaking story, they cover it in the same ways using the same themes and sources. (1989, 633)

They also observed that frequently the same unidentified administration news sources and international sources were used by each national newspaper, providing evidence of their reliance on routine news sources who did not want to be directly quoted (Danielian and Reese 1989). This is particularly troubling for Danielian and Reese, in that such findings have dramatic implications; they presented such a dilemma:

> This is potentially troublesome, for if we hear mostly the voices of national leaders on issues as they are first developed and defined, and if an issue becomes a story when national leaders speak, then they can frame the debate. For example, what happens when these leaders decide that the "cocaine epidemic" calls for military action in a foreign country? What other voices are heard? (1989, 65)

Such a speculation is not idle chatter, for U.S. military forces had joined Bolivian troops to raid cocaine-producing facilities in Bolivia in 1986. And during the first Bush administration, U.S. forces invaded Panama to capture Manuel Noriega, a purported cocaine kingpin.

Shoemaker, Wanta, and Leggett (1989) found that "the more the mass media emphasize drugs, the more the public is concerned with drugs as a problem—once again providing evidence to support the agenda-setting hypothesis" (79). During the fifteen years studied, "Increases in news coverage resulted in increased nominations of drugs as the most important problem facing this country. Decreased coverage resulted in fewer mentions of drugs" (D. L. Shaw and McCombs 1989, 114). In our own nationwide, statewide, and countywide surveying in the fall of 1986, we found that regardless of what governmental level was being discussed, when we addressed the question, we found that respondents viewed the most important problem facing the nation, state, and county as drugs. Clearly, the media had set the public's agenda.

In their study of nine national news organizations, Shoemaker, Wanta, and Leggett concluded:

> *The New York Times* and *The Los Angeles Times* were responsible for almost all of the variance in public opinion accounted for by all nine media. These two major newspapers may have had more influence on public concern with drugs than do all three major television networks and all three major news magazines combined. (1989, 79)

And Shoemaker, Wanta, and Leggett (1989) found that the relationships between news coverage and public opinion polls were closest during the one month before a poll and four months before a poll, illustrating the importance of recurring news reports on a four-month cycle. "Months 1 and 4 were the keys, accounting for more than three-fourths of all the variance explained" (Shoemaker, Wanta, and Leggett 1989, 79).

Such direct evidence of media coverage on public concern is also problematic in terms of policy decision making. Young (1981) observed that news assemblers cover drug-related issues in the United States as moral issues rather than as medical or health issues. Thus, according to Young, the media's condemnation of the "immoral drug user" serves to exacerbate public panic over drug use, "contribute[s] enormously to public hostility to the drug taker and precludes any rational approach to the problem" (1981, 334). And the cost is not inconsiderable. During the last fifteen years, our prison populations have more than doubled as a result of increased, mandatory, and habitual sentencing procedures. And with $18,000–30,000 a year going to support each prisoner, the cost to the nation has been very high indeed. In addition, the U.S. Congress responded to increased public and media pressure by passing the Omnibus Drug Bill, which was signed into law by Ronald Reagan in late 1986, costing the nation several billions of dollars (Johnston 1989). Drug enforcement rather than drug education or prevention featured prominently in the federal government's drug bill; as a result, "Television coverage made the raids familiar: a battering ram for the door; the heavily armed police; the drugs, money, and guns that were confiscated; and the handcuffed suspects being led away" (Johnston 1989, 103). The War on Drugs made for graphic and exciting television news footage.

But was the "cocaine summer" or the "cocaine epidemic of 1986" real? Johnston (1989) indicates that while news coverage of drug use peaked in the summer of 1986, the use of drugs by high school seniors had peaked in 1981 and the "*active* use of illicit drugs" by high school seniors had peaked in 1978 (see Johnston 1989, 99; emphasis in original). Moreover, national studies funded by the federal government indicated that between 1981 and 1986, active drug use among both high school seniors and young adults steadily declined (Johnston 1989).

It appears that what had happened and what influenced news media coverage was the relatively high level of cocaine use across all demographic categories, which remained stable throughout this time period. While the use of cocaine did not increase during this time, the incidence of more dangerous cocaine use in the form of crack did increase, resulting in a 250 percent increase in cocaine-related deaths during the five-year period (Johnston 1989). And this increase in cocaine-related deaths was significantly dramatized by the demise of noted sports and entertainment celebrities such as Len Bias and John Belushi during this same time period. Johnston observed:

> Despite all of this action and the expenditure of billions of dollars on enforcement, there was constant evidence that we were losing the war on drugs. Something was wrong. The public and the media both knew it, and both were increasingly frustrated and alarmed at the inability of their social institutions to handle the problem. (1989, 103)

For Johnston (1989), the news media's focus on crime and drug enforcement has prevented significant policy innovations. The fear and anxiety produced by such news reports interferes with more reasonable public debate and policy considerations. He writes:

> Prevention and demand-reduction strategies generally are getting increased lip service paid to them today in news coverage and in Congressional debates; but when you look at where the column inches, program minutes, and federal dollars go, only a very small portion goes to demand reduction. . . . The resulting inability of our society to deal effectively with such a serious problem among our young people is too high a price to pay for entertainment in the news. (Johnston 1989, 110)

Such demonstrated news convergence isn't a recent phenomenon.

References

Abelson, R. P. 1975. Representing mundane reality in plans. In *Representation and understanding*, ed. D. G. Bobrow and A. M. Collins, 273–309. New York: Academic Press.

Abramson, P. R., J. H. Aldrich, P. Paolino, and D. W. Rhode. 1992. "Sophisticated" voting in the 1988 presidential primaries. *American Political Science Review* 86: 55–69.

Adams, W. C. 1978. Local public affairs content of TV news. *Journalism Quarterly* 55: 690–695.

Adatto, K. 1990. *Sound bite democracy: Network evening news presidential campaign coverage, 1968 and 1988*. Cambridge, Mass.: Barone Center on the Press, Politics, and Public Policy, Kennedy School of Government, Harvard University.

Adler, J. 2002, December 23. A cardinal offense. *Newsweek* 140: 50–54.

———. 2004, January 12. Mad cow: What's safe now? *Newsweek*: 42–48.

Adoni, H., and A. A. Cohen. 1978. Television economic news and the social construction of economic reality. *Journal of Communication* 28: 61–70.

Adoni, H., and S. Mane. 1984. Media and the social construction of reality: Toward an integration of theory and research. *Communication Research* 11: 323–340.

Adoni, H., A. A. Cohen, and S. Mane. 1984. Social reality and television news: Perceptual dimensions of social conflict in selected life areas. *Journal of Broadcasting* 28: 33–49.

Alger, D. 1994. The media in elections: Evidence on the role and the impact. In *Media power in politics*, ed. D. Graber, 147–160. Washington, D.C.: CQ Press.

Allport, F. H. 1924. *Social psychology*. Boston: Houghton Mifflin.

———. 1937. Toward a science of public opinion, *Public Opinion Quarterly* 1: 7–23.

Althaus, S., J. A. Edy, and P. Phalen. 1994, April. The re-election motive and congressional oversight of U. S. force interventions: Debating the Libya crisis of 1986. Paper presented at the Midwest Political Science Association Annual Meeting, Chicago.

Altheide, D. L. 1976. *Creating reality: How TV news distorts events.* Beverly Hills, Calif.: Sage.

Altheide, D. L., and J. M. Johnson. 1980. *Bureaucratic propaganda.* Boston: Allyn & Bacon.

American Association of Public Opinion Research. n.d. Ethics code. www.aapor.org/ethics/code.html/ (accessed February 15, 2002).

Anderson, B. 1983. *Imagined communities: Reflections on the origin and spread of nationalism.* London: Verso Books.

Anderson, R., R. Dardenne, and G. M. Killenberg. 1994. *The conversation of journalism: Communication, community, and news.* Westport, Conn.: Praeger.

Aristotle. 1932. *The rhetoric of Aristotle.* Translated by L. Cooper. New York: Appleton-Century-Crofts.

Aronson, E., and D. Linder. 1965. Gain and loss of esteem as determinants of interpersonal attractiveness. *Journal of Experimental Psychology* 1: 156–171.

Arterton, F. C. 1984. *Media politics: The news strategies of presidential campaigns.* Lexington, Mass.: Lexington Books.

Åsard, E., and W. L. Bennett. 1997. *Democracy and the marketplace of ideas: Communication and government in Sweden and the United States.* Boston: Cambridge University Press.

Asen, R. 1996. Constructing the objects of our discourse: The welfare wars, the orphanage, and the silent welfare mom. *Political Communication* 13: 293–307.

Atkin, C. K. 1980. Political campaigns: Mass communication and persuasion. In *Persuasion: New directions in theory and research,* ed. M. E. Roloff and G. R. Miller, 285–308. Beverly Hills, Calif.: Sage.

Ault, P. H., and E. Emery. 1965. *Reporting the news.* New York: Dodd, Mead.

Bachrach, P., and M. Baratz. 1962. The two faces of power. *American Political Science Review* 56: 947–952.

Bailyn, B. 1967. *The ideological origins of the American Revolution.* Cambridge, Mass.: Harvard University Press.

Baird, R. N., A. T. Turnbull, and D. M. McDonald. 1987. *The graphics of communication,* 5th ed. New York: Holt, Rinehart, & Winston.

Baker, R. 1986, July 26. Same old junk. *New York Times,* 15.

Ball-Rokeach, S. J., and M. L. DeFleur. 1976. A dependency model of mass media effects. *Communication Research* 3: 3–21.

Ball-Rokeach, S. J., G. T. Power, K. K. Guthrie, and H. R. Waring. 1990. Value-framing abortion in the United States: An application of media system dependency theory. *International Journal of Public Opinion Research* 2: 249–273.

Ball-Rokeach, S. J., and M. Rokeach. 1987. Contribution to the future study of public opinion: A symposium. *Public Opinion Quarterly* 51: 184–185.

Ball-Rokeach, S. J., M. Rokeach, and J. W. Grube. 1984. *The great American values test: Influencing behavior and belief through television.* New York: Free Press.

Banks, L. 1978, April. Memo to the press: They hate you there. *Atlantic,* 241.

Barber, B. 1963. Some problems in the sociology of professions. *Daedalus* 92: 669–688.

———. 1984. *Strong democracy: Participatory politics for a new age.* Berkeley: University of California Press.

Barber, J. D. 1974. *Choosing the president.* Englewood Cliffs, N.J.: Prentice Hall.

———. 1978. *Race for the presidency.* Englewood Cliffs, N.J.: Prentice Hall.

Barnhurst, K. G., and D. Mutz. 1995. The new "long" journalism: *The New York Times* and the decline of event-centered reporting. Unpublished manuscript.

Bartels, L. M. 1988. *Presidential primaries and the dynamics of public choice.* Princeton, N.J.: Princeton University Press.

———. 1994. The American public's defense spending in the post–Cold War era. *Public Opinion Quarterly* 58: 479–509.

———. 1996. Uninformed voters: Information effects in presidential elections. *American Journal of Political Science* 40: 194–230.

Bartlett, F. C. 1932. *Remembering: A study in experimental and social psychology.* Cambridge: Cambridge University Press.

Bateson, G. 1972. A theory of play and fantasy. In *Steps to an ecology of mind,* ed. G. Bateson, 117–193. New York: Ballantine Books.

———. 1979. *Mind and nature: A necessary unity.* Toronto: Bantam Books.

Batscha, R. M. 1975. *Foreign affairs news and the broadcast journalist.* New York: Praeger.

Baudrillard, J. 1988. *Selected Writings.* Edited by Mark Poster. Stanford, Calif.: Stanford University Press.

Baus, H. M., and W. B. Ross. 1968. *Politics battle plan.* New York: Macmillan.

Becker, L. G., and D. C. Whitney. 1980. Effects of media dependencies: Audience assessments of government. *Communication Research* 7: 95–120.

Benedict, S. 1961. Changing the watch in Washington. *Virginia Quarterly* 37: 15–33.

Bennett, W. L. 1983. *News: The politics of illusion.* New York: Longman.

———. 1988. *News: The politics of illusion,* 2nd ed. New York: Longman.

———. 1996. An introduction to journalism norms and representations of politics. *Political Communication* 13: 373–384.

Bennett, W. L., and M. Edelman. 1985. Toward a new political narrative. *Journal of Communication* 35: 156–171.

Bennett, W. L., and R. M. Entman. 2001. *Mediated politics: Communication in the future of democracy.* Boston: Cambridge University Press.

Bennett, W. L., L. A. Gressett, and W. Halton. 1985. Repairing the news. *Journal of Communication* 35: 50–68.

Bennett, W. L., and R. G. Lawrence. 1995. News icons and the mainstreaming of social change. *Journal of Communication* 45: 20–39.

Bensman, J., and R. Lilienfeld. 1973. *Craft and consciousness: Occupational techniques and the development of world images.* New York: John Wiley & Sons.

Benson, L. 1967–1968. An approach to the scientific study of past public opinion. *Public Opinion Quarterly* 31: 522–567.

Berelson, B., and C. Steiner. 1964. *Human behavior: An inventory of scientific findings.* New York: Harcourt, Brace, & World.

Berger, P. L., and T. Luckman. 1966. *The social construction of reality: A treatise in the sociology of knowledge.* Garden City, N.Y.: Anchor Books.

Berke, R. L. 1994, October 3. In '94 "vote for woman" does not play so well. *New York Times,* 1A.

Berkman, R., and L. W. Kitch. 1986. *Politics in the media age.* New York: McGraw-Hill.

Berkowitz, D. 1992. Who sets the media agenda? The ability of policymakers to determine news decisions. In *Public opinion, the press, and public policy,* ed. J. D. Kennamer, 81–102. Westport, Conn.: Praeger.

Bettman, J. R., and B. A. Weitz. 1983. Attributions in the board room: Causal reasoning in corporate annual reports. *Administrative Science Quarterly* 28: 165–183.

Bird, S. E. 1992. Travels in nowhere land: Ethnography and the impossible audience. *Critical Studies in Mass Communication* 9: 250–260.

Bird, S. E., and R. W. Dardenne. 1988. Myth, chronicle, and story: Exploring the narrative qualities of news. In *Media, myths, and narratives,* ed. J. W. Carey, 67–86. Newbury Park, Calif.: Sage.

Birgersson, B. O. 1977. The service paradox: Citizen assessment of urban services in 36 communities. In *Comparing urban delivery systems,* ed. V. Ostrom and F. P. Bish, 243–268. Newbury Park, Calif.: Sage.

Bishop, G. F., R. W. Oldendick, A. J. Tuchfarber, and S. E. Bennett. 1980. Pseudo-opinions on public affairs. *Public Opinion Quarterly* 44: 198–209.

Black, J., ed. 1997. *Mixed news: The public/civic/communitarian journalism debate.* Mahwah, N.J.: Lawrence Erlbaum.

Blair, D., and R. Savage. 1980. *The rhetorical challenge of a gubernatorial transition: Constructing the image of statecraft.* Unpublished paper, University of Arkansas.

Blanchard, M. A. 1977. The Hutchins Commission, the press, and the responsibility concept. *Journalism Monographs* 49.

———. 1986. *Exporting the First Amendment: The press-government crusade of 1945–1952.* New York: Longman.

Blau, R. 2001. Retaining independence isn't easy for journalists: But protection of sources can cheat the public and betray the truth. *Nieman Reports* (summer): 62.

Block, L. G., and P. A. Keller. 1995. When to accentuate the negative: The effects of perceived efficacy and message framing on intentions to perform a health-related behavior. *Journal of Marketing Research* 32: 192–203.

Blumer, H. 1946. Collective behavior. In *New outlines of the principles of sociology,* ed. A. M. Le, 167–222. New York: Barnes & Noble.

———. 1969. *Symbolic interactionism: Perspective and method.* Englewood Cliffs, N.J.: Prentice Hall.

Blumer, J. G., and M. Gurevitch. 1981. Politicians and the press: An essay in role relationships. In *Handbook of political communication,* ed. D. Nimmo and K. Sanders, 467–493. Newbury Park, Calif.: Sage.

Bodtker, A. M., and J. K. Jameson. 1997. Mediation as mutual influence: Reexamining the use of framing and reframing. *Mediation Quarterly* 14: 237–249.

Bogart, L. 1980. Television news as entertainment. In *The Entertainment functions of television,* ed. P. H. Tannenbaum, 209–249. Hillsdale, N.J.: Lawrence Erlbaum.

———. 1991. *The American media system and its commercial culture.* Occasional Paper no. 8. New York: Gannett Foundation Media Center.

Boorstin, D. 1961. *The image: A guide to pseudo-events.* New York: Atheneum.

———. 1971. From news-gathering to news-making: A flood of pseudoevents. In *The process and effects of mass communication,* ed. W. Schramm and D. F. Roberts, 116–150. Urbana: University of Illinois Press.

Bormann, E. G. 1972. Fantasy and rhetorical vision: The rhetorical criticism of social reality. *Quarterly Journal of Speech* 58: 396–407.

———. 1985. Symbolic convergence theory: A communication formulation. *Journal of Communication* (autumn): 128–138.

Bower, G. H., and P. R. Cohen. 1982. Emotional influences in memory and thinking: Data and theory. In *Affect and cognition: The seventeenth annual Carnegie symposium on motivation*, ed. M. S. Clark and T. S. Fiske, 291–331. Hillsdale, N.J.: Lawrence Erlbaum.

Boyd-Barrett, O. 1970. Journalism recruitment and training: Problems in professionalization. In *Media sociology: A reader*, ed. J. Tunstall, 181–201. Urbana: University of Illinois Press.

Brady, H. E., and P. M. Sniderman. 1985. Attitude attribution: A group basis for political reasoning. *American Political Science Review* 79: 1061–1078.

Breen, M., and F. Corcoran. 1982. Myth in the television discourse. *Communication Monographs* 49: 127–136.

Brickman, P., V. C. Rabinowitz, J. Keruza, D. Coates, E. Cohn, and L. Kidder. 1982. Models of helping and coping. *American Psychologist* 37: 368–384.

Brody, R., and B. Page. 1975. The impact of events on presidential popularity: The Johnson and Nixon administrations. In *Perspectives on the presidency*, ed. A. Wildavsky, 136–148. Boston: Little, Brown.

Broh, C. A. 1980. Horse-race journalism: Reporting the polls in the 1976 presidential election. *Public Opinion Quarterly* 44: 514–529.

Brooks, B. S., G. Kennedy, D. R. Moen, and D. Ranly. 1999. *News reporting and writing*, 6th ed. Boston: Bedford/St. Martin's.

Brosius, H.-.B., and A. Bathelt. 1994. The utility of exemplars in persuasive communications. *Communication Research* 21: 48–78.

Brosius, H.-.B., and P. Eps. 1995. Prototyping through key events. *European Journal of Communication* 10: 391–412.

Brown, J. D., C. R. Bybee, S. T. Wearden, and D. M. Straughan. 1987. Invisible power: Newspaper news sources and the limits of diversity. *Journalism Quarterly* 64: 45–54.

Brummett, B. 1980. Towards a theory of silence as a political strategy. *Quarterly Journal of Speech* 66: 289–303.

Buchanan, B. 1996. *Renewing presidential politics: Campaigns, media, and the public interest*. Lanham, Md.: Rowman & Littlefield.

Buchanan, P. 1992, August 17. Republican national presidential convention speech, Houston, Texas.

Burka, P. 2000, January. The race is on. *Texas Monthly*, 103–114.

Burke, K. 1945. *A grammar of motives*. New York: Prentice Hall.

———. 1950. *A rhetoric of motives*. New York: Prentice Hall.

———. 1966. *Language as symbolic action*. Berkeley: University of California Press.

Burr, V. 1998. Overview: Realism, relativism, social constructionism and discourse. In *Social constructionism, discourse, and realism*, ed. I. Parker, 13–25. Thousand Oaks, Calif.: Sage.

Bybee, C. R. 1990. Constructing women as authorities: Local journalism and the microphysics of power. *Critical Studies in Mass Communication* 7: 197–214.

Califano, J. A., Jr., and H. Simons. 1979. The businessman and the journalist. In *The media and business*, ed. H. Simons and J. Califano Jr., ix–xxv. New York: Random House.

Campbell, A., P. E. Converse, W. E. Miller, and D. E. Stokes. 1960. *The American voter*. New York: Wiley.

Campbell, L. R., and R. E. Wolseley. 1961. *How to report and write the news*. Englewood Cliffs, N.J.: Prentice Hall.

Capella, J. A., and K. H. Jamieson. 1994. Broadcast adwatch effects. *Communication Research* 21: 342–365.

———. 1997. *Spiral of cynicism*. New York: Oxford University Press.

Carey, J. 1976. How media shape campaigns. *Journal of Communication* 26: 50–57.

———. 1986. Why: The dark continent of American journalism. In *Reading the news*, ed. R. K. Manoff and M. Schudson, 146–196. New York: Little, Brown.

———. 1987, March–April. The press and public discourse. *Center Magazine*, 4–16.

Cater, D. 1959. *The fourth branch of government*. Boston: Houghton Mifflin.

Ceasar, J., G. Thurow, J. Tulis, and J. Bessette. 1982. The rise of the rhetorical presidency. In *Rethinking the presidency*, ed. T. Cronin, 233–251. Boston: Little, Brown.

Chafe, W. 1977a. Creativity in verbalization and its implications for the nature of stored knowledge. In *Discourse production and comprehension*, ed. R. O. Freedle, 41–55. Norwood, N.J.: Ablex.

———. 1977b. The recall and verbalization of past experience. In *Current issues in linguistic theory*, ed. R. W. Cole, 215–246. Bloomington: Indiana University Press.

Chaney, D. 1986. The symbolic form of ritual in mass communication. In *Communicating politics: Mass communications and the political process*, ed. P. Golding, G. Murdock, and P. Schlesinger, 115–132. Leicester, UK: Leicester University Press.

Charity, A. 1995. *Doing public journalism*. New York: Guilford Press.

Chibnall, S. 1981. The production of knowledge by crime reporters. In *The manufacture of news: Social problems, deviance, and the mass media*, rev. ed., ed. S. Cohen and J. Young, 75–97. Beverly Hills, Calif.: Sage.

Childs, H. L. 1965. *Public opinion: Nature, formation, and role*. New York: D. van Nostrand.

Christenson, R. M., A. S. Engel, D. N. Jacobs, M. Rejai, and H. Walter. 1981. *Ideologies and modern politics*. New York: Harper & Row.

Cirino, R. 1971. *Don't blame the people: How the news media use bias*. Los Angeles: Diversity Press.

Clancey, M., and M. Robinson. 1985, December–January. General election coverage: Part I. *Public Opinion* 7: 49–54.

Clarke, P., and S. H. Evans. 1980. "All in a day's work": Reporters covering congressional campaigns. *Journal of Communication* 30: 112–121.

———. 1983. *Covering campaigns: Journalism in congressional elections*. Stanford, Calif.: Stanford University Press.

Clinard, M. B., and P. Yeager. 1980. *Corporate crime*. New York: Free Press.

Clines, F. X. 1993, August. See what you've done now, Camelot Dweeb? *New York Times Book Review*, 22.

Clymer, A. 1992, November 22. Tiff over governor's "Christian" remark underscores fault line in GOP. *New York Times*, 28.

Cobb, R. W., and C. D. Elder. 1971. The politics of agenda-building: An alternative perspective for modern democratic theory. *Journal of Politics* 33: 892–915.

———. 1972. Individual orientations in the study of political symbolism. *Social Science Quarterly* 53: 79–90.

———. 1981. Communication and public policy. In *Handbook of political communication*, ed. D. Nimmo and K. R. Sanders, 391–416. Newbury Park, Calif.: Sage.

———. 1983. *Participation in American politics: The dynamics of agenda-building*, 2nd ed. Baltimore: Johns Hopkins University Press.

Coffey, S. 1993, February 3. "Newspapers in the 90s." Lecture 28 in the Press-Enterprise Lecture Series, delivered at the University of California, Riverside.

Cohen, A. A., H. Adoni, and C. R. Bantz. 1990. *Social conflict and television news*. Newbury Park, Calif.: Sage.

Cohen, B. C. 1963. *The press, the public, and foreign policy*. Princeton, N.J.: Princeton University Press.

———. 1973. *The public's impact on foreign policy*. Boston: Little, Brown.

Cohen, J., D. Mutz, V. Price, and A. Gunther. 1988. Perceived impact of defamation: An experiment on third-person effects. *Public Opinion Quarterly* 52: 161–173.

Cohen, S., and J. Young, eds. 1981. Introduction. In *The manufacture of news: Social problems, deviance, and the mass media*, rev. ed., 15–33. Beverly Hills, Calif.: Sage.

Cohen, Y. 1986. *Media diplomacy*. London: Frank Cass.

Cole, M., and J. S. Bruner. 1971. Cultural differences and inferences about psychological processes. *American Psychologist* 26: 867–876.

Coleman, C.-L. 1997. Science, technology, and risk coverage of a community conflict. In *Social meanings of news*, ed. D. Berkowitz, 483–496. Thousand Oaks, Calif.: Sage.

Coleman, S. 2000. Meaningful political debate in the age of the soundbite. In *Televised election debates: International perspectives*, ed. S. Coleman, 1–24. New York: St. Martin's Press.

Combs, J. 1973. "The dramaturgical image of political man: A modernist approach to political inquiry." Ph.D. diss., University of Missouri.

———. 1980. *Dimensions of political drama*. Santa Monica, Calif.: Goodyear.

Combs, J., and M. Mansfield. 1980. *Drama in life*. New York: Hastings House.

Combs, J. E., and D. Nimmo. 1993. *The new propaganda: The dictatorship of palaver in contemporary politics*. New York: Longman.

Compaigne, B. M. 2000. Who owns the media companies? In *Who owns the media? Competition and concentration in the mass media industry*, 3rd ed., ed. B. M. Compaigne and D. Gomery, 481–506. Mahwah, N.J.: Lawrence Erlbaum.

Compaigne, B. M., and D. Gomery. 1982. *Who owns the media? Competition and concentration in the mass media industry*. Mahwah, N.J.: Lawrence Erlbaum.

———. 1995. *Who owns the media? Competition and concentration in the mass media industry*, 2nd ed. Mahwah, N.J.: Lawrence Erlbaum.

———. 2000. *Who owns the media? Competition and concentration in the mass media industry*, 3rd ed. Mahwah, N.J.: Lawrence Erlbaum.

Converse, P. 1962. Information flow and stability of partisan attitudes. *Public Opinion Quarterly* 26: 578–599.

———. 1964. The nature of belief systems in mass publics. In *Ideology and Discontent,* ed. D. Apter, 206–261. New York: Free Press.

———. 1970. Attitudes and non-attitudes: Continuation of a dialogue. In *The quantitative analysis of social problems,* ed. E. R. Tufte, 168–189. Reading, Mass.: Addison-Wesley.

———. 1987. Changing conceptions of public opinion in the political process. *Public Opinion Quarterly* 51: 12–24.

Cook, F. L. 1981. Crime and the elderly: The emergence of a policy issue. In *Reactions to crime,* ed. D. A. Lewis, 123–147. Newbury Park, Calif.: Sage.

Cook, F. L., and W. G. Skogan. 1991. Convergent and divergent voice models of the rise and fall of policy issues. In *Agenda setting: Readings on the media, public opinion, and policymaking,* ed. D. L. Protess and M. McCombs, 189–206. Hillsdale, N.J.: Lawrence Erlbaum.

Cook, F. L, T. R. Tyler, E. G. Goetz, M. T. Gordon, D. Leff, and H. L. Molotch. 1983. Media and agenda-setting: Effects on the public, interest group leaders, policy makers, and policy. *Public Opinion Quarterly* 47: 16–35.

Cook, T. E. 1996a. The negotiation of newsworthiness. In *The psychology of political communication,* ed. A. N. Crigler, 11–36. Ann Arbor: University of Michigan Press.

———. 1996b. Political values and production values. *Political Communication* 13: 469–481.

———. 1998. *Governing with the news: The news media as a political institution.* Chicago: University of Chicago Press.

Cooley, C. H. 1909. *Social organization: A study of the larger mind.* New York: Scribner's Sons.

Cornfield, M. 2003. Starting to click: Online campaigning in the 2002 elections. In *Midterm madness: The elections of 2002,* ed. L. Sabato, 57–66. Lanham, Md.: Rowman & Littlefield.

Cornwell, E., Jr. 1965. *Presidential leadership of public opinion.* Bloomington: Indiana University Press.

———. 1976. The president and the press: Phases in the relationship. *Annals of the American Academy of Political and Social Science* 427: 53–64.

Couldry, N. 2000. Media organisations and non-media people. In *Media organizations in society,* ed. J. Curran, 273–297. London: Oxford University Press.

Crespi, I. 1980. Polls as journalism. *Public Opinion Quarterly* 44: 462–476.

Crick, B. 1972. *In defense of politics,* 2nd ed. Chicago: University of Chicago Press.

Cromby, J., and D. J. Nightingale. 1999. What's wrong with social constructionism? In *Social constructionist psychology: A critical analysis of theory and practice,* ed. D. J. Nightingale and J. Cromby, 1–19. Philadelphia: Open University Press.

Crouse, T. 1972. *The boys on the bus.* New York: Ballantine Books.

Culbert, S. A., and J. J. McDonough. 1990. The concept of framing as a basis for understanding a blind spot in the way managers wield power. In *Advances in organizational development,* vol. 1, ed. F. Massarick, 57–82. Norwood, N.J.: Ablex.

Culbertson, H., and G. Stempel, III. 1985. Media malaise: Explaining personal optimism and societal pessimism about health care. *Journal of Communication* 2: 180–190.

Cunningham, L. G., and B. A. Henry. 1989. *The changing face of the newsroom*. Washington, D.C.: American Society of Newspaper Editors.

Curran, J. 1991. Rethinking the media as a public sphere. In *Communication and citizenship: Journalism and the public sphere in the new media age*, ed. P. Dahlgren and C. Sparks, 27–57. London: Routledge.

Curtin, P. A. 1999. Reevaluating public relations information subsidies: Market-driven journalism and agenda-building theory and practice. *Journal of Public Relations Research* 11: 53–90.

Cushman, D. P. 1977. The rules perspective as a theoretical basis for the study of human communication. *Communication Quarterly* 25: 30–45.

Dahl, R. A. 1989. *Democracy and its critics*. New Haven, Conn.: Yale University Press.

Dahlgreen, P. 1981. TV news and the suppression of reflexivity. In *Mass media and social change*, ed. E. Katz and T. Szecskö, 101–113. Beverly Hills, Calif.: Sage.

Dahlgren, P., and C. Sparks, eds. 1991. *Communication and citizenship: Journalism and the public sphere in the New Media Age*. London: Routledge.

Danielian, L. 1992. Interest groups in the news. In *Public opinion, the press, and public policy*, ed. J. D. Kennamer, 63–79. Westport, Conn.: Praeger.

Danielian, L. H., and S. D. Reese. 1989. A closer look at intermedia influences on agenda-setting: The cocaine issue of 1986. In *Communication campaigns about drugs: Government, media, and the public*, ed. P. J. Shoemaker, 47–66. Hillsdale, N.J.: Lawrence Erlbaum.

Darnton, R. 1975. Writing news and telling stories. *Daedalus* 104: 175–194.

Dautrich, K., and T. H. Hartley. 1999. *How the news media fail American voters: Causes, consequences, and remedies*. New York: Columbia University Press.

Davis, A. 2000. Public-relations campaigning and news production. In *Media organizations in society*, ed. J. Curran, 173–192. London: Oxford University Press.

Davis, D. K., and J. P. Robinson. 1986. The social role of television news: Theoretical perspectives. In *The main source: Learning from TV news*, ed. J. P. Robinson and M. R. Levy, 29–54. Beverly Hills, Calif.: Sage.

Davison, W. P. 1958. The public opinion process. *Public Opinion Quarterly* 21: 91–106.

———. 1983. The third-person effect in communication. *Public Opinion Quarterly* 47: 1–15.

DeFleur, M. L., and S. Ball-Rokeach. 1982. *Theories of mass communication*, 4th ed. New York: Longman.

Delli Carpini, M. X., and S. Keeter. 1996. *What Americans know about politics and why it matters*. New Haven, Conn.: Yale University Press.

Delli Carpini, M. X., and B. A. Williams. 2001. Let us infotain you: Politics in the new media environment. In *Mediated politics: Communication in the future of democracy*, ed. W. L. Bennett and R. M. Entman, 160–181. Cambridge: Cambridge University Press.

Dennis, D. K. 1990. News and politics. In *New directions in political communication: A resource book*, ed. D. L. Swanson and D. Nimmo, 147–184. Newbury Park, Calif.: Sage.

Deutschmann, P. J., and W. A. Danielson. 1960. Diffusion of knowledge of the major news story. *Journalism Quarterly* 37: 354–355.

Dewitt, J. 1997. Framing politicians. *American Behavioral Scientist* 40: 1139–1160.

Dexter, L. A. 1954. The use of public opinion polls by political party organizations. *Public Opinion Quarterly* 18: 53–61.

Diamond, E., F. Accosta, and L. Thornton. 1987, February 7. Is TV news hyping America's cocaine problem? *TV Guide*, 4–10.

Dionne, E. J. 1980, May 4. Experts find polls influence activists. *New York Times*, 26.

Dolbeare, K. M. 1981. *American political thought*. Belmont, Calif.: Wadsworth.

Domhoff, G. W. 1970. *The higher circles*. New York: Random House.

———. 1990. *The power elite and the state*. New York: Aldine de Gruyter.

Dominick, J. R. 1977. Geographic bias in national TV news. *Journal of Communication* 27: 94–99.

———. 1981. Business coverage in network newscasts. *Journalism Quarterly* 58: 179–185, 191.

Donohue, G. A., P. J. Tichenor, and C. N. Olien. 1975. Media and the knowledge gap: A hypothesis reconsidered. *Communication Research* 2: 2–23.

———. 1995. A guard dog perspective on the role of the media. *Journal of Communication* 45: 115–132.

Doob, A. N., and G. E. Macdonald. 1979. TV viewing and fear of victimization: Is the relationship causal? *Journal of Personality and Social Psychology* 37: 170–179.

Doob, L. W. 1948. *Public opinion and propaganda*. New York: Henry Holt.

———. 1966. *Public opinion and propaganda*, 2nd ed. Hamden, Conn.: Archon Books.

Doppelt, J. C. 1992. Marching to the police and court beats: The media-source relationship in framing criminal justice policy. In *Public opinion, the press, and public policy*, ed. J. D. Kennamer, 114–130. Westport, Conn.: Praeger.

Downs, A. 1957. *An economic theory of democracy*. New York: Harper & Row.

———. 1972. Up and down with ecology: The 'issue-attention cycle.' *Public Interest* 28: 2850.

Drechsel, R. E., and D. Moon. 1983. Libel and business executives: The public figure problem. *Journalism Quarterly* 60: 709–710.

Drudge Report. 2003, December 2. www.drudgereport.com/dean1.htm/.

Drummond, L. 1984. Movies and myth: Theoretical skirmishes. *American Journal of Semiotics* 3: 1–32.

Duhé, S. F., and L. M. Zoch. 1994. Framing the media's agenda during a crisis. *Public Relations Quarterly* 34: 42–45.

Duncan, H. 1962. *Communication and social order*. New York: Bedminister Press.

———. 1968. *Symbols in society*. New York: Oxford University Press.

Dunn, D. D. 1969. *Public officials and the press*. Reading, Mass.: Addison-Wesley.

Edelman, M. 1964. *The symbolic uses of politics*. Urbana: University of Illinois Press.

———. 1971. *Politics as symbolic action*. Chicago: Markham.

———. 1977. *Political language*. New York: Academic Press.

———. 1988. *Constructing the political spectacle*. Chicago: University of Chicago Press.

Edwards, D., M. Ashmore, and J. Potter. 1992. Death and furniture: The rhetoric and politics and theology of bottom line arguments against relativism. *History of the Human Sciences* 8: 25–49.

Edwards, G., III. 1976. Presidential influence in the House: Presidential prestige as a source of presidential power. *American Political Science Review* 73: 101–113.

Ehrlich, M. C. 1992. Competition in local television news: Rituals, enactment, and ideology. *Mass Communication Review* 19: 21–26.

———. 1995. The competitive ethos in television newswork. *Critical Studies in Mass Communication* 12: 196–212.

Eliasoph, N. 1988. Routines and the making of oppositional news. *Critical Studies of Mass Communication* 5: 313–334.

Elliot, P. 1980. Press performance as political ritual. In *Mass communication and society*, ed. J. Curran, M. Gurevitch, and J. Wollocott, 583–619. London: Arnold.

Elliott, M. 2002, December 30. The trouble with saving the world. *Time*, 108–112.

Entman, R. 1981. The imperial media. In *Politics and the Oval Office*, ed. A. Meltzer, 79–102. San Francisco: Institute for Contemporary Studies.

———. 1989a. *Democracy without citizens: Media and the decay of American politics*. New York: Oxford University Press.

———. 1989b. How the media affect what people think: An information processing approach. *Journal of Politics* 51: 347–370.

———. 1993. Framing: Toward clarification of a fractured paradigm. *Journal of Communication* 43: 51–58.

Entman, R. M., and A. Rojecki. 1993. Freezing out the public: Elite and media framing of the U.S. anti-nuclear movement. *Political Communication* 10: 155–173.

Epstein, E. J. 1973. *News from nowhere*. New York: Vantage Books.

Ericson, R. V., and P. M. Baranek. 1982. *The ordering of justice*. Toronto: University of Toronto Press.

Ericson, R. V., P. M. Baranek, and J. B. L. Chan. 1989. *Negotiating control: A study of news sources*. Toronto: University of Toronto Press.

Erikson, R. S., N. R. Luttbeg, and K. L. Tedin. 1988. *American public opinion: Its origins, content, and impact*, 3rd ed. New York: Wiley.

———. 1991. *American public opinion: Its origins, content, and impact*, 4th ed. New York: Macmillan.

Erikson, R. S., and K. L. Tedin. 1995. *American public opinion: Its origins, content, and impact*, 5th ed. Boston: Allyn & Bacon.

Ettema, J. 1988. *The craft of the investigative journalist*. Evanston, Ill.: Institute for Modern Communications Research Monograph.

———. 1997. Press rites and race relations. In *Social meanings of news*, ed. D. Berkowitz, 457–482. Thousand Oaks, Calif.: Sage Publications.

Ettema, J. S., and T. L. Glasser. 1988. Narrative form and moral force: The realization of innocence and guilt through investigative journalism. *Journal of Communication* 38: 8–26.

———. 1998. *Custodians of conscience*. New York: Columbia University Press.

Ettema, J. S., and F. G. Kline. 1977. Deficits, differences, and ceilings: Contingent conditions for understanding the knowledge gap. *Communication Research* 4: 179–202.

Etzioni, A. 1993. *The spirit of community: Rights, responsibilities, and the communitarian agenda*. New York: Crown.

Eulau, H., ed. 1956. *Political behavior*. Glencoe, Ill.: Free Press.

Eveland, W. P., Jr., and D. A. Scheufele. 2000. Connecting news media use with gaps in knowledge and participation. *Political Communication* 17: 215–237.

Evensen, B. J. 1997. *The responsible reporter: News gathering and writing with the highest standards of professionalism and personal conduct,* 2nd ed. Northport, Ala.: Vision Press.

Eyestone, R. 1974. *From social issues to public policy.* New York: John Wiley.

Fallows, J. 1997. *Breaking the news.* New York: Vintage.

Farnsworth, S. J., and S. R. Lichter. 2003. *The nightly news nightmare: Network television's coverage of U.S. presidential elections, 1988–2000.* Lanham, Md.: Rowman & Littlefield.

Fedler, F., and D. Jordan. 1982. How emphasis on people affects coverage of crime. *Journalism Quarterly* 59: 474–478.

Fejes, F., and K. Petrich. 1993, June. Invisibility, homophobia, and heterosexism: Lesbians, gays, and the media. *Critical Studies in Mass Communication* 10: 396–422.

Feldman, S. 1982. Economic self-interest and political behavior. *American Journal of Political Science* 26: 446–466.

Fenno, R. 1975. The president's cabinet. In *Perspectives on the presidency,* ed. A. Wildavsky, 318–338. Boston: Little, Brown.

Ferejohn, J. 1990. Information and the electoral process. In *Information and democratic processes,* ed. J. Ferejohn and J. Kuklinski, 3–19. Urbana: University of Illinois Press.

Festinger, L. 1950. Informal social communication. *Psychological Review* 57: 217–281.

———. 1954. A theory of social comparison processes. *Human Relations* 7: 117–140.

Fields, J. M., and H. Schuman. 1976–1977). Public beliefs about beliefs of the public. *Public Opinion Quarterly* 40: 427–448.

Fillmore, C. J. 1975. An alternative to checklist theories of meaning. In *Proceedings of the first annual meeting of the Berkeley Linguistics Society,* Institute of Human Learning, 123–131. Berkeley: University of California Press.

Fincham, F. D., and J. M. Jaspars. 1980. Attribution of responsibility: From man the scientist to man as lawyer. In *Advances in experimental social psychology,* vol. 13, ed. L. Berkowitz, 81–138. New York: Academic Press.

Fineman, H. 2004, January 7. The Dean dilemma. *Newsweek,* 18–28.

Fisher, B. 2000, January 13. Personal interview.

Fisher, W. 1984. Narration as a human communications paradigm: The case of public moral argument. *Communication Monographs* 51: 1–22.

———. 1970. A motive view of communication. *Quarterly Journal of Speech* 56: 131–139.

———. 1980. Rationality and the logic of good reasons. *Philosophy and Rhetoric* 12: 121–130.

———. 1985. The narrative paradigm: An elaboration. *Communication Monographs* 52: 347–367.

Fishkin, J. 1995. *The voice of the people: Public opinion and democracy.* New Haven, Conn.: Yale University Press.

Fishman, M. 1978. Crime waves as ideology. *Social Problems* 25: 531–543.

———. 1980. *Manufacturing the news.* Austin: University of Texas Press.

———. 1981. Crime waves as ideology. In *The manufacture of news: Social problems, deviance, and the mass media*, rev. ed., ed. S. Cohen and J. Young, 98–117. Beverly Hills, Calif.: Sage.

———. 1997. News and nonevents: Making the visible invisible. In *Social meanings of news*, ed. D. Berkowitz, 210–229. Thousand Oaks, Calif.: Sage.

Fiske, S. T., and S. E. Taylor. 1984. *Social cognition*. New York: Random House.

Fletcher, F. J. 1996. Polling and political communication. In *Political communication in action: States, institutions, movements, audiences*, ed. D. L. Paletz, 299–315. Cresskill, N.J.: Hampton Press.

Folkes, V. S. 1984. Consumer reactions to product failure: An attributional approach. *Journal of Consumer Research* 10: 398–409.

Foote, J. S., and A. C. Saunders. 1990. Graphic forms in network television news. *Journalism Quarterly* 67: 501–507.

Foote, J. S., and M. E. Steele. 1986. Degree of conformity in lead stories in early evening network TV newscasts. *Journalism Quarterly* 63: 19–23.

Forman, A., and S. B. Lachter. 1989. The National Institute on Drug Abuse cocaine prevention campaign. In *Communication campaigns about drugs: Government, media, and the public*, ed. P. J. Shoemaker, 13–20. Hillsdale, N.J.: Lawrence Erlbaum.

Frankel, M. 2000, January 9. The wall, vindicated: A sturdy barrier between news and commerce enhances both. *New York Times Magazine*, sec. 6, 24–25.

Frayn, M. 1981. The complete stylisation of news. In *The manufacture of news: Social problems, deviance, and the mass media*, ed. S. Cohen and J. Young, 71–74. London: Constable.

Frazier, P. J., and C. Gaziano. 1979. Robert Ezra Park's theory of news: Public opinion and social control. *Journalism Monographs* 64: 1–49.

Freiburg, P. 1993, April 23. Gays and the media. *Washington Blade* 25: 53–57.

Frentz, T. S., and T. B. Farrell. 1976. Language-action: A paradigm for communication. *Quarterly Journal of Speech* 62: 333–349.

Freud, S. 1952. *On dreams*. New York: Norton.

Friedland, L. A., and M. Zhong. 1996, April. International television coverage of Beijing spring 1989: A comparative approach. *Journalism & Mass Communication Monographs*, issue 156.

Fuller, J. 1996. *News values: Ideas for an information age*. Chicago: University of Chicago Press.

Galtung, J., and M. H. Ruge. 1965. The structure of foreign news. *Journal of International Peace Research* 1: 64–90.

———. 1970. The structure of foreign news. In *Media sociology*, ed. J. Tunstall, 259–298. London: Constable.

———. 1981. Structuring and selecting news. In *The manufacture of news: Social problems, deviance, and the mass media*, rev. ed., ed. S. Cohen and J. Young, 52–63. Beverly Hills, Calif.: Sage.

Gamson, W. A. 1985. Goffman's legacy to political sociology. *Theory and Society* 14: 605–622.

———. 1988a. Political discourse and collective action. *International Social Movement Research* 1: 219–244.

———. 1988b. The 1987 distinguished lecture: A constructionist approach to mass media and public opinion. *Symbolic Interaction* 11: 161–174.

———. 1989. News as framing. *American Behavioral Scientist* 33 157–161.

———. 1992a. The social psychology of collective action. In *Frontiers in social movement theory*, ed. A. D. Morris and C. McClurg Mueller, 53–76. New Haven, Conn.: Yale University Press.

———. 1992b. *Talking politics.* New York: Cambridge University Press.

———. 1996. Media discourse as a framing resource. In *The psychology of political communication*, ed. A. N. Crigler, 111–132. Ann Arbor: University of Michigan Press.

Gamson, W. A., D. Croteau, W. Hoynes, and T. Sasson. 1992. Media images and the social construction of reality. *Annual Review of Sociology* 18: 373–393.

Gamson, W. A., and K. E. Lasch. 1983. The political culture of social welfare policy. In *Evaluating the welfare state: Social and political perspectives*, ed. S. E. Spiro and E. Yuchtman-Yaar, 397–415. New York: Academic Press.

Gamson, W., and A. Modigliani. 1989. Media discourse and public opinion on nuclear power: A constructivist approach. *American Journal of Sociology* 95: 1–37.

Gamson, W., and D. Stuart. 1992. Media discourse as a symbolic contest: The bomb in political cartoons. *Sociological Forum* 7: 55–86.

Gandy, O. H., Jr. 1982. *Beyond agenda setting: Information subsidies and public policy.* Norwood, N.J.: Ablex.

———. 2001. Epilogue—Framing at the horizon: A retrospective assessment. In *Framing public life: Perspectives on media and our understanding of the social world*, ed. S. D. Reese, O. H. Gandy Jr., and A. E. Grant, 355–378. Mahwah, N.J.: Lawrence Erlbaum.

Gans, H. 1979. *Deciding what's news.* New York: Vintage Books.

Ganzach, Y., and N. Karahi. 1995. Message framing and buying behavior: On the difference between artificial and natural environment. *Journal of Business Research* 40: 91–95.

Garceau, O. 1951. Research in the political process. *American Political Science Review* 45: 69–85. (Quotation from the reprinted article in Eulau 1956, 44.)

Garcia, M. R. 1987. *Contemporary newspaper design: A structural approach*, 2nd ed. Englewood Cliffs, N.J.: Prentice Hall.

Gaventa, J. 1980. *Power and powerlessness.* Urbana: University of Illinois Press.

Gaziano, C. 1983. The knowledge gap: An analytical review of media effects. *Communication Research* 10: 447–486.

———. 1988. Communication knowledge gaps. *Critical Studies in Mass Communication* 5: 351–357.

———. 1997. Forecast 2000: Widening knowledge gaps. *Journalism and Mass Communication Quarterly* 74: 237–264.

Genova, B. K. L., and B. S. Greenberg. 1979. Interest in news and the knowledge gap. *Public Opinion Quarterly* 43: 79–91.

Gerbner, G., and L. Gross. 1976. Living with television: The violence profile. *Journal of Communication* 26: 182–190.

Gerbner, G., L. Gross, M., Morgan, and N. Signorielli. 1980a. Aging with television: Images on television drama and conceptions of social reality. *Journal of Communication* 30: 37–47.

———. 1980b. The "mainstreaming" of America: Violence profile no. 11. *Journal of Communication* 30: 10–29.

———. 1982. Charting the mainstreaming: Television's contributions to political orientations. *Journal of Communication* 32: 100–127.

———. 1986. Living with television: The dynamics of the cultivation process. In *Perspectives on media effects*, ed. J. Bryant and D. Zillmann, 17–40. Hillsdale, N.J.: Lawrence Erlbaum.

———. 1994. Growing up with television: The cultivation perspective. In *Perspectives on media effects*, ed. J. Bryant and D. Zillmann, 2nd ed., 17–48. Hillsdale, N.J.: Lawrence Erlbaum.

Gergen, K. 1982. *Toward transformation in social knowledge.* New York: Springer-Verlag.

———. 1985a. The social constructionist movement in modern psychology. *American Psychologist* 40: 266–275.

———. 1985b. Social constructionist inquiry: Context and implications. In *The social construction of the person*, ed. K. J. Gergen and K. E. Davis, 3–18. New York: Springer-Verlag.

———. 1998. Constructionism and realism: How are we to go on? In *Social constructionism, discourse, and realism*, ed. I. Parker, 147–155. Thousand Oaks, Calif.: Sage.

———. 1999. *Invitation to social construction.* Thousand Oaks, Calif.: Sage.

———. 2001. *Social construction in context.* Thousand Oaks, Calif.: Sage.

Gerhards, J., and D. Rucht. 1992. Mesomobilization: Organizing and framing in two protest campaigns in West Germany. *American Journal of Sociology* 98: 555–595.

Gibson, R., and D. Zillmann. 1994a. Exaggerated versus representative exemplification in news reports: Perceptions of issues and personal consequences. *Communication Research* 21: 603–624.

———. 1994b. The impact of quotation in news reports on issue perception. *Journalism Quarterly* 70: 793–800.

Gieber, W. 1960–1961. Two communicators of the news: A study of the roles of sources and reporters. *Social Forces* 39: 76–83.

Gill, R. 1995. Relativism, reflexivity, and politics: Interrogating discourse analysis from a feminist perspective. In *Feminism and discourse: Psychological perspectives*, ed. S. Wilkinson and C. Kitzinger, 165–186. London: Sage.

Gitlin, T. 1978. Media sociology: The dominant paradigm. *Theory and Society* 6: 205–253.

———. 1979. Prime time ideology: The hegemonic process in television entertainment. *Social Problems* 26: 251–266.

———. 1980. *The whole world is watching.* Berkeley: University of California Press.

———. 1990. Blips, bites, and savvy talk. *Dissent* (winter): 18–26.

Glasser, T. L., and S. Craft. 1996. Public journalism and the prospects for press accountability. *Journal of Mass Media Ethics* 11: 152–158.

Glasser, T. L., and J. S. Ettema. 1989. Investigative journalism and the moral order. *Critical Studies in Mass Communication* 6: 1–20.

Glenn, C. J., R. E. Ostman, and D. G. McDonald. 1995. Opinions, perception, and social reality. In *Public opinion and the communication of consent*, ed. T. L. Glasser and C. T. Salmon, 249–277. New York: Guilford Press.

Glenn, N. D. 1972. The distribution of political knowledge in the United States. In *Political attitudes and public attitudes*, ed. D. Nimmo and C. Bonjean, 273–283. New York: David McKay.

Glynn, C. J. 1989. Perception of others' opinions as a component of public opinion. *Social Science Research* 18: 53–69.

———. 1997. Public opinion as a normative process. In *Communication Yearbook 20*, ed. B. R. Burleson, 157–183. Thousand Oaks, Calif.: Sage.

Goffman, E. 1959. *The presentation of self in everyday life*. Garden City, N.Y.: Doubleday Anchor.

———. 1961. Role distance. In *Encounters*, by Erving Goffman, 85–152. New York: Bobbs-Merrill.

———. 1974. *Frame analysis: An essay on the organization of experience*. Cambridge, Mass.: Harvard University Press.

Goldenberg, E. N. 1975. *Making the papers: The access of resource-poor groups to the metropolitan press*. Lexington, Mass.: Lexington Books.

Golding, P. 1981. The missing dimensions: News media and the management of social change. In *Mass media and social change*, ed. E. Katz and T. Szecsko, 63–81. Beverly Hills, Calif.: Sage.

Goldstein, N. 1998. *The Associated Press stylebook and libel manual*. New York: Associated Press.

Gollin, A. E., ed. 1980. Polls and the news media: A symposium. *Public Opinion Quarterly* 44: 445–461.

Gordon, M. T., and L. Heath. 1981. The news business, crime, and public fear. In *Reactions to crime*, ed. D. A. Lewis, 227–250. Beverly Hills, Calif.: Sage.

Gorney, C. 1992. Numbers versus pictures: Did network television sensationalize Chernobyl coverage? *Journalism Quarterly* 69: 455–465.

Graber, D. 1976. *Verbal behavior and politics*. Urbana: University of Illinois Press.

———. 1980. *Mass media and American politics*. Washington, D.C.: Congressional Quarterly Press.

———. 1982. Introduction. In *The president and the public*, ed. D. Graber, 1–14. Philadelphia: ISHI.

———. 1989. *Mass media and American politics*, 3rd ed. Washington, D.C.: Congressional Quarterly Press.

———. 1994. Why voters fail information tests: Can the hurdles be overcome? *Political Communication* 11: 331–346.

———. 1997. *Mass media and American politics*, 5th ed. Washington, D.C.: Congressional Quarterly Press.

Gramsci, A. 1971. *Selections from the prison notebooks of Antonio Gramsci*. Edited by Q. Hoare and G. N. Smith. New York: International Publishers.

Grant, A. E. 1996. Media dependency and multiple media sources. In *The psychology of political communication*, ed. A. Crigler, 199–210. Ann Arbor: University of Michigan Press.

Gray, B. 1997. Framing and reframing of intractable environmental disputes. *Research on Negotiation in Organizations*, vol. 6, 163–188. Greenwich, Conn.: JAI.

Greenberg, J. 2002. Framing and temporality in political cartoons: A critical analysis of visual news discourse. *CRSA/RCSA* 39: 181–198.

Greenwood, E. 1957. Attributes of a profession. *Social Work* 2: 45–55.

Greider, W. 1976, November 7. What can Carter do? The limitations of presidential power. *Washington Post*, C1.

Groennings, S. 1970. Patterns, strategies, and payoffs in Norwegian coalition formation. In *The study of coalition behavior: Theoretical perspectives and cases from four continents*, ed. S. Groennings, 60–79. New York: Holt, Rinehart, Winston.

Grossman, M., and M. Kumar. 1981. *Portraying the president*. Baltimore, Md.: Johns Hopkins University Press.

Groth, A. J. 1971. *Major ideologies*. New York: John Wiley & Sons.

Grunig, J. E. 1983. Washington reporter publics of corporate public affairs programs. *Journalism Quarterly* 60: 603–614.

Gunter, B. 1987. *Poor reception*. Hillsdale, N.J.: Lawrence Erlbaum.

Gunther, A. C. 1991. What we think others think: Cause and consequence in the third-person effect. *Communication Research* 18: 355–372.

Gunther, A. C., and E. Thorson. 1992. Perceived persuasive effects of product commercials and public service announcements: Third-person effects in new domains. *Communication Research* 19: 574–596.

Gurevitch, M., and M. R. Levy, eds. 1985. *No nukes: Everyone's guide to nuclear power*. Boston: South End Press.

Hackett, R. A. 1984. Decline of a paradigm? Bias and objectivity in news media studies. *Critical Studies in Mass Communication* 1: 229–259.

———. 1985. Decline of a paradigm: Bias and objectivity in news media studies. In *Mass communication review yearbook*, vol. 5, ed. M. Gurevitch and M. Levy, 251–274. Beverly Hills, Calif.: Sage.

Halberstam, D. 1979. *The powers that be*. New York: Dell.

Hall, P. 1972. A symbolic interactionist analysis of politics. *Sociological Inquiry* 42: 35–75.

———. 1977, August. "The presidency and impression management." Paper presented at the American Sociological Convention, Chicago.

Hall, S. 1973. The determination of news photographs. In *The manufacture of news: A reader*, ed. S. Cohen and J. Young, 176–190. Beverly Hills, Calif.: Sage.

———. 1984. The narrative construction of reality: An interview with Stuart Hall. *Southern Review* 17: 3–17.

Hall, S., C. Critcher, T. Jefferson, J. Clarke, and B. Roberts. 1978. *Policing the crisis: Mugging, the state, and law and order*. London: Macmillan.

Hallahan, K. 1999. Seven models of framing: Implications for public relations. *Journal of Public Relations Research* 11: 205–242.

Hallin, D. C. 1986. *The "uncensored war."* Berkeley: University of California Press.

———. 1992a. Sound bite democracy. *Wilson Quarterly* 16: 34–37.

———. 1992b. Sound bite news: Television coverage of elections, 1968–1988. *Journal of Communication* 42: 5–24.

Hallin, D. C., and T. Gitlin. 1994. The Gulf War as popular culture and television drama. In *Taken by storm*, ed. W. L. and D. L. Paletz, 149–163. Chicago: University of Chicago Press.

Halloway, R. L. 2000. One nation, after all: Convention frames and political culture. In *The 2000 presidential campaign: A communication perspective*, ed. R. E. Denton Jr., 117–134. Westport, Conn.: Praeger.

Hannerz, U. 1969. *Soulside: Inquiries into ghetto culture and community*. New York: Columbia University Press.

Hansen, K. A., J. Ward, J. L. Connors, and M. Neuzil. 1994. Local breaking news: Sources, technology, and news routines. *Journalism & Mass Communication Quarterly* 71: 561–572.

Hardin, C. D., and E. T. Higgins. 1996. Shared reality: How social verification makes the subjective objective. In *Handbook of motivation and cognition*, vol. 3., ed. R. M. Sorrentino, and E. T. Higgins, 28–84. New York: Guilford Press.

Harré, R. 1999. Discourse and the embodied person. In *Social constructionist psychology: A critical analysis of theory and practice*, ed. D. J. Nightingale and J. Cromby, 97–112. Philadelphia: Open University Press.

Hart, R. P., D. Smith-Howell, and J. Llewellyn. 1990. Evolution of presidential news coverage. *Political Communication and Persuasion* 7: 213–230.

———. 1996. News, psychology, and presidential politics. In *The psychology of political communication*, ed. A. Crigler, 37–64. Ann Arbor: University of Michigan Press.

Hartz, L. 1955. *The liberal tradition in America*. New York: Harcourt Brace, Jovanovich.

Haskins, J. B. 1981. The trouble with bad news. *Newspaper Research Journal* 2: 3–16.

Hawkins, R. P., and S. Pingree. 1981. Using television to construct social reality. *Journal of Broadcasting* 25: 347–364.

Head, Sir H. 1920. *Studies in neurology*. Oxford: Oxford University Press.

Hennessey, B. C. 1965. *Public opinion*. Belmont, Calif.: Wadsworth.

Henry, W. A., III. 1981. News as entertainment: The search for dramatic unity. In *What's news: The media in American society*, ed. E. Abel, 133–158. San Francisco, Calif.: Institute for Contemporary Studies.

Herbst, S. 1993. The meaning of public opinion: Citizens' constructions of political reality. *Media, Culture, and Society* 15: 437–454.

Herman, E. S. 1985. Diversity in the news: "Marginalizing" the opposition. *Journal of Communication* 1 (summer): 135–146.

Hernandez, D. G. 1995, July 1. Are women being annihilated by the media? *Editor and Publisher*, 56–57.

Herrnstein Smith, B. 1981. Narrative versions, narrative theories. In *On narrative*, ed. W. J. T. Mitchell, 209–232. Chicago: University of Chicago Press.

Hertog, J. K., and D. M. McCleod. 2001. A multiperspectival approach to framing analysis: A field guide. In *Framing public life: Perspectives on media and our understanding of the social world*, ed. S. D. Reese, O. H. Gandy Jr., and A. E. Grant, 139–174. Mahwah, N.J.: Lawrence Erlbaum.

Hess, S. 1983. The golden triangle: The press at the White House, State, and Defense. *Brookings Review* (summer): 14–19.

———. 1986. *International news and foreign correspondents*. Washington, D.C.: Brookings Institution.

Hickey, N. 2003, July–August. *FCC: Ready, set, consolidate*. http://archives.cjr.org/year/03/4/hickey.asp (accessed December 3, 2003).

Hickman, H. 1991. Public polls and election participants. In *Polling and presidential election coverage*, ed. P. J. Lavrakas and J. K. Holey, 100–133. Newbury Park, Calif.: Sage.

Hiebert, R., D. Ungurait, and T. Bohn. 1982. *Mass media III*. New York: Longman.

Hilgartner, S., and C. L. Bosk. 1988. The rise and fall of social problems: A public arenas model. *American Journal of Sociology* 94(1): 53–78.

Hill, R., and C. M. Bonjean. 1964. News diffusion: A test of the regularity hypothesis. *Journalism Quarterly* 41: 336–342.

Hilliard, R. D. 1989. The graphics explosion: Questions remain about roles. *Journalism Quarterly* 66: 192–194.

Hilt, M. L. 1997. *Television news and the elderly: Broadcast managers' attitudes toward older adults.* New York: Garland.

Hinck, E. A. 1993. *Enacting the presidency: Political argument, presidential debates, and presidential character.* Westport, Conn.: Praeger.

Hirsch, S. 1969, July. On uncovering the great nerve gas coverup. *Ramparts* 3: 12–18.

Hofstetter, C. R. 1976. *Bias in the news: Network television coverage of the 1972 election campaign.* Columbus: Ohio State University Press.

Hofstetter, C. R., and T. F. Buss. 1978. Bias in television news coverage of political events: A methodological analysis. *Journal of Broadcasting* 22: 517–530.

Hofstetter, C. R., and D. M. Dozier. 1986. Useful news, sensational news: Quality sensationalism and local TV news. *Journalism Quarterly* 63: 815–820.

Hogwood, B. W., and B. G. Peters. 1985. *The pathology of public policy.* Oxford: Clarendon Press.

Holbrook, T. M. 1996. *Do campaigns matter?* Thousand Oaks, Calif.: Sage.

Holman, C. H. 1972. *A handbook to literature,* 3rd ed. New York: Odyssey Press.

Hornig, S. 1992. Framing risk: Audience and reader factors. *Journalism Quarterly* 69: 679–690.

Horton, D., and R. Wohl. 1956. Mass communication and para-social interaction: Observations on intimacy at a distance. *Psychiatry* 19: 215–229.

Howard Dean on media ownership. 2003. http://paleblue.us/archives/000404.html/ 12/3/2003.

Hoynes, W., and D. Croteau. 1989, January–February. Are you on the *Nightline* guest list? *Extra!* 1–15.

Hughes, E. C. 1963. Professions. *Daedalus* 92: 665–668.

Hurwitz, J., and M. Peffley. 1987. How are foreign policy attitudes structured? A hierarchical model. *American Political Science Review* 81: 1099–1119.

Hyman, H., and P. Sheatsley. 1947. Some reasons why information campaigns fail. *Public Opinion Quarterly* 11: 412–423.

Hynds, E. C. 1980. Business coverage is getting better. *Journalism Quarterly* 57: 297–304.

Iorio, S. H., and S. S. Huxman. 1996. Media coverage of political issues and the framing of personal concerns. *Journal of Communication* 46: 97–115.

Ito, Y. 1996. Masses and media influence on government decision-making. In *Political communication research: Approaches, studies, and assessments,* vol. 2, ed. D. L. Paletz, 63–90. Norwood, N.J.: Ablex.

Iyengar, S. 1987. Television news and citizens' explanations of national issues. *American Political Science Review* 81: 815–832.

———. 1989. How citizens think about national issues: A matter of responsibility. *American Journal of Political Science* 33: 878–900.

———. 1991. *Is anyone responsible? How television frames political issues.* Chicago: University of Chicago Press.

Iyengar, S., and D. R. Kinder. 1986. More than meets the eye: TV news, priming, and public evaluations of the president. In *Public communication and behavior,* vol. 1, ed. G. Comstock, 135–171. Orlando, Fla.: Free Press.

———. 1987. *News that matters: Television and American opinion.* Chicago: University of Chicago Press.

Iyengar, S., and A. Simon. 1993. News coverage of the Gulf crisis and public opinion: A study of agenda-setting, priming, and framing. *Communication Research* 20: 365–383.

Jack, I. 1998, August 8. "Now for the bad news." *Guardian, Saturday Review,* 3.

James, W. 1896. *The principles of psychology.* New York: Henry Holt.

Jamieson, K. H. 1992. *Dirty politics: Deception, distraction, and democracy.* New York: Oxford University Press.

Jamieson, K. H., and C. Adasiewicz. 2000. What can voters learn from election debates? In *Televised election debates: International perspectives,* ed. S. Coleman, 25–42. New York: St. Martin's.

Jamieson, K. H., and P. Waldman. 2000. Watching the adwatches. In *Campaign reform: Insights and evidence,* ed. L. M. Bartels and L. Vavreck, 106–121. Ann Arbor: University of Michigan Press.

———. 2003. *The press effect: Politicians, journalists, and the stories that shape the political world.* New York: Oxford University Press.

Janowitz, M. 1975. Professional models in journalism: The gatekeeper and the advocate. *Journalism Quarterly* 52: 618–626, 662.

Johnson, E. J., and A. Tversky. 1983. Affect, generalization, and the perception of risk. *Journal of Personality and Social Psychology* 45: 20–31.

Johnson (a.k.a. Johnson-Cartee), K. 1984. "Impression management during the presidential transitions of Nixon, Carter, and Reagan: A quantitative content analysis and thematic analysis." Ph.D. diss., University of Tennessee, Knoxville.

———. 1985. The honeymoon period: Fact or fiction? *Journalism Quarterly* 62: 869–876.

Johnson-Cartee, K., and G. A. Copeland. 1991. *Negative political advertising: Coming of age.* Hillsdale, N.J.: Lawrence Erlbaum.

———. 1997a. *Inside political campaigns: Theory and practice.* Westport, Conn.: Praeger.

———. 1997b. *Manipulation of the American voter: Political campaign commercials.* Westport, Conn.: Praeger.

———. 2004. *Strategic political communication: Rethinking social influence, persuasion, and propaganda.* Lanham, Md.: Rowman & Littlefield.

Johnson (a.k.a. Johnson-Cartee), K., G. Copeland, and M. Huttenstine. 1988. Perceived differences in men and women as expert news sources in analytical and historical presentations. Unpublished paper, University of Alabama.

Johnson-Cartee, K., G. A. Copeland, A. Marquez, J. Buford, and J. Stephens. 1998. Examining the demise of the National Republican Coalition. *International Harvard Journal of Press/Politics* 3(2): 34–54.

Johnson (a.k.a. Johnson-Cartee), K., and D. Nimmo. 1986. Commentary: Reporting political polling: Avoiding public "misinformation." *Newspaper Research Journal* 7: 69–76.

Johnston, L. D. 1989. America's drug problem in the media: Is it real or is it Memorex? In *Communication campaigns about drugs: Government, media, and the public*, ed. P. J. Shoemaker, 97–111. Hillsdale, N.J.: Lawrence Erlbaum.

Johnstone, J. W. C., E. J. Slawski, and W. W. Bowman. 1976. *The news people: A sociological portrait of American journalists and their work*. Urbana: University of Illinois Press.

Jones, E. T. 1976. The press as metropolitan monitor. *Public Opinion Quarterly* 40: 239–244.

Jones, N. 1995. *Soundbites and spindoctors*. London: Cassell.

Joslyn, M. R., and S. Ceccoli. 1994, April 14–16. "Media messages and voter judgments: Is there a link? Estimating the impact of news consumption and content on voters' judgments during the final months of the 1992 campaign." Paper presented at the Midwest Political Science Association 52nd Annual Meeting, Chicago.

Jowett, G. S., and V. O'Donnell. 1992. *Propaganda and persuasion*, 2nd ed. Newbury Park, Calif.: Sage.

Just, M., T. Buhr, and A. Crigler. 2000. Shifting the balance: Journalist versus candidate communication in the 1996 presidential campaign. In *Campaign reform: Insights and evidence*, ed. L. M. Bartels and L. Vavreck, 122–144. Ann Arbor: University of Michigan Press.

Just, M. R., A. N. Crigler, and W. R. Neuman. 1996. Cognitive and affective dimensions of political conceptualization. In *The psychology of political communication*, ed. A. N. Crigler, 133–148. Ann Arbor: University of Michigan Press.

Kahn, K. F. 1992. Does being male help? An investigation of gender and media effects in U.S. Senate races. *Journal of Politics* 54: 497–517.

———. 1994. Does gender make a difference? An experimental examination of sex stereotypes and press patterns in statewide campaigns. *American Journal of Political Science* 38: 162–195.

Kahn, K. F., and E. N. Goldenberg. 1991. Women candidates in the news: An examination of gender differences in U.S. Senate campaigns. *Public Opinion Quarterly* 55: 180–199.

Kahneman, D. 1982. The psychology of preferences. *Science* 246: 136–142.

Kahneman, D., and A. Tversky. 1979. Prospect theory: An analysis of decision under risk. *Econometrica* 47: 263–291.

———. 1984. Choices, values, and frames. *American Psychologist* 39: 341–350.

Kaid, L. L., M. McKinney, and J. C. Tedesco. 2000. *Civic dialogue in the 1996 presidential campaign*. Cresskill, N.J.: Hampton Press.

Kaid, L. L., M. McKinney, J. C. Tedesco, and K. Gaddie. 1999. Journalistic responsibility and political advertising: A content analysis of coverage by state and local media. *Communication Studies* 50: 279–293.

Kaid, L. L., J. C. Tedesco, and L. M. McKinnon. 1996. Presidential ads as nightly news: A content analysis of 1988 and 1992 televised adwatches. *Journal of Broadcasting and Electronic Media* 40: 297–308.

Kalbfeld, B., ed. 1998. *The Associated Press broadcast news handbook.* New York: Associated Press.

Katz, D., and F. H. Allport. 1931. *Student attitudes.* Syracuse, N.Y.: Craftsman.

Katz, E. 1983. Publicity and pluralistic ignorance: Notes on "the spiral of silence." In *Mass communication review yearbook 4,* ed. E. Wartella, D. C. Whitney, and S. Windahl, 89–100. Newbury Park, Calif.: Sage.

Katz, E., J. G. Blumer, and M. Gurevitch. 1974. Utilization of mass communication by the individual. In *The uses of mass communication: Current perspectives on gratifications research,* ed. J. G. Blumler and E. Katz, 19–32. Beverly Hills, Calif.: Sage.

Kellerman, K. 1984. The negativity effect and its implications for initial interaction. *Communication Monographs* 51: 37–55.

Kelley, H. H. 1952. Attitudes and judgments as influenced by reference groups. In *Readings in social psychology,* rev. ed., ed. G. E. Swanson, T. M. Newcomb, and E. L. Hartley, 410–414. New York: Holt, Rinehart, & Winston.

Kelly, J. D. 1993. The effects of display format and data density on time spent reading statistics in text, tables, and graphs. *Journalism Quarterly* 70: 140–149.

Kelman, S. 1987. *Making public policy.* New York: Basic Books.

Kendall, K. E. 1995. *Presidential campaign discourse: Strategic communication problems.* Albany: State University of New York Press.

———. 1997. Presidential debates through media eyes. *American Behavioral Scientist* 40: 1193–1207.

Kennamer, J. D. 1992. Public opinion, the press, and public policy: An introduction. In *Public opinion, the press, and public policy,* ed. J. D. Kennamer, 1–18. Westport, Conn.: Praeger.

Kerbel, M. R. 1997. The media: Viewing the campaign through a strategic haze. In *The elections of 1996,* ed. M. Nelson, 81–105. Washington, D.C.: Congressional Quarterly Press.

———. 1998. Parties in the media: Elephants, donkeys, boars, pigs, and jackals. In *The parties respond: Changes in American parties and campaigns,* ed. L. S. Maisel, 243–259. Boulder, Colo.: Westview.

Kerner, O. 1968. *Report of the national advisory commission on civil disorders.* Washington, D.C.: U.S. Government Printing Office.

Kerr, N. L., R. J. MacCoun, C. H. Hansen, and J. A. Hymes. 1987. Gaining and losing social support: Momentum in decision-making groups. *Journal of Experimental Social Psychology* 23: 119–145.

Kerr, P. 1986, November 1. Anatomy of an issue: Drugs, the evidence, the reaction. *New York Times,* 1.

Kessell, J. H. 1965. Cognitive dimensions and political activity. *Public Opinion Quarterly* 29: 377–389.

Key, V. O. 1961. *Public opinion and American democracy.* New York: Knopf.

Kierstead, R. 1988, December 12. Grading the election coverage. *Boston Globe,* 14.

Kimball, P. 1994. *Downsizing the news: Network cutbacks in the nation's capital.* Washington, D.C.: Woodrow Wilson Center Press.

Kinder, D. R. 1983. Diversity and complexity in American public opinion. In *Political science: The state of the discipline*, ed. A. W. Finifter, 389–425. Washington, D.C.: American Political Science Association.

Kinder, D. R., G. Adams, and P. Gronke. 1989. Economics and politics in the 1984 presidential election. *American Journal of Political Science* 33: 491–515.

Kinder, D. R., and L. M. Sanders. 1990. Mimicking political debate with survey questions: The case of white opinion on affirmative action for blacks. *Social Cognition* 8: 73–103.

Kinder, D. R., and D. O. Sears. 1985. Public opinion and political behavior. In *Handbook of Social Psychology*, ed. G. Lindzey and E. Aronson, 539–598. New York: Random House.

Kinnick, K. N., D. M. Krugman, and G. T. Cameron. 1996. Compassion fatigue: Communication and burnout toward social problems. *Journalism and Mass Communication Quarterly* 73: 687–707.

Kissinger, H. 1966. Conditions of world order. *Daedalus* 95: 503–529.

Klandermans, B. 1986. New social movements and resource mobilization: The European and the American approach. *International Journal of Mass Emergencies and Disasters* 4 (special issue, *Comparative perspectives and research on collective behavior and social movements*): 13–27.

———. 1988. The formation and mobilization of consensus. In *International Social Movement Research 1*, ed. B. Klandermans, H. Kriesi, and S. Tarrow, 173–198. Greenwich, Conn.: JAI.

Knight, G., and T. Dean. 1982. Myth and the structure of news. *Journal of Communication* 32: 144–161.

Knight, M. G. 1999. Getting past the impasse: Framing as a tool for public relations. *Public Relations Review* 25: 381–398.

Kopenhaver, L. L., D. L. Martinson, and M. Ryan. 1984. How public relations practitioners and editors in Florida view each other. *Journalism Quarterly* 61: 860–865.

Korte, C. 1972. Pluralistic ignorance about student radicalism. *Sociometry* 35: 576–587.

Kotz, (N.) 1969. *Let them eat promises: The politics of hunger in America*. Englewood Cliffs, N.J.: Prentice Hall.

Kraft, J. 1981, May. The imperial media. *Commentary*, 36–47.

Kraus, S., and D. Davis. 1976. *The effects of mass communication on political behavior*. University Park: Pennsylvania State University Press.

Kuhn, T. S. 1970. *The structure of scientific revolutions*, 2nd ed., expanded. Chicago: University of Chicago Press.

Kumar, M., and M. Grossman. 1982. Images of the White House in the media. In *The president and the public*, ed. D. Graber, 85–110. Philadelphia: ISHI.

Kurtz, H. 1996. *Hot air: All talk, all the time*. New York: Times Books Random House.

———. 1998. *Spin cycle: Inside the Clinton propaganda machine*. New York: Free Press.

Kuypers, J. A. 2002. *Press bias and politics: How the media frame controversial issues*. Westport, Conn.: Praeger.

Kwak, N. 1999. Revisiting the knowledge gap hypothesis: Education, motivation, and media use. *Communication Research* 26: 385–413.

Lachter, S. B., and A. Forman. 1989. Drug abuse in the United States. In *Communication campaigns about drugs: Government, media, and the public*, ed. P. J. Shoemaker, 7–12. Hillsdale, N.J.: Lawrence Erlbaum.

Lang, G. E., and K. Lang. 1981. Watergate, an exploration of the agenda-building process. *Mass Communication Review Yearbook* 2: 447–468.

———. 1983. *The battle for public opinion*. New York: Columbia University Press.

Langer, E. J. 1975. The illusion of control. *Journal of Personality and Social Psychology* 32: 311–328.

Lapham, L., and E. Rosenbush, eds. 2000. *An American album: One hundred and fifty years of Harper's magazine*. New York: Franklin Square Press.

Larson, J. 1984. *Television's window on the world: International affairs coverage on the U.S. networks*. Norwood, N.J.: Ablex.

Larson, M. S. 1989. Presidential news coverage and "All Things Considered": National Public Radio and news bias. *Presidential Studies Quarterly* 19: 347–353.

Lasorsa, D. L. 1989. Real and perceived effects of "Amerika." *Journalism Quarterly* 66: 373–378, 529.

———. 1991. Political outspokenness: Factors working against the spiral of silence. *Journalism Quarterly* 68: 131–139.

———. 1992. Policymakers and the third-person effect. In *Public opinion, the press, and public policy*, ed. J. D. Kennamer, 163–176. Westport, Conn.: Praeger.

Lasorsa, D. L., and S. D. Reese. 1990. News source use in the crash of 1987: A study of four national media. *Journalism Quarterly* 67: 60–71.

Lasorsa, D. L., and W. Wanta. 1988, May. "The effects of personal, interpersonal, and media experience on issue salience." Paper presented to the Political Communication Division of the International Communication Association, New Orleans, Louisiana.

Lasswell, H. 1935. *World politics and personal insecurity*. New York: Whittlesey House, McGraw-Hill.

———. 1936. *Politics: Who gets what, when, how*. New York: Whittlesey House, McGraw-Hill.

———. 1958. *Politics: Who gets what, when, how*, 2nd ed. New York: Meridian Books.

Latané, B., and J. M. Darley. 1969. Bystander "apathy." *American Behavioral Scientist* 57: 244–268.

———. 1970. *The unresponsive bystander: Why doesn't he help?* New York: Appleton-Century-Crofts.

Lau, R. R. 1980. *Negativity in political perceptions*. Unpublished manuscript, Department of Psychology, University of California, Los Angeles.

———. 1982. Negativity in political perception. *Political Behavior* 4: 353–378.

———. 1985. Two explanations for negativity effects in political behavior. *American Journal of Political Science* 29: 119–138.

Lau, R. R., and G. M. Pomper. 2001a. Effects of negative campaigning on turnout in U.S. Senate elections, 1988–1998. *Journal of Politics* 63: 804–819.

———. 2001b. Negative campaigning by U.S. Senate candidates. *Party Politics* 7: 69–87.

———. 2002. Effectiveness of negative campaigning in U.S. Senate elections. *American Journal of Political Science* 46: 47–66.

Lau, R. R., and D. P. Redlawsk. 1997. Voting correctly. *American Political Science Review* 91: 585–598.

Lau, R. R., L. Sigelman, C. Heldman, and P. Babbitt. 1999. The effectiveness of negative political advertising: A meta-analytic assessment. *American Political Science Review* 93: 851–875.

Lavrakas, P. J., and J. K. Holley, eds. 1991. *Polling and presidential election coverage.* Newbury Park, Calif.: Sage.

Lawrence, R. G. 1996. Accidents, icons, and indexing: The dynamics of news coverage of police use of force. *Political Communication* 13: 437–454.

———. 2000. Game-framing the issues: Tracking the strategy frame in public policy news. *Political Communication* 17: 93–114.

Lazarsfeld, P., B. Berelson, and H. Gaudet. 1948. *The people's choice: How the voter makes up his mind in a presidential campaign,* 2nd ed. New York: Columbia University Press.

Lazarsfeld, P., and R. Merton. [1948] 1960. Mass communication, popular taste, and organized social action. In *Mass communications,* ed. W. Schramm, 492–512. Urbana: University of Illinois Press.

Lee, M., and N. Solomon. 1990. *Unreliable sources: A guide to detecting bias in news media.* New York: Carol.

Leeper, M. S. 1991. The impact of prejudice on female candidates: An experimental study of voter inference. *American Politics Quarterly* 19: 248–261.

Leigh, D. 1982. Freedom of information and the criminal justice system. In *Crime, justice, and the mass media,* ed. C. Summer, 74–86. Cambridge: Institute of Criminology, University of Cambridge.

Leman, N. 1979, October 12. Florida caucuses: Media or message. *Washington Post,* 1.

Lemert, J. B. 1974. Content duplication by the networks in competing evening newscasts. *Journalism Quarterly* 51: 240–242.

Lemert, J. B., W. R. Elliott, J. M. Bernstein, W. L. Rosenberg, and K. J. Nestvold. 1988. *News verdicts, the debates, and presidential campaigns.* Westport, Conn.: Praeger.

Lester, M. 1971. "Toward a sociology of public events." Master's thesis, University of California, Santa Barbara.

———. 1980. Generating newsworthiness: The interpretive construction of public events. *American Sociological Review* 45: 984–994.

Levin, I. P. 1987. Associative effects of information framing. *Bulletin of the Psychometric Society* 25: 85–86.

Levin, I. P., and G. J. Gaeth. 1990. How consumers are affected by framing of attribute information before and after consuming the product. *Journal of Communication Research* 15: 374–378.

Levin, I. P., S. L. Schneider, and G. J. Gaeth. 1998. All frames are not created equal: A typology and critical analysis of framing effects. *Organizational Behavior and Human Decision Processes* 70: 149–188.

Levy, M. R. 1981. Disdaining the news. *Journal of Communication* 31: 24–31.

Lewis-Beck, M. S. 1988. *Economics and elections: The major Western democracies.* Ann Arbor: University of Michigan Press.

Leymore, V. L. 1975. *Hidden myth: Structure and symbolism in advertising.* New York: Basic.

Lichtenberg, J. 1996. In defense of objectivity revisited. In *Mass media and society*, 2nd ed., ed. J. Curran and M. Gurevitch, 225–242. London: Hodder Headline Group.

Lichter, S. R., and R. E. Noyes. 1995. *Good intentions make bad news: Why Americans hate campaign journalism.* Boston: Rowman & Littlefield.

Lichter, S. R., and S. Rothman. 1983. *The media elite: America's new power brokers.* Bethesda, Md.: Adler & Adler.

Lichter, S. R., S. Rothman, and L. Lichter. 1986. *The media elite.* Bethesda, Md.: Adler & Adler.

Liebler, C. M., and S. J. Smith. 1997. Tracking gender differences: A comparative analysis of network correspondents and their sources. *Journal of Broadcasting and Electronic Media* 41: 58–68.

Limerick, P. N. 1988, October 20. Polls are a liability for our democracy. *USA Today*, 6A.

Lindzey, G., and Aronson, E., eds. 1985. *The handbook of social psychology*, vol. 2, 3rd ed. New York: Random House.

Linsky, M. 1986. *Impact: How the press affects federal policymaking.* New York: Norton.

Lippmann, W. 1920. *Liberty and the news.* New York: Harcourt, Brace, Howe.

———. 1921. The world outside and the pictures in our heads. In *The processes and effects of mass communication*, 2nd ed., ed. W. Schramm and D. Roberts, 3–39. Urbana: University of Illinois Press, 1971.

———. [1922] 1965. *Public opinion.* New York: Free Press.

Littlejohn, S. W. 1992. *Theories of human communication*, 4th ed. Belmont, Calif.: Wadsworth.

Livingston, S., and T. Eachus. 1996. Indexing news after the Cold War: Reporting U.S. ties to Latin American paramilitary organizations. *Political Communication* 13: 423–436.

Locander, R. 1979. The adversary relationship: A new look at an old idea. *Presidential Studies Quarterly* 9: 266–274.

Lorenz, J. D. 1978, February 12. An insider's view of Jerry Brown. *Chicago Tribune.*

Lovrich, N. P., and J. C. Pearce. 1984. "Knowledge gap" phenomena: Effect of situation specific and transsituational factors. *Journal of Communication Research* 11: 415–434.

Lule, J. 2001. *Daily news, eternal stories: The mythological role of journalism.* New York: Guilford Press.

Luskin, R. 1987. Measuring political sophistication. *American Journal of Political Science* 31: 856–899.

MacDonald, L. C. 1969. Myth, politics, and political science. *Western Political Quarterly* 22: 141–150.

MacIntyre, A. 1981. *After virtue: A study in moral theory.* Notre Dame, Ind.: University of Notre Dame Press.

Mack, C. S. 1997. *Business, politics, and the practice of government relations.* Westport, Conn.: Quorum Books.

MacLean, E. 1981. *Between the lines.* Montreal: Black Rose Books.

Maher, T. M. 2001. Framing: An emerging paradigm or a phase of agenda setting? In *Framing public life: Perspectives on media and our understanding of the social world*, ed. S. D. Reese, O. H. Gandy, and A. E. Grant. Mahwah, N.J.: Lawrence Erlbaum.

Makay, J. J. 1970. The rhetorical strategies of Governor George Wallace in the 1964 Maryland primary. *Southern Speech Journal* 36: 164–175.

Mancini, P., and D. Swanson. 1996. Politics, media, and modern democracy: Introduction. In *Politics, media, and modern democracy: An international study of innovations in electoral campaigning and their consequences*, ed. D. Swanson and P. Mancini, 1–26. Westport, Conn.: Praeger.

Manheim, J. 1979. The honeymoon's over: The news conference and the development of presidential style. *Journal of Politics* 41: 55–74.

Mann, T. E., and G. R. Orren, eds. 1992. *Media polls in American politics*. Washington, D.C.: Brookings Institution.

Manning, P. 1998. *Spinning for Labour: Trade unions and the new media environment.* Aldershot, UK: Ashgate.

———. 2001. *News and news sources: A critical introduction.* London: Sage.

Manoff, R. K. 1987. Writing the news (by telling the "story"). In *Reading the news: A Pantheon guide to popular culture*, ed. R. Manoff and M. Schudson, 197–229. New York: Pantheon.

Maslach, C. 1982. *Burnout: The cost of caring.* Englewood, Cliffs, N.J.: Prentice Hall.

Matthews, D. R. 1960. *U.S. senators and their world.* Chapel Hill: University of North Carolina Press.

———. 1978. "Winnowing": The news media and the 1976 presidential nominations. In *Race for the presidency: The media and the nominating process*, ed. J. D. Barber, 55–78. Englewood Cliffs, N.J.: Prentice Hall.

McCamy, J. L. 1939. *Government publicity.* Chicago: University of Chicago Press.

McCombs, M. E. 1979. An address to the College of Communication at the University of Tennessee–Knoxville.

McCombs, M. E., E. Einsiedel, and D. H. Weaver. 1991. *Contemporary public opinion: Issues and the news.* Hillsdale, N.J.: Lawrence Erlbaum.

McCombs, M., and S. I. Ghanem. 2001. The convergence of agenda setting and framing. In *Framing public life: Perspectives on media and our understanding of the social world*, ed. S. D. Reese, O. H. Gandy, Jr., and A. E. Grant, 67–94. Mahwah, N.J.: Lawrence Erlbaum.

McCombs, M., and S. Gilbert. 1986. News influence on our pictures of the world. In *Perspectives on media effects*, ed. J. Bryant and D. Zillmann, 1–15. Hillsdale, N.J.: Lawrence Erlbaum.

McCombs, M. E., J. P. Llamas, E. Lopez-Escobar, and F. Rey. 1997. Candidate images in Spanish elections: Second level agenda-setting effects. *Journalism and Mass Communication Quarterly* 74: 703–717.

McCombs, M. E., and D. L. Shaw. 1972. The agenda-setting function of the mass media. *Public Opinion Quarterly* 36: 176–187.

———. 1977. Agenda-setting and the political process. In *The emergence of American political issues: The agenda-setting function of the press*, ed. D. L. Shaw and M. E. McCombs, 149–156. St. Paul, Minn.: West.

———. 1993. The evolution of agenda-setting research: Twenty-five years in the marketplace of ideas. *Journal of Communication* 43: 58–67.

McCombs, M. E., D. L. Shaw, and D. Weaver. 1997. *Communication and democracy: Exploring the intellectual frontiers in agenda-setting theory.* Mahwah, N.J.: Lawrence Erlbaum.

McGinniss, J. 1993. *The last brother.* New York: Simon & Schuster.

McLeod, D. M., and B. H. Detender. 1999. Framing effects of television news coverage of social protest. *Journal of Communication* (summer): 3–23.

McLeod, D. M., and J. K. Hertog. 1992. The manufacture of public opinion by reporters: Informal cues for public perceptions of protest groups. *Discourse and Society* 3: 259–275.

———. 1998. Social control and the mass media's role in the regulation of protest groups: The communicative acts perspective. In *Mass media, social control, and social change,* ed. D. Demers and K. Viswanath, 305–330. Ames: Iowa State University Press.

McLeod, J., L. Becker, and J. Byrnes. 1974. Another look at the agenda-setting function of the press. *Communication Research* 1: 131–167.

McManus, J. H. 1992. What kind of commodity is news? *Communication Research* 19: 787–805.

———. 1994. *Market-driven journalism: Let the citizen beware.* Thousand Oaks, Calif.: Sage.

McNair, B. 1998. *The sociology of journalism.* London: Arnold.

McQuail, D. 1994. *Mass communication: An introduction,* 3rd ed. Thousand Oaks, Calif.: Sage.

———. 2000. *McQuail's mass communication theory,* 4th ed. Thousand Oaks, Calif.: Sage.

Mead, G. H. 1934. *Mind, self, and society: From the standpoint of a social behaviorist.* Chicago: University of Chicago Press.

Meltzer, B. 1972. Mead's social psychology. In *Symbolic interaction,* 2nd ed., ed. J. Manis, and B. Meltzer, 4–22. Boston: Allyn & Bacon.

Merriam, J. 1989. National news media coverage of drug issues, 1983–1987. In *Communication campaigns about drugs: Government, media, and the public,* ed. P. J. Shoemaker, 21–28. Hillsdale, N.J.: Lawrence Erlbaum.

Merrill, J. 1997. Communitarianism's rhetorical war against Enlightenment liberalism. In *Mixed news: The public/civic/communitarian journalism debate,* ed. J. Black, 54–65. Mahwah, N.J.: Lawrence Erlbaum.

Merrill, J. C., P. J. Gade, and F. R. Blevens. 2001. *Twilight of press freedom: The rise of people's journalism.* Mahwah, N.J.: Lawrence Erlbaum.

Merton, R. K. [1957] 1968. *Social theory and social structures.* New York: Free Press.

Meyer, P. 1995, November–December. Discourse leading to solutions. *IRE Journal:* 3–5.

Meyrowitz, J. 1985. *No sense of place: The impact of electronic media on social behavior.* New York: Oxford University Press.

———. 1989a, September. The generalized elsewhere. *Critical Studies in Mass Communication:* 326–334.

———. 1989b. Using contextual analysis to bridge the study of mediated and unmediated behavior. In *Information and behavior,* vol. 3: *Mediation, information, and communication,* ed. B. D. Ruben and L. A. Lievrouw, 67–94. New Brunswick, N.J.: Transaction.

Michelson, S. 1972. *The electric mirror.* New York: Dodd, Mead.

Miller, A. H., E. N. Goldenberg, and L. Erbring. 1979. Type-set politics: Impact of newspapers on public confidence. *American Political Science Review* 73: 67–78.

Miller, D. 1994. *Don't mention the war: Northern Ireland, propaganda, and the media.* London: Pluto Press.

Miller, D. T., and C. McFarland. 1987. Pluralistic ignorance: When similarity is interpreted as dissimilarity. *Journal of Personality and Social Psychology* 53: 298–305.

Miller, M. M., and R. Hurd. 1982. Conformity to AAPOR standards in newspaper reporting of public opinion polls. *Public Opinion Quarterly* 46: 243–249.

Miller, M. M., and B. P. Riechert. 2001. The spiral of opportunity and frame resonance: Mapping the issue cycle in news and public discourse. In *Framing public life: Perspectives on media and our understanding of the social world,* ed. S. D. Reese, O. H. Gandy Jr., and A. E. Grant, 107–121. Mahwah, N.J.: Lawrence Erlbaum.

Miller, W. E., and D. E. Stokes. 1963. The politics of agenda-building: An alternative perspective for modern democratic theory. *Journal of Politics* 33: 892–915.

Mills, C. W. 1956. *The power elite.* New York: Oxford University Press.

Mintrom, M. 1997. Policy entrepreneurs and the diffusion of innovation. *American Journal of Political Science* 41: 738–770.

Mintz, L. 1986, September. Graphics networks. *Presstime,* 12–14.

Miroff, B. 1978, March. "Monopolizing the public sphere: The presidency as a barrier to democratic politics." Paper presented at the Southwestern Political Science Association, New Orleans, Louisiana.

———. 1982. Monopolizing the public space. In *Rethinking the presidency,* ed. T. Cronin, 218–232. Boston: Little, Brown.

Miyo, Y. 1983. The knowledge-gap hypothesis and media dependency. In *Communication Yearbook 7,* ed. R. N. Bostrom, 626–650. Beverly Hills, Calif.: Sage.

Mollenhoff, C. R. 1968. Lifeline of democracy. In *The press and the public interest,* ed. W. K. Agee, 175–190. Washington, D.C.: Public Affairs Press.

Molotch, H., and M. Lester. 1974. News as purposive behavior: On the strategic use of routine events, accidents, and scandals. *American Sociological Review* 39: 101–112.

Molotch, H., D. L. Protess, and M. T. Gordon. 1996. The media-policy connection: Ecologies of news. In *Political communication research: Approaches, studies, and assessments,* vol. 2, ed. D. L. Paletz, 41–62. Norwood, N.J.: Ablex.

Monge, P. 1977. The systems perspective as a theoretical basis for the study of human communication. *Communication Quarterly* 25: 19–29.

Moore, G., S. Sobieraj, J. A. Whitt, O. Mayorova, and D. Beaulieu. 2002. Elite interlocks in three U.S. sectors: Nonprofit, corporate, and government. *Social Science Quarterly* 83: 726–744.

Moore, S. F., and B. G. Meyerhoff. 1977. Secular ritual: Forms and meanings. In *Secular Ritual,* ed. S. F. Moore and B. G. Meyerhoff, 3–24. Amsterdam: Van Gorcum.

Moritz, M. J. 1995. The gay agenda: Marketing hate speech to mainstream media. In *Hate speech,* ed. R. K. Whillock, and D. Slayden, 55–79. Thousand Oaks, Calif.: Sage.

Morley, D. 1976. Industrial conflict and the mass media. *Sociological Review* 24: 245–268.

Muir, J. K. 1995. Hating for life: Rhetorical extremism and abortion clinic violence. In *Hate speech*, ed. R. K. Whillock and D. Slayden, 163–195. Thousand Oaks, Calif.: Sage.

Myerhoff, B. 1972. The revolution as a trip: Symbol and paradox. In *The new pilgrims: Youth protest in transition*, ed. P. G. Altbach and R. S. Laufer, 251–266. New York: David McKay.

Negrine, R. 1996. *The communication of politics*. London: Sage.

Neidhardt, F., and D. Rucht. 1991. The analysis of social movements: The state of the art and some perspectives for further research. In *Research on social movements: The state of the art in Western Europe and the USA*, ed. D. Rucht, 421–464. Boulder, Colo.: Westview.

Nelson, B. J. 1978. Setting the public agenda: The case of child abuse. In *The policy cycle*, ed. J. V. May and A. B. Wildavsky, 17–41. Beverly Hills, Calif.: Sage.

———. 1984. *Making an issue of child abuse*. Chicago: University of Chicago Press.

Nelson, T. E., R. A. Clawson, and Z. M. Oxley. 1997. Media framing of a civil liberties conflict and its effect on tolerance. *American Political Science Review* 91: 567–583.

Nelson, T. E., and Z. M. Oxley. 1999. Issue framing effects on belief importance and opinion. *Journal of Politics* 61: 1040–1067.

Nelson, T. E., Z. M. Oxley, and R. A. Clawson. 1997. Toward a psychology of framing effects. *Political Behavior* 19: 221–246.

Nerone, J. C., ed. 1995. *Last rights: Revisiting four theories of the press*. Urbana: University of Illinois Press.

Neuman, W. R. 1982. Television and American culture: The mass medium and the pluralist audience. *Public Opinion Quarterly* 46: 471–487.

Neuman, W. R., M. R. Just, and A. N. Crigler. 1992. *Common knowledge: News and the construction of political meaning*. Chicago: University of Chicago Press.

Neustadt, R. 1980. *Presidential power*. New York: John Wiley & Sons.

Newhagen, J. E., and B. Reeves. 1992. The evening's bad news: Effects of compelling negative television news images on memory. *Journal of Communication* 42: 25–41.

Nie, N. H., S. Verba, and J. R. Petrocik. 1976. *The changing American voter*. Cambridge, Mass.: Harvard University Press.

Nightingale, D. J., and D. Cromby. 1999. Reconstructing social constructionism. In *Social constructionist psychology: A critical analysis of theory and practice*, ed. D. J. Nightingale and J. Cromby, 207–224. Philadelphia: Open University Press.

Nimmo, D. 1974. *Popular images of politics*. Englewood Cliffs, N.J.: Prentice Hall.

———. 1978. *Political communication and public opinion in America*. Santa Monica, Calif.: Goodyear.

———. 1989. Episodes, incidents, and eruptions: Nightly network TV coverage of candidates '88. *American Behavioral Scientist* 32: 464–478.

Nimmo, D., and J. Combs. 1980. *Subliminal politics: Myths and mythmakers in America*. Englewood Cliffs, N.J.: Prentice Hall.

———. 1983. *Mediated political realities*. New York: Longman.

———. 1985. *Nightly horrors*. Knoxville: University of Tennessee Press.

———. 1992. *The political pundits*. New York: Praeger.

Nimmo, D., and A. J. Felsberg. 1986. Hidden myths in televised political advertising: An illustration. In *New perspectives on political advertising*, ed. L. L. Kaid, D. Nimmo, and K. R. Sanders, 248–267. Carbondale: Southern Illinois University Press.

Nimmo, D., and K. S. Johnson (a.k.a. Johnson-Cartee). 1980. Positions and images in campaign communication: Newsmagazine labeling in the 1980 pre-primary presidential contests. In *Communications Research Symposium: A Proceedings*, ed. J. P. McKerns, 3: 36–54. Knoxville: University of Tennessee Press.

Nimmo, D., and C. Newsome. 1997. *Political commentators in the U.S. in the 20th century: A bio-critical sourcebook.* Westport, Conn.: Greenwood.

Nimmo, D. and K. R. Sanders, eds. 1981. *Handbook of political communication.* Newbury Park, Calif.: Sage.

Nimmo, D., and Savage, R. 1976. *Candidates and their images: Concepts, methods, and findings.* Pacific Palisades, Calif.: Goodyear.

Nisbett, R. E., and L. Ross. 1980. *Human inference: Strategies and shortcomings of social judgment.* Englewood Cliffs, N.J.: Prentice Hall.

Niven, D. 2002. Bolstering an illusory majority: The effects of the media's portrayal of death penalty support. *Social Science Quarterly* 83: 671–689.

Noelle-Neumann, E. 1973. Return to the concept of powerful mass media. *Studies of Broadcasting* 9: 67–112.

———. 1977. Turbulences in the climate of opinion: Methodological applications of the spiral of silence theory. *Public Opinion Quarterly* 40: 143–158.

———. 1979. Public opinion and the classical tradition: A re-evaluation. *Public Opinion Quarterly* 43: 143–155.

———. 1981. Mass media and social change in developed societies. In *Mass media and social change*, ed. E. Katz and T. Szecsko, 137–166. Beverly Hills, Calif.: Sage.

———. 1983. The effect of media on media effects research. *Journal of Communication* 33: 157–165.

———. 1984. *The spiral of silence: Public opinion—Our social skin.* Chicago: University of Chicago Press.

———. 1985, September. Identifying opinion leaders. Paper presented at the 38th ESOMAR Conference, Wiesbaden, Germany.

———. 1991. The theory of public opinion: The concept of the spiral of silence. In *Communication Yearbook 14*, ed. J. A. Anderson, 256–287. Newbury Park, Calif.: Sage.

———. 1993. *The spiral of silence*, 2nd ed. Chicago: University of Chicago Press.

———. 1995. Public opinion and rationality. In *Public opinion and the communication of consent*, ed. T. L. Glasser and C. T. Salmon, 33–54. New York: Guilford Press.

Nordenstreng, K. 1997. Beyond the four theories of the press, In *Media and politics in transition*, ed. J. Servaes and R. Lie, 97–110. Leuven: Acco.

O'Gorman, H. J. 1975. Pluralistic ignorance and white estimates of white support for racial segregation. *Public Opinion Quarterly* 39: 311–330.

———. 1986. The discovery of pluralistic ignorance. *Journal of the History of the Behavioral Sciences* 22: 333–347.

———. 1988. Pluralistic ignorance and reference groups: The case of ingroup ignorance. In *Surveying social life*, ed. H. J. O'Gorman, 145–173. Middletown, Conn.: Wesleyan University Press.

O'Gorman, H. J., and S. L. Garry. 1976. Pluralistic ignorance: A replication and extension. *Public Opinion Quarterly* 40: 1–19.

O'Hara, R. 1961. *Media for the millions.* New York: Random House.

O'Keefe, G. J. 1980. Political malaise and reliance on media. *Journalism Quarterly* 57: 122–128.

Olien, C. N., G. A. Donohue, and P. J. Tichenor. 1995. Conflict, consensus, and public opinion. In *Public opinion and the communication of consent*, ed. T. L. Glasser and C. T. Salmon, 301–322. New York: Guilford Press.

Oncken, H. 1914. Politik, Geschichtsschreibung und öffentliche Meinung. In *Historisch-politische Aufsätze und Reden*, vol. 1, 203–243. Translated by E. Noelle-Neumann. Munich: R. Oldenbourg.

Orren, G. R., and N. W. Polsby. 1987. *Media and momentum: The New Hampshire primary and nomination politics*. Chatham, N.J.: Chatham House.

Oskamp, S. 1991. *Attitudes and opinions*, 2nd ed. Englewood Cliffs, N.J.: Prentice Hall.

Owen, D. 1997. The press' performance. In *Toward the millennium: The elections of 1996*, ed. L. Sabato, 205–223. Boston: Allyn & Bacon.

Oxford dictionary and thesaurus. 1996. Oxford: Oxford University Press.

Page, B. I. 1995. Speedy deliberation: Rejecting "1960s programs" as causes of the Los Angeles riots. *Political Communication* 12: 245–261.

Page, B. I., and B. I. Shapiro. 1992. *The rational public: Fifty years of trends in Americans' policy preferences*. Chicago: University of Chicago Press.

Page, B., R. Shapiro, and G. Dempsey. 1987. What moves public opinion? *American Political Science Review* 81: 23–42.

Paivio, A. 1971. *Imagery and verbal processes*. New York: Holt, Rinehart & Winston.

Paleologos, D. A. 1997. A pollster on polling. *American Behavioral Scientist* 40: 1183–1189.

Paletz, D. L. 2002. *The media in American politics*, 2nd ed. New York: Longman.

———, ed. 1996. *Political communication in action: States, institutions, movements, audiences*. Cresskill, N.J.: Hampton Press.

Paletz, D. L., and R. M. Entman. 1981. *Media power politics*. New York: Free Press.

Paletz, D. L., J. Y. Short, H. Baker, B. C. Campbell, R. J. Cooper, and R. M. Oeslander. 1980. *Public Opinion Quarterly* 44: 495–513.

Palmgreen, P., and P. Clarke. 1977. Agenda-setting with local and national issues. *Communication Research* 4: 435–452.

———. 1991. Agenda-setting with local and national issues. In *Agenda setting: Readings on media, public opinion, and policymaking*, ed. D. L. Protess and M. McCombs, 109–118. Hillsdale, N.J.: Lawrence Erlbaum.

Palmgreen, P., and J. D. Rayburn. 1985. An expectancy-value approach to media gratification. In *Media gratification research*, ed. K. E. Rosengren, L. A. Wenner, and P. Palmgreen, 61–72. Beverly Hills, Calif.: Sage.

Palmgreen, P., L. A. Wenner, and K. E. Rosengren. 1985. Uses and gratifications research: The past ten years. In *Media gratifications research: Current perspectives*, ed. K. E. Rosengren, L. A. Wenner, and P. Palmgreen, 11–37. Beverly Hills, Calif.: Sage.

Pan, Z., and G. M. Kosicki. 1993. Framing analysis: An approach to news discourse. *Political Communication* 10: 55–75.

———. 2001. Framing as a strategic action in public deliberation. In *Framing public life: Perspectives on media and our understanding of the social world*, ed. S. D. Reese, O. H. Gandy Jr., and A. E. Grant, 35–66. Mahwah, N.J.: Lawrence Erlbaum.

Parenti, M. 1970. Power and pluralism: A view from the bottom. *Journal of Politics* 32: 501– 530.

———. 1996. *Dirty truths: Reflections on politics, media, ideology, conspiracy, ethnic life, and class power.* San Francisco: City Lights Books.

Park, R. 1940. News as a form of knowledge: A chapter in the sociology of knowledge. *American Journal of Sociology* 45: 669–686.

Pateman, C. 1980. The civic culture: A philosophical critique. In *The civic culture revisited*, ed. G. Almond and S. Verba, 57–102. Boston: Little, Brown.

Paterson, C. A. 2001. The transference of frames in global television. In *Framing public life: Perspectives on media and our understanding of the social world*, ed. S. D. Reese, O. H. Gandy Jr., and A. E. Grant, 337–353. Mahwah, N.J.: Lawrence Erlbaum.

Patterson, T. E. 1980. *The mass media election: How Americans choose their president.* New York: Praeger.

———. 1991. More style than substance: Television news in U.S. national elections. *Political Communication and Persuasion* 8: 145–161.

———. [1993] 1994. *Out of Order.* New York: Alfred A. Knopf.

———. 1995, August 31–September 3. "News decisions: Journalists as partisan actors." Paper presented at the annual meeting of the American Political Science Association, Chicago.

———. 1996. Bad news, period. *PS: Political Science and Politics* 29: 17–20.

Patterson, T. E., and W. Donsbach. 1996. News decisions: Journalists as partisan actors. *Political Communication* 13: 455–468.

Patterson, T. L. 1992, September. Irony of the free press: Professional journalism and news diversity. Paper presented at the annual meeting of the American Political Science Association, Chicago.

Perloff, L. S. 1983. Perceptions of vulnerability to victimization. *Journal of Social Issues* 39: 41–61.

Perloff, L. S., and B. K. Fetzer. 1986. Self-other judgments and perceived vulnerability to victimization. *Journal of Personality and Social Psychology* 50: 502–510.

Perloff, R. M. 1989. Ego-involvement and the third-person effect of televised news coverage. *Communication Research* 16: 236–262.

———. 1996. Perceptions and conceptions of political media impact: The third-person effect and beyond. In *The psychology of political communication*, ed. A. N. Crigler, 177–197. Ann Arbor: University of Michigan Press.

———. 1998. *Political communication: Politics, press, and public in America.* Mahwah, N.J.: Lawrence Erlbaum.

Perloff, R. M., K. Neuendorf, D. Giles, T.-K. Chang, and L. W. Jeffres. 1992. Perceptions of "Amerika." *Mass Communication Review* 19: 42–48.

Perucci, R., and D. D. Knudsen. 1983. *Sociology.* New York: West.

Peterson, R. A., G. Albaum, G. Kozmetsky, and I. C. M. Cunningham. 1984. Attitudes of newspaper business editors and general public toward capitalism. *Journalism Quarterly* 61: 56–65.

Peterson, R. A., G. Kozmetsky, and I. C. M. Cunningham. 1982. Perceptions of media bias toward business. *Journalism Quarterly* 59: 461–464.

Pettigrew, T. F. 1979. The ultimate attribution error: Extending Allport's analysis of prejudice. *Personality and Social Psychology Bulletin* 5: 461–476.

Pfau, M., and A. Louden. 1994. Effectiveness of adwatch formats in deflecting political attack ads. *Communication Research* 21: 325–341.

Phillips, E. B. 1976. Novelty without change. *Journal of Communication* 26: 87–92.

Pollard, G. 1995. Job satisfaction among newsworkers: The influence of professionalism, perceptions of organizational structure, and social attributes. *Journalism and Mass Communication Quarterly* 72: 682–697.

Pool, I. 1965. *Candidates, issues, and strategies.* Cambridge, Mass.: MIT Press.

Popkin, S. L. [1991] 1994. *The reasoning voter: Communication and persuasion in presidential campaigns.* Chicago: University of Chicago Press.

Price, V. 1989. Social identification and public opinion: Effects of communicating group conflict. *Public Opinion Quarterly* 53: 197–224.

Price, V., and H. Oshagan. 1995. Social-psychological perspectives on public opinion. In *Public opinion and the communication of consent,* ed. T. Glaser, and C. T. Salmon, 177–206. New York: Guilford.

Price, V., and D. F. Roberts. 1987. Public opinion processes. In *Handbook of Communication Science,* ed. C. R. Berger and S. H. Chaffee, 781–815. Newbury Park, Calif.: Sage.

Price, V., and D. Tewksbury. 1997. News values and public opinion: A theoretical account of media priming and framing. In *Progress in communication sciences: Advances in persuasion,* vol. 13, ed. G. A. Barnett and F. J. Boster, 173–212. Greenwich, Conn.: Ablex.

Price, V., D. Tewksbury, and E. Powers. 1997. Switching trains of thought: The impact of news frames on readers' cognitive responses. *Communication Research* 24: 481–506.

Protess, D. L., F. L. Cook, T. R. Curtin, M. T. Gordon, D. R. Leff, M. E. McCombs, and P. Miller. 1987. The impact of investigative journalism on public opinion and policymaking: Targeting toxic waste. *Public Opinion Quarterly* 51: 166–185.

Protess, D. L., F. L. Cook, J. C. Doppelt, J. S. Ettema, M. T. Gordon, D. R. Leff, and P. Miller. 1991. *The journalism of outrage: Investigative reporting and agenda building in America.* New York: Guilford Press.

Protess, D. L., D. R. Leff, S. C. Brooks, and M. T. Gordon. 1985. Uncovering rape: The watchdog press and the limits of agenda-setting. *Public Opinion Quarterly* 49: 19–37.

Putnam, L. L., and M. Holmer. 1992. Framing, reframing, and issue development. In *Communication and negotiation: SAGE annual review of communication research,* vol. 22, ed. L. L. Putnam and M. E. Roloff, 128–155. Newbury Park, Calif.: Sage.

Qualter, T. H. 1985. *Opinion control in the democracies.* New York: St. Martin's.

Raghubir, P., and G. Menon. 1998. AIDS and me, never the twain shall meet: The effects of information accessibility on judgments of risk and advertising effectiveness. *Journal of Consumer Research* 25: 52–63.

Randall, D. M. 1987. The portrayal of corporate crime in network television newscasts. *Journalism Quarterly* 64: 150–153, 250.

Ratzan, S. C. 1989. The real agenda setters: Pollsters in the 1988 presidential campaign. *American Behavioral Scientist* 32: 451–463.

Rayburn, J. D., and P. Palmgreen. 1984. Merging uses and gratifications and expectancy value theory. *Communication Research* 2: 537–562.

Rayfield, J. R. 1972. What is a story? *American Anthropologist* 74: 1085–1106.

Reese, S. D. 1990. The news paradigm and the ideology of objectivity: A socialist at the *Wall Street Journal. Critical Studies in Mass Communication* 7: 390–409.

———. 1991. Setting the media's agenda: A power balance principle. In *Communication Yearbook 14*, ed. J. A. Anderson, 309–340. Newbury Park, Calif.: Sage.

———. 2001. Prologue—Framing public life: A bridging model for media research. In *Framing public life: Perspectives on media and our understanding of the social world*, ed. S. D. Reese, O. H. Gandy Jr., and A. E. Grant, 7–34. Mahwah, N.J.: Lawrence Erlbaum.

Reese, S. D., J. A. Daly, and A. P. Hardy. 1987. Economic news on network television. *Journalism Quarterly* 64: 137–144.

Reese, S. D., and L. H. Danielian. 1989. Intermedia influence and the drug issue: Converging on cocaine. In *Communication campaigns about drugs: Government, media, and the public*, ed. P. J. Shoemaker, 29–45. Hillsdale, N.J.: Lawrence Erlbaum.

———. 1994. The structure of news sources on television: A network analysis of "CBS News," "Nightline," "MacNeil/Lehrer," and "This Week with David Brinkley." *Journal of Communication* 44: 84–107.

Relph, E. 1976. *Place and placelessness*. London: Pion.

Rhee, J. W. 1997. Strategy and issue frames in election campaign coverage: A social cognitive account of framing effects. *Journal of Communication* 47: 26–48.

Rhodebeck, L. A. 1998, April. Framing policy debates on old age. Paper presented at the annual conference of the Midwest Political Science Association, Chicago.

Rich, A. 2001. The politics of expertise in Congress and the news media. *Social Science Quarterly* 82: 583–601.

Ricoeur, P. 1981. The narrative function. In *Paul Ricoeur: Hermeneutics and the human sciences*, ed. J. B. Thompson, 274–296. New York: Cambridge University.

Riley, J. W., Jr., and M. W. Riley. 1959. Mass communication and the social system. In *Sociology today*, ed. R. K. Merton, L. Broom, and L. S. Cottrell, 537–578. New York: Basic Books.

Robinson, J. P. 1974. The press as kingmaker. *Journalism Quarterly* 51: 587–594.

———. 1976a. Interpersonal influence in election campaigns: Two-step flow hypothesis. *Public Opinion Quarterly* 40: 304–319.

———. 1976b. Public affairs television and the growth of political malaise: The case of the "selling of the Pentagon." *American Political Science Review* 70: 409–432.

Robinson, J. P., and M. Levy. 1986a. Information flow in society. In *The main source: Learning from television news*, ed. J. P. Robinson and M. Levy, 13–27. Beverly Hills, Calif.: Sage.

———. 1986b. *The main source: Learning from television news*. Beverly Hills, Calif.: Sage.

Robinson, M. J. 1976. Public affairs television and the growth of political malaise: The case of "the selling of the Pentagon." *American Political Science Review* 70: 409–432.

Robinson, M. J., and A. Kohut. 1988. Believability and the press. *Public Opinion Quarterly* 52: 174–189.

Rock, P. 1981. News as eternal recurrence. In *The manufacture of news: Social problems, deviance, and the mass media*, rev. ed., ed. S. Cohen and J. Young, 64–70. Beverly Hills, Calif.: Sage.

Rogers, E. M., and J. W. Dearing. 1988. Agenda-setting research: Where has it been, where is it going? In *Communication Yearbook 11*, ed. J. A. Anderson, 555–594. Newbury Park, Calif.: Sage.

Rollberg, J. N., L. W. Sanders, and M. D. Buffalo. 1990. Down to the wire: How six newspapers reported public opinion polls during the 1988 presidential campaign. *Newspaper Research Journal* 11: 80–93.

Roper, E. 1957. *You and your leaders.* New York: Morrow.

Roper Starch Worldwide. 1995. *America's watching: Public attitudes toward television.* New York: Network Television Association.

Roscho, B. 1975. *Newsmaking.* Chicago: University of Chicago Press.

Rosen, J. 1996. *Getting the connections right: Public journalism and the troubles in the press.* New York: Twentieth Century Fund Press.

Roshier, B. 1981. The selection of crime news by the press. In *The manufacture of news: Social problems, deviance, and the mass media*, rev. ed., ed. S. Cohen and J. Young, 40–51. Beverly Hills, Calif.: Sage.

Ross, L., D. Greene, and P. House. 1977. The "false consensus effect": An egocentric bias in social perception and attribution process. *Journal of Experimental Social Psychology* 13: 279–301.

Rouner, D., M. D. Slater, and J. M. Buddenbaum. 1999. How perceptions of news bias in news sources relate to beliefs about media bias. *Newspaper Research Journal* 20: 41–51.

Rozell, M. J. 1994. Press coverage of Congress, 1946–92. In *Congress, the press, and the public*, ed. T. E. Mann and N. J. Ornstein, 59–139. Washington, D.C.: American Enterprise Institute and the Brookings Institution.

Rozwenc, E. C. [1961] 1972. *The causes of the American Civil War.* Lexington, Mass.: D. C. Heath.

Rubin, A. M., and S. Windahl. 1986. The uses and dependency model of mass communication. *Critical Studies in Mass Communication* 3: 184–199.

Rubin, R. B., and M. P. McHugh. 1987. Development of parasocial interaction relationships. *Journal of Broadcasting and Electronic Media* 31: 279–292.

Rubin, R. L. 1981. *Press, party, and presidency.* New York: W. W. Norton.

Rudd, R. 1986. Issues as image in political campaign commercials. *Western Journal of Speech Communication* 50: 102–118.

Rude, G. 1980. *Ideology and popular protest.* New York: Knopf.

Ryan, C. 1991. *Prime time activism: Media strategies for grassroots organizing.* Boston, Mass.: South End Press.

Sabato, L. 1991. *Feeding frenzy: How attack journalism transformed American politics.* New York: Free Press.

Sale, K. 1973, June. Myths as eternal truths. *More: A Journalism Review* 3: 3–5.

Salmon, C., and C.-Y. Moh. 1992. The spiral of silence: Linking individuals and society through communication. In *Public opinion, the press, and public policy*, ed. J. D. Kennamer, 145–161. Westport, Conn.: Praeger.

Salwen, M. B. 1985. The reporting of public opinion polls during presidential election years, 1968–1984. *Journalism Quarterly* 62: 272–277.

Salzman, J. 1998. *Making the news: A guide for nonprofits and activists.* Boulder, Colo.: Westview.

Sapir, E. 1934. Symbolism. *Encyclopedia of the Social Sciences* 14: 492–495.

Sapiro, V. 1982. If U.S. Senator Baker were a woman: An experimental study of candidate images. *Political Psychology* 3: 61–83.

Sartori, G. 1987. *The theory of democracy revisited.* Chatham, N.J.: Chatham House.

Saussure, F. 1966. *Course in general linguistics.* New York: McGraw-Hill.

Schamber, L. 1987, August 1–4. Visual literacy in mass communication: A proposal for educators. Paper presented at the Association for Education in Journalism and Mass Communication conference, San Antonio, Texas.

Schank, R. C., and R. P. Abelson. 1975. Scripts, plans, and knowledge. In *Advance papers of the Fourth International Joint Conference on Artificial Intelligence,* Tbilisi, Georgia, USSR, 151–157. Cambridge, Mass.: Artificial Intelligence Lab.

———. 1977. *Scripts, plans, goals, and understanding: An inquiry into human knowledge structures.* Hillsdale, N.J.: Lawrence Erlbaum.

Schattschneider, E. E. 1960. *The semi-sovereign people: An elitist's view of democracy in America.* New York: Holt, Rinehart, & Winston.

Scheufele, D. 1999. Framing as a theory of media effects. *Journal of Communication* (winter): 103–122.

Schiller, H. 1992. *Mass communications and American empire.* Boulder, Colo.: Westview.

Schlesinger, M., and R. R. Lau. 2000. The meaning and measure of policy metaphors. *American Political Science Review* 94: 611–625.

Schlesinger, P. 1978. *Putting "reality" together: BBC News.* London: Constable.

Schlesinger, P., and H. Tumber. 1994. *Reporting crime: The media politics of criminal justice.* Oxford: Clarendon Press.

Schneider, A., and H. Ingram. 1993. Social construction of target populations: Implications for politics and policy. *American Political Science Review* 87: 334–347.

Schneider, D. J., A. H. Hastorf, and P. C. Ellsworth. 1979. *Person perception.* Reading, Mass.: Addison-Wesley.

Schoenbach, K. 1983. News in the Western world. In *Comparative mass media systems,* ed. L. J. Martin and A. G. Chaudhary, 33–43. New York: Longman.

Schoenfeld, A. C., R. F. Meier, and R. J. Griffin. 1979. Constructing a social problem: The press and the environment. *Social Problems* 27: 38–61.

Scholes, R. 1982. *Semiotics and interpretation.* New Haven, Conn.: Yale University Press.

Schön, D. 1983. *The reflective practitioner: How professionals think in action.* New York: Basic.

Schorr, D. 1977. *Clearing the air.* Boston: Houghton Mifflin.

Schram, S. F. 1991. The post-modern presidency and the grammar of electronic electioneering. *Critical Studies in Mass Communication* 8: 210–216.

Schroeder, A. 2000. *Presidential debates: Forty years of high-risk TV.* New York: Columbia University Press.

Schudson, M. 1978. *Discovering the news.* New York: Basic.

———. 1982. The politics of narrative form: The emergence of news conventions in print and television. *Daedalus* 11: 97–112.

———. 1991. The sociology of news production revisited. In *Mass Media and Society,* ed. J. Curran and M. Gurevitch, 141–328. London: Edward Arnold.

———. 1995. *The power of news.* Cambridge, Mass.: Harvard University Press.

———. 2001. The objectivity norm in American journalism. *Journalism* 2: 149–170.

Schutz, A. 1962. *Collected Papers, vol. 1, The problem of social reality.* Edited by Maurice Natanson. The Hague: Martinus Nyhoff.

———. 1967. *The phenomenology of the social world.* Evanston, Ill.: Northwestern University Press.

———. 1970. *On phenomenology and social relations.* Chicago: University of Chicago Press.

Sego, M. A. 1977. *Who gets the cookies,* 3. Brunswick, Ohio: King's Court Communications.

Seib, P. 1994. *Campaigns and conscience: The ethics of political journalism.* Westport, Conn.: Praeger.

Semetko, H. A. 1995, August 31–September 3. Journalistic culture in comparative perspective: The concept of "balance" in U.S., British, and German TV news. Paper presented at the annual meeting of the American Political Science Association, Chicago.

Semetko, H. A., J. G. Blumler, M. Gurevitch, and D. H. Weaver, S. Barkin, and G. C. Wilhoit. 1991. *The formation of campaign agendas: A comparative analysis of party and media roles in recent American and British elections.* Hillsdale, N.J.: Lawrence Erlbaum.

Seymour-Ure, C. 1974. *The political impact of mass media.* Beverly Hills, Calif.: Sage.

Shafer, R. 1976. *A new language for psychoanalysis.* New Haven, Conn.: Yale University Press.

Shah, D. V. 2001. The collision of convictions: Value framing and value judgments. In *Communication in U.S. elections: New agendas,* ed. R. P. Hart and D. R. Shaw, 55–74. Lanham, Md.: Rowman & Littlefield.

Shah, D. V., D. Domke, and D. B. Wackman. 1996. "To thine own self be true": Values, framing, and voter decision-making strategies. *Communication Research* 23: 509–560.

———. 2001. The effects of value-framing on political judgment and reasoning. In *Framing public life: Perspectives on media and our understanding of the social world,* ed. S. D. Reese, O. H. Gandy Jr., and A. E. Grant, 226–243. Mahwah, N.J.: Lawrence Erlbaum.

Shah, D., M. D. Watts, D. Domke, and D. P. Fan. 2002. News frames and cueing of issue regimes: Explaining Clinton's public approval in spite of scandals. *Public Opinion Quarterly* 66: 339–370.

Shamir, J., and M. Shamir. 1997. Pluralistic ignorance across issues and over time: Information cues and biases. *Public Opinion Quarterly* 61: 227–260.

Shapiro, M. A. 1991. Memory and decision processes in the construction of social reality. *Communication Research* 18: 3–24.

Shapiro, M. A., and A. Lang. 1991. Making television reality: Unconscious processes in the construction of social reality. *Communication Research* 18: 685–705.

Shaw, D. 1989, August 25. How media gives [sic] stories same "spin." *Los Angeles Times*, reprint.

———. 1993, March 31. Trust in media on decline. *Los Angeles Times*, A1, A16–18.

Shaw, D. L., and M. E. McCombs. 1989. Dealing with illicit drugs: The power—and limits—of mass media agenda setting. In *Communication campaigns about drugs: Government, media, and the public*, ed. P. J. Shoemaker, 113–120. Hillsdale, N.J.: Lawrence Erlbaum.

———, eds. 1977. *The emergence of American political issues: The agenda-setting function of the press*. St. Paul, Minn.: West.

Shaw, E. F. 1977a. The agenda-setting hypothesis reconsidered: Interpersonal factors. *Gazette* 23: 230–240.

———. 1977b. The interpersonal agenda. In *The emergence of American public issues: The agenda-setting function of the press*, ed. D. L. Shaw and M. E. McCombs, 69–87. St. Paul, Minn.: West.

Shea, D. M., and M. J. Burton. 2001. *Campaign craft: The strategies, tactics, and art of political campaign management*, rev. ed. Westport, Conn.: Praeger.

Sherman, S. J., C. C. Presson, and L. Chassin. 1984. Mechanisms underlying the false consensus effect: The special role of threats to self. *Personality and Social Psychology Bulletin* 10: 127–138.

Shimanoff, S. B. 1980. *Communication rules: Theory and research*. Beverly Hills, Calif.: Sage.

Shoemaker, P. J. 1982. The perceived legitimacy of deviant political groups. *Communication Research* 9: 249–286.

———. 1984. Media treatment of deviant political groups. *Journalism Quarterly* 61: 66–78.

Shoemaker, P. J., T. Chang, and N. Brendlinger. 1987. Deviance as a predictor of newsworthiness: Coverage of international events in the U.S. media. In *Communication yearbook 10*, ed. M. McLaughlin, 348–365. Beverly Hills, Calif.: Sage.

Shoemaker, P. J., and S. D. Reese. 1991. *Mediating the message: Theories of influences on mass media content*. New York: Longman.

Shoemaker, P. J., W. Wanta, and D. Leggett. 1989. Drug coverage and public opinion, 1972–1986. In *Communication campaigns about drugs: Government, media, and the public*, ed. P. J. Shoemaker, 67–80. Hillsdale, N.J.: Lawrence Erlbaum.

Shrum, L. J., and T. C. O'Guinn. 1993. Processes and effects in the construction of social reality: Construct accessibility as an explanatory variable. *Communication Research* 20: 436–471.

Siebert, R., T. Peterson, and W. Schramm. 1956. *Four theories of the press*. Urbana: University of Illinois Press.

Sigal, L. 1973. *Reporters and officials*. Lexington, Mass.: D. C. Heath.

———. 1986. Sources make the news. In *Reading the news*, ed. R. Manoff and M. Schudson, 9–37. New York: Pantheon.

Sigal, L. V. 1978. Newsmen and campaigners: Organization men make the news. *Political Science Quarterly* 93: 465–470.

Silverstone, S., and C. L. Webb. 1986, April. Many newspapers, small and large, turn to the Mac. *Presstime*, 23–26.

Simon, A., and M. Xenos. 2000. Media framing and effective public deliberation. *Political Communication* 17: 363–376.

Simons, H. W., and A. A. Aghazarian. 1986. Genres, rules, and political rhetoric: Toward a sociology of rhetorical choice. In *Form, genre, and the study of political discourse*, ed. H. W. Simons and A. A. Aghazarian, 45–58. Columbia: University of South Carolina.

Singletary, M. W. 1982. Commentary: Are journalists "professionals"? *Newspaper Research Journal* 3: 75–87.

Skirrow, G. 1979. Education and television: Theory and practice. In *Media, politics, and culture: A socialist view*, ed. C. Gardner, 25–39. London: Macmillan.

Skogan, W. G., and M. G. Maxfield. 1980. *Coping with crime: Victimization, fear, and reactions to crime in three American cities*. Evanston, Ill.: Northwestern University Center for Urban Affairs.

Slater, D., and W. R. Elliot. 1982. Television's influence on social reality. *Quarterly Journal of Speech* 68: 69–79.

Slattery, K., and J. T. Tiedge. 1992. The effect of labeling staged video in the credibility of TV news stories. *Journal of Broadcasting and Electronic Media* 36: 279–286.

Smith, E. J., and D. J. Hajash. 1988. Informational graphics in 30 daily newspapers. *Journalism Quarterly* 65: 714–718.

Smith, K. A. 1987. Effects of newspaper coverage on community issue concerns and local government evaluations. *Communication Research* 14: 379–395.

Smith, K. B. 1997. When all's fair: Signs of parity in media coverage of female candidates. *Political Communication* 14: 71–82.

Snow, D. A., and R. D. Benford. 1988. Ideology, frame resonance, and participant mobilization. *International Social Movement Research* 1: 197–217.

Snow, D. A., E. B. Rochford, S. K. Worden, and R. D. Benford. 1986. Frame alignment processes, micromobilization, and movement participation. *American Sociological Review* 51: 464–481.

Sohn, A. B. 1978. A longitudinal analysis of local non-political agenda-setting effects. *Journalism Quarterly* 55: 325–332.

Soley, L. C. 1992. *The news shapers: The sources who explain the news*. New York: Praeger.

———. 1994. Pundits in print: "Experts" and their use in newspaper stories. *Newspaper Research Journal* 15: 65–73.

Spangler, M. B. 1986, August. *A preliminary codification of Chernobyl nuclear accident issues and their reporting by the media*. Unpublished draft report to U.S. Nuclear Regulatory Commission, Washington, D.C.

Speier, H. 1950. Historical development of public opinion. *American Journal of Sociology* 55: 376–388.

Sproule, J. Michael. 1989, September. Progressive propaganda critics and the magic bullet myth. *Critical Studies in Mass Communication* 6: 225–246.

Steele, C. A., and K. G. Barnhurst. 1996. The journalism of opinion: Network news coverage of U.S. presidential campaigns, 1968–1988. *Critical Studies in Mass Communication* 13: 187–209.

Stempel, G., III, and H. Culbertson. 1984. The prominence and dominance of news sources in newspaper medical coverage. *Journalism Quarterly* 61: 671–676.

Stephenson, W. 1967. *The play theory of mass communication*. Chicago: University of Chicago Press.

Stepp, C. S. 1991, April. When readers design the news. *Washington Journalism Review*, 20–25.

Stevenson, R., and D. E. Sanger. 2003, August 29. Bush vilifies Saddam, touts economic plan. *Tuscaloosa News*, A1, A12.

Stevenson, R. L., and M. T. Greene. 1980. A reconsideration of bias in the news. *Journalism Quarterly* 57: 121.

Streckfuss, R. 1990. Objectivity in journalism: A search and a reassessment. *Journalism Quarterly* 67: 973–983.

Strentz, H. 1989. *News reporters and news sources: Accomplices in shaping and misshaping the news*, 2nd ed. Ames: Iowa State University Press.

Swidler, A. 1986. Culture in action: Symbols and strategies. *American Sociological Review* 51: 273–286.

Sykes, A. J. M. 1965. Myth and attitude change. *Human Relations* 18: 323–337.

———. 1966. A study in attitude change. *Occupational Psychology* 40: 31–41.

———. 1970. Myth in communication. *Journal of Communication* 20: 17–31.

Tankard, J., L. Hendrickson, J. Silberman, K. Bliss, and S. Ghanem. 1991, August. Media frames: Approaches to conceptualization and measurement. Paper presented to the Association for Education in Journalism and Mass Communication, Boston.

Tankard, J. W., Jr. 2001. The empirical approach to the study of media framing. In *Framing public life: Perspectives on media and our understanding of the social world*, ed. S. D. Reese, O. H. Gandy Jr., and A. E. Grant, 95–106. Mahwah, N.J.: Lawrence Erlbaum.

Tannen, D. 1993. What's in a frame? Surface evidence for underlying expectations. In *Framing in discourse*, ed. D. Tannen, 14–56. Oxford: Oxford University Press.

Taylor, P. 1986, October 5. Negative ads becoming powerful political force. *Washington Post*, A1, A6–A7.

Taylor, S., and J. D. Brown. 1988. Illusion and well-being: A social psychological perspective on mental health. *Psychological Bulletin* 103: 193–210.

Tedesco, J. C. 2000. Network news coverage of campaign 2000: The public voice in context. In *The 2000 presidential campaign: A communication perspective*, ed. R. E. Denton Jr., 199–224. Westport, Conn.: Praeger.

———. 2001. Issue and strategy agenda-setting in the 2000 presidential primaries. *American Behavioral Scientist* 44: 2048–2067.

Tedesco, J. C., L. L. Kaid, and L. M. McKinnon. 2000. Network adwatches: Policing the 1996 primary and general election presidential ads. *Journal of Broadcasting and Electronic Media* 44: 541–555.

Tedesco, J. C., L. M. McKinnon, and L. L. Kaid. 1996. Advertising watchdogs: A content analysis of print and broadcast ad watches. *Harvard International Journal of Press/Politics* 1: 76–93.

Terkildsen, N., and F. Schnell. 1997. How media frames move public opinion: An analysis of the women's movement. *Political Research Quarterly* 50: 879–900.

Tewksbury, D., and S. L. Althaus. 2000. Differences in knowledge acquisition among readers of the paper and online versions of a national newspaper. *Journalism and Mass Communication Quarterly* 77: 457–479.

Thorson, J. A. 1995. *Aging in a changing society.* Belmont, Calif.: Wadsworth.

Tichenor, P. J., G. A. Donohue, and C. N. Olien. 1970. Mass media flow and differential growth in knowledge. *Public Opinion Quarterly* 34: 159–170.

———. 1980. *Community conflict and the press.* Newbury Park, Calif.: Sage.

Tilly, C. 1979. Repertoires of contention in America and Britain, 1750–1830. In *The dynamics of social movements: Resource mobilization, control, and tactics,* ed. M. N. Zald and J. D. McCarthy, 126–155. Cambridge: Winthrop.

Tipton, L. 1992. Reporting on the public mind. In *Public opinion, the press, and public policy,* ed. J. D. Kennamer, 131–144. Westport, Conn.: Praeger.

Traugott, M. 1992. The impact of media polls on the public. In *Media polls in American politics,* ed. T. E. Mann and G. R. Orren, 125–149. Washington, D.C.: Brookings Institution.

Trent, J. S., and R. V. Friedenberg. 1995. *Political campaign communication: Principles and practices,* 3rd ed. Westport, Conn.: Praeger.

Tuchman, G. 1972. Objectivity as strategic ritual: An examination of newsmen's notions of objectivity. *American Journal of Sociology* 77: 660–679.

———. 1973. Making news by doing work: Routinizing the unexpected. *American Journal of Sociology* 79: 110–131.

———. 1976. Telling stories. *Journal of Communication* 26: 93–97.

———. 1977. The exception proves the rule: The study of routine news practices. In *Strategies for Communication Research,* ed. P. Hirsch, P. Miller, and F. Kline, 43–62. London: Sage.

———. 1978a. *Making news.* New York: Free Press.

———. 1978b. Professionalism as an agent of legitimation. *Journal of Communication* (spring): 106–113.

———. 1981a. Myth and the consciousness industry: A new look at the effects of the mass media. In *Mass media and social change,* ed. E. Katz and T. Szecsko, 83–100. Beverly Hills, Calif.: Sage.

———. 1981b. The symbolic annihilation of women by the mass media. In *The manufacture of news: Social problems, deviance, and the mass media,* rev. ed., ed. S. Cohen and J. Young, 169–185. Beverly Hills, Calif.: Sage.

Tufte, E. R. 1983. *The visual display of quantitative information.* Cheshire, Conn.: Graphics Press.

Tuggle, C. A. 1998. The bias toward finding bias in television news. *Communication Reports* 11: 65–72.

Tumulty, K. 2004, January 12. Inside the mind of Howard Dean. *Time,* 24–29.

Turk, J. V. 1985. Subsidizing the news: Public information officers and their impact on media coverage of state government. Ph.D. diss., Syracuse University.

———. 1986a. Information subsidies and media content. *Journalism Monographs* 100: 1–29.

———. 1986b. Public relations' influence on the news. *Newspaper Research Journal* 7: 15–27.

Turner, J. 1974. *The structure of sociological theory.* Homewood, Ill.: Dorsey Press.

Turner, J. H., and L. Beeghley. 1981. *The emergence of sociological theory.* Homewood, Ill.: Dorsey Press.

Turner, V. 1982. Social dramas and stories about them. In *From ritual to theatre: The human seriousness of play,* by V. Turner, 61–88. New York: Performing Arts Journal Publications.

Tversky, A., and D. Kahneman. 1973. Availability: A heuristic for judging frequency and probability. *Cognitive Psychology* 5: 207–232.

Tyler, T., and F. L. Cook. 1984. The mass media and judgments of risk: Distinguishing impact on personal and societal level judgments. *Journal of Personality and Social Psychology* 47: 693–708.

Underwood, D. 1988. When MBAs rule the newsroom. *Columbia Journalism Review* 26: 23–30.

Valentino, N. A., M. N. Beckmann, and T. A. Buhr. 2001. A spiral of cynicism for some: The contingent effects of campaign news frames on participation and confidence in government. *Political Communication* 18: 347–367.

van Dijk, T. 1988. *News as discourse.* Hillsdale, N.J.: Lawrence Erlbaum.

———. 1991. *Racism and the press.* London: Routledge.

Viswanath, K., and J. Finnegan Jr. 1996. The knowledge gap hypothesis: Twenty-five years later. In *Communication Yearbook 19,* ed. B. R. Burleson, 187–227. Newbury Park, Calif.: Sage.

Viswanath, K., E. Kahn, J. Finnegan Jr., J. Hertog, and J. Potter. 1993. Motivation and the knowledge gap: Effects of a campaign to reduce diet-related cancer risk. *Communication Research* 20: 546–563.

Walker, J. L. 1977. Setting the agenda in the United States Senate: A theory of problem selection. *British Journal of Political Science* 1: 432–445.

Wallack, L., K. Woodruff, L. Dorfman, and I. Diaz. 1999. *News for a change: An advocate's guide to working with the media.* Thousand Oaks, Calif.: Sage.

Wallas, G. 1914. *The great society.* New York: Macmillan.

Wamsley, G., and R. Pride. 1972. Television network news: Re-thinking the iceberg problem. *Western Political Quarterly* 25: 433–450.

Ward, D. B. 1992. The effectiveness of sidebar graphics. *Journalism Quarterly* 69: 318–328.

Ward, J., and K. A. Hansen. 1993. *Search strategies in mass communication,* 2nd ed. White Plains, N.Y.: Longman.

Warren, R. P. [1946] 1953. *All the king's men.* New York: Random House, Modern Library Edition.

Watzlawick, P., J. H. Beavin, and D. Jackson. 1967. *Pragmatics of human communication.* New York: W. W. Norton.

Wayne, S. J. 2000. *The road to the White House.* Boston: Bedford/St. Martin's.

Weaver, D. 1996. Media agenda setting and elections: 1970s–1990s. In *Political communication research: Approaches, studies, and assessments,* vol. 2, ed. D. L. Paletz, 211–225. Norwood, N.J.: Ablex.

Weaver, D., and D. Drew. 2001. Voter learning and interest in the 2000 presidential election: Did the media matter? *Journalism and Mass Communication Quarterly* 78: 787–798.

Weaver, D. H., and G. C. Wilhoit. 1996. *The American journalist in the 1990's.* Mahwah, N.J.: Lawrence Erlbaum.

Weaver, P. 1974. The new journalism and the old: Thoughts after Watergate. *Public Interest* (spring): 67–88.

Weaver, P. H. 1972. Is television news biased? *Public Interest* 11: 67–68.

———. 1976, August 29. Captives of melodrama. *New York Times Magazine* 6: 48–51, 54, 56–57.

Wegner, D. M., R. Wenzlaff, R. M. Kerker, and A. E. Beattie. 1981. Incrimination through innuendo: Can media questions become public answers? *Journal of Personality and Social Psychology* 40: 822–832.

Weimann, G. 2000. *Communicating unreality: Modern media and the reconstruction of reality.* Thousand Oaks, Calif.: Sage.

Weimann, G., and H. Brosius. 1991. The newsworthiness of international terrorism. *Communication Research* 18: 333–354.

Weinberger, M. G., C. T. Allen, and W. R. Dillon. 1984. The impact of negative network news. *Journalism Quarterly* 61: 287–294.

Weiss, A. 1978, March. The future public opinion of business. *Management Review* 67: 8–15.

Wenner, L. A. 1985. The nature of news gratifications. In *Media gratifications research: Current perspectives*, ed. K. A. Rosengren, L. A. Wenner, and P. Palmgreen, 171–193. Beverly Hills: Sage.

Wertkin, J. A. 2002. Election 2000.com: Internet use and the American voter. In *The election of the century and what it tells us about the future of American politics*, ed. S. J. Wayne and C. Wilcox, 217–238. Armonk, N.Y.: Sharpe.

West, D. M. 1993. *Air wars: Television advertising in election campaigns, 1952–1992.* Washington, D.C.: Congressional Quarterly Press.

Westerståhl, J., and F. Johansson. 1985. *Bilden av Sverige* [The picture of Sweden]. Stockholm: Studieförbundet Näringsliv och Samhälle.

———. 1986. News ideologies as moulders of domestic news. *European Journal of Communication* 1: 13–149.

Whillock, R. K. 1997. Cyber-politics: The online strategies of '96. *American Behavioral Scientist* 40: 1208–1225.

Whillock, R. K., and D. E. Whillock. 2000. Digital democracy 2000. In *The 2000 presidential campaign: A communication perspective*, ed. R. E. Denton Jr., 167–181. Westport, Conn.: Praeger.

White, H. 1978. *The tropics of discourse: Essays in cultural criticism.* Baltimore: Johns Hopkins University Press.

———. 1980. The value of narrativity in the representation of reality. *Critical Inquiry* 7: 5–27.

———. 1987. *The content of the form: Narrative discourse and historical representation.* Baltimore: Johns Hopkins University Press.

Whitney, D. C., M. Fritzler, S. Jones, S. Mazzarella, and L. Rakow. 1989. Geographic and source biases in network television news 1982–1984. *Journal of Broadcasting and Electronic Media* 33: 159–174.

Whitney, D. C., and E. Wartella. 1988. The public as dummies. *Knowledge: Creation, diffusion, utilization* 10: 99–110.

Whorf, B. S. 1956. *Language, thought, reality.* New York: Wiley.

Wicks, R. H., and M. Kern. 1995. Factors influencing decisions by local television news directors to develop new reporting strategies during the 1992 political campaign. *Communication Research* 22: 237–255.

Wilcox, C. 1994. Why was 1992 the year of the women? Explaining women's gains in 1992. In *The year of the woman: Myths and realities,* ed. E. Cook, S. Thomas, and C. Wilcox, 1–24. Boulder, Colo.: Westview.

Wilensky, H. L. 1964. The professionalization of everyone? *American Journal of Sociology* 70: 137–158.

Wilhoit, G. C., and D. Weaver. 1996. *The American journalist in the 1990s: U.S. news people at the end of an era.* Mahwah, N.J.: Lawrence Erlbaum.

Wilkins, L. T. 1964. *Social deviance: Social policy, action, and research.* London: Tavistock.

Williams, P. N. 1978. *Investigative reporting and editing.* Englewood Cliffs, N.J.: Prentice Hall.

Williams, W., Jr., M. Shapiro, and C. Cutbirth. 1991. The impact of campaign agendas on perceptions of issues. In *Agenda setting: Readings on media, public opinion, and policymaking,* ed. D. C. Protess, and M. McCombs, 251–260. Hillsdale, N.J.: Lawrence Erlbaum.

Willis, W. 1991. *The shadow world: Life between the news media and reality.* New York: Praeger.

Wills, G. 1982. *Comments on the media-policy connection.* Remarks to the media cluster roundtable, Center for Urban Affairs and Policy Studies, Northwestern University.

Wittebols, J. H. 1996. News from the noninstitutional world: U.S. and Canadian television news coverage of social protest. *Political Communication* 13: 34–361.

Wober, G. M. 1978. Television violence and paranoid perception: The view from Great Britain. *Public Opinion Quarterly* 42: 315–321.

Wolfe, T. 1973. The new journalism. In *The new journalism by Tom Wolfe,* ed. T. Wolfe and E. W. Johnson, 2–52. New York: Harper & Row.

Wolfsfeld, G. 1984. Collective political action and media strategy. *Journal of Conflict Resolution* 28: 363–381.

———. 1997. *Media and political conflict: News from the Middle East.* New York: Cambridge University Press.

Woodward, G. C. 1997. *Perspectives on American political media.* Boston: Allyn & Bacon.

Wortman, C. B. 1976. Causal attributions and personal control. In *New directions in attribution research,* vol. 1, ed. J. H. Harvey, W. Ickes, and R. Kidd, 23–52. Hillsdale, N.J.: Lawrence Erlbaum.

Wu, H. D., and A. Bechtel. 2002. Web site use and news topic and type. *Journalism and Mass Communication Quarterly* 79: 73–86.

Wulfemeyer, T. K. 1982. Developing and testing method for assessing local TV newscasts. *Journalism Quarterly* 59: 79–82.

Wundt, W. 1907. *Outlines of psychology,* 7th ed. Leipzig: Engleman.

Young, J. 1981. The myth of drug takers in the mass media. In *The manufacture of news,* ed. S. Cohen and J. Young, 326–334. Beverly Hills, Calif.: Sage.

Zajonc, R. 1980. Feeling and thinking: Preferences need no inferences. *American Psychologist* 35: 151–175.

Zaller, J. 1994. Strategic politicians, public opinion, and the Gulf War. In *Taken by storm*, ed. L. Bennett and D. Paletz, 250–274. Chicago: University of Chicago Press.

———. 1998. Monica Lewinsky's contribution to political science. *PS: Political Science and Politics* 31: 182–189.

Zaller, J., and D. Chiu. 1996. Government's little helper: U.S. press coverage of foreign policy crises, 1945–1991. *Political Communication* 13: 385–405.

Zelizer, B. 1997. Journalists as interpretive communities. In *Social meanings of news*, ed. D. Berkowitz, 401–419. Thousand Oaks, Calif.: Sage.

Zettl, H. 1979. The graphication and personification of television news. In *Television studies: Textual analysis*, ed. G. Burns and R. J. Thompson, 137–163. New York: Praeger.

Zillmann, D., and H.-B. Brosius. 2000. *Exemplification in communication: The influence of case reports on the perception of issues*. Mahwah, N.J.: Lawrence Erlbaum.

Zillmann, D., R. Gibson, V. J. Ordman, and C. F. Aust. 1994. Effects of human-interest stories in broadcast news. *Journal of Broadcasting and Electronic Media* 38: 65–78.

Zillmann, D., R. Gibson, S. S. Sundar, and J. W. Perkins. 1994, August 10–13. Effects of exemplification in magazine journalism on the perception of social issues. Paper presented at the Association for Education in Journalism and Mass Communication national conference, Atlanta, Georgia.

———. 1996. Effects of exemplification in news reports on the perception of social issues. *Journalism and Mass Communication Quarterly* 73: 427–444.

Zillmann, D., J. W. Perkins, and S. S. Sundar. 1992. Impression-formation effects of printed news varying in descriptive precision and exemplification. *Medienpsychologie* 3: 168–185.

Zoch, L. M., and J. V. Turk. 1998. Women making news: Gender as a variable in source selection and use. *Journalism and Mass Communication Quarterly* 75: 762–775.

Zucker, H. G. 1978. The variable nature of news media influence. In *Communication Yearbook 2*, ed. B. D. Ruben, 225–240. New Brunswick, N.J.: Transaction Books.

Index

About the Author

Karen S. Johnson-Cartee is professor in the Department of Advertising and Public Relations at the University of Alabama. She has also taught at the University of Alabama at Birmingham and the Universitat Klagenfurt in Klagenfurt, Austria. Dr. Johnson-Cartee has coauthored *Negative Political Advertising: Coming of Age* (with Gary Copeland, 1991), *Manipulation of the American Voter: Modern Political Commercials* (with Copeland, 1997), *Inside Political Campaigns: Theory and Practice* (with Copeland, 1997), and *Strategic Political Communication: Rethinking Social Influence, Persuasion, and Propaganda* (with Copeland, 2003). Her research has appeared in such scholarly journals as *Presidential Studies Quarterly, Journalism and Mass Communication Quarterly, Newspaper Research Journal,* and the *Harvard International Journal of Press/Politics.* For nearly twenty years, Dr. Johnson-Cartee has worked as a political consultant for numerous federal, state, and local electoral campaigns. She teaches undergraduate and graduate courses in political communication theory, political advertising and public relations, political campaign communication, political news analysis, and lobbying.